CW01637596

RELIGION AND CULTURE IN THE MIDDLE AGES

Feminine Sanctity and Spirituality in Medieval Wales

religion & culture in the middle ages

Series Editors
Denis Renevey (University of Lausanne)
Diane Watt (University of Wales, Aberystwyth)

Editorial Board
Miri Rubin (Queen Mary, University of London)
Jean-Claude Schmitt (École des Hautes
Études en Sciences Sociales, Paris)
Fiona Somerset (Duke University)
Christiania Whitehead (University of Warwick)

RELIGION AND CULTURE IN THE MIDDLE AGES

Feminine Sanctity and Spirituality in Medieval Wales

JANE CARTWRIGHT

UNIVERSITY OF WALES PRESS
CARDIFF
2008

© Jane Cartwright, 2008

All rights reserved. No part of this book may be reproduced, stored in a retrieval system, or transmitted, in any form or by any means, electronic, mechanical, photocopying, recording or otherwise, without clearance from the University of Wales Press, 10 Columbus Walk, Brigantine Place, Cardiff, CF10 4UP.
www.uwp.co.uk

British Library Cataloguing-in-Publication Data
A catalogue record for this book is available from the British Library.

ISBN 978-0-7083-1999-4 (hb)

The right of Jane Cartwright to be identified as author of this work has been asserted by her in accordance with sections 77 and 78 of the Copyright, Designs and Patents Act 1988.

Typeset by Columns Design Ltd, Reading, Berkshire
Printed in Great Britain by Antony Rowe Ltd, Wiltshire

Contents

Series Editors' Preface

Religion and Culture in the Middle Ages aims to explore the interface between medieval religion and culture, with as broad an understanding of those terms as possible. It puts to the forefront studies which engage with works that significantly contributed to the shaping of medieval culture. However, it also gives attention to studies dealing with works that reflect and highlight aspects of medieval culture that have been neglected in the past by scholars of the medieval disciplines. For example, devotional works and the practice they infer illuminate our understanding of the medieval subject and its culture in remarkable ways, while studies of the material space designed and inhabited by medieval subjects yield new evidence on the period and the people who shaped it and lived in it. In the larger field of religion and culture, we also want to explore further the roles played by women as authors, readers and owners of books, thereby defining them more precisely as actors in the cultural field. The series as a whole investigates the European Middle Ages, from *c.*500 to *c.*1500. Our aim is to explore medieval religion and culture with the tools belonging to such disciplines as, among others, art history, philosophy, theology, history, musicology, the history of medicine, and literature. In particular, we would like to promote interdisciplinary studies, as we believe strongly that our modern understanding of the term applies fascinatingly well to a cultural period marked by a less tight confinement and categorization of its disciplines than the modern period. However, our only criterion is academic excellence, with the belief that the use of a large diversity of critical tools and theoretical approaches enables a deeper understanding of medieval culture. We want the series to reflect this diversity, as we believe that, as a collection of outstanding contributions, it offers a more subtle representation of a period that is marked by paradoxes and contradictions and which necessarily reflects diversity and difference, however difficult it may sometimes have proved for medieval culture to accept these notions.

Acknowledgements

I am grateful to a large number of people who have helped in a variety of different ways with this project over the years – some have offered support, advice, suggestions and constructive criticisms, others have shared their knowledge of medieval poetry, prose, manuscripts, relics and art, checked translations or discussed various aspects of this work with me at different points. I would particularly like to thank Cathryn Charnell-White, R. Iestyn Daniel, Luned Davies, Sioned Davies, Dylan Foster Evans, Helen Fulton, Marged Haycock, Tristan Gray Hulse, Daniel Huws, Rhiannon Ifans, Christine James, Jacqueline Jenkins, Dafydd Johnston, Christine M. Jones, John Koch, Barry Lewis, Katherine J. Lewis, Ceridwen Lloyd-Morgan, Elisa Moras, John Morgan-Guy, Ann Parry Owen, Owen Thomas and Diane Watt. Of course, I am solely responsible for any errors which remain. I am extremely grateful to the Guild of Graduates of the University of Wales for a grant towards the cost of printing the images in the book, as well as the Department of Welsh at the University of Wales, Lampeter for buying some of the images and the two maps. Many thanks to Antony Smith of the University of Aberystwyth for producing the maps and Lampeter's Pantyfedwen fund for financial assistance with fieldwork. I am also grateful to the many vicars, priests and parish councils who welcomed me into their churches and allowed me to photograph stained-glass windows, reliquaries and paintings of the saints. Many thanks to the staff at the University of Wales Press and particularly Sarah Lewis, Ennis Akpinar, Julian Roskams and Elisabeth Doyle for guiding the book through the Press. Especial thanks are due to my father, Albert Cartwright, who chopped wood, lit fires, cooked, looked after Ifan and offered all manner of practical assistance while I was finishing this volume. Thanks to my partner John who has provided continuous support throughout the project and, of course, to my son Ifan for making my heart sing with joy whenever I took a short break.

LIST OF ILLUSTRATIONS

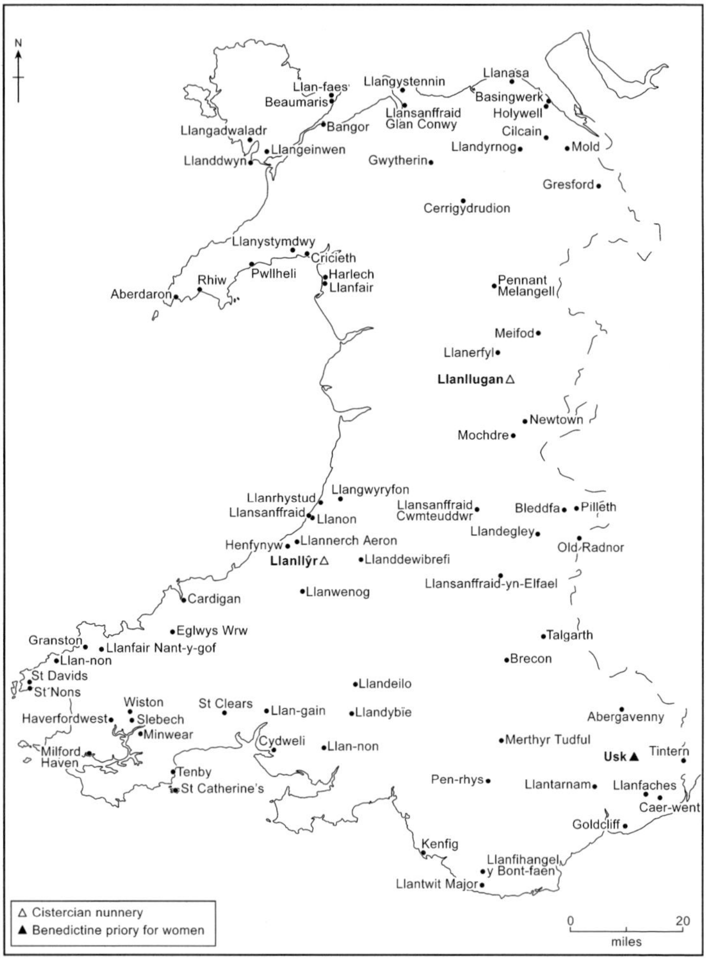

Map of Wales showing key places mentioned in the text

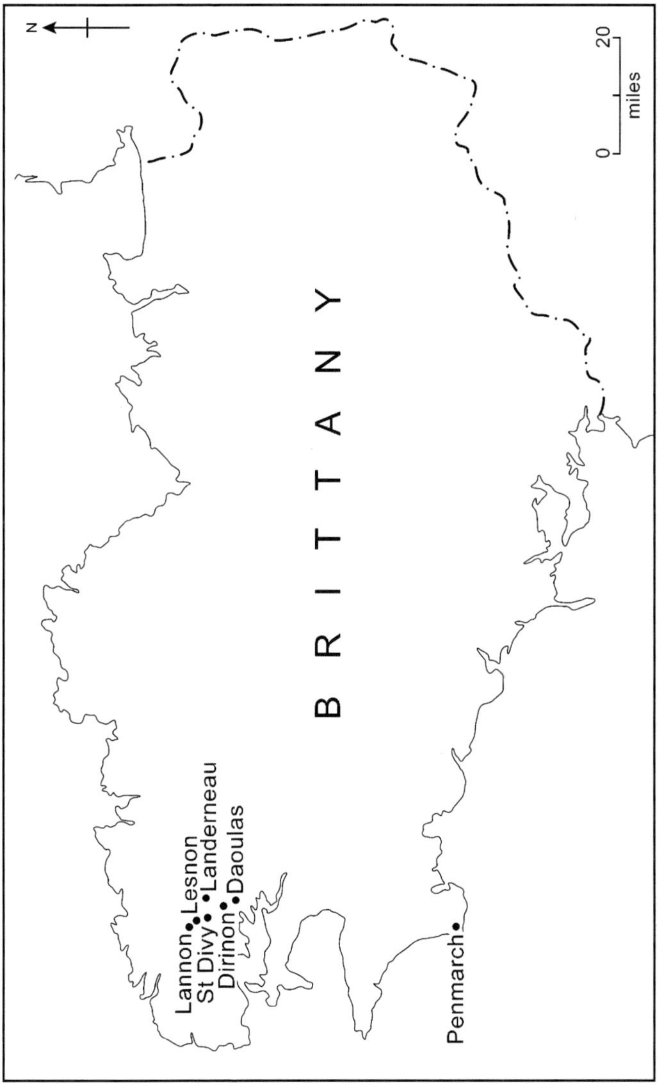

Map of Brittany showing key places mentioned in the text

ABBREVIATIONS

B	Bulletin of the Board of Celtic Studies
BL	British Library
CAWCS	University of Wales Centre for Advanced Welsh and Celtic Studies
EETS	Early English Texts Society
ES	extra series
fl.	*floruit*
NLW	National Library of Wales
OS	original series
RCAHMW	Royal Commission on the Ancient and Historical Monuments of Wales
SS	supplementary series

This book is dedicated to my family:
Albert, Glenys, Jue, Rob, Tom, Mike, Janet, Emily, Sylvia, Leslie, Paul, Liz, Anna, Bettina, Scott, John and Ifan.

Introduction

This volume brings together much of the research I have undertaken on women and religion in medieval Wales over the past decade. Drawing on a wide range of sources from saints' Lives and native poetry to holy wells and visual evidence, the volume explores feminine sanctity, its meanings, manifestations and related iconography in a specifically Welsh context. It does this via the study of a number of saints' cults – including both native Welsh saints and the universal saints of Christendom who became the subjects of Middle Welsh Lives – as well as considering the history of the Welsh nunneries and the experiences of 'real' noblewomen living and worshipping in various parts of Wales in the late Middle Ages. The period covered is a broad one, stemming from the fifth century to the mid-sixteenth century, that is from the period when the native female saints, if indeed they ever existed, are believed to have been active in Wales and the Dissolution, when a number of important saintly images were destroyed. The main focus, however, is on the period from the twelfth century to the end of the fifteenth century when the few nunneries that existed in Wales were founded and much of the material evidence (visual and literary) was produced. The aim is to investigate the roles women played in relation to religious life in Wales and highlight the wealth and variety of Welsh sources, many of which remain inaccessible to a non-Welsh-speaking audience.

The intersection of women's history and religion has proved a particularly popular field outside of Wales and there has been a proliferation of extremely valuable publications on feminine sanctity, virginity, female mysticism, anchoritism and the religious experiences of women in medieval Western Europe.[1] Saints' Lives and their relationship to women's literary culture, as well as detailed studies of individual saint's cults, have shed new light on the literary, linguistic and religious history of medieval England in particular.[2] Nevertheless, despite the fact that 'Gender and Medieval Studies' has proved such a fruitful and fashionable field elsewhere, this area of study has not, to date, attracted a great deal of attention in Wales, particularly in relation to women and religion.[3] While holiness and masculinity have recently attracted the attention of scholars working in the field of medieval studies, the topic remains largely virgin territory in Wales.[4]

The cult of the Virgin Mary and the influence the figure of Mary had on medieval devotional texts and women's religious experience more generally has been the subject of a variety of important studies.[5] In Wales Andrew Breeze has published a series of articles examining various *topoi* associated with Mary in medieval Welsh poetry: these poetic themes are frequently discussed in their wider European context.[6] Christine James has also provided a detailed study of the shrine to the Virgin at Pen-rhys in the Rhondda Valley and a discussion of the medieval Welsh poems which refer to this important pilgrimage site.[7] Madeleine Gray has discussed pilgrimage routes to Pen-rhys and focuses in some detail on images of the Virgin Mary and female saints in *Images of Piety: The Iconography of Traditional Religion in Late Medieval Wales*.[8] My own work on the Welsh cult of the Virgin Mary includes a chapter published in Welsh in 1999 which was the first study to trace the history and development of the cult of the Virgin Mary in Wales and discuss a wide range of sources including prose, poetry and visual representations.[9] The chapter has been substantially revised here and although it draws on many of the same Welsh sources, the focus is no longer predominantly on the importance of virginity and chastity (*agweddau ar wyryfdod a diweirdeb*) which appeared in the volume's subtitle. Rather than include subsections on Mary's relationship with Joseph, her virginity in partu and post partum and her perpetual virginity, the chapter has been expanded and rearranged so that it focuses on Middle Welsh translations of Marian texts, medieval poetry to the Blessed Virgin Mary and important images, shrines and holy wells.

Welsh poetry is an extremely important literary and historical source and, thus, excerpts of Welsh poetry and English translations feature throughout the volume. Our knowledge of medieval Welsh poetry and its accessibility has greatly improved over recent years thanks to the proliferation of scholarly editions of medieval Welsh poetry and, in particular, the projects on the Poets of the Princes and the Poets of the Gentry undertaken at the University of Wales Centre for Advanced Welsh and Celtic Studies. The chapter on the Virgin Mary has been able to take advantage of numerous editions from these series and, in addition, it discusses several unedited poems which were not analysed in the Welsh chapter, including an anonymous *cywydd* to an image of the Virgin at Llanystumdwy, a poem by Dafydd ap Hywel to a representation of Mary at Pilleth and an unusual love poem written by Hywel Dafi which describes the Virgin's physical appearance in remarkable detail.

Medieval Welsh literature is rich in hagiographical lore. A number of Latin and Middle Welsh Lives – *vitae* and *bucheddau* – survive which record the medieval traditions associated with many of the male Welsh saints, for example, SS. David, Beuno, Illtud, Cadog and Teilo.[10] Yet SS. Gwenfrewy and Melangell are the only native Welsh female saints for whom detailed prose narratives survive. Baring-Gould and Fisher in their remarkably comprehensive study, *The Lives of the British Saints*, have numerous entries dealing with individual female saints and Henken has valuable chapters on five female saints in her *Traditions of the Welsh Saints*.[11] Other useful studies focus on the legends associated with St Gwenfrewy (or Winefride) and her healing well at Holywell, Flintshire, and with St Melangell and her church and shrine at Pennant Melangell, Powys.[12] The sources for the female saints are disparate and varied and, as a result, one needs to adopt a multi-disciplinary approach in order to effectively evaluate the source material. Relevant primary sources include Welsh and Latin Lives, genealogies, calendars, prayers, *Cywyddwyr* poetry, law texts, place-names, holy wells, shrines, ecclesiastical seals and stained glass. The second chapter in this volume attempts to synthesize many of these sources and shed light on the medieval traditions associated with a number of sainted women, including Dwynwen, the Welsh patron saint of lovers, Melangell, the patron saint of hares and St Ursula, whose cult became firmly rooted at Llangwyryfon in Ceredigion. The biographical patterning of these *mulieres sanctae*, in so far as it can be ascertained from the limited extant sources, is explored and the reasons why so few official prose Lives of native women saints are extant are also considered.

Earlier versions of the chapters on female saints and Welsh nuns have appeared as separate studies elsewhere. It was felt that these articles and chapters would work well together in one convenient volume and that a book-length study of *Feminine Sanctity and Spirituality in Medieval Wales* would make a more significant contribution to this field than a series of separate studies on the Welsh evidence published in a variety of different places. Where chapters have appeared in a different form in edited volumes and journals, this is noted at the beginning of the chapter.

In Wales sanctity was locally conferred and none of the medieval Welsh saints appear to have been canonized by the Roman Catholic Church.[13] Oral traditions recounted locally in the vicinity of the saint's church appear to have performed an important function, establishing a focal point for veneration of the saint's cult, as well as generating and reinforcing popular belief in the saint's legend and miracles. Fragments of these traditions sometimes survive in medieval poetry (e.g. Iorwerth Fynglwyd's *cywydd* to San Ffraid), 'historical' accounts (such as Gerald of Wales's summary of the martyrdom of St Eluned) and pictorial narratives (such as the carved wooden roodscreen at Pennant Melangell depicting the legend of St Melangell).

One native saint whose popularity extended beyond Wales and whose legend was transferred wholesale to other Celtic regions, including Brittany, is St Non, the mother of St David.

Chapter 3 focuses in detail on the cult of St Non, who makes an interesting case study because, unlike many of the other virgin martyr saints, Non's sanctity is closely related to her maternity. Mulder-Bakker has noted that in the context of European hagiography, mother saints were generally the exception rather than the rule, despite obvious parallels with the Virgin Mary.[14] Yet in Wales a number of mother saints are recorded and this is particularly noticeable in the genealogies. Non is perhaps even more unusual within a European framework because she is not merely threatened with sexual violence, but she is actually raped and this is the central focus of her Breton *Buez*. It is argued that ultimately Non is a kind of honorary virgin and that in the context of Celtic hagiography, Non is not unique. Virginity was rendered violable when the maternity of an important male saint, such as St David, was at stake.

The volume then progresses from a detailed discussion of the material associated with one of the native saints to a more detailed consideration of the Middle Welsh Lives of some of the universal saints of Christendom. Chapter 4 analyses the vernacular accounts of the Lives of Mary Magdalene and her sister Martha and discusses their context within the Welsh manuscripts. According to their medieval legends, Mary Magdalene and Martha set sail with their brother Lazarus, St Maximinus and other Christians in a boat with no sail or oars, landed safely in Marseilles and evangelized Provence. Whilst the Welsh Life of Mary Magdalene (extant in twelve manuscripts), for the most part, closely resembles the standard medieval narrative best represented by Jacobus de Voragine's *Legenda aurea*, the Welsh Life of Martha (extant in eight manuscripts) omits important episodes such as the slaying of the odious dragon of Tarascon. This chapter examines ways in which Mary Magdalene and Martha became particularly relevant saints within the lay household. It proposes that these versions of the Lives were intended primarily for a lay audience, and challenges the frequent assumption that the Middle Welsh Lives of Mary Magdalene, Martha, Katherine, Margaret and Mary of Egypt were intended for an audience of religious sisters.

The Middle Welsh Life of Katherine of Alexandria is a particularly violent, fast-moving version of Katherine's *passio* which differs in certain details from the more well-known versions of Katherine's Life. For example, in the Welsh version of the legend, Porffir (Porphyrius) does not suffer martyrdom silently, but picks up a ladder and slays 4,000 of Maxentius' men and injures another 4,000 before he is put to death. When Katherine is buried oil flows from her breasts rather than her bones and this peculiar detail recurs in medieval Welsh poetry. The Welsh *Buched Seint y Katrin* most closely resembles an unusual fifteenth-century English verse Life of Katherine, although the Welsh version pre-dates its English equivalent. Both versions appear to have been produced for lay families and occur in household manuscripts. The Life of Katherine is a particularly visual text and this chapter will examine visual depictions of Katherine in Wales, as well as discuss the spread of her cult, church dedications and holy wells.

The final chapter focuses on the convents of medieval Wales, by examining the extant documentary and literary evidence. It considers attitudes towards nuns and pious women in Wales and discusses the poets' perception of the female religious as corruptible virgin. In Wales there were only three long-standing religious establishments for women: a Benedictine priory at Usk and two Cistercian houses at Llanllugan and Llanllŷr.[15] Possible reasons for the scarcity of nunneries in Wales are suggested. Women may have been too central within the political economy and too integrally connected to the vested interests of secular society to have been purposefully directed towards withdrawal into monastic seclusion. In practice few medieval Welsh women appear to have been encouraged to follow in the footsteps of the numerous Dark-Age virgins who became honoured as saints and other high-status Welsh women were forced into nunneries outside of Wales by the English crown. Spirituality played an important role in the Lives of many married Welsh noblewomen, but religion seems to have rarely been available as a formal vocation for women in medieval Wales. To date there appears to be a distinct lack of evidence concerning female anchoritic activity in Wales. However, it is not clear whether this mode of religious devotion remains undetected due to an absence of written documentation and the difficulties of detecting such activities within the archaeological record or whether it represents a real difference between religious practice in England and Wales. New evidence concerning women who lived semi-monastic lifestyles may yet be uncovered and it is hoped that the present volume will encourage further research on women and religion in medieval Wales.

1

The Welsh Cult of the Virgin Mary

It is perhaps impossible to overemphasize the importance of the Virgin Mary in medieval religious devotion. Mary, the paragon of feminine sanctity, was the most important of all female saints. As mother of the Redeemer, her unique role within the holy kinship made her an effective mediator between heaven and earth. Through her flesh Christ was made man: 'Mab o gnawd Mair' (a Son from Mary's flesh) in the words of the poet Siôn Ceri.[1] Her proximity to mankind ensured a special fondness for the Virgin Mary, a closeness which may be compared to the relationship Christians enjoyed with their local saints. Yet Mary was also 'brenhines nef a dayar ac vffern'[2] (queen of heaven, earth and hell). She alone was both a mother and a virgin and her virginity during (in partu) and after (post partum) the birth of Christ made her an object of wonder and special veneration: the emphasis placed on her physical purity had a far-reaching influence on attitudes towards female sanctity throughout the Middle Ages.

Devotion to the Blessed Virgin Mary permeated medieval Welsh culture in much the same way as it did the rest of medieval Christendom. She was omnipresent in Welsh churches and chapels: images of her abounded in wood, alabaster, stained glass and wall paintings. Famous images of her such as those found at Pen-rhys, Cardigan, St Davids, Pilleth, Pwllheli and Llanystumdwy attracted large numbers of pilgrims and, in the case of Pen-rhys and Cardigan, some of these were of sufficient importance to be specifically singled out in letters to Cromwell advising that they be destroyed during the Reformation.[3]

There were far more churches and holy wells dedicated to the Virgin Mary in Wales than any other saint. Glanmor Williams notes that at least 143 churches and chapels honoured her name.[4] Frances Jones lists 76 holy wells associated with Mary, remarking that many of these were located in areas of strong Norman influence.[5] While there is some evidence to suggest that there were churches dedicated to Mary in tenth-century Wales (e.g. the Book of Llandaf mentions 'Lann Meiripenn Ros' in a charter dated *c.*910 which has been identified with St Mary's, Monmouth),[6] it has generally been assumed that the cult of the Virgin Mary proliferated under Norman influence and that many churches in Wales were rededicated to Mary in the post-conquest period. While in many cases the original dedications to native saints would have been lost, occasionally Mary's name was added to the dedication. For example, some time after 1155 the Virgin Mary's name was added to the dedications to Tysilio and Gwyddfarch at Meifod. It is also likely that during the twelfth and thirteenth centuries new churches were built and it was perfectly normal for the Welsh (regardless of Anglo-Norman influence) to dedicate these to the Mother of Christ. It should perhaps be viewed not so much as a 'takeover' which diluted the influence of native Welsh saints as a natural progression and alteration in trends which affected the whole of Europe, Wales being no exception. The fabric of almost all extant Welsh churches post-dates the eleventh century and dedications are notoriously difficult to date.[7]

Due to a lack of extant early sources, it is extremely difficult to date the 'arrival' of the cult of the Virgin Mary in Wales. In England calendars, poems, liturgical and prose texts demonstrate that Mary was worshipped prior to the Norman Conquest and she is referred to in calendars in Ireland *c.*750–800.[8] Before the end of the sixth century festivals specifically dedicated to Mary were celebrated in Byzantium and by the eighth century a number of Marian feasts had been gradually introduced to the Roman calendar including the Purification (2 February), the Annunciation (25 March), the Assumption (15 August) and the Nativity of Mary (8 September). Mary Clayton has demonstrated that these four feasts were celebrated in England prior to the Conquest, but it is not known with any certainty when they began to be celebrated in Wales. The Welsh equivalents (Gŵyl Fair y Canhwyllau/Gŵyl Puredigaeth Mair, Gŵyl Fair y Gyhydedd/Gŵyl Cyfarchiad Mair, Gŵyl Fair Gyntaf/Gŵyl Dyrchafiad Mair, Gŵyl Fair Ddiwethaf/Gŵyl Fair Pan Aned) along with other feasts which were added to the Roman calendar later – Gŵyl Anna mam Mair (The Feast of St Anne) on 26 July, and Gŵyl Fair yn yr Haf (The Visitation) on 2 July – appear in medieval Welsh calendars, including some of the earliest calendars (e.g. London, British Library Cotton Vespasian A xiv),[9] but since these date from the thirteenth century, they shed little light on Mary's early cult in Wales. Although there appears to have been a new impetus in devotion to Mary in Wales from the twelfth century onwards, it is difficult to believe that the Welsh, already deeply implicated by the process of Christianization in the fifth century, did not venerate Christ's mother before the Norman Conquest.

Early Welsh poetic references to Mary appear to be Christological rather than Marian centred. One of the earliest extant Welsh *englynion* refers indirectly to Mary: 'nit guorgnim molim map meir'[10] (it is not too great a toil to worship Mary's son). This Old Welsh poem praising the Trinity is thought to have been added to the Cambridge Juvencus Manuscript in the early tenth century: it demonstrates that by this period Mary was worshipped for her association with Christ and it was enough to refer to Christ simply as 'map meir' (Mary's son). Nora Costigan has suggested that by the thirteenth century poets would frequently refer to 'Mary's son' in order to avoid using the holy name Jesus.[11] A large corpus of Middle Welsh poetry survives which is testimony to Mary's popularity in Wales. She is described by Bleddyn Ddu as 'crair crefydd'[12] (faith's treasure) and Hywel Swrdal's description of her as 'gwreichionen a phen y ffydd'[13] (the spark and head of the faith) is indicative of the constant source of inspiration that Mary provided to Welsh poets. The 'Golden Age' of Marian poetry in Welsh occurs in the fifteenth century. It is particularly during this period that poets not only invoke Mary, but praise all aspects of her life. It should, however, also be noted that more poetry survives from this period and in general praising the saints and providing poetic accounts of their lives and miracles was particularly in vogue. The poets focus on Mary's relationship with the Trinity, her role as intercessor and merciful mother, Mary as the antithesis of Eve, her early life with Anna and Joachim, her relationship with Joseph, the virgin birth, her joys and sorrows, her perpetual virginity and Mary as Immaculate Conception, as well as her death and corporeal Ascension into heaven.

While there is nothing specifically 'Welsh' about the cult of the Virgin Mary, a huge body of Welsh literature venerating Mary contributes to the medieval 'evidence' for the popularity of her cult and much of the Welsh material remains inaccessible to a non-Welsh-speaking audience. While it is not possible in one chapter to cover every aspect of Mary's cult in Wales, it is hoped that the present study will shed light on a number of the Welsh sources and highlight the importance of Wales's contribution to Marian devotion.

Middle Welsh translations of Marian texts: the apocryphal gospels of Mary, the Ascension, the Miracles of the Blessed Virgin Mary and the Little Office of Our Lady

Between the twelfth and the late fifteenth centuries a number of predominantly prose texts venerating Mary were translated or adapted into Middle Welsh. While the Latin origins of some of the Welsh translations may be traced and similarities between the Welsh versions and other versions highlighted, the immense popularity of many of these texts and the large numbers of extant manuscripts which preserve slightly different versions throughout Western Europe, mean that it is often difficult, if not impossible, to pinpoint from exactly which manuscripts the Welsh texts were translated. Indeed, to a certain extent, the Welsh versions are new creations, adaptations made for a specific sponsor or with a specific audience in mind. Characteristically typical of the *mouvance* of medieval literature is the fact that there are also sometimes slightly different versions of the same text extant in Welsh. The texts would have been recited orally and read aloud – particularly on feast days associated with Mary – and Welsh poets, as one might expect, demonstrate a familiarity with many of the apocryphal tales: often the details they provide are consistent with the Welsh prose versions and occasionally specific details in the poetry differ from the extant prose versions, demonstrating a general familiarity with these well-known tales and perhaps a tendency to draw on oral traditions.

At some point during the second century AD the *Protoevangelium Jacobi* was produced, originally in Greek. This apocryphal legend related details concerning Mary's parents (Anna and Joachim), her conception, birth and childhood, as well as the process of choosing Joseph as her husband and the miraculous birth of Jesus. This was translated into Latin as well as other languages and became a source for the *Pseudo Matthew*, a Latin text produced in the period 550–700 which added details relating to the flight into Egypt and various miracles associated with Jesus's childhood based on the *Infancy Gospel of St Thomas*.[14] It is from this corpus of apocryphal texts that the Welsh legends which have become known as *Buched Anna* (The Life of Anna), *Buched Meir Wyry* (The Life of the Virgin Mary) and *Llyma Vabinogi Iessu Grist* (The Infancy of Jesus Christ) were adapted.[15] They shall be referred to below as *Buched Meir Wyry* rather than by the titles given to them by their editors.

J. E. Caerwyn Williams has demonstrated that there were at least three independent Welsh translations of *Pseudo-Matthaei Evangelium sive de ortu Beatae Mariae et infantia Salvatoris*. These are found in manuscripts dating from the second half of the thirteenth century to the nineteenth century and they are given various titles in the medieval manuscripts including 'hwn yw prol yr esgyp' (This is the prologue of the bishops) and 'Llyma mal y treithir o vuched meir wyry. ac o vabolyaeth an harglyud ny iessu grist' (This is how it is narrated of the Life of the Virgin Mary and of the Infancy of Our Lord Jesus Christ).[16]

In Aberystwyth, NLW, MS Peniarth 5 Anna and Joachim have been married for twenty years but remain childless. When Joachim's sacrifice is refused he flees to the mountains and is visited by an angel who tells him to leave the mountain and return to his wife: 'A thitheu ae keffy hy eneit yn y chroth. yr argluyd Du6 a gyffroes hat yndi. ac ae g6naeth yn vam yr tragy6yaul vendith.'[17] (And you will find her with a living being in her womb. The Lord God has excited seed in her and made her the mother of the eternal blessing.) They are told to meet at the Golden Gate where Anna throws her arms around Joachim's neck and announces that she is pregnant. Nine months later she gives birth to Mary. Joachim's involvement in Mary's conception is deliberately ambiguous, but the suggestion appears to be that Anna becomes pregnant with Joachim's seed – made more potent by divine intervention.[18]

While some of the Church Fathers believed that Anna was a virgin, others disagreed. The feast relating to Mary's miraculous conception on 8 December was introduced in the ninth century, but throughout the Middle Ages celebrating this was a contentious issue. In the twelfth century Bernard, Bishop of St Davids, attempted to prevent the Welsh from celebrating the feast, arguing that it was against the Church's teaching.[19] When the Canons of Lyons celebrated the feast in 1128 St Bernard of Clairvaux reacted furiously, emphasizing that there was a world of difference between the conception of Mary and the miraculous conception of Christ:

> Pity him who tells himself that she was conceived by the Holy Spirit and not by a man. . . I say that she gloriously conceived by the Holy Spirit but was not conceived of it; I say that she has given birth as a virgin but was not born of a virgin. If not, where is the prerogative of the Mother of the Lord who is believed to exult in a way that is quite unique by reason of the nature of her offspring and her bodily integrity if the same privilege was granted to her mother as well?[20]

Some of the Church Fathers argued that Mary was conceived at the time that Anna and Joachim met at the Golden Gate.

Their embrace is depicted in medieval stained glass at the Church of All Saints, Gresford, near Wrexham (Plate 1). The image forms part of a visual narrative relating the apocryphal Life of Mary from her conception, birth and presentation at the temple to her death and Ascension into heaven. Despite the fact that Mary is born nine months after Anna and Joachim are reunited and Joachim spent a further six months away from home, in the Peniarth 47 version of the legend Joachim is informed that, although he had not realized it at the time, Anna was already pregnant when he left for the mountains, suggesting that Mary was conceived fifteen months prior to her birth.[21] A similar suggestion is made in a poem by Hywel Swrdwal (*fl.*1430–70) to Mary's parents:

> Siohasym was a heusor.
> Ffo'dd oedd, heb ffydd dda,
> A Mair wen ym mru Anna.[22]
>
> (Joachim servant and herdsman.
> He was fleeing, without good faith,
> And holy Mary in Anna's womb)

Although the birth of Mary is frequently depicted in medieval visual narratives of her life, including the stained-glass cycle at Gresford, *Buched Meir Wyry* provides no details regarding the labour and thus distances Anna from original sin without claiming that Mary's birth was miraculous. Medieval Welsh poets also tend to avoid describing Mary's birth, linking it only with the birth of Christ. Ieuan Tew, for example, in his *cywydd* to Anna refers to the fact that Anna and Joachim had remained childless for twenty years and provides a tender picture of the infant Mary in her mother's arms, but he chooses to focus on Christ's birth rather than Mary's:

> Morwyn yw Mair o Ann wen.
> Merch wen ym mraich Anna fu,
> Digyswyn y dug Iesu,
> Duw a aned ohoni
> Ac, er hyn, gwyryf yw hi.
> Gwyry wedi'i ddwyn ydoedd
> A chyn dwyn, Duw'n ei chnawd oedd.[23]

(Mary is a maiden from holy Ann.
A holy girl in the arms of Anna,
She gave birth to Jesus without calumny,
God was born of her
And, despite this, she is a virgin.
She was a virgin after giving birth
And before parturition God was in her flesh.)

According to the *Trinubium* Anna was certainly not a virgin, since she married three times and on each occasion had a daughter called Mary: Joachim was the father of her firstborn (the Virgin Mary), but she also had two further daughters with her subsequent husbands Cleophas and Salmon. The early fourteenth-century Peniarth 14 version of *Buched Meir Wyry* refers to Mary the daughter of Cleophas, but makes no mention of Mary the daughter of Salmon. It confirms the notion that Anna was given another daughter in order to compensate for the fact that the Virgin Mary was taken away from her because she was destined for divine service.[24] The *Trinubium* was translated into Welsh and is preserved in a seventeenth-century manuscript, but it was also current in the Middle Ages and poets such as Iolo Goch and Hywel Swrdwal demonstrate a familiarity with this tradition. It is also preserved in the Welsh place-name Llan-y-tair-Mair (literally the Church of the three Marys, but known in English as Knelston) where the church was originally dedicated to the three Marys before it became dedicated simply to Mary.[25]

Mary is taken to the temple at the age of three and remains there with other virgins until she marries Joseph. The Presentation is depicted in stained glass at Gresford: Anna is seen delivering Mary to the bishop (Plate 2) who receives Mary into the temple and ensures that she receives a religious education. The Presentation of Mary is highly significant because it marks a considerable shift in religious practice. She is portrayed as the pioneer of a new faith, a faith which puts particular emphasis on virginity. As Bishop Absychar himself notes when Mary later refuses to marry his son:

Meibon yr Israel heb ef. guerendeuch vy geireu. i. yn da. Yr pan adeila6d Selyf y temyl honn. y buant merchet y brenhined ar prophuydi. ar offeireit yn guedia6 yndi. A phan doethant y oet

> dedua6l wynt a gymerassant wyr. a her6yd y rei kyn nog 6ynt bodlaun vu Du6 vdunt. Y mae Meir e hun yn g6neuthur creuyd ne6yd yr honn yssyd yn ymrodi y Du6 yn wyry y tra vo by6.[26]
>
> ('Sons of Israel' he said. 'Listen to my words well. Since Selyf built this temple, the daughters of kings, prophets and priests have been praying in it. And when they reached legal age they took husbands. And because of their predecessors God was satisfied with them. Mary herself is creating a new religion – she who is giving herself to God and remaining a virgin while she lives.')

Mary is not in a nunnery and it is customary for her fellow virgins to marry at the age of fourteen; nevertheless, Mary makes a speech vowing that she will never take a husband and emphasizing the spiritual superiority of virginity over married life. Her speech is meant to be revolutionary and, in a sense, she is the first nun – a champion of monasticism. One senses in this section the strong presence of the monastic compiler/translator making the most of an opportunity to have Mary voice monastic propaganda, promoting a way of life which was, by the time the Welsh text was circulating, perfectly acceptable and commonplace.

The poet Iolo Goch (*c.*1325–*c.*1398) refers to Mary as 'fwyn fynaches' (tender nun) and in a poem to God Dafydd Nanmor (*fl.*1450–90) highlights her superiority over other virgins 'Gorrav oedd o'r gwerryddon' (She was the best of the virgins).[27] In *Buched Meir Wyry* the other virgins in the temple become jealous of Mary and tease her by calling her 'vrenhines y gwerydon' (Queen of Virgins). An angel descends and tells them that they should not make light of this, for it is true. In a *cywydd* to Mary Dafydd ab Edmwnd (*fl.*1450–97) refers to Mary's fame amongst virgins:

> Mair em ddiwair mam dduw ion
> Mawr enw wyd ir morynion.[28]
>
> (Mary, chaste gem, the mother of the Lord God
> You are a great name to the virgins.)

and Iolo Goch also emphasizes that Mary has become a role model for other virgins:

Mair edrych arnaf ymerodres,
Morwyn bennaf wyd, Mair unbennes,
Mair diornair wyd, Mair deÿrnes,
Mair oleudrem haul, Mair lywodres,
Misere mei, moes eryr;
Prydlyfr gweryddon wyd a'u priodles,

(Mary look upon me o empress,
you are the highest of maidens, sovereign Mary,
Mary you are blameless, queen Mary
noble bright-faced Mary, mistress Mary,
have mercy on me, manner of a hen-eagle;
you are the virgins' songbook and their own benefactor)[29]

Mary's behaviour thus set a pattern for the female religious to follow. She became the symbol of virginity – embodying the monastic ideal and setting an example for both monks and nuns. As Miegge notes, 'it is the value of virginity itself that comes to be celebrated in the virginity of Mary'.[30] Once Christianity had become accepted by the emperors Constantine and Licinius in Milan in 313, it was no longer necessary to die for one's faith. A new kind of martyrdom was needed and thus the first followers of the monastic life began to sacrifice their sexuality. In the words of W. B. Smith, 'the presentation of one's body as a living, unblemished sacrifice, is an offering distinctive and unique, comparable in the Church's Tradition to martyrdom'.[31]

Ironically following the passionate speech in which Mary vows never to marry, *Buched Meir Wyry* goes on to describe the process by which Joseph was chosen as her husband. Mary may have been placed on a pedestal as the pioneer of female asceticism, but unlike other nuns, she continued her chaste way of life within the confines of marriage. As Marina Warner succinctly notes, 'in a patriarchal society, even the Messiah can only be legitimate if his mother is properly married'.[32] Joseph, the oldest of all the unmarried men in the temple, and the possessor of the symbolic 'gwialen verraf' (shortest rod), is chosen when a white dove miraculously flies from his staff into heaven. The episode echoes events involving Aaron's staff in the Old Testament (Numbers 17:8) and emphasizes the fact that Joseph poses no sexual threat to

Mary: he is described as her guardian or keeper and it is stressed that he already has children and is old enough to be her grandfather. Epiphanius, Jerome and St Augustine all believed that Mary was given to Joseph so that he could protect her and guard her virginity. Although Jerome also claimed that Joseph was a virgin, *Buched Meir Wyry* makes it clear that Joseph had children from a previous marriage and that by the time he married Mary he was at the end of his reproductive abilities. Unlike the *De natiuitate Mariae* which claimed that Joseph had never been married before, the Welsh texts name Joseph's sons and do not claim, as suggested by Jerome, that they are Jesus's cousins.[33]

Joseph is typically depicted as an old man leaning on his staff in medieval Welsh art. For example, in Aberystwyth, NLW, MS Peniarth 23 (*c*.1500), he sits in a chair at the foot of Mary's bed, head bent forward resting on his staff, as Mary recumbent clutches her newborn son wrapped in swaddling clothes (Plate 3). Hywel Swrdwal in his *cywydd* to Anna, Joachim and Mary refers to the fact that Mary did not complain, although she was expected to marry the old carpenter: 'Er dyfod i'w phriodi/ Â saer hen, ni sorrai hi.'[34] (Although it came to her marrying an old carpenter, she did not sulk.)

Marina Warner argues that the emphasis on Mary's virginity developed when the Bible was translated from Hebrew into Greek *c*.300. She suggests that the word 'almah' (Hebrew for 'young girl of marriageable age') was mistranslated as 'parthenos' in Greek (meaning 'virgin') and that the original word 'almah' did not necessarily convey the notion of 'virgo intacta'. Indeed in the Song of Songs 'almah' is used to refer to the girls in the harem of the beloved (Song of Solomon 7:3; 6:8). It was, nevertheless, generally assumed that a young girl of marriageable age would be a virgin before she was betrothed.[35] Mary was awarded the title *Aeiparthenos* (Eternal Virgin) by the Council of Chalcedon in 451.

The notion that Mary was a virgin when she conceived Christ stems largely from her response to Gabriel at the time of the Annunciation: 'How can this be, since I am a virgin?' (Luke 1:34) and her virginal state echoes the prophecy of Isaiah in the Old Testament (Isaiah 7:14). According to both

Luke 1:35 and Matthew 1:18 Mary conceived of the Holy Ghost. Although the Bible was not translated into Welsh until 1588, certain sections of the Bible were available in Middle Welsh and the fact that more than one translation of Luke 1:26–38 was circulating demonstrates the importance of the Annunciation to both the clergy and the laity in medieval Wales. *Rybud Gabriel at Veir* (literally 'Gabriel's warning to Mary') was translated into Welsh *c.*1346 by the anchorite of Llanddewibrefi for Gruffudd ap Llywelyn ap Philip ap Trahaern, a nobleman living at Rhydodyn near Llansawel, and 'Llith o Veir' (Mary's Litany) also formed part of the Welsh translation of the Little Office of the Virgin Mary which was used in church services as well as by individuals during private devotion.

Gwassanaeth Meir (the Welsh version of *Officum Parvum Beatae Mariae Virginis*) was produced in the second half of the fourteenth century by an unknown author who appears to have been using a Dominican version of the Office. The majority of the Welsh translation is metrical and the author demonstrates an ability to compose in both strict and free metre Welsh poetry. A copy made by John Davies of Mallwyd (*c.*1565–1618) attributes the *Gwassanaeth* to Dafydd Ddu of Hiraddug, a fourteenth-century cleric poet who may have belonged to the Dominican Order.[36] Brynley F. Roberts has demonstrated that although it cannot be claimed with absolute certainty that Dafydd Ddu was responsible for the Welsh version of this popular service in honour of Mary, he definitely possessed all the necessary skills to make him a strong contender.[37] *Gwassanaeth Meir* contains some of the earliest Welsh translations of the Psalms and liturgical prayers and its content formed a large portion of the primer or Book of Hours popular amongst the laity. Although one would expect that the Welsh nobility and gentry would have desired Books of Hours in the vernacular, just as they requested Middle Welsh versions of saints' Lives and other religious texts, there are in fact no surviving Middle Welsh Books of Hours. These particularly finely decorated manuscripts tend to be written in Latin or French and surviving examples with Welsh connections were commissioned from skilled workshops outside of Wales.[38]

The Llanbeblig Hours which appears, at least partially, to be of Gwynedd provenance was owned by Isabella Godynogh whose obit in 1413 is entered in a calendar in the manuscript which refers to local saints, such as Deiniol and Peblig. Although the book may have been produced in England, the calendar and six full-page miniatures (including an image of St Peblig) appear to have been added in north Wales.[39] One of the illustrations depicts an Annunciation scene in which Gabriel appears kneeling holding a palm and Christ is illustrated crucified on a lily (Plate 4). Lily crucifixions occur in other media such as stained glass, alabaster and wall paintings, but the Llanbeblig Hours, which is thought to date to the late fourteenth century, may contain the earliest example of a lily crucifixion in a medieval manuscript.[40] Throughout the Middle Ages it was generally believed that Christ was crucified on the same date as the Feast of the Annunciation, that is 25 March, and thus the two incidents are crystallized in the one visual image. The inevitability of Christ's suffering on the cross is apparent from the time of the Annunciation and one event will automatically lead to the other – both forming part of the divine plan. Yet although the viewer is reminded of the horror of the Crucifixion and the anguish that Mary will suffer as a result of this, as Sarah Boss has shown, the lily in bloom suggests the cross transformed into the Tree of Life: the Resurrection is implicit in the Crucifixion in the same way as the Crucifixion is implicit in the Annunciation.[41]

The Annunciation is described in detail in *Buched Meir Wyry* and it is in the apocryphal gospels rather than the Bible that all aspects of Mary's virginity are examined. Mary's virginity and Joseph's conduct are subjected to scrutiny when they are made to drink the bitter waters of the temple in order to prove their innocence[42] and Mary's virginity is again tested by the midwife Salome following the birth of Christ. In the apocryphal gospels Jesus is born in an underground cave and not moved to a manger in a stable until three days later. The Welsh texts make no mention of the three wise men. When Mary is about to give birth, Joseph rushes off to find women who can assist with the birth, but when he returns they are amazed to see that Mary has brought forth her child with ease, without pain, blood or afterbirth. One of the midwives, Zelome, marvels at the fact that Mary is a virgin and confirms Mary's virginity in partu and post partum:

> Zelomy a dyuat 6rth Veir wynvydedic gat ti ymi gyhurd a thi. Pan gyhyrdod. o lef uchel hy ae dy6ot. Argluyd. Argluyd maur trugarha 6rthyf. ny chly6yt. ac ny welet bronneu yn lla6n o laeth. a geni mab ae mam yn wyry yn ymdangos. ac nat oes lygredigaeth guaet nae arll6ybyr yr ganedic. na dolur ar y neb ae hesgores. gwyry kynn escor a guyry yn trigyau guedy escor val y mae aml6c.[43]

> (Zelomy said to the blessed Mary 'Let me touch you'. When she touched her she proclaimed in a loud cry, 'Lord, great Lord, have mercy on me. This has never been heard of or seen before – breasts full of milk and a son born to a mother who appears to be a virgin. And there is no sign of bloody pollution or trace of the newborn, nor any sign of pain on the one who has just given birth to him – a virgin before giving birth and still a virgin after giving birth, as is obvious.')

The other midwife, Salome, however, doubts whether Mary can possibly be a mother and a virgin at the same time and requests 'gat ti y mi dy balualv ual y cretuyf y Zelomi or hynn a gly6af' (allow me to grope you so that I may believe what I have heard from Zelome), presumably wanting to subject the virgin's hymen to a physical examination. When she touches the virgin her hand instantly withers and she is not cured until she lays her hand on the child and believes in the miraculous virgin birth.[44]

The effect of the description of the virgin birth – with no pain, blood or afterbirth – is to distance Mary from the curse of Eve (Genesis 3:16) and emphasize that she is no ordinary mother. She is free from the pain and 'bloody pollution' which is present in all other births experienced by ordinary women. The description of the nativity in the apocryphal gospels is, of course, a declaration of the hagiographer's belief in the doctrine of the Immaculate Conception, announcing that Mary is free from original sin, but in addition to its serious theological implications, it also betrays the prejudices of the time concerning women's bodily fluids and the uncleanliness associated with normal births conceived in sin. The poet Iorwerth Fynglwyd stressed that Mary's maternity was different from all others, since she was 'feichiog heb ddim afiechyd' (pregnant without taint, literally without disease).

Ni chafad o lwyth Adam,
a'i gyfrif oll, gyfryw fam:
mam wyd, – rhai a'th broffwydodd –
morwyn a mam o'r un modd.
Rhagoraist – synhwyraist sôn –
Mair wen ar lu'r morynion.
O buost, er bost i'r byd,
feichiog heb ddim afiechyd,
cedwaist, – mawr egluraist glod –
Fair wendeg, dy forwyndod.[45]

(Such a mother was not had
from Adam's tribe, counting them all:
you are a mother – some prophesied you –
a virgin and a mother in the same manner.
You excelled all the host of virgins
– you sensed the rumour – Holy Mary.
O you were, despite the world's boast,
pregnant without disease,
you kept – great the praise you explained –
fair, holy Mary, your virginity.)

Gwilym Tew (*fl. c.*1470–80) uses the same phrase 'y bu feichiog heb afiechyd' in his *awdl* to Mary of Pen-rhys – here in association with feeding Christ.[46] The fact that Mary did not suffer any labour pains is revered by Iolo Goch who also confirms his belief in Mary's virginity in partu and post partum:

Dihareb rhwydded y dehores
Heb boen yn esgor pôr perffeithles,
Heb friw o'i arwain, nef briores,
Heb ddim godineb â neb yn nes,
Neu ogan o ŵr, nid oedd neges . . .
Rhyfedd fu'r gallu o Fair gyfeilles,
Ymddŵyn yn forwyn, Fair f'arglwyddes,

Morwyn cyn ymddŵyn, fwyn fynaches,
Morwyn yn ymddŵyn, gorllwyn geirlles,
Morwynaidd eto a meiriones.

(It is proverbial how easily the lord of perfect benefit
was delivered without birth pains,
without any wound from bearing him, prioress of heaven,
without any fornication with anyone intimately,
or disgrace from any man, there was no contact . . .
Marvellous was the power of Mary the companion,
a virgin bearing child, Mary my lady,
a virgin before bearing, tender nun,
a virgin whilst bearing, lying-in of a beneficial name,
still virginal and a mistress.)[47]

Thus, the poets praise Mary's virginity and confirm the beliefs proliferated in the apocryphal gospels of Mary. Yet, as one might expect, they also inevitably emphasize how different Mary's experience of childbirth was from other women. She was, as one anonymous Welsh poet described her, 'Gorau mam, gorau mamaeth'[48] (the best mother, the best nursing mother).

Marina Warner has argued that since Mary was paradoxically both a virgin and a mother, she was 'alone of all her sex' and any comparison between the Virgin Mary and the ordinary female condition would automatically lead one to conclude that the average woman was deficient and imperfect. Placing the Virgin Mary on a pedestal, she argues, has often been used to the detriment of women in Catholic countries. The Virgin's legend has had the power 'to heal and to harm'.[49] Sarah Boss, on the other hand, has argued that there is a variety of ways of interpreting Mary's virginity and that the belief that Mary gives birth without pain or injury has in fact been attractive to women in childbirth: rather than alienate ordinary women, Mary's experience has offered women hope that she will assist them to obtain a safe delivery.[50] My own view is that both of these readings contain elements which are useful and relevant when interpreting how the virgin birth was viewed and used by medieval society. On the one hand, details concerning blood and afterbirth are indicative of negative attitudes towards the female body which was considered to be inferior and impure, not only in theological tracts but also in medieval medical texts. Misogynist attitudes towards women in medieval texts have been well documented and will not be re-examined here.[51] Nevertheless, it was appropriate for medieval hagiographers and poets to marvel at the unique nature of the birth of Christ and it is unlikely that ordinary medieval women would have felt slighted or assumed that any negative comparison with them was intended. In none of the Welsh poems which praise Mary's motherhood is there any attempt to denigrate other women and when genuine Welsh noblewomen are compared to the Virgin Mary in brief references to sponsors' wives the aim is to elevate their status.

In the tale of the flight into Egypt one finds detail which is peculiar to the Welsh translation of the *Pseudo Matthew*, possibly due to a mistranslation. While travelling to Egypt Mary becomes tired and rests under the shade of a palm tree. Seeing that the tree is laden with apples, she asks Joseph to pick some for her. He complains that the tree is too tall and that he would prefer some water. Jesus, sitting on his mother's lap, asks the tree to bend and miraculously it lowers its branches to Mary's feet so that she can easily collect the apples.[52] In the majority of the Latin versions of the text the tree is either an unidentified fruit tree or a date tree. The Welsh version may be unique in claiming that the tree is an apple tree and it is possible that the translator mistook 'pomum' (fruit tree) for 'apple tree'.[53] Tudur Aled (*c*.1465–*c*.1525) in a *cywydd* to the abbot of the Cistercian abbey of Valle Crucis refers to the miracle and interestingly demonstrates a familiarity with the Welsh version of the text, describing the abundance of apples offered to Mary: 'Afalau i fair, fil, a fu/ Am i'r blagur mawr blygu'[54] (Apples for Mary, a thousand there were/ because the great branches bent). Other Welsh poets demonstrate a familiarity with different versions of the legend. For example, in an anonymous poem to Mary the fruit is simply described as 'aeron' (berries), but Joseph is depicted in a particularly unpleasant manner as he tells Mary to ask the one who got her pregnant to pick the fruit.[55] This portrayal of Joseph, although absent in *Buched Meir Wyry*, is found in other medieval versions of the story including the

Middle English play *Ludus Coventriae*.[56] Apples may have unconsciously occurred to the Welsh redactor as an obvious fruit to be growing on trees, despite the fact that in *Buched Meir Wyry* the tree is also described as 'pren palym' (a palm tree). Apples lend a certain relevance to the tale that other fruit do not. Although the Bible does not name the fruit consumed by Eve in the Garden of Eden, it was generally assumed to be an apple which led the first woman to be expelled from Paradise. As we shall see below, since Mary was frequently contrasted with Eve, it would be appropriate that the miracle in the apocrypha should echo Eve's expulsion. While the natural world recoiled from the sinner Eve, it would bend over backwards to serve the mother of the Redeemer. In the Welsh translation of *Historia Adam* (*Ystorya Adaf*) the grass is said to have shrivelled under Adam and Eve's feet as they walked from Paradise, as Adam himself noted: 'ac na thyuawd na blewyn na llessewyn y ffordd y sathryssam ac an traet y dayar'[57] (and neither a blade nor a herb grew where our feet trod on the ground). Favourable associations between Mary and the natural world have meant that numerous flowers and plants have been named after Mary in Welsh as in other cultures.[58]

An early anonymous Welsh poem found in the Black Book of Carmarthen (*c.*1250) describes the flight into Egypt and focuses on the miracle of the instantaneous harvest.[59] The holy family fleeing Herod's men pass a man ploughing a field and ask him to speak truthfully to their pursuers. When Herod's evil men arrive shortly afterwards the man is miraculously reaping his crop and since he informs them that the holy family passed him when he was preparing the field for sowing, they turn back disappointed, abandoning their mission. Although the tale became widespread in the thirteenth century, Kenneth Jackson dates the Welsh poem on linguistic grounds to the twelfth century and proposes that the miracle may have originated in the Celtic Church.[60] Andrew Breeze, however, demonstrates that the Welsh and Irish versions differ in their detail and that the Welsh poem has more in common with a thirteenth-century French poem. Although the Welsh poem pre-dates the French version of the instantaneous harvest, Breeze argues convincingly that the legend is more likely to stem from a French source than to be an archaic Celtic survival from early Christian times.[61] Relatively few visual depictions of the flight into Egypt survive from medieval Wales, but a badly defaced stone carving in St Davids Cathedral probably depicts the holy family's flight with Jesus perched on Joseph's shoulders.[62]

Various Welsh versions of the *Transitus Mariae* (*Y mod yd aeth meir y nef*) are preserved in twelve manuscripts dating from the second half of the thirteenth century onwards.[63] The earliest manuscripts which contain legends explaining how Mary died and ascended into heaven are written in Syriac and appear to date from the end of the fifth century. Mary Clayton has argued that since the Feast of the Assumption of Mary was being celebrated in Jerusalem in the fifth century, this would naturally have given rise to conjecture concerning the circumstances of Mary's death. A sermon by Bishop Theoteknos, which has been dated to the end of the sixth century, elaborates upon the legend, providing a theological explanation for the reasons why Mary should be assumed into heaven body and soul. It was not considered fitting that the mother of Christ should suffer the curse of Adam and Eve and therefore, although she experienced death, her body did not rot. Both Enoch and Elijah had been taken to heaven, and, thus, it was unimaginable that Christ would leave his own mother behind. Since Christ took his immaculate flesh from the immaculate flesh of his mother, her body 'was preserved incorrupt and undefiled and taken up into heaven with its pure and spotless soul by the holy archangels and powers and is above Enoch and Elijah and all the Prophets and Apostles and the heavens, except only God'.[64]

The Peniarth 5 version of *Transitus Mariae* was translated into Welsh in the thirteenth century by the cleric Madog ap Selyf for Gruffudd ap Maredudd ab Owain, a nobleman and descendant of the Lord Rhys whose family were great patrons of Welsh literature.[65] Gruffudd ap Maredudd, along with his brothers, was imprisoned in the Tower of London in 1283 during the Welsh Wars of Independence and it is likely, therefore, that the text was translated between 1265 and 1282.

In Peniarth 5 Mary is warned of her imminent death two years after Christ's Ascension. Mary removes her own clothes and carrying the palm from Paradise that the angel had given her she walks to the Mount of Olives with the bright light of the Holy Spirit shining all around her. First of all her soul is taken from her and entrusted to the Archangel Michael. Her valuable, shining soul 'na allei neb ryv dyn marvavl datgannv o'e tauot y decket. Tegach oed noc a vu o eiry na metal nac aryant nac eur yn echtywynnygu o eglurder diruaur'[66] (its beauty no mortal man could describe with his tongue. It was more beautiful than if it were snow or metal or silver or gold shining with intense brilliance). Then her body is prepared for the grave by three maidens, but before they begin cleaning the body it is already spotlessly clean and 'Vegys blodeu y lili oed lliv y hwynep'[67] (And the colour of her face was like the flowers of the lily). The Welsh text does not specify whether it was intended to bury her body on the Mount of Olives, Jehoshaphat or Gethsamene.[68] Her body is taken to a new graveyard to the south of the city facing east, where no man has ever been buried and three days later the Lord and angels descend and Christ placing his hands around her neck transports her corporeal body to heaven.

Emphasis throughout the text is placed on Mary's purity and virginity and at the beginning it is explained that Mary deserves a special send off 'yn bennaf canys megys y kettuis hi y gweryndaut a'e morwyndavt yr ymdvyn Crist a'e escor yn gorfforaul'[69] (principally because she kept her virginity and maidenhood since conceiving Christ and giving birth to him physically). The section which describes how the Jewish priest was punished when he tried to push Mary from her bier again highlights Mary's physical purity. While some versions of the text record that his deformed hand is healed when he touches the palm of Paradise, the Welsh version in Peniarth 5 notes that his hand is healed because he repeats after Peter a declaration of his belief in Mary's virginity in partu and post partum:

> Mi a gredaf yn Iessu Grist, Vab Duv, an Argluyd ni, yr hvnn a ymduc honn yn y bru ac a uu yr hynny wyry wedy escor mal kynn escor.[70]

(I believe in Jesus Christ, the Son of God, and our Lord, he who was brought forth from her womb and despite this she was a virgin after giving birth as she was before giving birth.)

Peter then gives him the palm and tells him to use it to heal blind people in the city, but in the Welsh text the palm plays no part in healing the Jew.

The Jew is depicted with his hands stuck to Mary's coffin in late medieval stained glass in the Lady Chapel at Gresford.[71] Images of the Assumption and Coronation of the Virgin Mary at Gresford have been much restored. On the carved alabaster tomb of Sir Richard Herbert of Ewias in the priory church of Abergavenny the Virgin is depicted ascending into heaven as St Thomas catches the girdle slipping from her waist.[72] This episode involving Thomas is not present in the majority of the Welsh versions of the *Transitus*, but an unusual version preserved in Aberystwyth, NLW, MS Llanstephan 117, in the hand of Ieuan ap William ap Dafydd ab Einws, refers to the episode and juxtaposes an account of the Ascension of Christ with Mary's Ascension. In Llanstephan 117 Thomas who is late for the funeral falls to his knees and begins to weep because he has missed the event, but the Blessed Virgin appears to him, cuts off the pendant on her girdle and puts it in his hand telling him that he should keep it as a sign that he was present and advises him that, because of this, the other apostles will not chastise him for missing the event. She then ascends into heaven.[73] It is noticeable that Mary places the relic in his hand before she begins her ascent (rather than throws it en route as is usually the case) and although she gives him the whole girdle, particular emphasis is placed on the pendant which she cuts off from the garment.

Although Iolo Goch refers to the incident in a poem to the twelve apostles and Judgement Day, he does not demonstrate a familiarity with any of the idiosyncrasies of the Llanstephan 117 version, describing instead how Thomas caught the girdle as it fell:

Degfed Tomas, hoywras hir,
A'r India yw ei randir;
Pan aeth Mair, fuddair addef,
Gyda nifer Nêr i nef,

O'i lleng hi a ollyngawdd
O nef i Domas ei nawdd,
Ei gwregys hi, wiw riain,
Orau modd o aur a main;
Hwnnw yw, iawnrhyw anrheg,
Ei warant ef, wiw rent teg.

(The tenth is Thomas, long vigorous grace,
and India is his territory;
when Mary went, utterance of a beneficial word,
with the Lord's host to heaven,
from her legion she let fall
from heaven to Thomas her protection,
her belt, good maiden,
finest form of gold and jewels;
that is, gift of good kind,
his warrant, fine fair payment.)[74]

In a separate poem to Mary Iolo again refers to Mary's Ascension and highlights the presence of her incorrupt body in heaven: 'Byw ydwyd yn nef fal abades/ Yn dy gorffolaeth, hoywgorff heules' (You are alive in heaven like an abbess/ in your bodily form, radiant body beneficial like the sun).[75] The poet Harri ap Hywel who was made archdeacon of Carmarthen in 1494 presents a similar idea in his *cywydd* to the Virgin Mary, claiming that Mary was still alive when she was taken to heaven.[76] Bleddyn Ddu (*fl. c.*1330–85) also refers to the fact that Mary's blessed body and soul were taken to heaven, possibly separately as in the Welsh prose versions: however, although he refers to those who transported the coffin he makes no mention of the Jew or of the incident involving St Thomas.[77] The episode involving Thomas and the girdle is only found in the *Transitus* of Pseudo-Joseph of Arimathaea which M. R. James traces to thirteenth-century Italy and the Llanstephan 117 version is unique amongst the Welsh manuscripts.[78] James, of course, makes no mention of the Welsh texts and I suspect that the Llanstephan 117 version, which was written by Ieuan ap William ap Dafydd 'ari gost i hvn' (at his own expense) is unusual even in a wider European context.[79]

Since Mary's entire physical body ascended into heaven, it could not be claimed that any of her bones remained on earth as relics. Mary was superior to other saints whose sanctity ensured that their bones possessed special healing powers – a means of compensating for the fact that, as descendents of Adam and Eve, their bodies remained on earth and only their souls joined Christ in heaven. It is claimed in an eighth-century document summarized by Hilda Graef that in 451 the Empress Pulcharia asked Bishop Juvenal of Jerusalem if she could have Mary's body. He replied that there were no corporeal relics of Mary since the apostles had only discovered her funeral clothes when they opened her tomb. Pulcheria then asked for these and Juvenal sent them to her in a sealed casket.[80] Throughout the Middle Ages relics associated with Mary, such as her veil, phials of her milk, tears, fragments of her hair or finger nails multiplied. Paris, Chartres, Constantinople, Le Puy and Assisi all claimed to possess the Virgin's girdle which she had given to St Thomas, but perhaps the most famous example is associated with Prato cathedral where it was claimed that Michele Dagomari donated the relic having acquired it when he married the daughter of a Greek priest whom he had fallen in love with during the first crusade. The girdle or belt which had been given as a dowry was said to aid conception and increase one's chances of becoming pregnant.[81] I have not come across any examples of references to Marian relics in Wales, although sections of the holy rood were said to have been owned by the royal house of Gwynedd.

In Peniarth 14 the account of Mary's death and Ascension form part of a larger text, the Middle Welsh account of the Miracles of the Blessed Virgin Mary (*Gwyrthyeu e Wynvydedic Veir*). In Peniarth 5 and Llanstephan 27 the *Transitus* precedes the miracles, whereas in the oldest version, Peniarth 14, the *Transitus* occurs between two miracles involving statues of the Virgin Mary. Lewis Haydn Angell notes that while the Peniarth 14 and Peniarth 5 versions of the *Gwyrthyeu* (Miracles) appear to stem from the same common original the accounts of the *Transitus* that they preserve are quite different. He proposes that the Welsh version of the *Transitus* found in Peniarth 14 most closely resembles version B printed in *Apocalypses Apocryphae*, edited by L. F. C. Tischendorf and suggests that the Welsh versions of the *Gwyrthyeu* closely resemble the Latin texts found in London, BL, MS Cotton Cleopatra C. X and Oxford, Balliol College, MS 240.[82] Ingo Mittendorf has argued that since the arrangement of the miracles in Balliol 240 most closely resembles Peniarth 14, that this should be considered its source.[83]

In all *Gwyrthyeu e Wynvyvedic Veir* recounts twenty-eight miracles which demonstrate that Mary is both powerful and merciful.[84] When all else fails, the repentant, no matter how great their sins, can turn to the Virgin Mary for assistance. Mary heals the sick, resurrects the dead, ensures that sinners are given proper burials, helps monks preserve their chastity, saves Jews, assists during battle, slays tyrants, converts sinners and reinstates dismissed clergy. The majority of the miracles involve priests, abbots, monks and knights, but some of the miracles involve female protagonists and in particular emphasize the Virgin's efficacy when it comes to assisting with childbirth.

One of the most popular miracles which is found in almost every collection, including the Welsh versions, is the tale of the pregnant abbess who attempts unsuccessfully to conceal her pregnancy. Surprisingly the text includes no moral condemnation of the errant abbess and it makes no reference to the father of her baby or any long-standing affair. She is merely tricked by the devil and 'gvander y chnavt' (the weakness of her flesh), almost as though the author sympathises with her. The image presented of the nunnery is, however, fairly unfavourable and although there is no direct criticism of the abbess, the sisters of the convent do not fare as well. It is suggested from the beginning that the sisters are spiteful towards the abbess because they resent her authority over them: 'Manaches a oed cas gan y chuioryd a oed darystyngedic idi.'[85] (The female religious was hated by the sisters who were subordinate to her.) She confides in one of the nuns who immediately betrays her and goes to inform the archdeacon: it is suggested that the nun should have kept the secret and it is her betrayal rather than the abbess's conduct which is criticized. On the day when the baby is due to be delivered the abbess weeps and prays to Mary before the altar. 'Ac ny phallws idi hitheu Mam y Drugared' (And the Mother of Mercy did not fail her). The highlight of the tale, as in the majority of the miracle stories, is the notion that when everyone else has turned against you, the Virgin will never let you down. The Virgin appears and delivers the baby boy, so that when the bishop's messengers arrive 'y deimlav e chroth' (to feel her womb), there are no signs that she is pregnant. On the third day, when the bishop himself arrives, he believes that she has been wrongly accused and is about to burn her accusers when the abbess confesses and tells him all. The boy is not entrusted to a hermit in the Welsh version (as is usually the case), but a kind friend of the Virgin's and at the age of seven he attends the bishop's palace, succeeding the bishop when he dies.[86]

Another miracle, which again is well known in these collections, relates how the Virgin helps a pregnant woman give birth while on pilgrimage to the Mont St Michel. The other pilgrims think only of saving themselves when the waves rush towards them and they pretend not to hear her cries for help, but the Virgin appears and shelters the woman with her sleeve ensuring that not a single drop of sea water touches the poor pilgrim as she gives birth: 'Ac ena yd enghis e wreic ar vab heb ovyn arnei no chet bei en e cartref diogelaf'[87] (And then the woman gave birth to a son and she was no more afraid than she would have been had she been in the safest home). Pregnancy features once more in the miracles when the Virgin restores a woman's sanity when she loses her mind shortly after giving birth. Thus, the miracles which were available in Welsh during the second half of the thirteenth century appear to confirm popular belief in the Virgin Mary's eagerness to support pregnant women and assist during childbirth. Although miracles concerning preserving male chastity are present in the collection, it is noticeable that the miracles involving women are predominantly associated with pregnancy and sexual transgression. The only other miracle which involves a female protagonist is the legend of Mary of Egypt which is included here as one of the Virgin's miracles, since Mary of Egypt is an active prostitute until she experiences a conversion in front of a statue of the Virgin Mary in Jerusalem.[88]

One miracle which appears in the Welsh Peniarth 14 and Peniarth 5 collections, but is not found in the Latin version in Balliol 240, relates how a thief attempted to steal a golden crown from an image of Christ sitting on his mother's knee. The statue of the Virgin comes alive as she reaches out her hands to prevent the thief robbing her Son's crown. The thief angrily takes out his bow and arrow and attempts to shoot the statue, but the carving of Christ catches the arrow and the statue is said to have remained thus, with Christ sitting on his mother's knee clutching the thief's arrow.[89] No equivalent for this Welsh miracle has thus far been found and, although it is possible that this is unique to the Welsh collection, it is likely that this brief miracle which is sandwiched between the *Transitus* and the Welsh collection of the miracles of St Edmund comes from another Latin source, or that the Welsh version is not a direct translation of Balliol 240, but stems from an intermediary very similar to this. Moving images of the Virgin are well known in modern Ireland and some are said to have existed in medieval Wales, such as 'delw fyw yr Wyddgrug' the living image at Mold which is discussed in greater detail below.[90] Although little is known of this particular image in the Virgin's church at Mold, it is possible that it was thought to have miraculously come to life and moved. Neither the church nor the location of the miracle are mentioned in the *Gwyrthyeu* and, since a number of the miracles involve statues of the Virgin Mary, it is unlikely that the miracle in the Middle Welsh account is based on a tale involving a specific Welsh statue. Although medieval Welsh poets refer to events described in the apocryphal gospels of Mary and the *Transitus*, the legends related in the vernacular prose accounts of the Miracles of Blessed Virgin Mary do not appear in poetic form.

Medieval Welsh poetry to the Virgin Mary

Since Middle Welsh poetry is such a rich and important source, in addition to referring to bardic references to the apocryphal gospels and important shrines and images from Wales, the poetic evidence also warrants its own section in this discussion of Marian devotion in medieval Wales. Nevertheless, since a vast corpus of poetry survives from this period, it will only be possible to refer to a representative sample of Welsh poetry and a fraction of the poetic allusions to Mary.

As mentioned above, early references to Mary in Welsh poetry tend to focus on her relationship with Christ. Although there are numerous references to Mary in the work of the Poets of the Princes (*Beirdd y Tywysogion*) who flourished from the first half of the twelfth century until 1282 when the last of the Welsh princes, Llywelyn ap Gruffudd, was killed, no complete poems to the Blessed Virgin Mary are extant from this period. This is perhaps surprising considering that some of the Marian prose texts appear to have been translated into Welsh during the second half of the thirteenth century. Nevertheless, a number of important Marian themes are developed in the poetry of the Poets of the Princes, such as her relationship with her Son and the Holy Trinity, the doctrine of the Immaculate Conception, details relating to the nativity and Mary's efficacy as mediatrix. These, along with a variety of other Marian themes including details from the apocryphal legends, are further developed in the work of the Poets of the Gentry (*Beirdd yr Uchelwyr*) who superseded the Poets of the Princes and flourished until the end of the sixteenth century.[91] Numerous poems to Mary are extant from this period and all aspects of her cult are venerated.

Gwynfardd Brycheiniog (*fl.*1170s) in his famous *awdl* to Saint David is possibly the first Welsh poet to refer to Mary as 'Mam Rhadlonedd' (Mother of Graciousness) and, if the anonymous poem discussed above, which describes the instantaneous harvest, can be dated to the twelfth century, then this contains an early reference to Mary as 'dinam' (faultless or immaculate).[92] Einion Wan (*fl.*1200–45) also describes Mary as 'Mair ddinam' (faultless Mary) in his elegy to Prince Llywelyn ap Iorwerth who died in 1240 and by the time of the Poets of the Gentry the epithet 'dinam' and variations on this were frequently used by medieval Welsh poets.[93] For example, Casnodyn (*fl.*1320–40) in his *englynion* to Mary emphasises that Mary is not tainted by sin: 'Cain firain forwyn ddibech' (Beautiful, excellent and sinless virgin) and Bleddyn Ddu refers to her as 'Mair berffaith' (perfect Mary).[94] Although there are references in Middle English poetry from the thirteenth century onwards which suggest that Christ died to save the sins of Mary as well as the rest of mankind, there do not appear to be any instances in medieval Welsh poetry which doubt that Mary was free from original sin.[95]

The Immaculate Conception, the notion that Mary was untainted by original sin from the time of her own conception to her death and Ascension into heaven, was a contentious issue throughout the Middle Ages and it was not made dogma by the Catholic Church until 1854 when Pope Pius XI declared it an article of Catholic faith. Ambrose (339–97) emphasized Mary's perfect purity and was one of the first to give direction to Mariology in the West, although he did not necessarily teach the Immaculate Conception, a doctrine peculiar to the Western Church. Mary, he claimed, is a personification of the Church:

> betrothed, yet a virgin, because she is the type of the Church, which is immaculate yet married. The virgin [Church] has conceived us by the Spirit, the Virgin brings us forth without pain. And therefore perhaps is the holy Mary married to one [Joseph], but filled with another [the Holy Spirit], because the individual Churches, too, are filled by the Spirit and his grace, but are externally joined to a mortal priest.[96]

In Mary's body the mystic body of Christ, as well as his physical body, was formed. Since Christ's humanity was largely dependant upon the notion that he took his flesh from the flesh of Mary, his only human parent, it was appropriate that Mary should be granted a special grace and that her body, unlike all the other descendants of Eve, should be free from original sin. St Augustine (354–430) is usually credited with being one of the first exponents of the doctrine of the Immaculate Conception; other Church Fathers disagreed and felt that extending Christ's perfection to Mary impaired his humanity.

While Eve was blamed for the fall of mankind, Mary was considered to be the antithesis of Eve, the woman prophesied in Genesis 3:15 as the mother who would stamp on the head of the serpent and introduce salvation to Christendom. As stated in the Middle Welsh translation of the *Elucidarium* (*Historia Lucidar*), a compendium of Christian doctrine attributed to Honorius Augustodunensis: 'a megys ydoeth anghev yr byt drwy eua yn vor6ynn. velly ydoeth Iechyt yr byt dr6y yrwy veir'[97] (and as death came to the world through Eve a virgin, so salvation came to the world through the Virgin Mary). Jerome claimed that Eve was a virgin before the Fall, thus he naturally contrasted Eve and Mary and associated virginity in particular with women: 'In paradise Eve was a virgin . . . Death came through Eve, but life has come through Mary. And thus the gift of virginity has been bestowed most richly upon women, seeing as it had its beginning from a woman.'[98]

Numerous Welsh poets contrasted Eve's sinfulness and Mary's sinlessness, as one might expect. The Anglesey poet Iorwerth ab y Cyriog associated himself with Eve's natural propensity to sin, and emphasized that Christ, in contrast, was a descendant of Mary and free from sin because of her special grace:

> Un wyf a hanwyf o hen Efa,
> Ynof nawd pechawd, pechais ddirdra;
> Un wyd a hanwyd (dyuna – â'm plaid)
> O Fair, ras enaid fawr reisina.[99]
>
> (I am one descended from Eve of old,
> Sinful nature is in me. I have committed wicked sins;
> You are one who is descended (agree with my cause)
> from Mary, great queen of grace-filled soul.)

Since Gabriel's salutation 'Ave' spelled 'Eva' backwards, the poets frequently played with this palindrome in their poetry, juxtaposing Eve and Mary and contrasting these two extreme representatives of femininity. As Andrew Breeze suggests, it is likely that Gruffudd ap Maredudd (*fl.*1342–82) was the first Welsh poet to use the topos:[100]

> Tair llythyren, wen windud,
> A'n dug yng nghyfrgoll golled;
> A thair, Fair, o fawr gariad
> A'n dug nef o'n dygn ofid . . .

EFA bu pla ym mhob plas – i'n bwrw
I berygl gyweithias;
AFE, urddedig urddas,
A'n dug yn faith o gaith gas.

Golau fydd, Fair fam Geli,
Golwg radlon heb gelu;
Gofwy nef oedd deg Afe,
Gofal fu afal Efa.[101]

(Three letters, holy one of the country of wine,
Brought us to total loss in damnation
And three [letters] Mary, through immense love,
Brought us to heaven out of our severe affliction . . .

EVA was a plague everywhere – casting us
into dangerous company;
AVE, noble honour,
Brought us far away from evil enslavement.

Bright will your graceful appearance be, Mary mother of the Lord,
without concealment;
The fair AVE was a manifestation from heaven,
[whereas] Eve's apple was an affliction).

In an *awdl* to Christ and Mary Gruffudd Fychan contrasts Eve's foolishness and culpability with Mary's righteousness and role in the Incarnation. Gabriel's address at the Annunciation is cleverly extended over seven *englynion* – positioned at the beginning of lines and the address stands out from the rest of the poem as Gabriel's words are in Latin, whereas the rest of the poem is in Welsh. The familiarity of the Latin 'Ave Maria' which played a central role in the service of mass meant that it was possible for the poet to weave two texts together and for both to be understood by a lay audience. Gruffudd Fychan also makes full use of wordplay as he brings together the different meanings of 'gair' (word): the word 'Ave' uttered by Gabriel, the Word of God incarnate in Mary's womb and the Word made flesh (Christ).[102] The poem also reflects the popular belief that the Annunciation and the

Incarnation were simultaneous events: Mary became pregnant as she heard the Word of God.

The striking image of Mary becoming pregnant as she listened intently to Gabriel's message was popular in both medieval poetry and art. In the miraculous conception of Christ words replaced seed. As Iolo Goch stated: 'Efo â chwegair a'th feichioges' (he with a sweet word made you pregnant).[103] In Gruffudd Llwyd's praise poem to the Holy Trinity Gabriel's words become embodied in Mary's womb at the time of the Annunciation and, as a result of this, she gives birth to God's Word:

Gabriel, o radd gyfaddef,
A wnaeth, drwy arch Duw o nef,
Anfon i Fair Air arab,
A'r Gair aeth i Fair yn fab:
A'r Gair oedd hawdd Ei garu,
A'r Gair mab i Fair a fu:
Gair o nef yn gâr i ni.[104]

(Gabriel, of the acknowledged grade [of angels],
sent the gentle Word to Mary, at the request of God of heaven,
And the Word became a son in Mary:
And it was easy to love the Word,
And the Word was Mary's son:
A Word from heaven [became] our friend.)

The Holy Spirit, frequently depicted as a bird in Christian iconography, is often illustrated flying into Mary's ear at the time of Christ's conception, as in the following refrain by Ieuan Deulwyn (*fl.*1460): 'Mal y bu ymru mair wenn/ wedi yrru yn yderyn'[105] (As it was in holy Mary's womb/ driven [there] in the form of a bird). This, of course, was a simple and convenient way of visually depicting the complex notion of the Incarnation. In late medieval stained glass at Llandyrnog the Holy Spirit is depicted in the form of a bird swooping down towards Mary's ear at the time of the Annunciation (Plate 5). The presence of a potted lily, ubiquitous in Annunciation scenes, reminds the viewer of Mary's purity and physical virginity at the moment of conception: for the bird is penetrating Mary's ear, not any other part of her body, and thus the image emphasizes the sexless generation of Christ. In the Middle Welsh Life of St Collen, the saint is given a lily by the pope which had previously regenerated from a withered stem in front of the pagans as proof of Mary's perpetual virginity.[106] Madeleine Gray has suggested that the Annunciation scene depicted in an alabaster panel on the tomb of Sir William ap Tomas and his wife Gwladus at the priory church of St Mary at Abergavenny contains an image of God blowing the Word into Mary's ear (Plate 6).[107] The section of the carving between God the Father and the Virgin Mary in this scene appears to have been vandalized and it is difficult to determine whether Gray's interpretation is correct or whether the scene originally depicted a dove flying towards Mary's ear as in the Llandyrnog image. Something appears to have been removed from the 'cloud-like thread blowing across the panel' and the vandal has initialled the scene. God the Father is raising his hand in a blessing motion rather than cupping his hand around his breath in a blowing motion and he is standing on a balcony not leaning from a cloud. Ephraem (*ob.* 373) appears to have been the first in the East to suggest that Mary became pregnant through her ear and in the West this idea was promoted by Zeno of Verona.[108]

Another popular means of depicting Christ's conception, particularly in poetry, is to create an image of the Holy Spirit penetrating Mary as a ray of light penetrates through glass. Sunshine passes through glass without breaking or damaging it and this image provided a useful means of explaining how Mary's virginity – or rather her hymen – remained intact despite conceiving a son. In the words of Iolo Goch:

> A Duw o fewn aeth yn dy fynwes
> Fal yr â drwy'r gwydr y terydr tes.
>
> (and God went into your bosom
> as the sunbeam goes through glass.)[109]

A similar image is found in a *cywydd* of uncertain authorship to Joachim, Mary and Anna. The light passes through the glass to the fountain: the image of Mary's body as a sealed fountain – symbolic of her unbroken virginity – stems from the Song of Songs (4:12).

Mal yr haul y molir hon
Drwy ffenestr wydr i'r ffynnon.
Yr un modd, iawnrhodd anrheg,
Y daeth Duw at famaeth deg,
Gorau mam, gorau mamaeth,
Gorau i nef y gŵr a wnaeth.[110]

(She is worshipped like the sun
passing through a glass window to the fountain.
In the same way, just gift,
God came to a fair nursing mother,
The best mother, the best nursing mother,
Best was the man [she] made for heaven.)

Glass is again used in poetic imagery both as a means of shielding and protecting the Virgin from external pollution and as a means of conveying her purity and perpetual virginity. In Gruffudd Fychan's *awdl* to Christ and Mary, Christ is born of the Holy Spirit in a glass bedchamber:

Ganed Ef, gwn nad ofer,
Ganedigaeth deg segur,
O Fair ac un gair gan gâr
A Glân Ysbryd heb gyd gŵr.

Morwyn fu Fair fwyn o fywn hundy – gwydr,
  Yn gwiw ddal Mab Duw fry,
Morwyn gyn no hyn gain hy,
(mirain wawd) morwyn wedy.[111]

(He was born, I know that this was not in vain,
beautiful and effortless birth,
from Mary and one word from a relationship
With the Holy Spirit without intercourse with a man.

Tender Mary was a maiden in a glass bedchamber,
worthily holding God's Son aloft
A beautiful, undaunted virgin before this
(fair poetry) and a virgin afterwards.)

R. T. Davies has argued that the image of the Virgin sleeping in a glass bedchamber is unique to Welsh poetry.[112] However, without a thorough, international survey of poetry from this period it is not possible to confirm whether this is the case. Glass, of course, was a precious commodity in the Middle Ages and the implication here is that Mary is precious and deserves to be protected from original sin. As noted in the Middle Welsh version of Gabriel's warning to Mary (*Rybud Gabriel at Veir*): 'yr yspryt glan odyarnatiada6 ynot. Agrym ygoruchaf auyd gysca6t ac amddiffyn yti rac pob pecha6t.'[113] (and the Holy Spirit from upon you will come into you. And the power of the Almighty will be a shelter and shield you from every sin). The poem emphasizes Mary's effortless labour and her perpetual virginity, thus, implicitly acknowledging Mary as Immaculate Conception.

Although I prefer to take 'gwydr' here to mean 'glass' (its literal meaning, which is appropriate for the imagery in the poem), another interpretation of 'hundy – gwydr' is 'a bright bedchamber'.[114] In *Buched Meir Wyry*, Mary gives birth in a dark cave which fills with a bright, shining light as Christ is born. The miraculous, radiant light which appears at the moment of birth is a common motif in the Lives of saints, but Mary in particular is associated with bright light and the sun.[115] Mary has frequently been associated with the woman clothed with the sun with a crown of twelve stars and the moon beneath her feet, the pregnant Woman of the Apocalypse in Revelation 12:1–16 who it is prophesied will give birth to the Redeemer.[116] In *Buched Meir Wyry*, the blinding light coming from the cave prevents the midwives from hurrying in to assist Mary. She is frequently described as having such radiance that it is difficult to look at her, as in the following excerpts from the apocryphal Life of Mary: 'a chyn echtywynediket oed y hwyneb ac yd oed vreid y nep edrech arnei'[117] (and so bright was her face that it was pointless anyone looking at her), 'kyndecket oed hitheu ac na allei neb yn hawd edrych yn y hwyneb'[118] (she was so beautiful that no one could easily look at her face). This, of course, prevents Mary from becoming a victim of the unchaste gaze, a fate which befalls many female saints and threatens their spirituality, as we shall see in the next chapter.

The poets frequently associate Mary with the sun. Gruffudd ap Maredudd describes her as 'Meir hoen haul hirddydd, hefelydd haf . . . Mair o'r Israel hael, haul oruchaf'[119] (Mary [like the] brightness of the sun on a long day, [you are] similar to summer . . . Mary from noble Israel, almighty sun); Rhys Goch Eryri refers to 'A Mair yn haul yn eu mysg'[120] (And Mary a sun in their midst) and in *englynion* of uncertain authorship she is called 'Gwargain haul firain, hael Fair . . . Mair, gwâr hael grair, gwir haul Gred'[121] (Gentle and bright [like the] splendid sun, noble Mary . . . Mary, gentle and generous treasure, the true sun of Christendom). These *englynion* which were added to the Hendregadredd Manuscript, probably in the second quarter of the fourteenth century when it was owned by Ieuan Llwyd of the Aeron Valley in Ceredigion, also refer to the idea that Mary is the source responsible for bringing light into the world, since she gives birth to the Redeemer. Numerous other poets refer to the fact that Mary brings light (i.e. the hope of salvation) into the world as she gives birth and Bleddyn Ddu refers to her as one 'a lenwid o oleuni'[122] (who was filled with light). The image of Mary's body filling with light at the time of conception is totally appropriate for the mother of the Redeemer and Bleddyn Ddu describes the process in more detail in another of his *awdlau* to Christ:

> Iesu a ddyfu o ddefawd – gwarder
>   I osod lleufer ffydd, iawnder ffawd,
> Oeswedd dangnefedd yng nghawd – Mair berffaith,
>   Eisyddyn gobaith gwirdaith gwyrdawd.[123]

> (Jesus came to place faith's light, gentle custom,
> fortune's justice, in perfect Mary's flesh, everlasting peace,
> the home of hope is the true journey of virginity.)

In his poem to the Virgin's mother, Hywel Swrdwal employs three metaphors from the Old Testament to describe Mary's virginity. The rod of Aaron which flowered miraculously without water, producing buds and ripe almonds, may be taken as a sign of Mary's fertility (Numbers 17.8). Gideon's fleece wet with dew may be interpreted as the Virgin Mary having conceived whilst the dry threshing floor beneath represents her inviolate virginity (Judges 6.37) and the flames of fire in the burning bush which burned but did not consume the bush are taken as a metaphor for Mary's perpetual virginity (Judges 6.37):

> Mawr oedd broffwydo Mair wen
> Mam Iesu ym myw Moesen.
> Y tân oedd fawr anianol
> Yn y berth; ni bu ei ôl.
> Arwydd ydoedd – pand oedd deg? –
> O'i morwyndod, Mair wendeg.[124]
>
> (Great was the prophecy of holy Mary,
> Jesus's mother, during the lifetime of Moses.
> The fire in the bush was very great;
> It did not leave its mark.
> It was a sign – was it not reasonable?
> Of her virginity, fair holy Mary.)

Mary's perpetual virginity is one of the accomplishments listed in *Gramadegau'r Penceirddiaid* (the Bardic Grammars) as a specific reason why Welsh poets should praise Mary. The Bardic Grammars provided professional poets with information relating to their craft, such as the twenty-four strict metres, metrical faults to be avoided and guidance on writing praise poetry consisting of lists of appropriate reasons for praising individual subjects. The Virgin Mary was deemed an appropriate person to praise and brief guidance on how to praise Mary is given in the Grammars. The Peniarth 20 version of the Grammars is generally attributed to Dafydd Ddu of Hiraddug and thought to be his reworking of Einion Offeiriad's original version which was composed *c.*1320.[125] Dafydd Ddu, as we have already seen, is a possible contender for having translated the Little Office of the Blessed Virgin Mary into Welsh. He expands the section on Mary providing additional reasons for praising the Virgin:

> Meir y vam a volir o achaws y morwynawl weryndawt, a'y santeidrwyd, a'y gleindyt buched, ac o'y bot yn vam y drvgared, ac yn vrenhines nef a dayar ac vffern, a haydu ohonei ymdwyn yn y gwerynawl groth kreawdyr hollgyuoethawc y kreaduryeit oll, a'y bot yn wyry kynn esgor a gwedy esgor.[126]

> (Mary his mother is praised because of her virginal virginity, and her sanctity, and her cleanliness of life, and because she is the mother of mercy, queen of heaven, earth and hell, and because she deserved to conceive the Almighty Creator of all creatures in her virginal womb, and because she was a virgin before giving birth and after giving birth.)

It is in his version that Mary's 'gwerynawl groth' (virginal womb) is given specific attention and details added relating to her virginity in partu and post partum. Neither the Red Book of Hergest nor the Llanstephan 3 version of the Bardic Grammars mention this or refer to Mary as 'queen of heaven, earth and hell'. They merely add that Mary should be praised for all the same reasons as Christ and suggest that she should also be praised for her great beauty – an attribute which is omitted incidentally in Dafydd Ddu's Grammar.

Although Welsh poets frequently allude to Mary's beauty, her physical appearance is in fact rarely described in any detail. As discussed above, she is often associated with the sun and depicted as being surrounded by a bright light which makes it difficult to view her. Unlike Christ whose appearance is described in detail in 'Pryd y Mab' (the face of the Son), a particularly intense section of the Welsh mystical text *Ymborth yr Enaid*, in which the Dominican author vividly portrays his vision of Jesus,[127] Mary's appearance is not described in Welsh religious prose and, despite the fact that some versions of the Bardic Grammars specifically recommend that poets should praise Mary's beauty, her face and physical attributes are rarely mentioned.

One particularly unusual exception to this rule is an unedited poem by Hywel Dafi (*fl.*1450–80) which praises the Virgin in much the same way as noblewomen are praised in Welsh courtly love poetry. The poem begins with a detailed description of the girl he loves and it is not immediately apparent that he is referring to the Virgin. She is described from tip-to-toe in a style which is deliberately typical of *amour courtois*: she has a beautiful, high, golden forehead, yellow hair, unblemished lime-white skin, red cheeks, a thin swan-like neck, dark eyebrows which resemble blackbirds' wings, excellent teeth, snow-white breasts and arms and golden legs. It is impossible, says the poet, to convey in words her great beauty. He then reveals that the name of the girl he loves is Mary – Joseph's wife and Joachim's daughter. Unlike other women described in this way, the Virgin's love is more loyal and her gifts, the poet is keen to emphasize, are greater. He would rather stand and admire the Virgin Mary than any other girl, and thus what initially appears to be a courtly love poem is transformed into a praise poem to the Virgin.[128] Although the predominant colours – gold, white and red – are typical of the stylized colours used in courtly love poetry, here they are also used in a way that is reminiscent of painted statues of the Virgin Mary (e.g. golden nose and golden legs). This coupled with the fact that the poet mentions 'gwell gennyf . . . gael sefyll a gweled honn/ yr eneth bleth gwyn/ Gwenn Vair nag ag un vorwyn'[129] (I prefer . . . to stand and see her/ the gentle, fair-haired girl/ Holy Mary than any other maiden) perhaps suggests that he is standing in front of a familiar image of the Virgin. Although he made no mention of this poem, Gilbert Ruddock suggested that images of the Virgin may have affected the way in which the poets described idealised beauty in Welsh poems.[130] It seems equally likely – perhaps even more likely – that current ideas concerning fashion and beauty would have determined how Mary was depicted in the visual arts in Wales. Poetry to the statue of Mary at Pen-rhys, which will be discussed in greater detail in the next section, also contains similar brief references to the statue's beauty which are reminiscent of courtly love poetry.[131] Hywel Dafi's poem is, nevertheless, unique in providing a lengthy description of the Virgin.

Another unusual poem to the Virgin Mary is an *awdl* attributed to Ieuan ap Hywel Swrdwal which, it is claimed, he wrote while a student at Oxford in order to prove that Welsh poets could compose poetry in English that far excelled anything an Englishman could write in his own language.[132] The fifteenth-century poem which is composed in strict-metre Welsh *cynghanedd* is written in English in Welsh orthography. The poet appeals to the Virgin Mary and Christ to assist him in his quest for salvation. The first section of the poem consists of seven *englynion* to the Virgin, our 'michti ladi' (mighty lady), and focuses on her intercessory powers and her relationship with God the Father and the Son:

> Kwin od off owr God, owr geiding – mwdyr,
> Maedyn notwithstanding,
> Hwo wed syts with a ryts ring
> As God wod ddys gwd weding.
>
> Help ws, prae ffor ws, preffering – owr sowls;
> Asoel ws at owr ending.
> Mak ddat awl wi ffawl tw ffing
> Iwr Swns lwf, owr syns lefing.[133]
>
> (Sole queen of our God, our guiding mother
> yet still a maiden: because God wanted this good wedding,
> he married you with a rich ring.
>
> Help us, pray for us, advance our souls
> give us at the end absolution.
> Make all of us receive your Son's love,
> leaving sin behind us.)

Mary's authority and sovereignty are stressed, as well as her fertility and humanity: she is 'queen of our God' and a 'fruit-bearing blossom'. Particular emphasis is placed on the fact that she fed Christ with her own breasts and, as a result, she is justly rewarded in heaven:

> Owr ffadyrs ffadyr, owr ffiding, – owr pop,
> on iwr paps had swking;
> in hefn-blys i haf thys thing,
> attendans wythowt ending.[134]
>
> (There sucked at your breast
> our father's father; our food, our pope.
> Now [the angels] serve you in heaven for ever.)

The poetic image strongly resembles the visual image of Mary on the Throne of Wisdom: Mary crowned queen of heaven is seated on a throne with the Christ child on her knee. Christ's humanity is emphasized by the fact that Mary frequently has one breast revealed and is in the process of nourishing Jesus, as in the late fourteenth-century image from the Llanbeblig Hours (Plate 7). The image venerates Mary's maternity, but her throne and crown dominate the miniature and it is a powerful expression of her power and authority. Mary is frequently associated with Wisdom (Sophia) and, as a type of the Church, Mary's milk may be seen as a life-giving force, nourishing all Christians and offering the possibility of Redemption.

Lactation is one of the few physical features of childbearing that Mary shared with all women, since, as we have seen, she was exempt from intercourse, labour and its associated bodily fluids. Yet according to medieval medical theory breast milk was made from menses: menstrual blood travelled to the breasts where it was transformed into breast milk. Thus the curse of Eve is again transformed into salvation via the body of Mary. As Teresa Reed notes:

> In this scenario the reminder of the death curse is turned into nourishment, locally with each infant born and nursed and culturally in each picture or poem in which the Virgin offers her breast to Christ. The incorporation of the forbidden fruit and, thus, of sin and death in Genesis is, therefore, translated via the formless matter of the menses into salvation.[135]

According to Aristotelian medical theory, while the father provided the important genetic material determining the sex and characteristics of the child, the mother provided physical matter in the form of menstrual blood. The fact that Christ took his flesh and blood from Mary is frequently referred to by Welsh poets, who are keen to emphasize Christ's humanity, and she is not assigned the more passive role which, according to Galenic theory, meant that the mother was a mere vessel in which the child grew.[136] The Welsh poet Gruffudd ap Maredudd refers to Mary's 'diwair waed'[137] (chaste blood) and the Middle Welsh translation of *Domine Ihesu Christe* (*Gweddi Boneffas Bab*) confirms the belief via prayer that Christ took his blood from Mary's womb: 'Arglwydd Jessu Grist, yr hwnn a gymereist y kyssegrediccaf gnawt hwnn a'th werthuawroccaf waet o vru y wyry Arglwyddes Veir . . .'[138] (Lord Jesus Christ, who took this the most sacred flesh of all and the most valuable blood from the womb of the Virgin Lady Mary . . .). Cynddelw Brydydd Mawr refers to the growth of Christ in the womb in the following manner:

Dyfu Grist yng nghawd, Priawd prifed,
Dyfu ym mru Mair Mab dymuned;[139]

(Christ came in flesh, Proprietor of supremacy,
There came in the womb of Mary the Son of expectation;)[140]

and Ieuan Deulwyn and other anonymous poets associate Christ's humanity and the Incarnation with Mary's role as breastfeeding mother, as in the following examples:

knawd oedd kynn y dioddef
os o gnawd y sugna ef
mair onn a vagai mhrynnwr
gwedi gael heb gyd a gwr.[141]

([he was] flesh before suffering
if from flesh he suckled
Mary raised our Redeemer
having had [him] without intercourse with a man.)

Y ganed Duw o gnawd hon.
Hon a fagodd o'i bronnau.[142]

(God was born of her flesh.
She raised him with her breasts.)

Mary is also depicted bare-breasted in the late fifteenth-century nativity scene in Peniarth 23 (Plate 3). In this image Mary is relaxing, lying in bed following the birth of Christ and Joseph, the ox and the ass are depicted at the foot of the bed. The image occurs in a Welsh version of Geoffrey of Monmouth's *Historia Regum Britanniae* at a point in the text which refers to the tradition that Cynfelyn was on the throne in Britain when Christ was born. The text emphasizes that Christ, born of the Virgin Mary, redeemed mankind with his 'werthvawr waet' (valuable blood) and freed the human race from hell; the particularly important event in this 'historical' chronology which has been picked out in red and deemed worthy of illustration is the moment 'pan aned iessu grist or wyry vair' (when Jesus Christ was born of the Virgin Mary). The newborn baby is wrapped in swaddling clothes – a sign of Christ's humility and the presence of the animals suggest the lowly surroundings of Christ's birth. However, the Virgin reclines on luxurious cushions decorated with tassels and the bed is covered in a black and red patterned bedspread. Johan Henrik Cornell has argued that this kind of nativity scene was popular in Europe until the end of the fourteenth century when, under the influence of the visions of St Brigitta of Sweden, the Virgin began to be depicted kneeling by Christ's crib.[143] As Peter Lord has demonstrated, the old iconography persisted in Wales and Brittany throughout the fifteenth century.[144] The image is at odds with the thirteenth-century description of the Nativity given by the poet Madog ap Gwallter (*fl.*1250):

Ych ac asen,	Arglwydd presen,	preseb piau,
A sopen wair	yn lle cadair	i'n Llyw cadau;
Pali ny myn,	nid uriael gwyn	ei ginhynnau,
Yn lle syndal	ynghylch ei wâl	gwelid carpau[145]

(An ox and an ass, Lord of this world,
  Their manger is his,
A bundle of hay instead of a cradle
  For our Lord of hosts.
No silk he wishes, no fine fabrics
  Are his swaddlings;
Instead of sendal around his bed
  Were seen tatters.)[146]

Madog ap Gwallter was a Franciscan friar and, true to the Franciscan emphasis on poverty, has chosen to highlight the humility of Christ's birth. Unlike the popular, medieval account of the birth of Christ in the apocryphal gospels where Christ is born in a cave and no mention is made of the three wise men, the poem describes what might be considered by a modern audience to be a more familiar account of Christ's nativity in a lowly stable: Herod's plans are thwarted and the three kings bearing gifts are guided by a star to the Son of God on Christmas night:

Gwelsont seren o liw amgen ac amgylchau
Ac amgen nod no'r sêr uchod uch eu pennau:
Geni yna y Brenin da, arwydd diau
Fu gysefin gan dri brenin, fawr eu breinau.
Yna credant, yna cyrchant cyrch goddeau,
Ac eu manag seren o'u rhag yn rhoi golau;
Caerusalem a chaer Fethlem (nid er methlau)
Doethan' yn rhwydd ar feirch ebrwydd, wiw ebrannau.
Disgyn yn ffysg (seren a'u dysg, wir ei dysgau),
I'r tŷ ydd ânt, heb ddôr, heb gant, gwynnawg ddrysau;
Y Mab ydoedd a anydoedd dan ei nodau,
A'i fam ar lawr, a'i bron werthfawr wrth ei enau . . .
Nos Nadolig: nos annhebyg i ddrygnosau,
Nos lewenydd i lu bedydd: byddwn ninnau![147]

(They saw a star, of a different hue,
  Having a halo,
With a different goal than the stars above,
  Over their heads:
He was being born then, the good king,
  Certain the portent
That first and foremost was seen by three kings,
  Greatly privileged.

Then they believed, then they go in quest,
  A successful quest,
And their epiphany a star before them
  Sending forth light:
To Jerusalem and Bethlehem town,
  Expecting no tricks,
They came swiftly on speedy horses,
  Proper their fodder.

Alighting in haste, the star instructs them,
  True its instructions,
To the house they go, without door, without frame,
  Windy doorways:
The Son was there, the One who was born
  Beneath his signs,
And his mother resting, her precious breast
  Pressed to his lips . . .
The Nativity's night, a night unlike
  Nights of wickedness,

A night of joy for Christendom:
Let us too be joyful.)[148]

The poem has been described by Henry Lewis as the first Christmas carol.[149] It ends with a simple affirmation of the poet's faith in Mary's ability 'to do us good and prevent our pains' as well as ensure a place for us in heaven.

The belief that Mary was an effective mediator and that praising Mary would ultimately assist the poet in his search for salvation is of paramount importance in Marian praise poetry. From the end of the eleventh century onwards Mary is named among other saints and martyrs capable of offering intercession, as, for example, in the following early poem attributed to 'Elaeth' in the Black Book of Carmarthen:

Y Duv y harchaw, arch aton dihev
rac poenav gelinion:
Y'm eneid, o pleid cofion,
Naut Meir gwiri a'r gueriton.[150]

(I ask of God, a request [for] sure blessings
Against the pains of enemies:
For my soul, through the medium of [their] thoughts,
[To receive] the support of chaste Mary and the virgins.)

The Poets of the Princes also cast Mary in this role in their religious poetry. Llywelyn Fardd II (*fl.* *c.*1215–*c.*1280) requests that Mary guide his soul to the Trinity and support him as he is judged at the Last Judgement.[151] Meilyr ap Gwalchmai (*fl.* second half of twelfth century) emphasizes Mary's authority amongst other saints and suggests that she is the most effective mediator in the pantheon of Christian saints:

Gan Dduw yn lleufer, llewychant, – llu bedydd,
Llewenydd a gaffant.
Rhag bron Mair, mwyaf ei meddiant,
Gweryddon gwirion fydd ein gwarant,
A Mihangel deg, dygant – yn ganllaw
I'r canllu o'r difant.[152]

(With God in light, they [will] shine, host of Christendom,
Happiness they [will] have.

In the presence of Mary of greatest authority,
Spotless saints will our surety be,
And fine Michael, they will bring him as a helper
To the hosts from perdition.)[153]

The theme continues and by the fifteenth century poets such as Dafydd Epynt and Harri ap Hywel stress the pre-eminence of Mary amongst saints. In the words of Dafydd Epynt: 'Lliw ynod a llawenydd yr holl saint eraill y sydd'[154] (The colour and joy of all the other saints [is found] in you) and according to Harri ap Hywel: 'Mair uwch saint ei braint a'i brig'[155] (Mary whose privilege and position is above [other] saints). Because of her unusual position bridging heaven and earth and her unique sphere of influence within the heavenly host, Mary is often depicted as the most effective and most merciful mediator. By the fifteenth century she is also depicted placing her rosary in the Archangel Michael's scales as he weighs the souls of the dead on Judgement Day and Mary tries to counteract the weight of the individual's sins by tipping the balance in favour of the sinner.[156]

The *Mater Dolorosa* who wept tears of blood at the foot of the Cross and mourned the loss of her Son, was considered to be most likely to empathize with sinners and recognize the pain and suffering of others who had lost loved ones and friends. In an elegy to Dafydd Fychan, the poet Ieuan Deulwyn expresses his own grief by comparing it to Mary's as she wept tears of blood on seeing her Son's wounds:

ail Mair am weliau i mab
gwaed oedd or llygaid iddi
ag ail gwaed o'm golwg i.[157]

(A second Mary [who] for the wounds of her Son
[wept] blood from her eyes
and blood again [comes] from my eyes.)

A number of other Poets of the Gentry, including Guto'r Glyn (*c*.1435–*c*.1493), Dafydd Llwyd (*c*.1395–1486), Gutun Owain (*fl*.1450–98) and Dafydd Epynt (*fl*. *c*.1460), refer to Mary's tears of blood.[158]

The Virgin is depicted weeping visibly large tears in an early sixteenth-century Crucifixion scene in stained glass at the Church of St Mary, Cilcain, Flintshire (Plate 8). Although her tears are not necessarily of blood, they are nevertheless pronounced. The overall impression created by this figure of the Virgin standing with her head slightly bowed and her hands together in an attitude of prayer is to both evoke emotion in the viewer who naturally sympathizes with the Virgin's suffering and also to suggest that the Virgin will sympathize with any emotions or difficulties experienced by the viewer.

Mary's efficacy as mediator and the immense faith placed in Mary's abilities to ensure salvation are encapsulated in this anonymous fifteenth-century *cywydd* which highly recommends singing Mary's praises:

Mair a'n tyn o'r mieri,
Ac wedi hyn gyda hi
Cawn wenfyd, canu i Wenfair,
Cawn nef oll – canwn i Fair![159]

(Mary will pull us from the briars,
And after this with her
We will attain bliss, singing to holy Mary,
We will have the whole of heaven – let us sing to Mary!)

Although in the vast majority of Welsh poems Mary is expected to react sympathetically towards all sinners and offer protection, in an unusual fourteenth-century *cywydd* the poet Gruffudd Llwyd suggests that Mary is also capable of cursing and punishing individuals. In 1385 Morgan ap Dafydd ap Llywelyn of Rhydodyn in the parish of Caeo, Carmarthenshire, was accused of the murder of John Lawrence, a deputy magistrate who had been killed whilst travelling between Carmarthen and Cardigan. Gruffudd Llwyd (*c*.1380–*c*.1420) composed a poem appealing to the judge, Sir Dafydd Hanmor, to come and hear the case in Carmarthen and find Morgan not guilty. The bard appears keen to sit on the jury and lists other poets who would be suitable jurors in this case. The poem ends with a request that Mary curse all those who turn their backs on Morgan and abandon him in his hour of need.[160]

Far more common are the poems which claim Mary as protector and mediator. Her powers of protection extended over sea and land and, as *Stella Maris* (Star of the Sea), she afforded special protection to seafarers and pilgrims. The hymn 'Ave Maris Stella' was translated into Middle Welsh and formed part of the Little Office of the Virgin Mary. The poets Lewys Glyn Cothi (*c*.1420–89) and Lewys Morgannwg (*fl*.1520–65) refer to Mary's ability to ensure safe passage for seafaring pilgrims and Deio ap Ieuan Ddu (1460–1500) appeals to 'Mair Arglwyddes y moroedd' (Mary Lady of the Seas) for the safe return of Siancyn ap Maredudd kidnapped at sea by pirates and imprisoned on a French boat.[161] Ieuan ap Gruffudd gives an account of a pilgrimage to Santiago when Siancyn Hafart of Breconshire and three Welsh women – Gwenllian, Mawd and Elen – sailed from Bristol to La Corogne in a boat named 'Mair o Fryste' (Mary of Bristol).[162] Mary not only afforded protection to pilgrims, but various sites throughout Wales associated with Mary also attracted large numbers of pilgrims and many of her images and shrines also became the subject of Welsh poetry.

Places of pilgrimage: images, shrines and holy wells

One of the most well-documented medieval shrines to the Virgin is found at Pen-rhys in the Rhondda Valley. No fewer than nine Middle Welsh poems survive praising the Virgin's image and holy well at Pen-rhys and the shrine is also referred to briefly in a number of other poems from the period *c*.1450–1535.[163] The shrine appears to have been situated in a clearing in dense steeply sloping woodland. According to Gwilym Tew 'Ynys yw Pen-rhys yn nhrwyn – y fforest'[164] (Pen-rhys is an island on the ridge of the forest) and in the words of Lewys Morgannwg:

> Yna daethost, fendithfawr,
> I'r lle hwn o'r nef i'r llawr.
> Dy ddelw bob dydd a welynt
> Yn fyw a gad o nef gynt.[165]

(Then you came, great blessing,
To this place from heaven to the ground.
Your image, which came previously from heaven,
is alive [and] seen every day.)

As is often the case with miraculous images of the Virgin, it was claimed that the figure was not a man-made image but a gift sent directly from heaven. It was found, according to Lewys Morgannwg, in the hollow trunk of an oak tree and refused to be removed: 'o fôn dâr ni fynnai'i dwyn'[166] (from the trunk of the oak it did not wish to be taken).

As Christine James has demonstrated in her detailed discussion of the poetry to Pen-rhys, the image was probably a gilded and painted wooden figure of the Virgin, crowned, enthroned, wearing a cloak and depicted holding her Son: 'Yn dy fraich mae'r un Duw fry', (In your arms is the one almighty God), possibly bending as though to kiss the infant 'magu Iesu am gusan'[167] (nursing Jesus for a kiss), although this could also be a figurative poetic image rather than a literal description of the statue. 'Magu' (nursing/rearing) could simply refer to the fact that the statue was holding the baby or it could also imply that Mary was depicted breast-feeding Jesus, since 'magu' can also mean 'maethu' (to nourish) and in the lines preceeding this Rhisiart ap Rhys (*fl. c.*1485–1515) refers to the milk flowing from Mary's breasts. Gwilym Tew also refers to the Virgin at Pen-rhys nourishing the child at her breast.[168]

It is likely that the statue stood in the chapel which was erected on the summit of the mountain ridge with the well further down the slope. The site was owned by the Cistercian abbey of Llantarnam and no doubt provided the abbey with a considerable source of income: other buildings included a grange, a hostelry where pilgrims could stay, a brewery, a bake-house and a malt-house.[169] The Cistercians were keen on promoting veneration to Mary and they became the premier religious Order in Wales, fostering close links with the native princes, gentry and local poets. All of their houses were dedicated to Mary and she is frequently depicted on Cistercians seals.[170] The Cistercian abbey of Tintern possessed a statue of the Virgin Mary which was visited by a 'very great multitude' and in 1414 indulgences were granted to those who visited the chapel and left alms. The statue's fame seems to focus on a characteristic it shared with the images at Pen-rhys and Cardigan – miraculously it could not be moved from its original location.[171]

At the Dissolution it would appear that the abbey of Llantarnam was deriving one-fifth of its income from Pen-rhys, including rents and spiritualities, so it is little wonder that the monks were keen on proliferating the statue's fame.[172] According to Lewys Morgannwg pilgrims came from afar and crossed sea and land in order to visit Pen-rhys.[173] Llywelyn ap Hywel ab Ieuan ap Gronw describes how all visitors were healed of both spiritual and physical afflictions at the well:

Dwyn enaid pob dyn uniawn
A wna, a chorff, yn iach iawn.
Rhoi clywed a dywedyd,
Y mae i fyddar a mud.
Aed dall i gyty â hon,
O'i phlegid caiff olygon.[174]

She causes the body and soul
of every righteous man to become very healthy.
She gives [the power of] hearing and speech
to the deaf and dumb.
A blind man goes to commune with her,
And, as a result, gains [his] sight.)

As well as visiting local sites such as Pen-rhys, the poet Llywelyn ap Hywel was capable of going on pilgrimage far further afield, including visiting some of the most important pilgrimage sites of Christendom in Rome. In another *cywydd* which recounts his experiences in Rome he refers to the fact that one of the sites he visited was the church of Santa Maria Maggiore where he saw the famous painting of the Virgin which was reputedly executed by St Luke: 'A wnaeth Luc unwaith â'i law'[175] (which Luke once made with his [own] hand).

The fame of Mary's image at Pen-rhys meant that she became equated with other popular statues such as Our Lady of Walsingham and Our Lady of Worcestre. In June 1538 Hugh Latimer, Bishop of Worcestre, wrote to Thomas Cromwell condemning the statue in his own cathedral and suggesting that the Worcestre image, along with others, including Pen-rhys, be destroyed:

> She hath been the devil's instrument to bring many, I fear, to eternal fire; now she herself, with her old sister of Walsingham, her young sister of Ipswich, with their other two sisters of Dongcaster and Penryesse, would make a jolly muster in Smithfield. They would not be all day in burning.[176]

In September of the same year the image at Pen-rhys was sent to London and burned – probably in the courtyard of Thomas Cromwell's house at Chelsea. Cromwell had ordered that the statue be removed 'as secretly as might be' for fear of local revolt.

Another Welsh image of the Virgin which was brought to Cromwell's attention was Our Lady of Cardigan with its miraculous taper which burned continuously for nine years without ever being extinguished. Cromwell appears to have originally enquired about an image of Our Lady and taper at Haverfordwest, but Bishop William Barlow was keen to point out that the Cardigan taper was of much greater significance:

> I chaunced apon another taper of moch greater credyte and of more shamefull detestacion, called our ladyes taper of Cardigan, which I have sent here to your lordship with convenyent instructyons of that develish delusyon.[177]

Barlow had been prior at Haverfordwest before becoming bishop of St Davids.

The legend associated with the image from Cardigan is recorded by Thomas Hore, the last prior of the Benedictine house at Cardigan, who believed the taper to be 'a holy relyque . . . And then he confesseth hym selfe to have be deceaved therin'.[178] Unfortunately the legend does not appear to have been preserved in the work of medieval Welsh poets and Gerald of Wales did not refer to Our Lady of Cardigan in the twelfth century, although he visited Cardigan and referred to many miracles performed near the River Teifi which, he claimed, he did not have time to describe.[179] The statue of the

Virgin, according to Thomas Hore, was miraculously found standing on the River Teifi with the taper burning in one hand and her son on her lap. Three or four attempts were made to move the statue to Christ Church, Cardigan, but on each occasion the statue disappeared and made its way back to the banks of the Teifi. A church was then erected on this spot to house the statue and its burning candle.

The taper rather than the statue itself appears to have become the principal focus of devotion and the candle which burned continuously but was never consumed was, no doubt, taken as a sign of Mary's perpetual virginity, as well as a powerful symbol reminding the faithful that Mary was responsible for bringing light (the Redeemer) into the world. As a punishment to a pilgrim who swore a false oath in front of the image, the flame was extinguished, but the taper continued to be worshipped. Thomas Hore notes that 'sence the ceasinge of burnynge of the sayd taper, it was enclosed and taken for a greate relyque, and so worshipped and kyssed of pylgremes, and used of men to sweare by in difficill and harde matters'. The church, he remarks, 'ys used for a greate pilgemage to this presente daye', yet the taper, he confessed, appeared to be made of wood.[180] Morgan Meredith, vicar of the Church of Our Lady, solved the mystery by confirming that Prior John Frodsam, presumably Hore's predecessor, had either replaced or encased the taper in wood because pilgrims kept taking the wax away with them.[181] H. Maynard Smith in *Pre-Reformation England* refers to Our Lady of the Taper and the fact that 'the Welsh were always stealing the wax'.[182] However, this was presumably an act of veneration rather than irreverance. Since the taper itself became a holy relic, then the wax was, no doubt, believed to possess special powers and pilgrims keen to possess a fragment of the relic would presumably break off pieces of wax and take them home with them in much the same way that they chipped off fragments of Gwenfrewy's reliquary casket at Gwytherin long after her relics had been transferred to Shrewsbury.[183] John Frodsam's main concern appears to have been 'that the people shuld not dyminesh the substance of the taper', rather than to fool them by replacing it with wood, as suggested by the reformers.

The current bronze statue of Our Lady of the Taper was installed in the modern church in May 1986 and a taper blessed by Pope John Paul II was placed in the statue's hand and lit. The shrine has been designated the Welsh National Shrine of Our Lady and remains a popular place of pilgrimage.[184] The most recent shrine to Mary in Wales is found in a church at Bala which was consecrated in 1948 and dedicated to Our Lady of Fatima. At a convent at Llanycil near Bala the Poor Sisters of Nazareth prayed for a church and vowed to dedicate it to Our Lady of Fatima. A reasonably priced chip shop became available and, thanks largely to the efforts of Father Koenan, was converted with great enthusiasm. The statue of Our Lady at Bala is a copy of Our Lady in Cova da Iria, Fatima, and arrived in Bala in an open-top car before being taken in procession to the church.[185]

Amongst the various medieval images of the Virgin which survived the Reformation in Wales one finds a carved wooden figure of the Virgin which presumably formed part of the rood-screen at the Church of All Saints, Mochdre, in Montgomeryshire (now in the National Museum and Galleries, Cardiff) and a carved alabaster image of the Virgin and child at the priory church of St Mary, Cydweli, Carmarthenshire. Both images are thought to date to the mid- to late fourteenth century and depict Mary standing and wearing a crown, long flowing dress and mantle (Plates 9 and 10). The sculpture at Cydweli appears to have been concealed during the Reformation. It was later found and, in the eighteenth century, placed in a niche in the porch above the main entrance to the church. Ladies entering the church would curtsey to the figure of our Lady and this appears to have caused such consternation in one of the vicars who served at the church in the nineteenth century that he had it taken down and buried in the church grounds. It was only exhumed when the Cambrian Archaeology Society visited the church in 1875 and it was reinstated in the church in 1922.[186]

In a *cywydd* known as 'Dagrau Serch' (Love's Tears) Dafydd ap Gwilym (*fl.*1315/20–1350/70) appears to compare his lover Dyddgu to an image of the Virgin Mary somewhere in Maelienydd:

Dyddgu liw dydd goleuaf,
Dy nawdd, er Unmab Duw Naf,
Deurudd Mair o diredd Mael,
Duon lygaid a dwyael . . .
Dylyy fawl, myn delw Fair.[187]

(Dyddgu, colour of the brightest day,
Help me, for Lord God's Only Son,
Two cheeks like Mary, from Mael land;
Your eyes and brows are black . . .
You're worthy of praise by Mary's image.)[188]

There would have been images of Mary in almost every church in Maelienydd and we know nothing of the majority of these, simply because there is no mention of them in the surviving written record. Thomas Parry suggests that Dafydd may have been referring to an image at Cwm Hir abbey or Llanbister church.[189] Although it is impossible to say with any certainty to which image he is referring (if indeed he is referring to a specific image or statue of Mary), it is at least plausible that he could have had an image of Mary at the foot of the cross in mind, perhaps a figure such as the carved rood image previously found at Mochdre in Maelienydd (Plate 9). The emphasis in the poem on the poet's tears which have excoriated his face, as well as his wounds and physical suffering could be interpreted as being reminiscent of the sadness and suffering depicted in a rood scene. The bent, anguished figure of Christ with a caved chest still survives from Mochdre and it is not beyond the realms of possibility that Dafydd meant to evoke a scene such as this in the poem:[190] he refers to Dyddgu as having wounded him with a spear beneath his broken breast and, although the pain suffered as a result of unrequited love is a common topos in medieval poetry, the emphasis on wounds and tears in this poem is particularly intense. Did Dafydd imagine that Dyddgu would be more merciful towards him if he compared her to an image of Mary? Since there is some uncertainty regarding the date of Dafydd's death, as well as the dating of the rood figure at Mochdre, one cannot be certain that the figure was even in the church at the time that Dafydd composed the *cywydd*. If it were, then it is likely that it was a relatively new image.

There was also a celebrated statue of the Virgin at Pilleth Church, also in Maelienydd. In an unedited *awdl* to Mary of Pilleth Dafydd ap Hywel (1480–1510) describes visiting the enthroned statue with a golden crown on its head on one of the Marian feasts. The poet associates the pilgrimage site with miracles and healing, stating that the blind, dumb and mad were all cured at Pilleth. The holy well at Pilleth – 'y vawr ffynnon' (the large well) appears to have once been a substantial structure which attracted numerous pilgrims into its waters and, no doubt, as at Pen-rhys, the well coupled with the statue led to the success of the site. Once again, Mary is depicted as being particularly merciful and willing to use her rosary to speed the soul's passage into heaven.[191] The main emphasis in the poem is on Mary's generosity and there is very little description of the statue itself. The church at Pilleth was destroyed by fire in 1402 during the revolt of Owain Glyndŵr and it was again burned in 1894. The area is now well known for being the site of the Battle of Bryn Glas, rather than the location of a famous statue of the Virgin Mary. Even if Dafydd ap Gwilym (*c*.1315/20–1350/70) had been referring to the staute at Pilleth, which is highly unlikely, he was not referring to the same statue as Dafydd ap Hywel (1480–1510).

In medieval Wales there would have been numerous brightly painted, carved wooden images of the Virgin, often forming part of a rood scene, depicted standing at the foot of the cross with St John. Some of these holy roods, their screens and attendant figures became objects of worship throughout Wales and were venerated by Welsh poets. Notable examples were found at Brecon, Carmarthen and Llangynwyd.[192] No doubt the figures, as well as the rood itself, were believed to have special healing and intercessory powers and some of the 'delwau byw' (living images) from Wales may have been rood figures. There were reputedly living images of the Virgin at Rhiw, Gresford and Mold, and although relatively little is known of these figures, it has often been suggested that they were capable of moving mechanically in some way: perhaps in a similar fashion to the famous figure of Christ on the Rood of Grace at Boxley in Kent which could bow its head, snap its jaws and roll its eyes.[193] Occasionally it is difficult to ascertain whether the 'living images' in question were figures of the Virgin Mary or Christ depicted on the Rood. Tudur Aled mourning the death of his patron Siôn Wynn places specific emphasis on Mary's role, guiding Siôn's soul to heaven. No individual in Mold is said to have escaped grief on this sad occasion and the mourning cries extend as far as heaven's gates:

Mae'r llef hyd ym mhyrth nefoedd,
Marw Siôn Wynn, mor resyn oedd;
Mair wyrf, ar bawb, mawr fu'r bâr,
Marw eginyn mor gynnar;
I nef ydd âi, 'n ufudd iawn,
Mair a'i enaid mor uniawn,
A'i ddwyn, hawdd uddun heddyw
Ar ddwy law Fair a'r Ddelw Fyw![194]

(The wail extends to heaven's gates,
Siôn Wynn's death was such a pity;
Virgin Mary, great was everyone's anxiety,
So early has the young shoot died;
To heaven very obediently did Mary go,
her soul [being] so righteous,
and [Siôn shall be] carried, it is easy for them [to do that] today,
on Mary's hands and the Living Image!)

It is not, however, clear whether the living image referred to here is a living image of Mary, or a separate image, possibly the rood itself. In the Church of St Mary at Mold there is a medieval stone canopy and pedestal which, according to John Ray in 1662, was 'where they say stood a living or quick image'. The current statue of the Virgin and child was installed on the pedestal in 1922. It has previously been assumed that the pedestal was destroyed as a 'popish relic' in 1768,[195] but it is possible that this is a reference to the destruction of the statue.

Poets such as Hywel Swrdwal and Dafydd Nanmor refer to another famous image of the Virgin which stood in the Lady

Chapel at St Davids Cathedral, although they provide very little description of the statue, mentioning only that it had thin eyebrows and an abundance of fine hair.[196] Both Bishop Fastolfe who died in 1361 and Bishop Benedict Nicholls who died in 1433 requested that they be buried near Mary's image at St Davids.[197]

Other images of the Virgin which attracted local interest included statues at Llanystumdwy and Pwllheli. An anonymous *cywydd* to 'Mair o'r Trŵn'[198] (Mary of the Throne) emphasizes the intense spirituality to be experienced at Llanystumdwy:

> Llys Ddüw yn llawes y ddol
> llys bradwys lle ysbrydol.
> Down i'r lann dirion ar wledd
> Mair o honn i mae rinwedd.
> Llan vaen wenn lliw nef waneg
> ystyndwy ywch ystyn deg.[199]

> (God's court on the edge of the meadow,
> court of paradise, a spiritual place.
> We come to the gracious river bank on Mary's feast
> From her is [had] virtue.
> Llanystymdwy,[200] white stone church the colour of a heavenly wave
> above the fair meander in the river.)

As in many of the Welsh poems to images of the Virgin, the poet focuses on events throughout Mary's lifetime, rather than the statue itself. She is praised for being free from sin and for having 'dwyn y grog dan ei gwregis' (reared the cross under her girdle). The Annunciation and Crucifixion are again brought together in one image. Mary weeps tears of blood at the foot of the cross as Christ is crucified wearing a crown of thorns, but her intercessory powers are also emphasized in a lighter tone as she places her rosary on the scales in an attempt to speed souls to heaven: 'hwpo enaid heb boeni/ i nef hwnn a vynno hi' (giving the soul a quick push into heaven, without worrying. This is what she wants). The poem was composed in order to celebrate one of the Marian feasts at Llanystymdwy – 'ar wledd Mair' (on Mary's feast) –

although the poet does not specifically indicate which feast: perhaps the Feast of the Annunciation on 25 March, since this is highlighted in the poem.[201]

Hywel Rheinallt's *cywydd* to Mary's image at Pwllheli does refer specifically to the Feast of the Annunciation and states that crowds seeking help visited the church on her feast. One can easily imagine that the poem was read aloud on the feast and its main aim seems to be to celebrate the wondrous image which, like the statue at Pen-rhys, was believed to be a divine gift rather than a man-made object: 'Duw a roddes, da wreiddyn,/ Delw deg heb waith dwylo dyn.'[202] (God donated the fair image, of good origin, /[which] had not been worked by man's hand.) The statue holds Christ in her arms and Mary is depicted as a life-giving force providing the earth with sun and water. She is, on the one hand, a goddess, a lady sent from heaven: 'Arglwyddes . . . wen o nef' (Holy Lady from heaven), but she is also 'frenhines fro' (a local or regional queen). The emphasis placed on the locality is particularly significant in this poem, as it is in the poem to the image at Llanystumdwy. Mary of Pwllheli attracts crowds of people – some from the countryside and some from the sea – but one is left with the distinct impression that the vast majority of pilgrims are locals drawn from surrounding areas in north Wales:

> Llu a eilw ym Mhwllheli
> I gael help ar ei gŵyl hi.
> Gwŷr o wlad ragorol wen,
> Gwŷr o fôr i gaer fawrwen;
> Gwŷr Llŷn ac eraill unair.
> Craig euraid, cwyr ac arian,
> Can llaw'n dwyn canhwyllau'n dân.
> Dinas fal penrhyn Dwynwen,
> Daear i Fair yw'r dre' wen.[203]

> (Crowds call at Pwllheli
> to receive help on her feast.
> Men from the excellent holy region,
> Men from the sea [come] to the great holy fortress;
> Girls visiting Mary,
> Men from Llŷn and others of like persuasion.

Golden rock[s], wax and money,
A hundred hands carrying lit candles.
A citadel like Dwynwen's promontory,
This holy town is Mary's ground.)

Pwllheli becomes Mary's region and Mary acting through local images and statues becomes a local saint. Rhisiart ap Rhys noted in a poem to the Virgin's image at Pen-rhys that the statue was almost as effective as Mary herself and Llywelyn ap Hywel in another poem to Pen-rhys notes: 'Mair a gynnail Morgannwg'[204] (Mary supports Glamorgan). Mary acting through the agency of local images became closer to the people and her cult took on a regional significance. Although the poets refer to the great numbers of pilgrims attracted to the individual sites, it is noticeable that most of the poets venerating the images are local poets associated with the counties where the images appear. With the exception of Huw Cae Llwyd and his son, all five of the other Pen-rhys poets are drawn from Glamorgan.[205] Hywel Rheinallt's poetry may be taken as a reflection of popular religious practice in fifteenth-century Caernarvonshire and north Wales: other poems celebrate the cults of St Cawrda at Aber-erch, Einion Frenin at Llanengan and Dwynwen on Llanddwyn island, Anglesey. In the poem to Mary of Pwllheli he compares the pilgrimage site at Pwllheli with 'penrhyn Dwynwen',[206] the promontory leading to Dwynwen's church and the holy well on Llanddwyn island. Dwynwen, Welsh patron saint of lovers, was one of the many daughters of Brychan Brycheiniog and her church at Llanddwyn was another important local pilgrimage site.[207] In a poem to Dwynwen he again emphasizes this association, claiming 'Mair a'th gâr'[208] (Mary loves you). He requests a blessing from Mary for Rhisiart Cyffin, Dean of Bangor Cathedral and Rector at Llanddwyn, and in this instance Dwynwen is asked to act as mediator. Mary thus becomes associated with the local saints of Wales and becomes embedded in Wales.

Indeed Mary was believed to have come to Wales. Traditions survive that she visited Cydweli, Aberdaron, Rhiw and Llanfair. At Llanfair in Meirionethshire where a church is dedicated to her she reputedly walked towards Hafod-y-llyn and knelt at the roadside two miles south-east of Harlech. Her knee prints were left on the rock where she knelt and a holy well sprang forth from the ground. When she arrived at the lake she bathed in the water with her maidens and thereafter water lilies grew at Hafod-y-llyn.[209] Pilgrims crossing to Bardsey Island, 'Ynys Fair firain'[210] (fair Mary's island), would climb down Mary's steps at Aberdaron, Llŷn, and drink from her well, a natural spring in the rocks marking the spot where she was supposed to have visited and left her hand print.[211]

'Mair y dawn yng Nghymru deg'[212] (Mary of grace in fair Wales) thus became a 'brenhines fro'[213] (local or regional queen), as well as 'brenhines nef a dayar ac vffern'[214] (queen of heaven, earth and hell). This particularly potent combination ensured immense popularity in a country which placed particular importance on its local saints, of which there were many, for, as we shall see in the next chapter, in Wales sanctity was locally conferred. Mary's humanity, her eagerness to intercede on behalf of all sinners, meant that she was particularly amenable and her local shrines, holy wells and images, helped reinforce the belief that Mary cared for ordinary folk. Gwilym Tew in his poem to Our Lady of Pen-rhys refers to the fact that the shrine was visited by a host of labourers[215] and Iolo Goch in his *cywydd* to the ploughman working in the fields refers to Mary's close spiritual relationship with labourers and the special protection she offered workmen: 'Llaw Fair dros bob llafurwr' (the hand of Mary over every ploughman'.[216] For Llywelyn ap Hywel Mary was the patron of ordinary people: 'Morwyn yw am werin nef'[217] (She is a maiden to the ordinary folk of heaven). Given the range of services offered by Mary and the array of outlets for her cult in medieval Wales, it is little wonder that such a large corpus of Middle Welsh literature venerating Mary survives.

2

Dead Virgins: Feminine Sanctity in Medieval Wales[1]

The 'Age of the Saints' has frequently been depicted as a period of intense religious activity when 'Celtic' missionaries travelled back and forth across the western seaways establishing early religious communities in Wales, Scotland, Cornwall, Ireland, Brittany and the Isle of Man.[2] In Wales these religious enclosures were known as 'llannau', and many place-names reflect the names of both male and female saints: for example, Llanddewibrefi, Llan-non, Llanddwyn, Llangain, Llandudno, Llandegla and Llanilltud Fawr. Whilst some scholars, such as E. G. Bowen, once argued that place-names and church dedications possibly reflected a saint's missionary activities, most now suggest that they indicate the spread of a saint's cult.

Although south-east Wales was Christianized during Roman times, the fifth to the eighth centuries have traditionally been considered as the formative period in the founding of a 'Celtic Church' with its own specific infrastructure of monastic communities following a strict, ascetic regime. The notion of a unified Celtic Church has been justifiably challenged by Kathleen Hughes and largely demolished by Wendy Davies.[3] Ian Bradley, who was previously one of the chief supporters of the concept of 'Celtic Christianity', has more recently altered his views quite considerably. His book *The Celtic Way* referred to Celtic Christianity as 'a gentle, mystical, affirmative and holistic faith, firmly biblical and strongly influenced by Desert Fathers, while assimilating many pagan beliefs and practices',[4] whereas his subsequent volume *Celtic Christianity: Making Myths and Chasing Dreams* provided a valuable critique of the concept of Celtic Christianity, noting that: 'it is tempting to suggest that Celtic Christianity is less an actual phenomenon defined in historical and geographical terms than an artificial construct created out of wishful thinking, romantic nostalgia and the projection of all kind of dreams about what should and might have been.'[5]

Nevertheless, for many years archaic views of a male-dominated Celtic Church has led to the dismissal of the disparate and sometimes partial sources which deal with the female saints of Wales and this, coupled with the fact that very few official prose Lives survive for the native women saints, has meant that the important role they played in medieval belief and religious practice has not always been fully acknowledged.[6] J. W. Willis Bund, more than a century ago, claimed that women rarely became saints in Wales and Ireland 'for a woman would not be the head of a monastery, the chief of a tribe of a Saint, and so could never become a Saint or entitled to be so called . . . a woman could never fill the office which certainly among the Welsh entitled a person to become a saint'.[7] Sainthood was, in his view, gender specific and incompatible with the traditional roles played by women. G. H. Doble, author of numerous articles on the Cornish and Welsh saints, also found it difficult to accept that women could have travelled great distances in order to establish religious foundations. There are dedications to St Cain (or Keyne) in South Wales, Anglesey, Somerset, Herefordshire and Cornwall, and Doble, whilst perfectly willing to accept that Cain could have visited these locations had the saint been male, was somewhat reluctant to concede that this would be the case if Cain was female:

> It seems difficult to believe that a woman could, in those wild ages, travel so far, and found so many settlements, and St. Keyne may quite well have been a man, in spite of the later universally accepted tradition of *Cain Wyry* [Cain the Virgin].[8]

Doble also suggests that Non (St David's mother) and Efrddyl (St Dyfrig's mother) were originally male saints, despite the fact that *Vita Dauidis* and *Vita Dubricius* record that both saints were undoubtedly believed to be female and, as saintly mothers, they played an important role in the biographical patterning of the saint, a point which will be discussed in greater detail in the next chapter.[9] Doble's suggestions are indicative of a school of thought that assumed that male saints were much more likely to have been historical figures than were the female saints: needless to say, maleness alone is not admissible as evidence of historicity.

Similar gender-biased assumptions can be found in *The Oxford Dictionary of Saints*. David Farmer assumes that the fourteenth-century Welsh Life of Beuno 'may contain genuine elements', but dismisses the twelfth-century Latin Life of Beuno's niece, Gwenfrewy (Winifred) as 'a tissue of improbabilities'.[10] No explanation is given. Both legends deal with the same episode and it is unclear why one medieval narrative, relating how a Dark-Age, Welsh saint resurrected seven people from the dead (*Hystoria o Uched Beuno*), is more likely to record historical events than another medieval narrative which relates how the same saint resurrected Gwenfrewy (*Vitae sanctae Wenefrede/Buched Gwenfrewy*). The aim here is not to claim that the female saints were historical characters, nor to assess the historical accuracy of the Lives, but simply to challenge the frequent assumption that the *vitae* of almost all male saints contain a core element of historical 'truth'. Nor is it appropriate to dismiss the legendary material associated with the female saints as 'worthless'.[11] The vast majority of relevant sources belong to the medieval period and thus they will be considered as an accurate, albeit incomplete, record of medieval beliefs and traditions concerning the Welsh saints. As J. Wyn Evans concisely points out:

> The Lives of the saints appear then to tell us more of the cult of a saint at a particular place in the medieval period rather than

about the saint himself or herself. They are based on criteria which were valid for the cyfarwydd or the ecclesiastic in writing of their own past as they perceived it, rather than those which the twentieth century normally uses in writing history.[12]

The daughters of Brychan Brycheiniog

According to *Trioedd Ynys Prydein*, a Middle Welsh compendium of triads thought to have been assembled in the twelfth century, Brychan Brycheiniog's family was one of the Three Saintly Lineages of the Island of Britain (un o 'dri Santeidd Linys Ynys Prydein').[13] His genealogy in *De situ Brecheniauc* records that he married three times and had eleven sons and twenty-five daughters all of whom were saints.[14] It is interesting to note that E. G. Bowen maps the dedications to Brychan's sons in *Settlements of the Celtic Saints in Wales*, but neglects to provide a similar study of dedications to Brychan's daughters, despite the fact that they were more numerous.[15] Brychan's genealogy varies from one manuscript to the next. For example, the Vespasian A xiv version of *Cognacio Brychan* lists eleven sons and twenty-four daughters, while the Domitian i version lists thirteen sons and twenty-five daughters.[16] Although numerous medieval traditions survive concerning some of the daughters of Brychan (for example St Dwynwen, who will be discussed in a separate section below), the genealogies are an important source because they also preserve the names of saints of whom very little is now known.

St Mabyn (Mabena), for example, is referred to in the twelfth-century Hartland list of Brychan's children recorded in Cornwall and she is depicted in stained glass *c.*1528 at St Neot, Cornwall, although no Welsh traditions regarding Mabyn appear to have survived (Plate 11). In the wives' window at St Neot parish church Mabyn is depicted wearing a blue mantle, crowned one of Christ's virgins, holding a book in one hand and a palm in the other suggesting that she was probably martyred. The portrait is a rare example of surviving late medieval stained glass depicting one of Brychan's daughters. The church and holy well at St Mabyn are dedicated to her and a fragment of her shrine survives. The shrines of two of her sisters, St Endellion and St Issey, are well preserved and Joanna Mattingly has argued convincingly that the shrine at St Issey, Cornwall, depicts sculpted figures of Brychan Brycheiniog's children.[17]

St Eluned (Eliwedd or Elvetha) who is mentioned in the Welsh genealogies was martyred, according to *Cognacio Brychan*, for her love of chastity.[18] Gerald of Wales who also attributes twenty-four daughters to Brychan provides a more detailed account of Eluned's martyrdom in the *Itinerarium Cambriae* *c.*1188:

> The Welsh annals bear witness to the fact that he had twenty-four daughters. From their youth upwards they were all dedicated to the religious life, and they ended their days blissfully in this state of sanctity. There are still many churches in Wales which have the honour of being named after them. One is on the top of a hill in Brecknockshire, not far from the main castle of Brecon. It is called the church of Saint Eluned, after the name of the saintly virgin who on that spot refused the hand of an earthly ruler and married instead the King Eternal, thus triumphing in an ecstasy of self-denial. Each year on the first day of August her feast-day is celebrated with great solemnity in this same place.[19]

Were it not for his summary of the Life of Eluned, the specific traditions associated with this saint may well have been lost, since neither *vita* nor *buchedd* are extant and Eluned is not mentioned in native Welsh poetry. Surprisingly her feast-day is not entered under 1 August in any of the Welsh calendars.[20] However, there is a reference to Eluned in the work of William Worcestre (*c.*1415–85). He refers to the saint's remains as being housed in the priory church at Usk, home to a community of Benedictine nuns founded sometime before 1135 by Richard de Clare.[21] Worcestre also relates the tale of Eluned's martyrdom on a hill near Brecon, adding that a spring of water welled forth at the time of her decapitation and that whoever drinks from the water or recites the Lord's Prayer shall find one of Eluned's hairs on a stone near the site of her martyrdom.[22]

St Gwenfrewy

Eluned's mythos is somewhat reminiscent of the traditions associated with one of the most renowned Welsh saints – Gwenfrewy – a virgin martyr who was, according to the various versions of her medieval legend, decapitated at Sychnant (from then on known as Holywell) in Flintshire, because she refused to have sexual intercourse with a local prince called Caradog. As mentioned earlier, she is resurrected by St Beuno who places the virgin's head back on her shoulders, and a holy well, with curative powers, springs forth from the pool of saintly blood spilled on the ground. Tudur Aled, in an early sixteenth-century *cywydd*, draws attention to the unusual stones stained with blood at the bottom of the well.[23] The medieval *vitae* also emphasize the importance of the blood-stained stones and refer to fragrant moss found at the well, which was, according to Baring-Gould and Fisher, known as St Winefride's Hair.[24]

Gwenfrewy's legend is well attested in medieval sources and she is one of the few native female saints for whom official prose Lives survive. Two twelfth-century Latin Lives and a fifteenth-century Welsh *buchedd* are extant and a summary of Gwenfrewy's martyrdom and decollation is also given in the Welsh Life of Beuno, *Hystoria o Uuched Beuno* (*c.*1346). The Welsh version of the Life of Gwenfrewy preserved in Llanstephan 34 most closely resembles the Latin *vita* attributed to Prior Robert of Shrewsbury and concludes with an account of the translation of Gwenfrewy's relics from Gwytherin to Shrewsbury.[25] The Welsh version preserved in Peniarth 27, however, omits the account of the translation to Shrewsbury and focuses instead on the importance of the burial site at Gwytherin, emphasizing that countless other saints were also buried there, including local saints such as Cybi, Sanan and Theon. While this version emphasizes the importance of the Welsh sites at Holywell and Gwytherin, Prior Robert's Life adds Shrewsbury to the list and the anonymous twelfth-century Latin Life, which is brief to the point of being curt and abrupt, contains a lengthy appendix devoted to posthumous miracles performed at the well and church at Holywell. The anonymous *vita* is quite different from the other versions and it is only in this text that it is claimed that Gwenfrewy went on pilgrimage to Rome and also attended an important synod in Britain.[26]

Gwenfrewy's legend was translated into Middle English and included in a number of extremely popular hagiographical collections such as certain versions of the *South English Legendary* (which was in wide circulation between *c.*1270–85 and the fifteenth century), the *Gilte Legende* (1438) and William Caxton's printed edition of the *Golden Legend* (1483).[27] Medieval Welsh poetry relating Gwenfrewy's legend and recording miraculous healings at her holy well are to be found in the work of Ieuan Brydydd Hir (*fl.*1450–85), Tudur Aled (*c.*1465–*c.*1525), Siôn ap Hywel ap Llywelyn Fychan (*fl. c.*1490–1532), as well as in two medieval *cywyddau* of uncertain authorship.[28]

Having spent seven years residing over a community of nuns at Holywell, Gwenfrewy, according to her medieval Lives, moved to Gwytherin where she succeeded St Theon as Abbess. In 1138 her relics were translated to the Benedictine priory of SS. Peter and Paul at Shrewsbury. Gwytherin appears to have attracted pilgrims even after the removal of her relics since Edward Lhuyd, on a visit to Gwytherin *c.*1690, sketched a drawing of her empty reliquary, a piece of which was found by Tristan Gray Hulse in 1991 and is thought to date from the eighth or ninth century. It appears that pilgrims visiting Gwytherin cut off small fragments of the wooden box, until it gradually disintegrated.[29]

The vigorous spring at Holywell, now claimed to be one of the seven wonders of Wales, attracts pilgrims to this day and, at the height of the pilgrimage season, as well as on special occasions such as the saint's feast-days, the reliquary of St Gwenfrewy is displayed (Plate 12). A fragment of finger bone, presumed to be Gwenfrewy's, is encased in a silver monstrance: the relic which had been sent to Rome was returned to Holywell in 1855. From 1240 to the Dissolution the holy well was a source of considerable income for the Cistercian monks of Basingwerk to whom it was appropriated and, throughout the Middle Ages, it attracted eminent visitors such as Henry V, Edward IV and Richard III. A statue of Gwenfrewy appears in Henry VII's chapel at Westminster

Abbey and the building of the well chapel at Holywell has frequently been attributed to the generosity and religious convictions of Henry VII's mother, Margaret Beaufort (1441–1509), although one should also emphasize the importance of Thomas Pennant's sponsorship of the rebuilding work at Holywell, during his time as Abbot of Basingwerk (1481–1522). Medieval Welsh poetry certainly gives the impression that the building of the current Perpendicular well chapel was overseen and financed by Pennant. Tudur Aled, for example, wishes that Pennant may soon finish enclosing the well and be rewarded for his endeavours by being made either Bishop of York or Bishop of St Davids[30] and Siôn ap Hywel in his *awdl* to Gwenfrewy states that:

> O law Tomas urddaswin
> Yr aeth y gost ar waith Gwen:
> Diwan adeilad, da iawn y dylud,
> Da y darparwyd, iti darperir.[31]

> (From the hand of Thomas [provider of] noble wine
> came the cost of Gwen's work:
> A sturdy building, full well do you deserve it,
> well was it prepared, prepared for you.)

Gwenfrewy was certainly of sufficient political importance to warrant the production of medieval *vitae* and a Welsh *buchedd*. Her high-ranking status within the diocese of St Asaph is also confirmed by a fifteenth-century ecclesiastical seal, the second seal of the Chapter of St Asaph, which appears to depict Gwenfrewy, veiled as a bride of Christ, holding her abbess's crosier and a reliquary (Plate 13). To her left, stands another saint, probably St Asaph, and a third figure kneels under a canopy. Gwenfrewy is also depicted on a fifteenth-century seal from the Church of the Holy Cross at the priory of SS. Peter and Paul, Shrewsbury. This seal focuses on Gwenfrewy's decapitation and depicts an angry Caradog brandishing his sword above the virgin's neck. It bears the initials of Thomas Mynde, Prior of Shrewsbury 1459–99.[32] Gwenfrewy is depicted clutching a sword in late medieval stained glass at the church of St Tyrnog, Llandyrnog, Denbighshire. She appears in the tracery lights of the east window alongside St Marchell (Tyrnog's sister), St Frideswide of Oxford and St Katherine of Alexandria. It is possible that the virgin martyr depicted in medieval glass at Llanasa church may originally have been intended to be Gwenfrewy, and that the label 'Sca Katharina', along with the sword and the wheel were added when the glass was reconstructed in the nineteenth century. Neither the label nor Katherine's attributes appear in a sketch of the window in 1825. The saint (whoever she may be) has a visible scar around her neck and this is consistent with Gwenfrewy's iconography and the emphasis placed on her scar in medieval Welsh poetry.[33]

Scholars have frequently noted the political importance of saints' Lives and the way in which these narratives were used to empower the medieval dioceses, assert rights and privileges, define ecclesiastical boundaries and establish rights of sanctuary, as well as to promote the cult of a particular patron saint and establish a locus of pilgrimage with a view to both financial and spiritual gain.[34] The dioceses of St Davids and Llandaf were not only competing against each other in the struggle for archiepiscopal primacy, but were also attempting to fend off Norman influence. It is interesting to note that the anonymous Latin Life of Gwenfrewy remarks that, as an expression of celebration, Gwenfrewy's well flowed with a milky liquid for three days following the expulsion of the French from Gwynedd.[35]

As we saw in the previous chapter, it has generally been assumed that in post-conquest Wales numerous churches were rededicated to the Virgin Mary or to universally popular saints (particularly in areas of strong Norman influence) and that some of the original dedications to local Welsh saints have been lost or altered.[36] However, further, more detailed work on Welsh dedications is urgently needed if we are to test these theories and analyse to what extent this was in fact due to Norman influence. Certainly by the fourteenth century internationally popular saints, such as the Virgin Mary, Katherine of Alexandria and Mary Magdalene were as fashionable in Wales as they were elsewhere in Europe. Nevertheless hagiographical texts strongly associated native saints with a particular foundation and, in general, sanctity seems to have been locally conferred. The vast majority of the native saints' cults (and in particular the female saints) were confined to a particular locality, often having only one or two church dedications. With the exception of Gwenfrewy, few of the native female saints of Wales appear to have been considered of major political importance and this perhaps explains why so few Lives are extant. Naturally some may have been lost, but one cannot altogether discount the possibility that many of these hagiographical 'stories' were never committed to writing and may only have been current in oral tradition. Since medieval literature was generally intended for oral delivery and public performance rather than private reading, one could reasonably speculate that the local saints' Lives were frequently recounted on special days such as feast days, or on pilgrimages to the saint's holy well or shrine, and that the local population were familiar with these traditions, despite never having read an official *vita* or *buchedd*. This hypothesis is further supported by the nature of the evidence for the female saints. Remnants of their medieval traditions are found in native Welsh poetry, prayers and genealogies yet few Lives survive.

St Melangell

A noteworthy example of a female saint whose legend appears to have been current in oral tradition, possibly before being recorded in writing, is Melangell (or Monacella) – the patron saint of hares. In her church at Pennant Melangell stands a twelfth-century, Romanesque shrine, which was reconstructed in 1958, and again in 1991, from fragments found in the church walls and lych gate.[37] The shrine may once have contained the saint's relics or, alternatively, it may have been positioned over a cist grave found in the eastern apse of the church. Certainly by the twelfth century the church at Pennant Melangell was believed to honour the relics of the holy virgin Melangell.[38]

By the eighteenth century the relics appear to have found their way to France. Father Louis de Sabran, rector of the Jesuit College of St Omer, believed that the college possessed 'St Monacella's body' and referred to the saint in a series of letters between 31 October 1713 and 2 July 1715.[39] His letter book suggests that the relics remained intact and that the entire skeleton of Melangell was venerated at the college and dressed in clothes suitable for a saintly princess. In February 1714 he commissioned 'a flower crowne for St. Monacella' from Lady Knatchbull, Abbess of the English Benedictine nuns at Ghent, and she replied that she would send him a crown of gold and silver silk flowers.[40] Attempts were made to obtain an indulgence to venerate the body on Melangell's feast and Louis de Sabran was keen to learn more about Melangell and obtain a copy of her Life. During the period that the letters were written the Jesuits appear to have known very little about Melangell, assuming incorrectly that she was a martyr.[41] A play was performed in her honour at the college, but unfortunately it would appear that neither the play nor the relics have survived.[42]

Melangell is referred to by the fifteenth-century poet Lewys Glyn Cothi and mentioned three times in the poetry of Guto'r Glyn (*c*.1435–93).[43] Three complete copies and two incomplete copies of her Latin Life, *Historia divae Monacellae*, are extant in manuscripts dating from the late sixteenth century and there is also a printed copy of a seventeenth-century manuscript which was destroyed in a fire in 1858.[44] Radford and Hemp suggest that the Life was composed in the late fourteenth or fifteenth century, possibly when the church was enlarged and modernized, but Pryce proposes that it was composed sometime between the end of the fifteenth and the beginning of the sixteenth century and that it draws on oral sources as well as earlier written material.[45] The earliest record of Melangell's legend is pictorial rather than textual, since a carved, late fifteenth-century rood-screen in her church at Pennant Melangell depicts a large hare running towards the abbess, in order to seek protection from the pursuing hounds (Plate 14). On the left of the screen, Brochfael Ysgithrog is depicted on horseback clutching a sword and one of his men sounds the hunting horn.[46]

According to the *Historia divae Monacellae*, Melangell fled from Ireland to Wales in order to avoid an arranged marriage. She settled in a remote hamlet at Pennant Melangell and enjoyed a quiet and peaceful, contemplative existence for fifteen years during which time she never 'looked at the face of a man'.[47] Then one day she came face to face with Brochfael Ysgithrog hunting a hare. His hounds cowered and refused to approach the hare which peered out from under the hem of Melangell's skirt. Brochfael, made aware of Melangell's sanctity, decided to grant her a considerable portion of land on which to establish a nunnery and protective sanctuary for anyone seeking asylum. It was not until after Melangell's death that the peace at Pennant Melangell was broken when:

> a certain person by the name of Elise, came to Pennant Melangell, who, desiring to ravish, seize and defile the same virgins, came to an end most wretchedly and perished suddenly. Whoever has violated the aforementioned liberty and protected holy place of the said virgin has rarely been said to avoid divine vengeance in this region, as one can perceive every day.[48]

The message put forward in the *Historia* is crystal clear. Anyone who attempts to violate one of Christ's virgins risks divine retribution. Those who threaten or harm the female saints are frequently cursed, swallowed up by the earth, melted, frozen or suffer excruciating sudden death. In the *Vita sancte Wenefrede*, for instance, Beuno curses Gwenfrewy's murderer who immediately melts and disintegrates.[49] Melangell is fortunate in that she has already departed her earthly existence, before the would-be rapist visits Pennant Melangell with evil intent, but other female saints (such as Gwenfrewy and Eluned) are not as fortunate.

Martyrs: violence and torture

A number of Welsh female saints are reputed to have been martyred including Dunod, Tudful, Tybïe, Gwen, Enfail and Maches. Dunod, who is only mentioned in the Lives of St David, is brutally murdered by her stepmother Satrapa:

> Sef a oruc y vorwyn da, diweir, war, gymenn, rodi y phenn yn arffet y llysuam. Sef a oruc y llysuam, tynnv kyllell a llad penn y vorwyn santes. Ac yn y gyfeir y dygwydawd y gwaet y'r llawr,

> yd ymdangosses ffynnyawn. A llawer o dynyon a gauas yechyt a gwaret yno. A hyt hediw y gelwir y ffynnawn honno Ffynnawn Dunawt, kanys Dunawt oed enw y vorwyn.[50]
>
> (The good, chaste, civilized, eloquent maiden placed her head in her stepmother's lap. The stepmother took out a knife and cut off the saintly virgin's head. And in the very place where the blood fell to the ground, a holy well appeared. And many people were healed there and granted salvation. And today this well is still named Dunod's Well, for Dunod was the virgin's name.)

Four of Brychan Brycheiniog's daughters were murdered by pagan Saxons, according to Iolo Morganwg (1747–1826), namely Tybïe of Llandybïe, Tudful of Merthyr Tudful, Gwen of Talgarth and Enfail of Merthyr Enfail. Although the first three women appear consistently in Brychan's medieval genealogies, Iolo Morganwg's manuscripts are the only source which mentions their martyrdom, and in most cases Iolo simply adds the following formula to the genealogies: 'lle ai llas gan y Paganiaid Saeson' (where she was killed by pagan Saxons).[51] However, in the case of Tudful he elaborates upon the tale, claiming that Tudful was slain whilst visiting her ageing father Brychan. Her brothers, having witnessed her martyrdom, became involved in the conflict and hurried after the pagans to avenge her death, but Rhun, one of Brychan's sons, was killed in the onslaught. The pagans were eventually driven away by Tudful's young nephew, Nefydd ap Rhun, who was outraged by his father's death. Here Iolo makes Tudful of Glamorgan the mother of Brochfael Ysgithrog, a hero who is usually associated with Powys and who, as we have seen, grants lands for St Melangell's sanctuary.[52] Although Iolo Morganwg was an avid collector of Welsh manuscripts and a keen copyist, one must exercise caution when using his notes on the Welsh saints, since he is renowned for skilfully faking 'medieval' material and embellishing certain traditions, particularly those associated with Glamorgan.

One example of the manner in which Iolo Morganwg's narratives differ from medieval traditions is demonstrated in the account of the martyrdom of Maches. According to Iolo

Morganwg, Maches, who was fond of offering alms to the poor, was stabbed in the chest by a pagan Saxon who had disguised himself as a beggar. Iolo claims that Maches was St Cadog's sister and St Gwynllyw's daughter, yet neither the *Vita sancti Cadoci* nor the *Vita sancti Gundleii* mentions Maches.[53] However, an account of the martyrdom of the virgin Maches (Machuta) is given in the twelfth-century Latin Life of St Tathan (Tatheus) where it is related that Maches was beheaded by thieves who were eager to steal a ram from her flock. The murderers confess all to St Tathan who visits the spot where the virgin was martyred:

> In that same place he founded a church built in honour of the virgin Machuta. He refused to allow there the virgin's body, but only in the place where alone it ought to lie. Therefore it was carried to Caer-went, and buried in the floor of the church, and may her soul rest in eternal rest.[54]

Her role as shepherdess may have led to her misidentification with St Margaret of Antioch, a more popular and well-known saint who is depicted caring for her foster mother's flock of sheep at the beginning of her medieval Life. In an intriguing fifteenth-century *cywydd* to St Margaret the poet Thomas Derllysg (*fl.*1460–90) suggests that the saint from Antioch lies buried at Llanfaches, near Caer-went, and that the local Welsh parishioners will benefit spiritually from their association with Margaret since this is where she suffered:

> Sôn am eurgrair Sain Margred,
> Uwch Caer Went i iachau cred.
> Un ferch wen o Vorach oedd
> I Dewdus, a da ydoedd.
> Llyma ferch lle mae i fedd
> Llan faches, lleian fuchedd.
> Dywedaf i'm diwydion,
> Fuchedd hoff, o achoedd hon
> Un Dewdus un da ydoedd . . .
> . . . Margred sydd yn arwydd nef.
> Am iddi yma oddef,
> Mae nef yn gartref i gyd
> I'w phlwyogion o'i phlegyd.[55]

(Talking of the golden relic [of] St Margaret,
to heal faith, above Caer-went,
she was the only holy daughter of Theodosius
from Vorach [Antioch?] and she was good.
Here's a girl whose grave is at
Llanfaches, holy Life of a nun.
I will tell the faithful, favourite Life,
one Theodosius of her lineage, and good was she . . .
. . . Margaret who is a sign from heaven.
For since she suffered here,
heaven is home to her parishioners,
because of her.)[56]

The remainder of the poem is reasonably straightforward and recounts the standard narrative associated with St Margaret of Antioch, her imprisonment and persecution by Olibrius, her encounter with the devil disguised as a dragon and her heroic martyrdom.

The Lives of the universally popular saints Margaret of Antioch, Katherine of Alexandria, Mary of Egypt, Mary Magdalene and Martha were translated into Welsh sometime before the mid-fourteenth century. Chapters 4 and 5 in the present volume will provide a detailed study of the vernacular versions of these Lives, focusing in particular on the Welsh evidence for the cults of St Katherine, Mary Magdalene and her sister Martha. As in the traditions associated with the Welsh female saints, many of these universal saints' Lives are brutal and violent and most centre around the perpetual struggle to preserve the female saints' virginity. Both Gwenfrewy and Margaret refer to Christ as their protector, the man responsible for guarding their virginity and ensuring that they remain physically undefiled. With the exception of the repentant prostitutes, Mary Magdalene and Mary of Egypt, all of these holy women are virgins and their sanctity and spiritual strength are inextricably linked with their physical purity. Margaret of Antioch (Margred) and Katherine of Alexandria (Catrin) suffer an appalling array of tortures, but stoically refuse to bow to their tormentors' will. In *Buched Margred*, for example, Margaret is thrown in prison, beaten with large sticks until her flesh is ripped apart, stripped, set alight and tortured in boiling water:

> 'Noethwch hi a chroguch ynn yr awyr, ac ennynnwch y hystlyssev a ffaglev gwressauc' . . . Ac yna yd erchis y pennyadur dvynn llestreit o dvfyr brvt, a rvymav y phenn a'e thraet a'e dienydyav a'e phoeni yn hvnnv.[57]

> ('Undress her and suspend her in the air and set the sides of her body alight with red-hot firebrands' . . . And then her tormentor requested that vessels of boiling water be brought and that her hands and feet be bound and that she be tortured and put to death in them.)

Her tormentors are referred to as 'kiccydyon' (butcherers) and at one point during the series of vicious attacks perpetrated against her, even her torturer, Olibrius, has to look away because the scene is so horrific:

> Y kiccydyonn, hagen, voe voe a oed yn dinev y gvaet ac ynn dienydyav y chorff hi. Hynny a oruc y creulaun treissvr cudyav y llygeit a'e mantell cany allei edrych arnei rac meint yd yttoedit ynn gordinev o'e guaet hi.[58]

> (The butcherers, however, were increasingly causing her blood to flow and torturing her body. The cruel perpetrator of violence hid his eyes in his cloak since he could not bear to look at her, since the amount of blood flowing from her body was so immense.)

Margaret is eventually swallowed by the devil disguised as a dragon, but emerges from his body unharmed when the crucifix around her neck miraculously grows and splits the dragon in two. It is presumably for this reason, as well as the fact that she promises before she is beheaded that no lame or blind child will ever be born into any household which possesses a copy of her Life, that she became known as the patron saint of childbirth.

Of the numerous methods of torture described in saints' Lives, one of the most horrific is amputation of the saint's breasts. As we shall see in Chapter 5, in the Life of St Katherine it is the perpetrator's wife rather than St Katherine who has her breasts removed. In the continental versions of the Lives of Barbara and Agatha the saints have their breasts ripped off because, like Katherine, they refuse to sacrifice to pagan gods and refuse to marry their tormentors. Both are imprisoned and eventually decapitated.[59] Agatha's breasts heal miraculously during her incarceration. Neither the Lives of Barbara or Agatha appear to have been translated into Middle Welsh, although both saints were known in Wales. Agatha is invoked by the poet Dafydd Nanmor (*fl.*1450–90) in a long list of 'saint yr ynys hon' (saints of this island, i.e. Britain) whom he hopes will offer protection to Henry Tudor.[60] Barbara is one of the female saints invoked in a poem by Lewys Morgannwg (*fl.*1520–65) which was composed on behalf of Margred Siôn of Coety who appears to have been suffering from breast cancer:

> Bo ar weddi, bêr addef,
> beri bron iach, Barbra nef;
> San Ffred, Sant Margred a Mair,
> Sant Ann a'r holl saint unair.
> Galw o nefoedd, glain afiach,
> Gwenvrewy nerth, gwna vronn iach.[61]
>
> Heavenly Barbara, Ffraid, Margaret and Mary,
> St Ann and all the saints united,
> may this sweet prayer
> cause the breast to be healed.
> Call strong Gwenfrewy from holy heaven
> [in order to] heal the sick breast.)

St Apollonia, another 'foreign' saint who suffered physical torture when her teeth were brutally extracted one by one by her pagan tormentor, certainly seems to have been popular in Wales. The patron of toothache sufferers is depicted holding one of her teeth in a pair of pliers in two late fifteenth-century stained-glass windows at Gresford parish church.[62] She is also mentioned in a charm in one of the Middle Welsh medical texts which advises that the patient write a short prayer to Jesus, Mary and Apollonia and tie it around the neck in order to relieve toothache.[63]

St Ursula

Another saint of international repute who has a particular connection with Wales is St Ursula. According to Welsh tradition, Ursula and her 11,000 virgins set sail from Llangwyryfon (the church of the virgins) near Aberystwyth, Ceredigion, on their final pilgrimage to Rome and were martyred at Cologne. Her legend was translated from Latin into Welsh *c.*1514 by Huw Pennant and is preserved in a single manuscript, Aberystwyth, National Library of Wales, MS Peniarth 182. According to *Hystoria Gweryddon yr Almaen*, Ursula refused to marry a pagan prince, but was forced to compromise for the sake of her father 'un o brenhinoedd Ynys y Kedyrn' (one of the kings of the Island of the Mighty, that is to say Britain).[64] She agreed that she would marry on returning from her pilgrimage. Ursula set sail with her 11,000 maidens and having visited Cologne, they arrived in Rome where they received a rapturous welcome from the British Pope Curig. However, on their return to Cologne they discovered that the city was under siege and it was not long before all of Ursula's virginal companions were brutally murdered. The pagan prince responsible for the murders apologized to Ursula when he noticed her great beauty and requested her hand in marriage, but since she adamantly refused his offer, he took out his bow and arrow and shot her. Ursula is depicted shielding her companions under her cloak and holding the arrow with which she was martyred in modern stained glass at her church in Llangwyryfon.[65] The present church was erected in 1883, and built opposite the site of the medieval church which formerly stood in the circular cemetery at Llangwyryfon.

Gwerful Mechain (*fl.*1462–1500), the only Welsh female poet for whom a corpus of medieval poetry survives, refers to the 11,000 virgins in a poem she wrote to defend Anni Goch (and women in general) from a vitriolic attack by another poet called Ieuan Dyfi. Her 'Cywydd i Ateb Ieuan Dyfi am ei Gywydd i Anni Goch' (poem responding to Ieuan Dyfi for his poem to Anni Goch) lists particularly virtuous women, and was written in direct response to Ieuan Dyfi's *cywydd* which criticized, not only his lover Anni Goch, but the whole of womankind, listing numerous examples of female sinners and wrongdoers.[66] Other Welsh poets refer to the 11,000 virgin martyrs, but do not specifically praise St Ursula. For example, Tudur Aled compares Gwenfrewy to the 11,000 virgins rather than Ursula,[67] and, with the exception of Gwerful Mechain, most poets who name Cologne (Cwlen in Welsh) refer to the relics of the three wise men in Cologne cathedral, rather than the relics of Ursula and her virginal companions.[68] It is possible that the Life of Ursula (which follows the traditional *vita*) was not translated into Welsh until the sixteenth century and that the version which was perhaps more widely disseminated in Wales was Geoffrey of Monmouth's *Historia Regum Britanniae* (1136) and its Welsh translations.[69] In this version Ursula is not specifically named: she is the daughter of Dunod (Dionotus), King of Cornwall, and is martyred along with 11,000 noble virgins by the Picts and the Huns. The virgins and 60,000 women of lower status set sail for Brittany, whither they have been summoned by Cynan Meiriadog (Conanus Meridiadocus), who is eager for his men to marry Britons. The unnamed Princess and her companions are blown off course and a number are drowned before the remainder eventually land in Germany only to be martyred by Winwas (Wanius) and Melwas (Melga), the leaders of the Picts and the Huns. *Gŵyl y Gweryddon* (the feast of the Virgins) on 21 October is entered in almost all of the Welsh calendars.

Virginity and feminine sanctity

Virginity may almost be considered a prerequisite for feminine sanctity, and one begins to see a pattern emerging in the traditions of the female saints that is quite different from the male saints' Lives. Henken notes that the unusual birth and conception of the male saint is similar to that of the secular hero; that the childhood of the saint usually demonstrates his greatness; he often performs a miracle illustrating his 'coming out into the world'; he is learned, usually precocious and receives a good education; performs many miracles; heals the sick; punishes unbelievers; lives to a ripe old age and usually dies of natural causes.[70] Most of the Welsh male saints' Lives follow this pattern (the holy abbot/bishop model) rather than the alternative model of male martyr saints found in numerous Lives from England and the Continent. There is no Welsh equivalent, for example, of St George whose Life, in many ways, resembles that of a female saint (in particular St Katherine). George, like Katherine, is summoned to sacrifice to Roman gods and when he refuses he is detained by a heathen ruler, tortured in a variety of ways including being strapped to a wheel with knife-like blades and eventually he is decapitated. Although George appears to have been a relatively popular figure in medieval Welsh art, his Life was not translated into Middle Welsh. Medieval images of both SS. George and Katherine are extant from Llangystennin church, although the painted glass is no longer *in situ*.[71]

Of the Welsh female saints Henken says:

> Tradition pays no, or virtually no, attention to their lives until they are confronted with male sexuality . . . The encounter with male sexuality is the only major element in the biographical pattern which appears with any consistency for the Welsh women saints.[72]

One may add a number of details to the biographical pattern of the female saints: their Lives usually begin at puberty, when they decide to dedicate their virginity to Christ and refuse to marry; they are frequently of noble birth and often have to flee their native land in order to avoid an arranged marriage; sometimes this involves a journey across the Irish sea; they seek a simple ascetic lifestyle, worshipping Christ (their eternal husband), and either live alone or establish a community of religious females; however, they unwittingly become the objects of male desire and are frequently abducted, threatened with rape or forced marriage, tortured and decapitated.[73]

Only in death does the female saint attain perpetual virginity and eternal salvation, for whilst on earth there is a constant risk that she may be seen, admired and polluted. As Bloch notes 'a certain inescapable logic of virginity, most evident in medieval hagiography, leads syllogistically to the conclusion that the only good virgin – that is, the only true virgin – is a dead virgin'.[74] The confrontation with male sexuality is usually introduced to the narrative account via a description of the pagan suitor gazing or staring at the saint's beauty, as in the following example from the Life of Gwenfrewy:

> So Caradog gazing at the countenance of the girl made up of white and red and admiring the whole of her, fair in form and face, his heart in desire of her began to burn exceedingly.[75]

Another of Bloch's definitions of the medieval concept of a virgin is a woman who not only has never slept with a man, nor desired to do so, but 'a woman who has never been seen by a man'.[76] Interestingly, Melangell manages to lead a peaceful existence at Pennant Melangell since she has been hidden from the male gaze for fifteen years. The female saint welcomes physical punishment or torture because it is the prelude to her elevation from the corporeal world of the senses to the plane of spiritual fulfilment.

San Ffraid

San (St) Ffraid, a composite saint in Welsh tradition (that is a fusion of the Irish St Brigid of Kildare and St Birgitta of Sweden), is temporarily deprived of one of her senses in order to preserve her virginity. When her father tried to force her to marry she prayed to God for assistance. Miraculously, one of her eyes popped out of her head, presumably rendering her so physically repulsive that no one would wish to marry her and, when the threat of marriage subsided, her face healed. This episode (which stems from the Life of Brigid of Kildare) is related in a Welsh *cywydd* by Iorwerth Fynglwyd (*fl.*1485–1527):

> dydd, y ceisiodd dy dad
> wra yt, a'i roi atad,
> un o'th lygaid a neidiawdd
> o'th ben, hyn a'th boenai'n hawdd;
> a thrannoeth aeth yr wyneb
> oll yn iach, ni bu well neb.[77]

(The day your father attempted
to find you a husband, and give him to you,
one of your eyes jumped
out of your head, and this inevitably hurt you;
but the next day, all your face healed,
no one had ever felt better.)

There are numerous examples of saints and nuns who plucked out their eyes or cut off their noses in order to avoid marriage or rape. Schulenburg describes how nuns frequently mutilated their faces during Viking invasions in order to avoid sexual violation.[78] In Britain at least forty nunneries were destroyed during Viking raids, and by the time of the Norman Conquest only nine houses for women remained.[79] Saintly self-mutilation appears to have continued well into the High Middle Ages, for St Ffraid's method of avoiding an arranged marriage recurs in the thirteenth century. St Margaret of Hungary (who died in 1270) refused to marry the Duke of Poland, the King of Sicily and the King of Bohemia, and when she heard that the Pope intended to arrange a marriage for her she threatened to pluck out her eyes and cut off her nose.[80]

St Dwynwen

Numerous other female saints escape unwanted marriages, but one Welsh saint in particular has become associated with marital alliances and unrequited love. Dwynwen, the patron saint of lovers, whose cult has recently enjoyed a revival as the Welsh St Valentine, is perhaps the best known of Brychan Brycheiniog's unmarried daughters. Her feast day is still celebrated in Wales on 25 January and it is listed in most medieval calendars on this date, although one sixteenth-century manuscript refers to her feast on 13 July.[81] Hywel Rheinallt in a *cywydd* to the saint praises Dwynwen's noble lineage and emphasises her pre-eminence amongst the other saintly daughters of Brychan Brycheiniog:

Pab mewn côr o'th [ch]wiorydd,
Bob cares yn santes sydd.
Un wyd er dy fod yn iau
Sy'n tywyso santesau.[82]

(A pope in a choir of your sisters
Every loved one is a female saint.
Although you are younger, you are the one
who leads female saints.)

According to the legend recounted in the Iolo Morganwg manuscripts, Dwynwen fell in love with Maelon Dafodrill, but was heartbroken when he broke off their engagement on the grounds that she refused to have sexual intercourse before marriage. God punished Maelon by turning him into a block of ice and gave Dwynwen three wishes. She requested that Maelon be defrosted; that she would always be able to hear the anguished prayers of anyone suffering from unrequited love; and that she herself would never again suffer the pangs of love, but rather that she would live a solitary existence as a nun on Llanddwyn island.[83] In the sixteenth century three Latin prayers invoking Dwynwen were added to the Bangor missal (1494). These record very different traditions associated with Dwynwen, for they claim that Dwynwen miraculously walked across the Irish Sea for fear of Maelgwn Gwynedd.[84] Maelgwn, a common secular adversary in the Lives of the saints, may well have come into conflict with the saintly virgin, possibly requesting her hand in marriage and causing Dwynwen to flee. In the Latin Life of Cadog Maelgwn abducts the daughter of one of Cadog's prefects and is temporarily blinded as a punishment for insulting behaviour towards the saint.[85]

Throughout the Middle Ages Llanddwyn island was a popular place of pilgrimage. Hywel Rheinallt refers to her church there as 'seren y sir' (the star of the county) and describes how crowds of people from Gwynedd Is-conwy and Gwynedd Uwch-conwy visited the church and holy well in August leaving offerings of gold and wax. Dafydd Trefor (*c*.1460–*c*.1528) in his *cywydd* to Dwynwen gives the impression that the image of the saint was draped in gold and valuable offerings and provides a vivid description of miraculous healings that took place at the holy well:

Minteioedd ym min tywyn:
Merched o amrafael wledydd,
Meibion fil fyrddion a fydd,
Cleifion rhwng ei ffynhonnau,

Crupliaid a gweniaid yn gwau,
Bronnydd fel lluoedd brenin,
Pobl o'r wlad, pawb ar ei lin,
Taprau cwyr, pabwyr er pwyll,
Pibau gwin, pawb â'i gannwyll,
Crysau'n llawn brychau gerbron,
Miragl wrth godi meirwon![86]

(Crowds on the edge of the seashore:
Girls from various regions,
An innumerable myriad of men are to be found [there]
Sick people, cripples and the weak
bustling between the holy wells,
Hill slopes [covered with people] like a king's army,
People from the countryside, everyone on his knees,
Wax tapers, candle wicks for health of mind,
Pipes of wine, everyone with his candle,
Shirts covered in stains nearby,
A miracle as the dead are resurrected!)

The remains of Dwynwen's chapel on the island probably date from the sixteenth century. However, there was certainly an earlier chapel on the island and the fourteenth-century poet Dafydd ap Gwilym refers to a golden statue of the saint in her church. He invokes Dwynwen, requesting that she act as a *llatai* (love messenger) and persuade his lover Morfudd to arrange a tryst with him:

Dwynwen, pes parud unwaith
Dan wŷdd Mai a hirddydd maith,
Dawn ei bardd, da, wen y bych;
Dwynwen, nid oeddud anwych.
Dangos o'th radau dawngoeth
Nad wyd fursen, Ddwynwen ddoeth.[87]

(Dwynwen, if you would allow it once
Under May woods on a long, lingering day
Her poet's gift, [O] fair one, you'd be blessed.
Dwynwen, you were [never] wretched!
With your rich-gifted graces show,
Wise Dwynwen, you're not prudish.)[88]

The mischievous tone of the poem is characteristic of Dafydd ap Gwilym's love poetry. He is more than willing to take advantage of Dwynwen's reputation as a chaste holy virgin in order to arrange an unchaste, adulterous meeting with his married lover. In a satirical poem by Dafydd Llwyd of Mathafarn (*c*.1395–1486) Dwynwen is described as an extremely chaste saint who will, nevertheless, not prevent others from committing adultery.[89]

Although various references in medieval poetry refer to Dwynwen assisting in matters of the heart as well as the soul, it is not clear exactly when Dwynwen became specifically associated with lovers. By the eighteenth century people were not only visiting the well at Llanddwyn to obtain cures for physical ailments, but also in order to obtain information about relationships. An old woman from Newborough would sit near the well and having placed a suitor's handkerchief on the surface would predict from the movements of eels that lived in the bottom of the well, whether or not the relationship would be successful.[90]

Abduction

Whilst the majority of female saints are virgins who manage to avoid marrying, others are abducted against their will by their would-be suitors and some eventually become mothers to important male saints. St Tegfedd, according to Dafydd Llwyd of Mathafarn's *cywydd* to her brother St Tydecho, was abducted by Cynan, but later returned, maidenhead intact, and restored to her brother who was also given lands at Arthbeibio in the form of apology.[91] St Gwladys, one of Brychan Brycheiniog's daughters, was abducted by King Gwynllyw eager to make her his wife. En route to Gwynllyw's court she was spotted by King Arthur and his men and, for a brief moment, was actually in danger of being abducted from her abductors, since King Arthur:

> immediately very inflamed with lust in desire for the maiden, and filled with evil thoughts, said to his companions, 'Know that I am vehemently inflamed with concupiscence for this girl,

> whom that soldier is carrying away on horseback.' But they forbidding him said, 'Far be it that so great a crime should be perpetrated by thee, for we are wont to aid the needy and distressed. Wherefore let us run together with all speed and assist this struggling contest that it may cease.'[92]

Gwladys is never restored to her father, since King Arthur's interpretation of 'aiding the needy' involves assisting Gwynllyw in his abduction. However, after the birth of their son, St Cadog, Gwladys and Gwynllyw separate and she leads a holy life akin to that of a nun. The female saint's virginity, it appears, can be compromised when the conception of a male saint is at stake, a point which will be discussed in detail in the next chapter. Gwladys's ordeal is recounted in the Latin Life of her son Cadog and a different version of events is given in her husband Gwynllyw's Life.[93]

The notion of holy kinship is prevalent in the genealogies of Welsh saints, and many of the saints' families are interrelated. The lineages of the two eponymous kings, Ceredig and Brychan, who gave their names to Brycheiniog (Breconshire) and Ceredigion, include numerous Welsh saints: Ceredig who is purported to have been St David's grandfather is related to SS. Ina, Dogfael, Tyssul, Pedr and Afan Buellt and, one of his saintly daughters, Gwawr, is claimed to be the mother of St Gwynllyw. As we have already seen, Brychan Brycheiniog was credited with twenty-five holy daughters, some of whom mothered male saints. The genealogies *De situ Brecheniauc* and *Progenies Keredic* even link these two extended holy Welsh families claiming that Ceredig married St Meleri, one of Brychan's daughters, and thus St David's grandmother united the two most prominent holy families of Wales via a marital alliance.[94]

Conclusions

Thus we have seen that the biographical patterning of the female saint is somewhat different from that of the male saint and that feminine sanctity (with the exception of the maternal saints) is closely linked with the saint's virginity.[95] Whilst chastity is an important component in the male saint's make-up (and the Celtic saints are frequently described as sitting in icy cold water to extinguish lustful urges), their legends do not revolve around the struggle to maintain their virginity. The female saint is usually depicted as sexless. She is not troubled by the physical yearnings of the flesh, yet she is always described as being very beautiful and is also depicted as very feminine. Femininity and virginity are central to the female saint's iconography and she is usually depicted veiled and crowned Christ's bride. The nature of the female saint is, on the whole, paradoxical: she is, on the one hand, an innocent, fragile victim, but on the other, an independent and powerful victor who triumphs 'in an ecstasy of self denial' and is ultimately united with her heavenly groom.

Contrary to Willis Bund's claim that women rarely became saints in Wales, we have seen that there were in fact a significant number of Welsh women saints.[96] These Dark-Age virgins and maternal saints were revered in medieval Wales for a host of different reasons and offered valuable services and practical assistance to the faithful including healing, guidance in marital affairs and protection to animals. Above all, the intercessory powers of these *mulieres sanctae*, many of whom had themselves suffered torment and persecution, ensured their popularity with the local populace. Explanatory medieval legends accrued to these holy women who, in the main, led exemplary virginal lifestyles and were either nuns or abbesses. The extent to which their medieval traditions survive varies considerably. Whilst some are well attested in medieval sources, others have all but vanished from the written record. Their names may only be recorded in place-names (Llanllŷr, Llanerfyl, Eglwys Wrw, for example), or mentioned briefly in the Welsh calendars or genealogies (Rhyddlad, Callwen, Gwenfyl and Gwenfaen, for example).[97] Some of the lesser-known saints are occasionally invoked in the poetry of the *Cywyddwyr* or in medieval law texts (Tegfedd and Gwenog, for example), whilst others are mentioned only in the Lives of male saints (Gwladys, Dunod, Maches, for example).[98] Certain characters such as Helen (the mother of Constantine the Great) and Thecla of Iconium appear to have been amalgamated into Welsh tradition because of the similarity between their names and the names of Welsh characters (Elen and Tegla). St Helen became conflated with Elen Luyddog, a mythological character who marries the Roman Emperor Macsen Wledig (Magnus Maximus) in the Middle Welsh tale *Breudwyt Maxen*. The Invention of the True Cross was also translated into Middle Welsh – *Val a Cauas Elen y Grog*.[99] In an early thirteenth-century manuscript, Lambeth Palace MS 94, a number of miracles associated with St Tegla of Llandegley, Powys, form an appendix to *Passio S. Theclae*, the passion of St Thecla of Iconium.[100]

The immense popularity of the Welsh women saints might lead one to assume that medieval Wales was a favourable environment for the female religious, but this, surprisingly, was not the case. As we shall see in Chapter 6, there were only three long-standing nunneries in medieval Wales and they were small, poor and probably had very few inmates.[101] Despite the fact that the Welsh princes and nobility appear to have been particularly fond of sponsoring male Cistercian houses, there does not seem to be have been quite the same impetus to provide long-term investment in houses for religious women. No doubt Eluned's relics had a special significance for the Benedictine nuns of Usk, but it appears that only to a very limited extent were the female saints of Wales viewed as appropriate role models for medieval Welsh women. All of these female saints were purported to have been alive in the fifth, sixth and seventh centuries and the tradition of according sanctity did not continue in Wales into the Middle Ages.[102] Elsewhere holy women such as Margaret of Scotland (*c*.1045–93), Christina of Markyate (*c*.1097–*c*.1161), Malfada of Portugal (1184–1257) and Margaret of Cortona (1247–97) continued to be regarded as saints. However, in Wales, few noblewomen appear to have been encouraged to follow in the footsteps of the saints and retire to a contemplative existence. One could argue that for medieval Welsh society, the best kind of *holy* virgin was indeed a *dead* virgin.

3

St Non: Rape, Sanctity and Motherhood in Welsh and Breton Hagiography[1]

St David's mother, Non, the daughter of Cynyr of Caer Gawch, is a somewhat unusual saint whose cult warrants special attention, since she makes a particularly interesting case study. Unlike the vast majority of the Welsh female saints, her popularity was not confined to one particular locality. She was commemorated at several different locations in south Wales, and her cult was also transferred to Brittany, Ireland, Cornwall and Devon. In Wales her feast was celebrated on 3 March and it is listed in most medieval Welsh calendars.[2] In Brittany Non's principal pardon is celebrated on the Sunday following the octave of Corpus Christi and a minor pardon is held in her honour at Dirinon on the second Sunday after Easter.[3]

Non is also unusual, in the context of European hagiography, in that she is a rare example of a raped female saint. As we have seen in the previous chapter, the menaced virgin is a common topos in hagiography, and numerous female saints are threatened with rape or physical abuse. They frequently have to flee arranged marriages and are abducted, beaten, burned and tortured (occasionally having their breasts torn off) before eventually being decapitated. However, at no point during their torturous ordeals is their virginity violated, since virginity is almost a prerequisite for feminine sanctity, and the image of the female saint as the bride of Christ, a veiled, consecrated nun, is inextricably linked with her physical purity. In the Middle Welsh Life of Gwenfrewy (St Winifred), for example, Gwenfrewy's tormentor rather ironically announces that: 'oni byddi di vn a mi *oth vodd*, y lleddir dy benn a'r cleddyf hwnn'[4] (if you will not become one with me [i.e. have intercourse with me] *willingly* I'll cut off your head with this sword). Gwenfrewy chooses martyrdom rather than defilement, yet, as outlined in the previous chapter, she is resurrected by St Beuno and later becomes abbess of a community of women first of all at Holywell and then at Gwytherin.

In an extensive study, Corinne Saunders confirms that in medieval English hagiography 'in no instance is the virgin actually raped'.[5] And Kathleen Coyne Kelly states categorically that there are no rape narratives in hagiography:

> *Virginity* always outlasts the *virgin* . . . I have never read a narrative which describes rape, or says that rape was committed, or even creates a 'before and after' scenario . . . It is possible to argue that rape is 'represented' in hagiography through a rhetoric of silence, if not displacement and substitution, but the fact remains that there are no direct narratives of rape in hagiography.[6]

Although Non's case is unusual and deviates from the standard pattern found in the biographies of most candidates for feminine sanctity, as we shall see in this chapter, she is not the only example of a raped female saint. Whilst the Catholic Church continues to canonize women for defending their virginity and choosing martyrdom rather than rape, in medieval hagiography there are instances when the violation of a pure, devout virgin was deemed not only appropriate, but necessary, in order to explain the conception of certain, powerful male saints – notably, although not necessarily exclusively, in the Celtic regions. Maria Goretti of Ancona, who was stabbed to death whilst resisting rape in 1902, was canonized by Pope Pius XII in 1950 for the heroic defence of her virginity and for forgiving her oppressor. She is the patron saint of rape victims.

Most of what is known of St Non is derived from the various versions of the Life of St David. Other sources include Middle Welsh poetry, local folklore, oral traditions, pictorial narratives and the impact of Non and David's cults on the ritual landscape. One particular manuscript copy of Giraldus Cambrensis' Life of St David, which has attracted little attention to date, contains an appendix including various miracles associated with David (performed up to the year 1388) and five short readings for the feast of St Non. London, BL, MS Royal 13 C1 appears to be a compilation collected by William Worcestre in the fifteenth century. Folio 180^{v} summarizes the rape of St Non, the story of the conception of David, Non's encounter with Gildas who is struck dumb in the presence of the pregnant mother and the tale which parallels the massacre of the innocents. The readings associated with Non's pregnancy were obviously intended to be read aloud on Non's feast-day and were meant specifically to celebrate the life of David's mother, here referred to as 'our mother':

> De sancta Nonita leccio prima. Diem fest*i* beate Nonita selebremus hunc psalmu*m* resonent inde concrepent lecciones hinc populorum turbe letent*ur* unde paup*er*es Christi subleuent*ur*. Igitur et nos g*ra*tulemur in domino et de vita ipsius matris n*ost*re ad laude*m* et honor*em* dei aliqua p*er*stringamus ad gl*or*iam quippe laud*is* eius credimus impensu*m* quicquid s*anct*is suis fu*er*it solempnit*er* exhibitu*m*.[7]

> (First reading about St Non. Let us celebrate the feast of the blessed Non. Let them shout out this psalm, then let them call forth the readings, hence let the crowds of people be happy, whereby the poor of Christ may be uplifted. Therefore, let us too rejoice in the Lord and narrate some things about the life of our mother herself to the praise and honour of God. Indeed, we believe that whatever has been performed solemnly for his saints is supplied to the glory of his praise.)

The readings, which appear to be incomplete, break off before the birth of St David. They presumably once formed part of a service designed to celebrate the feast of St Non.

Although there is no Welsh prose Life of St Non, there is a late medieval Breton miracle play, *Buez Santez Nonn hac ez map Deuy*, extant in a unique fifteenth-century manuscript (Paris, Bibliothèque Nationale de France, MS fonds celtique 5) which elaborates upon the life of Non and embellishes the brief account of Non's experiences given in the Latin and Welsh Lives of David.[8] The *Buez* relocates the majority of the tale to Brittany and provides a dramatic and detailed account of the rape of Non – 'before, during and after'.

Having briefly outlined the principal sources for the cult of Non, the aim of this chapter is to shed light on much of the extant evidence available for her cult in Wales and Brittany, before analysing in more detail the significance of Non's role as a raped female saint. Although Non's popularity spread to Ireland and Cornwall, a detailed study of these regions is beyond the scope of the present volume.[9] This chapter, therefore, will focus primarily on the Welsh and Breton sources.

Ceredigion

The strong links between the cult of St David and Ceredigion have frequently been emphasized. E. G. Bowen calculated that there were eleven dedications to David and his mother in Ceredigion and that they ceased abruptly along a line marked by the Upper Ystwyth and Wyre rivers.[10] Rhygyfarch's Life of St David is generally assumed to have been composed at Llanbadarn Fawr in Ceredigion and the later Welsh Life, *Hystoria o Uuched Dewi*, is believed to have been composed by an anchorite at Llanddewibrefi *c.*1346.

Llanddewibrefi is one of the few locations mentioned in David's Life which remains easy to identify in modern Wales: many of the others, such as Vallis Rosina/Glyn Rhosyn and Hoddnant (all used to describe the site of David's principal monastery) require interpretation. Rhygyfarch's *Vita Dauidis* states that David was educated at Vetus Rubus, whilst the Welsh Life refers to his education at Henllwyn.[11] The Cotton Vespasian version of Rhygyfarch's Life, as well as the *vita* by Giraldus Cambrensis, interpret Vetus Rubus as Hen Vynyw/

Hen-meneu (Old Menevia) and this has traditionally been taken to refer to Hen Fynyw in Ceredigion.[12] Oral tradition and local folklore claim that David was born and brought up by his mother at Llanon in Ceredigion (formerly Llan-non) and that he began his education at Hen Fynyw. The tradition is commemorated and reinforced by a modern stained-glass window in the parish church of Llansanffraid: Non is depicted as a caring mother and her young son David holds a book, reminding the viewer that this is reputedly the area in which he received his early education.[13] The windows which were given to the church by the Thomas family of Belmont, Llanon, also include an image of San Ffraid, the church's patron saint.

In 1912 three anonymous articles appeared in the *Welsh Gazette* which attempted to 'prove' that David was born in Ceredigion and that he only left for spiritual work in Pembrokeshire in later life:

> St Non, undoubtedly, spent the whole of her life-time in Llan-non. The whole evidence of present-day Non survivals points to this, and again, this mass of evidence points to the fact that Dewi himself was born here and educated here as a young man, but that towards late manhood he left for spiritual work in Pembrokeshire.[14]

The same author paints a rather romantic picture of Non preaching from a rostrum at Llwyn Non in Llanon and converting the local populace to Christianity. Interestingly this author happily accepts that Non was a historical character and that she played an active role as a missionary. Pádraig Ó Riain, on the other hand, states that Non is a fabrication: 'as with many mothers of saints, Non shows signs of having been invented with a view to fleshing out the story of Dewi's birth and youth in Ceredigion'.[15] This is certainly plausible; however, whilst not wishing to suggest that Non was a historical character, I wonder why this particular element in the Life of St David has been singled out as a piece of pure fabrication. Why not focus on other elements in the medieval narrative such as the episodes in which David heals the blind, raises the dead or eats poisoned bread – all of which, along with his unusual conception and birth – 'flesh out' the story of St David and form important components in the biographical patterning of the saint?[16]

Gerald of Wales noted in his *Journey Through Wales* that the miraculous birth and conception of David were some of the most important and remarkable elements in the Life of the saint.[17] Later authors, however, appear to have been uncomfortable with the story of David's conception and this has led to the suggestion that Non and Sant were married or that Non became a nun in widowhood.[18] The assumption that Non was a nun, it has been suggested, is based on a confusion stemming from the fact that her name is similar to 'nonna', Latin for 'nun'. The fact that most female saints (regardless of their names) are nuns or abbesses seems to have been overlooked, not to mention the fact that the rape of Non appears consistently in all of the medieval accounts. G. H. Doble goes a step further and argues that St Non was originally a male saint – perhaps a companion to St David – who was later changed into a female saint and became known as his mother. This conjecture is partly based on the assumption that St Non is the same saint as St Nonna, the male patron of Penmarch in Brittany.[19] Doble also interprets the name Nonnita, which occurs on an inscribed stone at Tregony in Cornwall, as a male name, although, as Charles Thomas points out, since 'TRIS FILI' can be interpreted as 'TRES FILII' (three children), the name most probably refers to a daughter named Nonnita.[20] The principal reason, however, which motivated Doble's search for alternative origins for St Non appears to have been the fact that he found Rhygyfarch's account of the rape of Non distasteful:

> One day she fell into the power of Sant, the King of Ceredigion, the country in which she lived, – a violent, brutal man, like so many of those old Celtic chieftains. By him she became the mother of S. David . . . It is a sad story, but the great comfort is that it is probably not true. I suggest in all humility a different answer to the question.[21]

And thus he proposes that Non was originally a male figure.

Returning to Ceredigion we note that for many years a ruined building in Heol Non, Llanon, was believed to be the medieval chapel of St Non and it was identified as such largely on the basis that a holy water stoup was found on the site.[22] Ceredigion County Council even announced plans to give the historic chapel a facelift and open it up to the public in 1988.[23] However, in 1998 Richard Suggett of the Royal Commission on the Ancient and Historical Monuments of Wales visited the site and confirmed that the building, known locally as 'Neuadd' (Hall), was in fact not a chapel but a sixteenth-century house.[24] What had been claimed to be a tomb recess was quite simply a fireplace, and the stoup must have been moved there from elsewhere. The chapel of St Non appears to have been pulled down around 1906. An article in the *Welsh Gazette* in 1912 records that Homerton House was built on the old site of the chapel and that a statue of Non formerly stood outside the building above the entranceway. It recalls that young boys from the village used to throw stones at the statue and that in this way it probably became defaced.[25] Samuel Meyrick visited Non's chapel in 1808 and it was also described by George Eyre Evans in 1903 shortly before it was demolished:

> The ruins of the chapel of St. Non, – in the part of the village rightly called Llanon – are well worthy of a visit. The massive walls of unhewn stones, and one small, pointed arch, attest their former sacred use; whilst on the exterior wall, well protected by thatch of the roof immediately above it, is a stone, 14 inches tall, and 12 inches broad, on which is carved the face of a woman with a child in her arms, traditionally reputed to be that of St. Non with her boy. Certain is it the face of the mother is unlike any other known to me, as intended for the Virgin Mary.[26]

Various articles on the stone carving have appeared, some claiming that the statue is a representation of St David in his mother's arms and others proposing it is more likely to be the Virgin Mary and child.[27] The statue is now kept at the Ceredigion museum in Aberystwyth and the museum's curator, Michael Freeman, has proposed that it may in fact be a Sheela-na-gig: the size of the statue and its curved arms are reminiscent of other examples of Sheela-na-gigs.[28] Although statues of native saints are a rarity in Wales, there is a sixteenth-century statue – presumably of St Non – above the entranceway to her church at Dirinon in Brittany. Ritual abuse of saintly figures – including throwing stones at images of the saints – is quite commonplace in folk tradition.[29] The Llanon stone, however, in my view, is in too poor a state of repair to say anything with certainty about the figure it represents.

As far as the place-name is concerned, whilst Iwan Wmffre supports the view that Llanon reflects the name of the saint, Pádraig Ó Riain suggests that the name consists of the elements 'Llan' and 'on(n)' (church of the ash tree) and that the name may originally have had no connection with the saint.[30] Dirinon in Brittany has also been interpreted as reflecting the name of a tree, although in this instance it is the first element in the place-name which is of relevance, not the name of the saint – 'diri' (oak trees).[31] The dedication to Non at Llannerch Aeron does appear to be relatively modern and perhaps stems from the association of her name with the second element in the name of the river – aeron. A similar confusion may have led to Non's association with Caron/Tregaron, for the fifteenth-century poet Ieuan Llwyd Brydydd refers to 'Non Wen o Gaer Garon' (Holy Non of Caer Garon) rather than the more usual Non of Caer Gawch in a poem to St Doged. He visits Doged's well in the hope that washing in the holy water will enable him to see clearly again and envokes Doged's Ceredigion ancestors (Cedig, Ceredig and Cunedda – ancestors he shares, incidentally, with St David) as well as other saints associated with Ceredigion (Curig and Cynddylig).[32] The church at Tregaron is traditionally associated with another saint, Caron, whose feast-day was celebrated two days after St Non's on 5 March.

Carmarthenshire

Llanon in Ceredigion is not the only place in Wales to lay claim to being St David's birthplace. Llan-non in Carmarthenshire is another contender. Once again no textual evidence supports this view or allows us to date these traditions, and none of the Middle Welsh poems which record the tale of David's birth and boyhood refer specifically to any of the places called Llan-non. In a poem praising Siôn ab Ieuan and his wife Margred on St David's Day Lewys Glyn Cothi refers to numerous miracles performed at Llan-non in Carmarthenshire and links the place with David's mother.[33] Unfortunately, however, he fails to elaborate upon these specific Carmarthenshire traditions. The parish church at Llan-non is still dedicated to Non and in the garden of a house named Ffynnon Non (Non's Well) at Beidr Non (Non's Lane) is a holy well associated with the saint. It is claimed that Non drew water from the well when she was thirsty and that thereafter the water had healing properties.[34] According to another Carmarthenshire tradition, Non was reputed to have had a vision in a field named Eisteddfa Non (Non's Seat) at Llan-non. An angel appeared to her and told her to found a nunnery on the site. Needless to say, there are no records that there was ever a nunnery at Llan-non. Although the farmhouse at Eisteddfa still exists, the field is now hidden by a housing estate.[35]

Pembrokeshire

In all of the medieval Latin Lives of David the place of David's birth is preordained and an evil ruler who hears the prophecy vows to kill anyone who rests on the said spot. There are obvious parallels here with the biblical Herod (Matthew 2:1–19), and Thomas O'Loughlin has demonstrated that not only do the events in the *Vita Dauidis* mirror the scriptures, but the phraseology of scripture also permeates Rhygyfarch's narrative.[36] Non gives birth in a terrific thunderstorm which apparently prevents the evil king from venturing outside, thus ensuring that David remains unharmed:

> But the place, wherein the mother cried in her travail, shone with so serene a light that it glistened as though the sun was visible and God had brought it in front of the clouds. The mother in her labour had a certain stone close by, whereon, when urged by pain, she had leaned with her hands, for which reason the stone shows to those who examine it traces impressed as on wax. Dividing in the middle, it condoled with

> the sorrowing mother, one part leaping above the nun's head as far as her feet, when the child-bearer was bringing forth. In this place a church is situated, and in the foundation of its altar this stone lies covered.[37]

Although the Life does not specify the location of the church, it is traditionally believed to be in a field near St Non's well in Pembrokeshire, above St Non's Bay. The stone which bears Non's fingerprints has been eagerly sought in Pembrokeshire and, apparently, its location is often enquired of the vicar of St Divy in Brittany.[38] In 1898 Sabine Baring-Gould visited the remains of the medieval chapel in Pembrokeshire expecting to find an Ogham stone there, the indents on which could have been mistaken for Non's fingerprints. He was, however, disappointed.[39] Wade-Evans suggested that the stone was more likely to have been incorporated into a church at nearby Llan-non in the parish of Llanrhian.[40] No church or chapel is extant at the Pembrokeshire Llan-non.

An early Christian monument with a simple incised cross, thought to date from the seventh or eighth century, currently stands in the ruins of Non's chapel, above St Non's Bay.[41] Although it is possible that this cross-incised stone was moved here from elsewhere, it is interesting to note that the fifteenth-century poet Ieuan ap Rhydderch refers to the tradition that David was born at 'eglwys y groes' (the church of the cross). On the other hand, a more plausible interpretation of these lines could be simply that David was born into the Christian church:

> Yn eglwys y groes oesir
> Y ganed hwn, ganiad hir.
> Pan esgores y pennaeth,
> Y llech yn ddwylech ydd aeth.[42]
>
> (At the church of the cross, long life
> he was born, long stanza.
> When the chief was born,
> the stone became two stones.)

The events mentioned in the poem mirror the condensed Middle Welsh Life which omits the episode involving the evil king altogether. Both sources refer only to the fact that the stone miraculously split in two in sympathy with Non and make no reference to her pressing on the stone to relieve the agony of her labour pains. The Breton *Buez* is unique in that it provides additional detail and has three tyrants flee in terror from the storm as Non kneels on the stone and presses her hands into the rock as though it were made from wax.[43] The additional detail in the Breton *Buez* is likely to have been added at the time of the *Buez*'s compilation or it may stem from oral tradition.

Whilst the Latin, Welsh and Breton narratives associate David's baptism with the appearance of a holy well, none of the written accounts refer to a holy well which appeared miraculously as he was born. Nevertheless, according to oral tradition, St Non's well, near the ruins of the medieval chapel in Pembrokeshire, reputedly issued forth at the time of his birth, whilst another well at Capel-y-Pistyll in Porth Clais is claimed to be associated with his baptism. Although Capel-y-Pistyll (Well Chapel) no longer exists, remnants of the well can still be found in undergrowth near the car park at Porth Clais. Browne Willis records that the chapel took its name from the spring which ran under it into a cistern at the east end.[44] Laurence Butler has proposed that a similar system may originally have existed at Non's well above St Non's Bay. Since the orientation of the building currently believed to be the chapel is unusual in that it faces north-south, rather than east-west, it has been suggested that the medieval chapel may originally have stood nearer the well where there are now loose stones in a field, and that the water from the well may have flowed through the chapel as at Capel-y-Pistyll.[45] The ruins now believed to be Non's chapel could in fact have been a dwelling – perhaps the priest or the well keeper's house. Alternatively, as Richard Fenton suggested in 1811, the well keeper's house may have stood where the loose stones are found in a field and another building appears to have once surrounded the holy water.[46] Although the orientation of the 'chapel' is unusual, it does have particularly large foundation stones and appears to consist of different phases of building.[47]

The only extant medieval description of the chapel and holy well is found in the work of Lewys Glyn Cothi. In his fifteenth-century *cywydd* to Edudful ferch Gadwgon and her sons he provides a valuable description of Edudful's pilgrimage to St Davids. She visits Non's chapel and washes her head in the holy water, worships an image (possibly of St Non) and leaves candles on the altar at St Non's before proceeding to St Davids where she leaves an offering. The description of the building is not detailed enough to substantiate Lawrence Butler's claims, but the juxtaposition of the church and the well water in the poem could suggest that the washing, worshipping and lighting of candles all take place at the same location. At any rate, the poem certainly provides us with a rare glimpse of late medieval pilgrimage to the site and stresses the importance of Non's well and chapel in association with the cathedral:

Edudful Dduwsul a ddaw
ar Dduw i wir weddïaw;
bwrw ei phwys yn eglwys Non,
bwrw ei phen lle bo'r ffynnon,
dyrchaf dwylaw yn llawen,
addoli oll i'r ddelw wen,
ennyn y cwyr melyn mawr,
a'i roi oll ar yr allawr;
oddyno heibio'dd â hi
i glos da eglwys Dewi;
offrymu, cusanu'r sant,
iddo gŵyr rhudd ac ariant;[48]

(On Sunday Edudful comes
to pray sincerely to God;
She visits Non's church,
puts her head in the well
raises her hands merrily,
worships the holy image,
lights the large, yellow candles,
and puts all of them on the altar;
From there she passes to
the good close of St David's church;
makes an offering of crimson wax
and money and kisses the saint;)

In the sixteenth century George Owen of Henllys described the well in his memoirs which were quoted by Browne Willis (1717): 'There is a fine Well beside it [the chapel], cover'd with a Stone-Roof, and inclos'd within a Wall, and Benches to sit upon round the Well.'[49] The well and its surrounding construction appear to have been more substantial than that which exists at the site today. The cowl-shaped hood over the present well may have been constructed in the late eighteenth century and it was restored in 1951. In his *Historical Tour Through Pembrokeshire* (1811) Fenton recalls being dipped in the well as a child:

> . . . a most redundant spring arched over, and at one time inclosed with a wall. The fame this consecrated spring had obtained is incredible, and still is resorted to for many complaints. In my infancy, as was the general usage with respect to children at that time, I was often dipped in it, and offerings, however trifling, even of a farthing or a pin, were made after each ablution, and the bottom of the well shone with votive brass.[50]

As with many of the wells associated with St David, it was believed that the water was particularly beneficial for those suffering from eye complaints. Non's holy well at Altarnun, nevertheless, appears to have been associated with quite a different affliction – insanity or possibly epilepsy. In 1601 Carew provided a colourful description of what took place at the well:

> The water running from S. Nunn's well fell into a square and close-walled plot, which might be filled at what depth they listed. Upon this well was the frantic person set to stand, his back turned toward the pool, and from thence, with a sudden blow in the breast, tumbled headlong into the pond; where a strong fellow, provided for the nonce, took him, and tossed him up and down, alongst and athwart the water, until the patient, by foregoing his strength, had somewhat forgot his fury. Then was he conveyed to the church, and certain masses sung over him; upon which handling, if his right wits returned, S. Nun had the thanks; but if there appeared small amendment, he was

> bowssened again and again, while there appeared in him any hope of life, or recovery.[51]

The modern chapel which now stands nearby the well in Pembrokeshire was built in 1934 from stones recycled from old cottages and possibly monastic buildings at Whitehall. Mr Morgan-Griffiths, a solicitor from Carmarthen, had the Chapel of Our Lady and St Non erected near his house for his wife, since she had converted to Catholicism.[52] The chapel contains a number of stained-glass windows which depict native Welsh saints and above the altar is a representation of St Non in stained glass of the William Morris School. Clad in a blue gown, she clutches a book and her modern well can be seen in the background. According to the Sisters of Mercy who now manage the house as a religious retreat, this window was originally located in the house and later moved to the chapel.[53] In the detail at the base of the window, Non is depicted arriving in Brittany in a boat accompanied by her son, David – here depicted as a young boy. The artist responsible for the windows seems to have been aware of the tradition that Non travelled to Brittany following the birth of St David, and the window, therefore, attempts to link both the Breton and the Welsh traditions.

Brittany

A similar window in Non's church at Dirinon, Finistère, depicts Non and David's arrival in Brittany – again in a boat (Plate 15). The Breton *Buez*, which provides considerably more detail than the episodes involving Non in the Welsh Lives, suggests in its prologue that Non was raped in Ireland and that because of this shameful event she travelled to Brittany.[54] It is not clear whether the artist responsible for the windows at Dirinon intended to depict Non leaving Ireland or Wales. The four scenes depicted in the nineteenth-century windows appear to be based on local oral tradition at Dirinon, rather than on specific events found in the Latin and Welsh Lives of David or the Breton Life of Non. Non, for example, is depicted baptizing her own son in the presence of angels (Plate 16). This links the church and the legend of St Non with other topographical features at Dirinon: for instance, the holy spring where she prayed for water to baptize the infant which later became known as Non's well. In Rhygyfarch's Life of David the saint is baptized by Ailbe and a blind man who holds David as he is baptized miraculously gains his sight. Neither the Vespasian version of the *vita* nor the Welsh Life name this character, but in the Nero E. i version he is called Movi.[55] The Breton *Buez* goes a step further and has David cure two blind men, including one who was born without a nose or eyes.[56]

In the next scene in the stained-glass cycle Non is depicted with the infant Divy resting on a rock (Plate 17). This is presumably the stone known locally as St David's cradle, for it is claimed that when David's mother placed him on a nearby rock it melted like wax under the baby's body and formed a natural cradle (Plate 18).[57] Although *Vita Dauidis* and *Buez Santez Nonn* mention the stone which 'melted' under the pressure of Non's hands, neither refers to a similar miracle providing a cradle for her infant son. Non then hands over David to a group of monks so that he can receive a monastic education and, in the background of the scene, the church and chapel at Dirinon can be clearly seen.[58] In the tracery lights Non is depicted ascending into heaven holding a book, mirroring the image of Non found on a fifteenth-century carved tomb in the sepulchral chapel at Dirinon, just a few feet south of the parish church.

Although the rather confusing prologue to the *Buez* suggests that Non returned to Brittany only after she was raped, all of the events in the play appear to take place in Brittany. The author of the *Buez* demonstrates a lack of awareness of certain locations, particularly those derived from Wales. Kereticus is described as both king of Keretic and Demetri (Ceredigion and Dyfed), whereas the Latin and Welsh Lives mention only that he is king of Ceredigion. Although Non leaves the place where she is raped (Demetri), no mention is made in the *Buez* of a lengthy maritime journey to Brittany. It is claimed that Non descended from good Breton stock: 'tut fier a britonery / a noblanc a tj piuizic'[59] (powerful people from Brittany, nobles of a rich house), that she lived and died at Dirinon and her bones were interred in a tomb there: 'he corff so hep gaou entre landerneau ha daoulas'[60] (her body is to be found, without doubt, between Landerneau and Daoulas). Interestingly, the *Buez*, which obviously postdates the elaborate tomb, also states that her body was buried in a brand new tomb at Dirinon where there was both a chapel and a church and where it had been preordained that her body would rest.[61] Thus, the Breton Life was composed shortly after the tomb was commissioned and its primary purpose appears to have been to elevate the status of Dirinon and emphasize the importance of the tomb and its sponsors. One post-mortem miracle is recorded in which a perjurer suddenly drops dead in a nearby field having sworn a false oath at the tomb of St Non.

When the monument in question was taken apart it was found to contain merely a few bones belonging to an adolescent. R. Perrot visited the tomb and wrote an account of his adventures at Dirinon in *Archaeologia Cambrensis* in 1857. He was under the impression that the original tomb had been destroyed during the French Revolution and that only the recumbent figure of St Non had survived. This was based largely on information he was given locally over a glass of wine:

> On adjourning to the contiguous cabaret for our usual demi-chopine de vin, and to obtain some information respecting the 'personality' of the statue, our suspicions as to the originality of the sarcophagus were confirmed. The grandmother of the house, and an octogenarian who was sipping his 'modicum', informed us that, during the great Revolution, the tomb was pulled down, the statue only escaping. In more tranquil times the tomb was re-erected, and then, probably, the remains of some other sarcophagus were collected for the purpose.[62]

The tomb has certainly been taken apart and reconstructed in a rather bizarre manner, which has led to one of the apostles being jammed in the middle of the tomb rather than positioned at the end, but the angels which hold Non's pillow (on the carving on top of the tomb) are far too similar to the angels bearing the heraldic shields (on the base of the tomb) to be part of a separate monument. As Yves-Pascal Castel suggests, only the coats of arms appear to have been defaced during the Revolution. It is, nevertheless, possible to make out some of the heraldry and Castel concludes that the tomb was commissioned in the fifteenth century by Simon de Kerbringal and Maufuric de Lézuzan, Abbot of Daoulas, who died in 1468.[63] In 1218 the Acts of the abbey of Daoulas mention an 'ecclesia sanctae Nonnitae' amongst the abbey's possessions and Bernard Tanguy has proposed that the Breton Life of Non was probably composed at the abbey.[64] It has been claimed that the manuscript containing the Breton *Buez Santez Nonn* was discovered inside her tomb; in fact, it was found at the presbytery at Dirinon.

In the parish church at Dirinon there is also a silver reliquary which is reputed to contain some of the relics of St Non. Inside the reliquary, wrapped in silk, are two fragments of bone – probably a tibia – and a note from the bishop of Quimper (1805–23) authenticating the relics. The reliquary box is thought to have been made in Morlaix *c.*1450 and on top of the reliquary is a small image of St David (Plate 19). Given that David rather than Non is depicted on the reliquary, there is some uncertainty as to whose relics were originally believed to have been preserved at Dirinon.[65] In the Welsh Lives of St David Non disappears from the narrative when David begins his formal education, whereas the Breton *Buez* has a lengthy episode in which Non prepares for her death, makes her final confession and prays to the Virgin Mary for forgiveness. No references to Non's relics are extant in Welsh sources, and although the relics at St Davids Cathedral have attracted a great deal of attention, it does not appear to have been claimed that any of Non's relics were kept at the cathedral.[66] Around 1480 William Worcestre noted in his *Itineraries* that Non's body lay at Altarnun in Cornwall, six miles from Launceston where St David was born.[67] In 1281 the Commisary of the Dean and Chapter of Exeter carried out a visitation at Altarnun and recorded that there was a Life of St Non in a service book kept there, but unfortunately this is no longer extant.[68]

In Brittany there are numerous chapels and churches dedicated to St David (St Divy), particularly in Basse-Bretagne, although Non's cult appears to have centred on

Dirinon. Near Dirinon one also finds the place-names Lannon and Lesnon, although there are no extant chapels or holy wells in these villages. Bernard Tanguy, who has provided a detailed study of Divy dedications in Brittany, proposes that many of the chapels now dedicated to Divy were originally associated with another Breton saint, St Ivy.[69] One location in Brittany which has firm associations with St David is the church at St Divy, several miles from Dirinon.

Welsh traditions relating to St David have become firmly rooted at St Divy thanks to a seventeenth-century visual narrative (dated 1676) painted on wooden panelling on the vaulted ceiling.[70] The visual narrative depicts several scenes from the Life of St David and appears to be based on a version of Rhygyfarch's Life of St David rather than the Breton Life of Non. In 1668, shortly before the paintings were conceived, two *epitomae* of Rhygyfarch's Life of St David were made widely available by the Bollandists,[71] and it is certainly plausible that these early printed versions of the Life may have been the source of inspiration for the artist. At any rate, the images and the fragments of texts and labelling interspersed in the images give the impression of drawing on a written source rather than local oral tradition, unlike the nineteenth-century stained-glass cycle at Dirinon. Included in the painting are a number of Welsh place-names, such as Portvs Mavgan (Porth Maugan/Mawr) and Brevy (Llanddewibrefi), which are not mentioned in the Breton miracle play. David, for example, is depicted at the synod of Brefi with the earth miraculously rising beneath his feet. In the Breton *Buez* he is made archbishop at Lyons and there is no mention of the miracle which allowed the adoring crowd to hear his every word. Non is raped by Xanctvs/Sant (as in *Vita Dauidis*), rather than Kereticus/Ceredig (as in *Buez Santez Nonn*). In Welsh tradition Ceredig, the eponymous ruler of Ceredigion, is St David's grandfather, but the Breton *Buez* omits a generation, referring to his father as Kereticus.

The paintings at St Divy illustrate various scenes from the *Vita* including:

i St Patrick's angelic visitation when he is instructed that he must leave Vallis Rosina and go to Ireland, since God has assigned the valley to the unborn David. En route he resurrects Crvnither (usually known as Crumither);

ii Sant's dream in which the king is warned of the coming of St David and told that he must go hunting near the river Teifi and collect three gifts for David. Depicted in the background of the scene is the Monastery of the Deposit mentioned in the *Vita*, not the nunnery visited by St Non in the *Buez*;[72]

iii Sant's encounter with St Non in a rural landscape (Plate 20). He is depicted in regal hunting garb on horseback, whereas Non is clad in a nun's habit with a rosary tied around her waist and a glowing aureola. The two rocks which rose to hide Non's shame as she was raped are suggestive of the event which is about to take place;

iv the birth of St David. Non kneels in an attitude of prayer with the newborn baby at her knees and the inscription records the miracle which caused the rock to split in two;

v David's baptism by Belve (usually Ailbe);

vi the synod of Brefi mentioned above; and

vii David's death at the ripe old age of 107 (usually 147).

The sixth-century characters in the paintings are dressed in seventeenth-century costume, most notably in the hunting scene where Sant and his men seek the three gifts in preparation for the coming of St David.

Whilst it is generally assumed that the cults of St Non and her son David were transferred from Wales to Brittany at an unknown date during the Middle Ages, it is extremely difficult (if not impossible) to provide an accurate chronology for these cults in their entirety. Which came first: saints, place-names or cults? Did the proximity of the place-names St Divy and Dirinon give rise to their association with these related saints, or did well-rooted traditions associated with David and Non influence the choice of place-names?[73] The frequency of recurrent adjacency in the Brittonic world has been highlighted by Olson and Padel who point out that two saints with adjacent dedications in one country often recur near each other in other Celtic-speaking regions: the cult of one reinforcing and strengthening the other.[74] Frequent contacts between Wales and Brittany throughout the Middle Ages, as well as common cultural inheritance – often including hagiographical sources – meant that the legendary material associated with Non and David was easily transferred between the two regions.[75] Whilst Rhygyfarch's Life of St David seems to have been the predominant source, regional variations have given rise to different versions of the legend which appear to have happily co-existed: as we have seen, these are attested in oral tradition and visual depictions, as well as written sources such as the Breton *Buez*. Non's predominance in the title of the *Buez Santes Nonn hac ez map Deuy*, along with the central role she plays in the first three-quarters of the play, has given rise to the impression that Non was possibly more popular than David in Brittany and that the cult of the mother figure appears to have overshadowed that of her son. Nevertheless, there are in fact more dedications to David than Non in Brittany and there is some uncertainty regarding the appropriation of relics at Dirinon, since, as we have seen, the reliquary features a statuette of David (Plate 19).

Rape, sanctity and motherhood

Only in the Breton *Buez* is the rape of Non fully dramatized and Non's reaction to the rape voiced. There is a lengthy scene building up to the event in which Non calls at a nunnery and asks the abbess if she can join the convent and take a vow of virginity. She enters the chapter house and is accepted by the other sisters who all consider her to be a wise, pure virgin. On her way to mass, hurrying through an area of lonely woodland she meets Kereticus and is raped.[76] In the Welsh Lives there is no moral condemnation of the incident, since David's birth has been foretold thirty years in advance and Sant is merely enacting part of the divine plan:

> When the aforesaid thirty years were done, divine power sent Sant, king of the country of Ceredigion, as far as a community of the people of Dyved. And the king met a nun, a virgin called Nonnita, a very beautiful and graceful girl, whom desiring he took by force and violated. And she conceived her son, holy

> David, who neither before nor after knew a man, but continuing in chastity of mind and body, led a most faithful life, for from that time of conception she lived on bread and water only.[77]

The Breton play, on the other hand, describes Non as being mortified by the attack:

> Ach Autrou Doe so guir roe bet // me so oppre(ss)et an pret man digracc voar an placc discascun // ha me hoaz voar un ma hunan. Ne gorreif ma drem a breman // gant mez ha souzan voar an bet guerch voann ha glan ha leanes // me cret bout certes brasset. E nebeut spacc dre digracdet // ezof forzet violet tenn gant vn tirant hep consantj // ne gallenn muy ma mem difenn. Me ia sider da offerenn // hac ahannenn a mem tenno.[78]

> (Oh Lord God, who is the true king of the world, I have just been abused. Hatefully in a moment, disgracefully, when I was alone and still fasting. I am now overwhelmed with shame and sadness. I was a virgin – pure and religious: I am almost certain that I'm pregnant. In an instant I have been forced and violated with brutality by a tyrant, against my will, without being able to defend myself. I will go to mass and then leave this place.)

Keretic's followers chastise the king for his loathsome conduct. He immediately repents and dashes off to confession.

For the virgin bride of Christ rape is a fate worse than death, and in medieval hagiography the female saint, obsessed by the preservation of her virginity, usually welcomes martyrdom. For only in death is the virgin saint released from her worldly prison of sensuality ascending to the spiritual world where she will join her heavenly bridegroom. Virginity is a virtue extolled by the Church Fathers as the most admirable physical state: the only physical state that bears resemblance to the *vita angelica*, the asexual angelic life enjoyed before the Fall. A number of early treatises on virginity persuade religious men and women to avoid marriage and opt for virginal maintenance. Jerome suggests that only when one's chastity is jeopardized should you contemplate suicide: thus, putting forward the idea that the consecrated virgin should welcome death rather than allow her virginity to be violated. Augustine, on the other hand, states that:

> the consecrated body is the instrument of the consecrated will; and if that will continues unshaken and steadfast, whatever anyone else does with the body or to the body, provided that it cannot be avoided without committing sin, involves no blame to the sufferer.[79]

In the Breton *Buez* Non tells Ceredig that she would prefer to suffer a cruel death than allow her virginity to be violated: 'guell ve dif meruell hep dellit / eguet dren sceurt lit acuitaff'[80] (I would prefer to die cruelly than to submit myself to such an embrace). It is also worth recalling that both the *Vita Dauidis* and *Hystoria o Uuched Dewi* emphasize that Non is chaste of mind and body – 'diwair oedd hi o feddwl a gweithred'. More significantly, the five readings designed to celebrate the feast of St Non also add, in words which echo St Augustine's, that the body is not stained without the consent of the mind, and if a woman who is in love with Christ is violated against her will, her chastity is still 'woven into a crown'.[81] Virginity then, as depicted by the both the Early Church and medieval hagiography, is a mental as well as a physical attribute. Non is described as 'dinam' – blameless or faultless – in a medieval Welsh *cywydd* of uncertain authorship and Dafydd Llwyd of Mathafarn refers to her as 'diwair – feichiog' (chastely – pregnant).[82] Thus, Non is a kind of honorary virgin for, as Jocelyn Wogan-Browne points out, in the medieval period virginity was both gradable and negotiable.[83] Non's devotion to the ascetic life is confirmed not only by her decision never to have intercourse with any man, but also by her appropriate choice of food: 'for from the very time of her conceiving she lived on bread and water alone'. Interestingly, the Irish Penitentials also suggest that virginity may be restored through penance. According to the Penitential of Finnian, a nun who becomes pregnant should undertake penance for seven years living on bread and water alone. After this time her crown may be restored and she may don a white robe and be pronounced a virgin.[84]

Rather than taint St David's character in any way his unusual conception highlights his greatness and makes him an object of wonder. His importance, even whilst still in the womb, is made evident when Gildas is struck dumb in the presence of the pregnant Non. Although the episode is also recounted in the twelfth-century Life of Gildas, thought to have been composed by Caradog of Llancarfan, it is not mentioned in the earlier Breton Life of Gildas.[85] This seems to suggest either that the traditions about St Non were not known in Brittany by the ninth century, or that the anonymous Breton hagiographer was reluctant to include an episode which made St David appear to be more powerful than Gildas. Non's encounter with the preacher is referred to by a number of medieval Welsh poets including Dafydd Llwyd of Mathafarn:

> Non a ddôi i'r deml yn ddiwair – feichiog
> O Dywysog dewisair,
> A'r Prelad aeth o'r gadair
> Heb allu pregethu gair.[86]

> (Non was coming to the temple chastely – pregnant
> with a splendid Prince,
> and the Prelate went from the chair
> without being able to preach a word.)

Dafydd Llwyd's reference to Non as being 'diwair' (chaste) and 'beichiog' (pregnant) is echoed in the work of Iorwerth Fynglwyd who describes the Virgin Mary as 'feichiog heb ddim afiechyd'[87] (pregnant without taint – literally without disease). Unable to claim a virgin birth for David, Rhygyfarch resorts to the next best thing – his mother is a professed nun and remains a virgin up until the time of his conception. David's genealogy, found at the end of the Vespasian version and the beginning of the Middle Welsh Life, links David to the Virgin Mary and claims that he is related to Eugen or Euddolau the son of the Virgin Mary's sister.[88] Other Welsh genealogies link the saints to Mary and it is frequently claimed that the saints' parents only have intercourse on one occasion. One senses, perhaps, a certain unease on the part of the hagiographer when dealing with the sexual conception of the saints. Since it was inappropriate – even blasphemous – to suggest sexless generation, the medieval hagiographer usually opted for the symbolic, miraculous or unusual conception. *Hystoria o Uuched Beuno* recounts how the saint's parents, who have been sleeping in the same bed for twelve years, do not have intercourse until ordered to do so by an angel:

> Ac val y gorchynnawd yr angel vdunt, wynt ae gwnaethant. A beichiogi a gauas Beren y nos honno.[89]

> (They did it just as the angel had instructed them and Beren became pregnant that night.)

Buched Collen describes St Collen's conception in symbolic terms, thus avoiding any mention of intercourse. In a dream Ethinen sees a dove carry her womb to heaven, return with it in her beak and place it back in her body. The next day she discovers that she is pregnant.[90]

In this context we can more easily understand why Non is raped: in order for her to conceive without experiencing sexual pleasure. Nor is Non unique – for she is not the only example of a raped female saint. According to a fragmentary, twelfth-century Life of St Kentigern, Thaney, Kentigern's mother, wished to imitate the Virgin Mary and give birth to a son whilst still a virgin. Her wish, however, was not granted since she was brutally raped by Ewen son of Erwegende (Owain ab Urien). Beardless and dressed in female attire Ewen manages to convince her that she is still a virgin, even though she becomes pregnant. When her father discovered that she was pregnant he had her thrown off a cliff in a cart, and, since she survived the fall, he had her cast adrift in a boat. Again Thaney miraculously survived and gave birth to Kentigern, founder and patron of Glasgow cathedral. This anonymous life is incomplete and breaks off after Kentigern's birth.[91] There is, however, another complete Life of Kentigern which was written by Jocelin of Furness towards the end of the twelfth century.[92] Interestingly, in this Life the rape of Thaney is omitted. Jocelin instead has a rather ambiguous account which avoids naming the father and suggests that Thaney may have had some sort of encounter with a soothsayer. In his prologue he criticizes his source which he feels is contrary to the Catholic faith. Alan Macquarrie interprets this as a refererence to another Life (now lost) which must have claimed a virgin birth for Kentigern.[93] My own reading, however, leads me to believe that Jocelin is referring to the fragmentary Life and what he considers to be – in his words – 'tainted' and 'perverse' is the rape of Thaney. In the prologue he states: 'I deem it absurd that so precious a treasure should be swathed in vile wrappings, and therefore I have endeavoured to clothe it if not in gold tissue and silk, at least in clean linen.' Kentigern, he claims, was sanctified in the womb, 'so that he might prove that the special gift of the holy spirit is not constrained by the chain of original sin'.[94]

Neither Thaney nor Non, however, is free from original sin, and, unlike the Virgin Mary, both bring forth their progeny in pain. As we have seen, Non in her agony grasps a nearby rock and presses it so hard that the imprints of her hands are left on the rock as if it she had sunk her hands into wax. The Breton *Buez* places particular emphasis on Non's anguish during her labour: 'quen sempl ezaff na gallaf quen // gant guentl hac anquen em bener ma na vezaf mam e berr amser // ez rentif sider ma speret'[95] (I feel so ill; I can no longer be tortured by these labour pains. If I do not become a mother soon, I will surely give up the ghost). She prays to the Virgin Mary for assistance and laments the fact that no wise or married woman is present to assist with the birth. This reminds the viewer of the birth of Christ who, according to the apocryphal gospels of Mary, was born without the presence of a midwife, since the two women, Selome and Zelomy, arrived after the birth had taken place. The fundamental difference here is that whilst Non is afflicted with pain, Mary uniquely shows no signs of pain or afterbirth.[96]

Thus, it seems that the virginity of the female saint is rendered violable when the maternity of an important male saint is at stake. Numerous scholars have stressed the importance of saintly genealogies in the Celtic regions, and Pádraig Ó Riain has proposed that the importance of familial relationships which often creates a network of saints is 'by and large an exclusively Celtic phenomenon'.[97] St David, through his paternal line, is linked with Cunedda Wledig whose family, according to the Welsh triads, is one of the three saintly lineages of the island of Britain. His grandmother, Meleri, was one of the twenty-four daughters of Brychan Brycheiniog – all of whom were Welsh saints and many of whom were mothers of male saints.[98] Thus, the two most prominent holy families of Wales were united and St David was born into a vast network of saints.

Whilst not wishing to state categorically that this is a specifically Celtic phenomenon,[99] I would like to stress that there are a significant number of mother saints in Welsh hagiography and that within a European context, this is somewhat unusual. There are indeed saintly mothers such as Monica (the mother of St Augustine) and Ida of Boulogne (the mother of the leaders of the First Crusade) who, like St Non, are accorded sanctity because of their relationship with their holy sons. However, as Anneke B. Mulder-Bakker points out in *Sanctity and Motherhood*:

> The usual corpus of 'sacred biographies' contains almost no mother saints, that is, saints whose sanctity is based on motherhood . . . There were, of course, saints who were mothers, but they were honored at the altar despite rather than because of their children.[100]

The vast majority of female saints venerated in medieval hagiography are virgins. Even the patron saint of childbirth – St Margaret of Antioch – was a virgin who had never experienced childbirth.[101] Although most female saints are threatened with rape, it is usually prevented by divine intervention. In the Life of St Lucy of Syracuse, for example, Lucy's pagan tormentor announces that she is to be sent to a brothel where she will be repeatedly raped until she dies. However, Lucy miraculously roots to the spot and a thousand strong men with ropes fail to remove her to the brothel.[102] Whereas in the majority of the *vitae* the inviolate virgin functions as a metonym for the institution of the Church,[103] and her inviolate body can therefore under no circumstance be polluted, this is not the case with St Non. Her legend is not meant to be read allegorically and her body does not stand for the Church. She merely imitates the holy family, and is accorded sanctity purely on the basis of her association with her holy progeny, in much the same way that St Anne is accorded sanctity because of her importance within the holy kinship. In Wales Non is a second Anne, and in Brittany also Non appears to have become associated with St Anne.[104] At Dirnon and St Divy images of Anne teaching the virgin to read accompany images of Non and St David. In Wales, although St Non is not accredited with David's education she has become associated with his youth and formative years in Ceredigion and in this capacity performs a pedagogical function.

Perhaps because of her role as a maternal saint Non made a more relevant role model for medieval Welsh women than some of the virgin martyrs. In the poetry of the *Cywyddwyr* married noblewomen are more frequently compared to Non than to any other single female saint (with the obvious exception of the Virgin Mary). Lewys Glyn Cothi alone invokes Non forty-four times in his poetry. In one particular poem, an elegy to Gwenllian ferch Rhys, he refers to Gwenllian's ascent 'i'r nef ac i gôr Non ac i radd y gweryddon'[105] (to heaven and to Non's choir and to the rank of virgins). Gwenllian, like Non, was not a virgin, since she was married to Dafydd ap Tomas and had a son called Rhys. It is possible, but by no means certain, that she retired to a nunnery following the death of her husband, and (like Non) she appears to have been accorded the status of honorary virgin by the poet.[106] Thus, Non's maternity appears not only to form the origin of her sanctity, but also to be the root of her relevance and appeal. It remains possible, yet ultimately inconclusive, that the rape element in Non's story is due to a Celtic bias towards the sanctity of familial ties and the legitimizing cult of lineage.

4

The Harlot and the Hostess: The Middle Welsh Lives of Mary Magdalene and her Sister Martha[1]

As opposed to focusing on the traditions associated with 'native' saints, the next two chapters attempt to highlight the importance of medieval vernacular hagiography which relates the legends of internationally popular saints in Middle Welsh. Indeed although there were numerous Welsh women saints, the vast majority of the medieval vernacular Lives which survive focus on 'foreign' saints. To what extent these saints were viewed as 'foreign' by a medieval Welsh audience is debatable and it is certainly likely that their provenance was of secondary importance to the usefulness of the services they provided, their intercessory powers and the genuine respect their spirituality commanded amongst the faithful. One could argue that it is modern scholarship that has tended to focus on 'native' Welsh texts and ascribe particular importance to texts such as the Mabinogion, viewing the Lives of saints as mere 'translations' and therefore categorizing them as somehow less important than texts which are uniquely Welsh. Although to a modern audience texts which were originally composed in Welsh and which are unique to Wales may be considered as intrinsically more interesting than texts which are common to a number of cultures, this is not necessarily the view held by a medieval audience which may not have shared the same ideas concerning the concept of 'originality'. As we shall see, in some of the medieval Welsh manuscripts, the Lives of internationally popular saints happily sit alongside secular legends, such as the Mabinogion, and it is even possible that they were produced with similar audiences in mind.

Before discussing *Buched Meir Vadlen* and *Buched Martha* in detail, it would be useful to consider their context within the Welsh manuscripts. Since Mary Magdalene and Martha were considered to be sisters in the medieval period, and both women feature in each other's Lives, it is appropriate that these two Lives should be discussed together.

Middle Welsh Lives of 'foreign' female saints

Sometime before the mid-fourteenth century the Lives of Katherine of Alexandria, Margaret of Antioch, Mary of Egypt, Mary Magdalene and Martha were translated into Middle Welsh and were subsequently copied in a number of Welsh manuscripts. These Lives are grouped together as a distinct corpus in several articles which provide an overview of Welsh religious prose and Welsh hagiography, and it has frequently been suggested that they were written for an audience of religious women. J. E. Caerwyn Williams, Glanmor Williams and D. Simon Evans all link the Welsh Lives with the Middle English Katherine Group and texts such as *Ancrene Wisse*, thus suggesting that they are indicative of a renewed 'interest in the virgin life and the education of devout women'.[2] Unfortunately very little is known of the education of religious women in medieval Wales and one needs to take care when drawing direct comparisons between the Welsh evidence and the situation in England. *Ancrene Wisse* was produced originally for three female anchorites who had chosen to withdraw from their communities and spend the rest of their days in chaste and devotional contemplation. However, the same does not appear to be true of the audience of the Welsh Lives, nor do the Welsh manuscripts in question contain guides for recluses or texts such as *Hali Meiðhad* which place particular emphasis on the virgin life.[3] Whilst in medieval England there were at least 150 nunneries, in medieval Wales there were only three long-standing religious houses for women and, as we shall see in Chapter 6, these appear to have been poorly endowed and had relatively few inmates. In England examples are extant of Lives of virgin martyrs composed by women, as well as for women, and manuscripts containing predominantly female saints' Lives are known to have belonged to communities of religious women.[4] In Wales, on the other hand, no records have yet come to light regarding libraries or manuscripts kept in the nunneries and there is nothing in the manuscripts that specifically suggests that these Lives were produced for an audience of religious sisters. The purpose here is not to discount the relevance of the Lives of female saints within a religious milieu, be that the parish church, the monastery or indeed the convent, but merely to suggest that, within the specific context of medieval Wales, these Lives were probably read or heard and appreciated by far more laywomen than consecrated virgins. Katherine Lewis has shown that, although the female saints were considered as appropriate role models for young virgins, married women seeking to elevate both their social and spiritual stature also adopted them as exemplars.[5] Although this group of female saints' Lives had a particular relevance for women, the primary roles the saints played as powerful intercessors ensured that they enjoyed a wide popularity amongst men, women and children, and the medieval miscellanies which contain these *buchedddau* would have been used by lay families for the combined purposes of entertainment, education and spiritual edification.

The Middle Welsh Lives of Katherine, Margaret, Mary of Egypt, Mary Magdalene and Martha do not always appear together as a complete series, nor do they always occur in the same manuscripts or in the same order (see Table 1).[6] The Welsh Life of Gwenfrewy has also been included in this Table, since it occurs in some of the same manuscripts. Gwenfrewy, as we saw in Chapter 2, is the only native female saint for whom an official Middle Welsh prose *buchedd* survives. Although there are variations in the different Welsh manuscript versions of her Life, the Middle Welsh *Buched Gwenfrewy* is largely an adaptation of Robert of Shrewsbury's twelfth-century Latin Life.[7] The saints' Lives in question usually form part of a compendium of predominantly religious texts which are occasionally accompanied by secular legends and medical, scientific or genealogical material. Other religious texts which occur in these compendia include Middle Welsh translations of the Lives of St Thomas the Apostle, John the Evangelist, Martin, David, St Patrick's Purgatory, the Creed of Athanasius, the Miracles of the Blessed Virgin Mary and the Invention of the Cross by St Helen.

Table 1 Manuscripts containing the Welsh Lives of female saints

Manuscript	**Date and scribe (if known)**	**Lives of female saints**
Peniarth 14	SAEC. XIII[2]	Mary of Egypt
Peniarth 14	SAEC. XIV[1]	Margaret
Peniarth 5 (+ Peniarth 4 = the White Book of Rhydderch)	SAEC. XIV med.	Katherine, Margaret, Mary Magdalene, Martha, Mary of Egypt
Peniarth 15	SAEC. XIV XV	Margaret, Katherine
Llanstephan 27 (the Red Book of Talgarth)	SAEC XIV XV Hywel Fychan	Katherine, Mary Magdalene, Martha
Cardiff 3.242 (Hafod 16) detached portion of Llanstephan 27	SAEC XIV XV Hywel Fychan	Mary of Egypt
Cotton Titus D. xxii	SAEC XV[1]	Katherine, Margaret
NLW 5267B	1438	Katherine
Llanstephan 28	⩾1456 Gutun Owain	Margaret, Katherine
Peniarth 27iii	SAEC XV[2] Gutun Owain	Katherine
Peniarth 27ii	SAEC XV XVI	Mary Magdalene, Gwenfrewy

Manuscript	Date and scribe (if known)	Lives of female saints
Cardiff 2.629 (Hafod 19)	1535–6 Ieuan ap William ap Dafydd	Margaret, Katherine, Mary Magdalene
Llanstephan 117	1548 Ieuan ap William ap Dafydd	Margaret, Katherine, Mary Magdalene
Llanstephan 34	SAEC XVI[2] Roger Morris Thomas Evans	Katherine, Gwenfrewy, Mary Magdalene, Martha, Mary of Egypt, Margaret
NLW 6209E	SAEC XVII David Parry	Katherine, Mary Magdalene, Martha
NLW 552B	SAEC XVII	Margaret, Katherine
Peniarth 225	1594–1610	Mary Magdalene, Margaret, Gwenfrewy
Cardiff 2.633 (Hafod 23)	1604 John Jones of Gellilyfdy	Mary Magdalene, Martha, Mary of Egypt, Katherine, Margaret
Peniarth 217 (Llyfr Siôn ap William ap Siôn o Fucheddau Apostolion a Seintiau)	1611 John Jones of Gellilyfdy	Mary Magdalene, Martha, Mary of Egypt, Katherine
Llanstephan 187	1634 John Jones of Gellilyfdy	Katherine
Llanstephan 104	SAEC XVIII[1] Moses Williams Thomas Evans	Katherine, Gwenfrewy, Mary Magdalene, Martha, Mary of Egypt, Margaret
Cwrtmawr 1155	1810–80 Robert Williams of Rhydycroesau	Katherine, Margaret, Mary Magdalene, Martha

Peniarth 14 is the earliest extant manuscript to contain any of the Lives of this group of female saints. The portion that belongs to the second half of the thirteenth century contains the Welsh Life of Mary of Egypt, which here is not a text in its own right, since it forms part of a larger text *Gwyrthyeu e Wynvydedic Veir* (The Miracles of the Blessed Virgin Mary).[8] The Life of Margaret occurs in the portion of Peniarth 14 that belongs to the first half of the fourteenth century. The Lives of all the female saints mentioned above occur in Peniarth 5, Llanstephan 34, Llanstephan 104 and Cardiff 2.633 (*olim* Hafod 23); whereas in Llanstephan 27, otherwise known as the Red Book of Talgarth, the Lives of Mary Magdalene and Martha are accompanied only by the Life of Katherine. Mary of Egypt, however, occurs in a detached portion of the Red Book of Talgarth, now known as Cardiff 3.242 (*olim* Hafod 16). Thus, the earliest extant manuscript which contains all of these Lives is Peniarth 5. Originally MSS Peniarth 5 and Peniarth 4 formed one volume known as 'Llyfr Gwyn Rhydderch' (the White Book of Rhydderch) which as Daniel Huws has shown appears to have been compiled *c.*1350 for Rhydderch ab Ieuan Llwyd of Parcrhydderch, Llangeithio, who belonged to a long line of important Welsh literary patrons.[9] Although the White Book appears to have been commissioned by Rhydderch himself, or on his behalf, it contains texts that had been translated into Welsh for his forbears in the third quarter of the thirteenth century. A colophon in the White Book notes that Brother Gruffudd Bola translated the Creed of Athanasius from Latin into Welsh for Efa ferch Maredudd ab Owain, since she desired to read the text in her native tongue.[10] Another religious text which appears in the White Book is a vernacular translation of the Assumption of the Virgin Mary, commissioned by Efa's brother, Gruffudd ap Maredudd ab Owain, from the translator Madog ap Selyf.[11] Unfortunately, no indication is given as to who commissioned the translations of the Lives of women saints which would, no doubt, have been appreciated by both brother and sister. It is conceivable that they were produced in the thirteenth century for the same family, or alternatively at a later date nearer the time that the White Book was compiled for Maredudd ab Owain's great-great-grandson, Rhydderch. Of course, one does not necessarily need to assume that all of these Lives were translated at the same time or for the same family.

The second oldest extant manuscript that contains the Lives of Mary Magdalene and Martha, 'Llyfr Coch Talgarth' (the Red Book of Talgarth), also appears to have been owned by a lay family which was keen on sponsoring Welsh literature. This is a compendium of religious prose and poetry which does not contain the secular legends found in the White Book of Rhydderch. Brynley F. Roberts suggests that the Red Book of Talgarth was produced for Rhys ap Tomas who is mentioned in the manuscript.[12] His more renowned brother, Hopcyn ap Tomas, commissioned the same scribe (and others) to produce an important companion volume (the Red Book of Hergest) which, like the White Book, included the corpus of tales known as the Mabinogion.[13]

Most of the Welsh Lives of the universally popular saints have been edited at some time or another. The Life of Margaret has been edited by William J. Rees and Melville Richards;[14] the Life of Katherine by William J. Rees, Idris Bell and J. E. Caerwyn Williams and a new edition, based on all the extant manuscripts, is currently being compiled by Catherine E. Byfield;[15] editions of the Life of Mary of Egypt have been made available by Lewis Haydn Angell, Gwenan Jones, Melville Richards and Ingo Mittendorf;[16] the Life of Martha, however, has never been edited and only one version of the Welsh Life of Mary Magdalene, based on a relatively late manuscript, has been published. In 1929 Gwenallt published an edition of *Buched Meir Vadlen*, based on Peniarth 225, which can be dated to the late sixteenth/early seventeenth century.[17] Although this includes some of the variants from other manuscripts, it does not refer to all of the most significant variants and it does not discuss the relationship between the different manuscripts. Idris Foster may have had the intention of publishing an edition of the Life of Martha, since there are unpublished notes on the Life amongst his papers at the National Library of Wales.[18] On the whole, the Life of Martha appears to have been completely ignored and this is one of the reasons why I have chosen to focus on this particular Life and that of her sister Mary Magdalene in this chapter.[19]

In all *Buched Meir Vadlen* is extant in twelve handwritten manuscripts dating from the mid-fourteenth century to the nineteenth and *Buched Martha* is extant in eight of the same manuscripts (see Table 2). The Life of Mary Magdalene always precedes the Life of Martha and, although the Life of Mary Magdalene occurs on its own, the Life of Martha never occurs in any of the Welsh manuscripts without the Life of Mary Magdalene. Both Lives are incomplete in the earliest extant manuscript – Peniarth 5. Folio 26 (recto and verso) contains the first section of the Life of Mary Magdalene and a blank folio, which presumably replaces missing leaves, follows this. Folio 28 then follows with the end of the Life of Martha. The sorry state of Peniarth 5, in this section of the manuscript, has given rise to some confusion and may possibly explain why the Life of Martha has been ignored. In a footnote to his edition of the Peniarth 225 version of *Buched Meir Vadlen*, Gwenallt states that the ending of the Life of Mary Magdalene is 'different in Peniarth 5', but in fact what he is referring to is not the end of the Life of Mary Magdalene but that of Martha.[20] J. Gwenogvryn Evans does not provide titles for the Lives of Mary Magdalene and Martha in his description of the contents of the White Book, and he also appears to assume that the surviving texts comprise the beginning and end of the same Life.[21] This, in turn, led Ingo Mittendorf, in his study of Mary of Egypt, to state that in Peniarth 5 the Life of Mary of Egypt was separated from the other miracles of the Blessed Virgin Mary; that it followed the Lives of Katherine and Margaret but was separated from them 'by another short text'.[22] This unidentified 'text' is, of course, the incomplete Lives of Mary Magdalene and Martha. There is good reason why the Life of Mary of Egypt should have been associated with the Lives of Mary Magdalene and her sister Martha, since the legends of Mary of Egypt and Mary Magdalene have a great deal in common. Both women were reputed to be reformed harlots who spent many years in the wilderness and attained sanctity through a strict ascetic regime of self-deprivation and penance.

Both are nourished by celestial beings and avoid human contact until their final encounter with a priest. They both make preparations for their death, receive their last communion and expire. It is generally recognized that the episode relating Mary Magdalene's sojourn in the desert was added to the Life of Mary Magdalene as a result of her association with Mary of Egypt.[23] Misrahi demonstrates that the annexed episode was widespread by the eleventh century.[24] As early as the eighth century Anglo-Saxon martyrologies refer to the Magdalene's eremitical life,[25] and there is evidence to suggest that she may have become associated with Mary of Egypt in at least one of the Celtic regions from the early ninth century. Pádraig Ó Riain states that the entry for Mary Magdalene in the Martyrology of Tallaght (28 March rather than 22 July) was 'at the expense of Mary of Egypt', since Mary of Egypt's feast-day appears as 28 March in other martyrologies.[26] In the majority of the Welsh calendars Mary Magdalene's feast-day is entered consistently for 22 July, but in Peniarth 187 a feast for the Magdalene appears on 1 April, that is the day preceding Mary of Egypt's feast in the Roman Martyrology (2 April).[27] Before looking in detail at the content of the Welsh *bucheddau* and the relationship between the different Welsh manuscripts, it would perhaps be beneficial to provide a brief history of the development of the legends of Mary Magdalene and Martha.

Table 2 Manuscripts containing the Middle Welsh Lives of Mary Magdalene and Martha

Buched Meir Vadlen	Date and scribe (if known)	*Buched Martha*
Peniarth 5, fol.xxvi^{r}–xxvi^{v} (+ Peniarth 4 = the White Book of Rhydderch)	SAEC. XIV med.	Peniarth 5, fol. xxviii^{r} (+ Peniarth 4 = the White Book of Rhydderch)
Llanstephan 27, fols 132^{r}–135^{v} (the Red Book of Talgarth)	SAEC XIV XV Hywel Fychan	Llanstephan 27, fols 136^{r}–137^{r} (the Red Book of Talgarth)
Peniarth 27ii, pp. 51–9	SAEC XV XVI	

Buched Meir Vadlen	**Date and scribe (if known)**	*Buched Martha*
Cardiff 2.629 (Hafod 19), fols 68^{r}–72^{r}	1535–6 Ieuan ap William ap Dafydd	
Llanstephan 117, pp. 177–80	1548 Ieuan ap William ap Dafydd	
Llanstephan 34, pp. 365–78	SAEC XVI^{2} Roger Morris	Llanstephan 34, pp. 378–82
NLW 6209E, pp. 605–10	SAEC XVII	NLW 6209E, pp. 610–12
Peniarth 225, pp. 252–9	1594–1610	
Cardiff 2.633 (Hafod 23), pp. 331–46	1604 John Jones of Gellilyfdy	Cardiff 2.633 (Hafod 23), pp. 346–52
Peniarth 217, pp. 449–76 (Llyfr Siôn ap William ap Siôn o Fucheddau Apostolion a Seintiau)	1611 John Jones of Gellilyfdy	Peniarth 217, pp. 479–89 (Llyfr Siôn ap William ap Siôn o Fucheddau Apostolion a Seintiau)
Llanstephan 104, pp. 395–409	SAEC XVIII^{1} Moses Williams	Llanstephan 104, pp. 410–15
Cwrtmawr 1155ii, pp. 73–6	1810–80 Robert Williams of Rhydycroesau	Cwrtmawr 1155ii, p. 76

The development of the legends of Mary Magdalene and Martha and the notion of the composite Magdalene

Unlike most of the other female saints whose Lives were translated into Welsh in the Middle Ages, Mary Magdalene and Martha are biblical characters, not virgin martyrs. Their Lives do not follow the usual hagiographic pattern of the martyred female saint who stoically refuses to marry a pagan suitor and then has to suffer an appalling array of tortures, culminating in decapitation, in order to preserve her virginity and defend her Christian faith.[28] The medieval legends which accrued to Mary Magdalene and Martha and claimed that they evangelized Provence, bear little relation to their characters in the Gospels. The medieval Mary Magdalene is a particularly interesting character in that she is a conflation of various women mentioned in the New Testament. Today Roman Catholicism and Protestantism agree with the early Eastern Church in distinguishing between Mary Magdalene, Mary of Bethany and the penitent in Luke 7:36–50. However, throughout the Middle Ages, the Western Church, on the whole, regarded these women as one.[29] Thus it was believed that Mary Magdalene, from whom Christ drove out seven devils and who later witnessed the risen Christ, was the same person as Mary of Bethany, sister of Martha and Lazarus, who anointed Christ's feet and dried them with her hair (John 12:1–8). This led to her association with the unnamed sinner in Luke's Gospel who washed Christ's feet with her tears, wiped them with her hair and anointed them with ointment in the house of Simon the Pharisee. To confuse the issue further, Mark 14:3–9 and Matthew 26:6–13 also recount an episode involving an anointing, when an unnamed woman pours precious ointment on Christ's head in the house of Simon the Leper at Bethany. To a lesser extent, Mary Magdalene became associated with the woman of Samaria who was not legally married, although she had had five 'husbands' (John 4:18), and the woman taken in adultery (John 8:3): on both occasions Christ refuses to condemn publicly these women's sexual misdemeanours. The seven devils, driven out of Mary Magdalene, have been equated with the Seven Deadly Sins and it has frequently been assumed that the penitent's sin in Luke's Gospel was of a sexual nature. Thus, it was Mary Magdalene's conflation with women who had committed sexual crimes that led to her association with prostitution and the idea that she was a reformed harlot. In addition, Susan Haskins points out that Mary's surname, *Magdalini* in Greek, may have contributed to her promiscuous reputation, since it links her with el Mejdel, a village on the north-west bank of Galilee which was 'destroyed in AD 75 because of its infamy and the licentious behaviour of its inhabitants'.[30] By the thirteenth century Mary Magdalene had become firmly associated with prostitution and the reforming of prostitutes, since the Order of the Penitents of Mary

Magdalene was founded *c.*1225 by Rudolf of Worms.[31] These religious houses for reformed prostitutes became extremely popular in Germany, France and Italy, although there is no evidence to suggest that the Order ever existed in Wales. The notion of the composite Magdalene, although prevalent before the sixth century, was sanctioned by Gregory the Great (*c.*540–604) in his homilies. In the West this theory of unity remained relatively unchallenged until the sixteenth century when Jacques Lefèvre d'Etaples wrote a treatise on Mary Magdalene which refuted ecclesiastical tradition and suggested that there were in fact three separate women called Mary. He was apparently excommunicated as a result.[32]

The first coherent narrative relating the pre-ascension life of Mary Magdalene appears in a tenth-century sermon attributed to Odo of Cluny. Shortly after this a Latin *vita* appeared which gave an account of Mary Magdalene and Martha's voyage to Marseilles, and focused on Mary Magdalene's career in Gaul and her death and burial at Aix en Provence. Whilst in the East the most widely accepted legend claimed that Mary Magdalene died at Ephesus where she had fled with John and the Virgin Mary following the Ascension, in the West it was the Provençal legend that became popular. To the *vita apostolica*, set in Provence, were added further episodes including the Magdalene's sojourn in the wilderness and the story of the prince of Marseilles. The legend was to take on many different forms before evolving into the standard medieval narrative best represented by Jacobus de Voragine's thirteenth-century *Legenda aurea*.[33] The Life of Mary Magdalene, described by Victor Saxer as 'a medieval best-seller', was included in a number of important hagiographic collections. Saxer identifies over two hundred Latin versions of the legend and about the same number of vernacular translations.[34] The Lives of both Mary Magdalene and Martha occur in the *Legenda aurea*,[35] the South English Legendary,[36] Nicholas Bozon's Anglo-Norman legendary,[37] Jehan de Vignay's *Legende Dorée*, various French and Spanish collections,[38] the Middle English *Gilte Legende*[39] and Caxton's *Golden Legend*.[40] In addition, Mary Magdalene's Life is also found in the Northern Homily Collection,[41] the Auchinleck Manuscript,[42] John Mirk's *Festial*,[43] Osbern of Bokenham's *Legendys of Hooly Wummen*[44] and *Speculum Sacerdotale*.[45] There are also two French verse Lives and various German prose and verse versions of the Life of Mary Magdalene some of which appear to stem from the French poems.[46] Texts produced in the Celtic regions include the fourteenth-century vernacular verse Lives of Mary Magdalene and Martha in the Scottish Legendary and an incomplete Irish homily on Mary Magdalene.[47] The lengthy prologue, which precedes the Life of Mary Magdalene in the Scottish Legendary, is unique to this text and refers to St David (Dewi) alongside Mary Magdalene and Mary of Egypt in a list of sinners.

Buched Meir Vadlen and Buched Martha

The Middle Welsh Lives of Mary Magdalene and Martha do not correspond exactly to any of the versions listed above. Although the Welsh texts mirror certain sections of the *Legenda aurea* almost word for word, they omit other key episodes, some of which are essential to the structure of the *vitae*: it is probable, therefore, that the Welsh Lives are translations of incomplete texts rather than direct adaptations of the *Legenda aurea*. *Buched Meir Vadlen* does not conform to the criteria set out by David Mycoff for identifying *Legenda aurea* influence on vernacular texts:[48] for example, it omits the lengthy etymologies of Mary's name, the mention of the pseudo-Ambrose's view on the identity of the woman who blessed the Virgin's womb and the *post mortem* translation and miracles. Since numerous texts mirror the wording of the *Legenda aurea*, it is difficult to decipher the exact relationship between the Welsh Lives and Jacobus de Voragine's work. However, the *bucheddau* are more likely to be translations of an intermediary (or intermediaries) affiliated to the *Legenda aurea*, than to be direct adaptations of its versions.

All of the medieval versions of the Welsh texts, *Buched Meir Vadlen* and *Buched Martha*, have a great deal in common, although they also possess a significant number of variants. The two oldest extant manuscripts, Peniarth 5 and Llanstephan 27, appear to stem from the same common original, although a substantial part of both Lives is missing in Peniarth 5. However, on occasions their phraseology differs and this is reflected in later copies of the texts. Interestingly, although the sixteenth-century Llanstephan 34 version of *Buched Martha* closely follows variants in Peniarth 5, the Llanstephan 34 version of *Buched Meir Vadlen* does not follow either Peniarth 5 or Llanstephan 27 exactly. This seems to suggest that Llanstephan 34 drew on more than one source. Since the Life of Martha is incomplete in Peniarth 5, it is tempting to suggest that the sixteenth-century Llanstephan 34 may preserve a complete copy of the original Welsh *Buched Martha* that may once have existed in the mid-fourteenth-century Peniarth 5.[49] NLW 6209E is a copy of Llanstephan 27 and Cwrtmawr 1155ii is a copy of Peniarth 5 since it contains the same incomplete texts: in Cwrtmawr 1155ii Robert Williams of Rhydycroesau notes the start of each new page in his source which corresponds to the layout of the texts in Peniarth 5. The most notable difference between the Welsh versions of *Buched Meir Vadlen* is that Peniarth 27, Llanstephan 34, Peniarth 217 and Llanstephan 104 all contain an extra section of text relating details of Mary Magdalene's pre-ascension Life, noting her special relationship with Christ and identifying her as the sinner who anointed Christ's feet in the house of Simon. Here it is suggested that Mary Magdalene was due to marry John the Evangelist, but John decided to follow Christ and, as a result, Mary Magdalene threw herself into a Life of sexual promiscuity and carnal pleasure:

> Ḷaụer o lyfreü y syḍ yn dyụedüd pan dylysseü Ieüan Evangylụr briodi Mair Vagdalen ryerchi or Iessü iḍo i ga[n]lyn ef a chadụ i forụyndaụd ac feḷy y gụnaeth. Am hynny sorri a ụnaeth + Mair Vagdalen ac ymroḍi i bechodaü ac yn fụya i odineb.[50]

> (There are many books which say that when John the Evangelist should have married Mary Magdalene Jesus asked him to follow Him and retain his virginity, and so he did. Because of that + Mary Magdalene sulked and gave herself to [a life of] sin – and above all lust/adultery.)

Peniarth 27 does not specifically mention 'godineb' (lust or adultery); instead it claims that Mary Magdalene devoted herself to the Seven Deadly Sins.[51] Whilst in the *Legenda aurea* Jacobus de Voragine emphatically denies the relationship between Mary Magdalene and John the Evangelist declaring that 'these tales are to be considered false and frivolous', the Welsh *buchedd* makes no comment on the accuracy of this information. The additional section in the Welsh account is a summary of certain details found at the beginning and end of Jacobus de Voragine's legend. Indeed, this part of *Buched Meir Vadlen* has more in common with John Mirk's *Festial* than it does with the *Legenda aurea*, for Mirk's verse homily contains a similar concise account of the pre-ascension life combined with details of the Magdalene's failed relationship with John.[52] As in Mirk's *Festial*, this section is positioned at the beginning of the Life in Peniarth 27, but in all the other Welsh versions the additional material is appended to the Welsh Life. It appears that this additional section of text did not form part of the oldest extant versions preserved in Peniarth 5 and Llanstephan 27, for although Peniarth 5 is incomplete, its beginning is intact and the post ascension Life of Mary Magdalene follows hard on the heels of *Buched Margred* (the Welsh Life of Margaret of Antioch). The additional section, then, may have been added to the Welsh Life possibly at the end of the fifteenth century at the time that Peniarth 27 was compiled.

With the exception of Peniarth 27, the Welsh *Buched Meir Vadlen* begins with the tale of how Mary Magdalene, Maximinus, Cedonius (Acedemus), Lazarus, Martha and Maximista (Maximilla), Martha's handmaid, were put to sea with a number of other Christians in an old boat without oars, sails or ropes and how they miraculously arrived at the port of Marseilles ('Marsli'). The same event is narrated at the beginning of the Life of Martha – only *Buched Martha* does not mention Cedonius or Martha's handmaid who is usually claimed to be the author of the text. Having arrived in Marseilles, they discover that no one is willing to offer them accommodation. This is only achieved when Mary Magdalene succeeds in terrifying the prince of Marseilles and his wife by appearing to them in their dreams. Her face aflame with rage, Mary Magdalene accuses the prince and his 'cymar wennwynic' (venomous wife) of allowing the saints to starve to death. A peculiarity of the Welsh Life is that Mary not only complains that the saints have been left to die of hunger and thirst, but also that they are naked. Eventually the married couple offer hospitality to Mary and her companions and agree to be converted to Christianity if Mary Magdalene grants them a son. The princess immediately becomes pregnant, and the prince decides to set out to visit Peter in Rome. His wife insists that she must accompany him on the pilgrimage, ignoring his protestations that the journey is far too dangerous for a pregnant woman:

> 'Ot ey di minneu a af y gyt a thi' heb y wreic. 'Nac ef argl6ydes' heb ynteu. 'Kanys beichia6c 6yt ti a llawer y maent o berigleu yn y mor. Namyn tric di gartref y synnya6 ar yn kyuoeth an da a minneu a af ragof.' A hitheu dan wyla6 a dyg6yda6d y draet ef ac adol6yn y gadel y uynet gyt ac ef. A hynny a gafas.[53]

> ('If you go, I'm coming with you,' said his wife. 'No, Lady,' he said. 'For you are pregnant and there are many perils at sea. You stay at home and look after our wealth and possessions and I'll go on my way.' And she fell at his feet weeping and begged him to let her go with him. And she was granted that.)

The Welsh text perhaps depicts the woman in a slightly more favourable light than the *Legenda aurea*, since she is politely addressed as 'argl6ydes' (Lady). The *buchedd* also refrains from using this episode as a misogynistic device to generalize about womankind. The *Legenda aurea*, on the other hand, notes that 'she insisted, doing as women do. She threw herself at his feet, weeping the while, and in the end won him over'.[54] At the opposite end of the spectrum, Nicholas de Bozon's Anglo-Norman Life portrays the woman in a very favourable light, and suggests that God performed a miracle indicating that she should indeed accompany her husband.[55]

Cardiff MS 2.629 breaks off after the prince's protestations omitting the pilgrimage and continues, in a rather disjointed manner, with subsequent events at Aix and Marseilles. In all of the other versions the woman dies in childbirth at sea. Rather than allow the mariners to throw his wife's body to the sea monsters, the prince persuades them to leave her body and the distraught, hungry infant on a small hill-like island ('brynn bychan ual ynys'). On his return from Rome he passes the same place and sees a small boy playing with pebbles on the beach. Mary Magdalene, having cared for the child for two years, then revives the woman who immediately showers the Magdalene with praise and thanks her for assisting at the birth and feeding the child with her own breasts: 'Ti a doethost attaf 6rth vyng govit a mi yn esgor ac a wassaneytheist y mi dy vronneu di yn vfud.'[56] ('You came to me when I was troubled and in labour and obediently you served me with your breasts.')

It transpires that not only has Mary Magdalene cared for the couple's household during their absence and wet-nursed their child, but she has also accompanied the woman on a spiritual pilgrimage and visited all the same sites as the prince. On their return to Marseilles they are baptized by Maximinus. Lazarus is declared Bishop of Marseilles and Maximinus becomes bishop of Aix en Provence. Mary Magdalene then retires to the wilderness for thirty years, where every day at the seven canonical hours she is attended by angels who lift her up into the sky. One day a priest who lives twelve miles from Mary Magdalene's abode witnesses the event. The *Legenda aurea* notes only that his cell is a few miles from Mary Magdalene's cave and it also specifically states that her eremitic retreat was in an empty wilderness devoid of trees and streams.[57] Whilst the majority of the Welsh versions refer to her as living in a cave ('ogof') in the wilderness ('yn y diffeith'), Cardiff 2.629 has her retire to a wooded wilderness ('y diffeith goed') and the priest comes across her as he performs penance in the woods ('yn y koed').[58] Given that in medieval Welsh literature encounters with otherworldly beings and saintly figures frequently take place in woodland, it is not surprising that remote woodland would have been deemed a more relevant setting for a Welsh audience than the desert or a cave at Sainte Baume.[59] None of the Welsh versions mention Sainte Baume in the *massif* of Provence.[60] The Magdalene asks the priest to contact Maximinus and inform him that she is about to die and that he should meet her in church on the feast of the Lord's passion. Maximinus meets her, as arranged, and having taken her last communion, Mary lies down in front of the altar and passes away. Maximinus anoints the body with precious balm and requests that when he dies he is to be buried near Mary Magdalene. Both Peniarth 27 and Cardiff 2.629, like the *Legenda aurea*, add that for seven days following her burial a sweet smell pervaded the church. *Buched Meir Vadlen* ends here. It does not recount the translation of her relics to Vézelay or describe miracles performed after the saint's death. Although Jacobus de Voragine's legend was composed before Vézelay's claim to the Magdalene's relics was discredited, the Welsh Life was possibly compiled after the 'discovery' of an alternative set of relics at the church of St Maximin in 1279.

Buched Martha is an extremely short Life which recounts only the perilous journey to Marseilles in the boat with no oars or sail, the description of the saint's death and burial at Tarascon and the miracle involving Bishop Fronto's white gloves. Although *Buched Martha* has a great deal in common with the *Legenda aurea*, it omits some of the most interesting episodes in the *vita* such as Martha's encounter with the dragon of Tarascon, born of a creature capable of shooting burning excrement for up to an acre at its enemies. In the vast majority of the Latin and vernacular versions of Martha's Life the saint subdues the dragon, sprinkles holy water on the fiend and ties him up in her girdle. The inhabitants of Tarascon then promptly stone him to death:

> The dragon had come from Galatia in Asia, begotten of Leviathan, an extremely ferocious water-serpent, and Onachus, an animal bred in the region of Galatia, which shoots its dung like darts at pursuers within the space of an acre: whatever this touches is burned up as by fire. The people asked Martha for help, and she went after the dragon. She found him in the forest in the act of devouring a man, sprinkled him with blessed water, and had a cross held up in front of him. The brute was subdued at once and stood still like a sheep while Martha tied him up with her girdle, and the people killed him then and there with stones and lances. The inhabitants called the dragon *Tarasconus*, and in memory of this event the place is still called Tarascon.[61]

Since this is the highlight of the Life of Martha, its absence from the Welsh version is surprising. It is unlikely that the Welsh translator or copyist would voluntarily censor the episode. Margred's feisty wrestling match with the devil disguised as a dragon plays a central role in the Welsh Life of Margaret of Antioch:

> Ac yna y kymerth y vorvynn santes y kythreul gyr guallt y penn ac y trevis vrth y dayar ac y dodes y throet ar y war ef ac y dyvat vrthav, 'Peit bellach a dyvedut am vy morwyndaut i'.[62]

> (And then the saintly virgin took hold of the devil by the hair of his head and threw him to the ground, put her foot on the nape of his neck and said, 'Don't you mention my virginity again!')

The only explanation for the concise nature of *Buched Martha* is that the Welsh text is a translation of an incomplete Life. It also omits the account of how a young boy, eager to hear Martha preaching on the other side of the river, jumps into the water and attempts to swim across. He is drowned en route, but later resurrected by Martha.

In the Welsh *buchedd*, following their arrival in Marseilles, Martha and her companions travel to Aix where they convert large numbers of people to Christianity. In Llanstephan 34 Martha is described as 'doeth oeḍ a chymen a rhadlaụn a charedic gan baụb'[63] (she was wise, eloquent and full of grace and was loved by everyone). Her chastity is emphasized at the beginning of the *buchedd* where it is stated that she never married or had a relationship with a man. No sooner have the companions begun on their mission to preach and convert than Martha learns that she is to die within a year and begins to suffer from a terrible fever. A week before she passes away the ghost of her sister Mary Magdalene appears to her and she realizes that her time is nigh. She requests that the lanterns around her be lit, but at midnight a strong gust of wind extinguishes the lights and she is surrounded by evil spirits carrying written lists of her sins. She prays to Christ for forgiveness and a man appears and relights the lanterns. In the *Legenda aurea* it is Mary Magdalene that relights the lanterns. Christ offers her comfort saying that since she acted as his host and welcomed her into his house, so shall he welcome her into his. Martha's role as Christ's hostess ('llettywreic') is continuously stressed throughout the *buchedd*. She is taken out of the house, read a section from Luke's Gospel and passes away. At the same time far away in Perigueux ('Pentagores') Bishop Fronto, who is celebrating mass, falls asleep and dreams that he is called to bury Martha in Tarascon. Since all of the Welsh versions omit Martha's adventures with the dragon Tarasconen who gave his name to Tarascon, the location of Martha's funeral is not explained in the Welsh text. The *buchedd* jumps rather confusingly from one location to another. A deacon in his own church later wakes the bishop and Fronto, annoyed that the deacon has interrupted his dream, tells him to hurry to Tarascon because he has left his gold ring and pair of white gloves at Martha's funeral. True enough, when the deacon arrives at Tarascon he finds the objects that Fronto had lost in his dream. One of the white gloves is retained by the sacristan at Tarascon as proof of the miracle. The *buchedd* ends by stressing Martha's intercessory powers: 'A phoet tr6y eiryol y santes honno y delom ninneu i vuched dragywyda6l.'[64] (And through intercession with that saint may we attain everlasting life.)

Other sources: medieval Welsh poetry, church dedications, holy wells and visual representations

Whilst Mary Magdalene has an important role in the Welsh Life of Martha, Martha is a minor character in the Life of Mary Magdalene. Since *Buched Martha* omits many of the miracles that depict Martha as an active heroine performing miracles in her own right (e.g. slaying the dragon, preaching by the river and resurrecting the drowned boy), Martha does not develop into a fully autonomous heroine in the Welsh Life. *Buched Martha* is a mere shadow of *Buched Meir Vadlen* and, as we have seen, it never occurs in the Welsh manuscripts unless it is preceded by the latter (see Table 2). As one might expect, Mary Magdalene's pre-eminence is obvious in other sources such as medieval Welsh poetry, church dedications, holy wells and the visual arts. Martha seems only to have been introduced into Wales because of her association with her more prominent and flamboyant sister. Mary Magdalene's feast-day on 22 July is mentioned in nearly all of the Welsh calendars, but it is noticeable that Martha's feast on 29 July is not included.[65] Mary Magdalene's feast-day appears to have been widely celebrated in Wales and, as one might expect, its celebration was not confined to towns and villages where the local church was dedicated to her. At Llan-non in Ceredigion, a village traditionally associated with St Non (the subject of Chapter 3), a fair was held annually in the fourteenth century in honour of Mary Magdalene and the festivities lasted for three days.[66]

Although there appear to be no Welsh churches dedicated to Martha, there are thirteen churches dedicated to Mary Magdalene. Of these, Kenfig, Goldcliff and Cerrigydrudion appear to be medieval foundations and there was once a medieval town chapel in her honour at Pembroke. There was also a chapel dedicated to Mary Magdalene at the priory church at Usk and a sixteenth-century, free-metre Welsh poem, written in the form of a dialogue between Mary Magdalene and a pilgrim sinner, addresses the Magdalene as 'Mair Fadlen o Frynbuga' ('Mary Magdalene of Usk'). G. Hartwell Jones assumed that the pilgrim was specifically addressing a statue of Mary Magdalene at Usk which is certainly plausible, but it is equally possible that prayer is the medium of conversation between saint and sinner and that the sinner visualizes Mary mentally. Mary Magdalene 'priod Ifan' (John's wife) offers the pilgrim advice on spiritual matters and steers his thoughts away from financial concerns.[67] The chapel at Llanfair Nant-y-gof is recorded as being dedicated to Mary Magdalene *c.*1600 in a document listing churches that had been appropriated to the Knights Hospitallers of Slebech in the twelfth and thirteenth centuries. It is possible, therefore, that the holy well at Llanfair Nant-y-gof was dedicated to the Magdalene rather than the Virgin Mary.[68] In addition there were holy wells associated with Mary Magdalene at St Clears, Cerrigydrudion and Harlech (close to the castle walls).[69] Bleddfa and Wiston, previously dedicated to the Virgin Mary, were rededicated to Mary Magdalene in the early twentieth century, and the medieval

1. Anna and Joachim meet at the Golden Gate, stained glass, Church of All Saints, Gresford, Denbighshire, 1498. Charles and Patricia Aithie, ffotograff.

2. The Presentation of Mary, stained glass, Church of All Saints, Gresford, Denbighshire, 1498. Charles and Patricia Aithie, ffotograff.

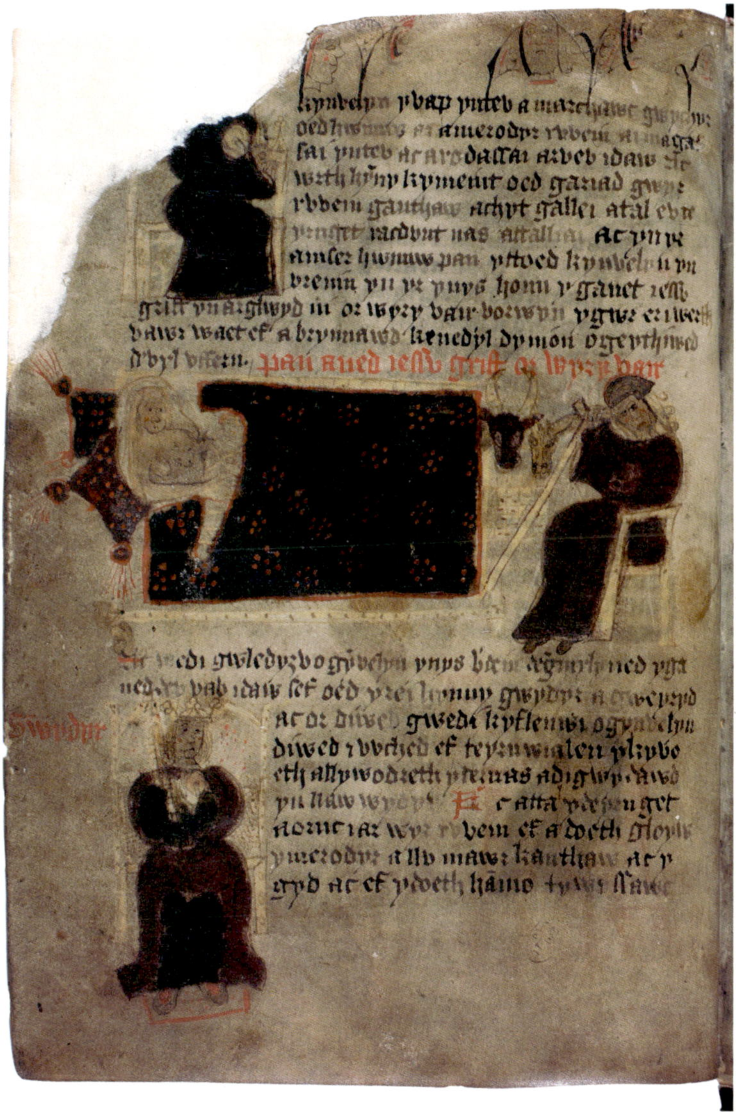

3. The Nativity of Christ, Aberystwyth, NLW, MS Peniarth 23, fol. 36v c.1500. National Library of Wales.

4. The Annunciation with lily crucifixion, Llanbeblig Hours (NLW, MS 1750A, fols 1v-2r), late fourteenth century. National Library of Wales.

5. The Annunciation, Church of St Tyrnog, Llandyrnog, Denbighshire, *c.*1500. Peter Lord.

6. The Annunciation, tomb of Sir William ap Tomos and his wife Gwladus, Priory Church of St Mary, Abergavenny, Monmouthshire, mid-fifteenth century. Jane Cartwright.

7. The enthroned Virgin nourishing Christ, the Llanbeblig Hours (NLW, MS, 1750A, fol. 4^r), late fourteenth century. National Library of Wales.

8. The Virgin weeping at the foot of the cross, stained glass Church of St Mary, Cilcain, Flintshire, early sixteenth century. Jane Cartwright.

9. Carved wooden image of the Virgin, probably from the rood-screen, Church of All Saints, Mochdre, Montgomeryshire, late fourteenth century. National Museum of Wales.

10. Stone sculpture of the Virgin and Child, Priory Church of St Mary, Cydweli, Carmarthenshire, late fourteenth century. Jane Cartwright.

11. St Mabyn, one of the daughters of Brychan Brycheiniog, stained glass at St Neot Parish Church, Cornwall, 1528. Jane Cartwright.

12. St Gwenfrewy's reliquary, Holywell Parish Church, Flintshire. Jane Cartwright.

13. The second seal of the Chapter of St Asaph depicting St Gwenfrewy, St Asaph, and an unknown bishop, fifteenth century. National Museum of Wales.

14. Illustration of the late fifteenth-century rood-screen at Pennant Melangell depicting the legend of St Melangell, sketch by John Parker, 1837. National Library of Wales.

15. Non and David arrive in Brittany, nineteenth-century stained glass, Church of St Non, Dirinon, Brittany. Jane Cartwright.

16. Non baptises David, nineteenth-century stained glass, Church of St Non, Dirinon. Jane Cartwright.

17. David resting on a rock, nineteenth-century stained glass, Church of St Non, Dirinon. Jane Cartwright.

18. St David's cradle, Dirinon. Jane Cartwright.

19. The reliquary of St Non, Dirinon, *c*.1450. Jane Cartwright.

20. Non meets Sant, ceiling painting, Church of St Divy, St Divy, Brittany, 1676. Jane Cartwright.

21. St Katherine of Alexandria, wall painting, Church of St Teilo, Llandeilo Tal-y-bont, now at the National History Museum, St Ffagans (formerly the Museum of Welsh Life). John Morgan.

22. St Katherine with the wheel, stained glass Church of St Stephen, Old Radnor, Radnorshire, *c.*1461–83. Jane Cartwright.

23. St Katherine tramples on Maxentius, the tomb of John White and his wives Margaret Phelp and Christina Einon at St Mary's Church, Tenby, Pembrokeshire, fifteenth century. Jane Cartwright.

24. Nun/abbess/donor figure, convent church Llanllugan, Montgomeryshire, late fifteenth century. Jane Cartwright.

25. Owain ap Meurig ap Llywelyn and his wife Elen, stained glass, Llangadwaladr Church, Anglesey, *c.*1490. Charles and Patricia Aithie, ffotograff.

foundations at Kenfig and Cerrigydrudion appear to have had earlier dedications to Cynfig and Ieuan Gwas Padrig respectively.[70]

St Ieuan Gwas Padrig appears to have once been depicted in medieval stained glass at the church in Cerrigydrudion, although the glass is no longer extant. Edward Lhuyd refers to the tradition, recorded in the parish register in 1503, that Ieuan Gwas Padrig founded the church in 440 and that the saint himself decided to dedicate his church to Mary Magdalene.[71] The sixteenth-century Welsh Life of Ieuan Gwas Padrig has an angel instruct him to build a church on the spot where he sees a roebuck.[72] This, of course, occurs at Cerrigydrudion, and the church is dedicated to Mary Magdalene and Ieuan.[73] Ieuan is also associated with Mary Magdalene and Cerrigydrudion in a poem by Gutun Ceiriog. The *cywydd* recounts the same events as the Middle Welsh Life, referring to the journey to Marseilles and the conversion of the populace in Provence. It also relates the miraculous events concerning the prince of Marseilles's pilgrimage to Rome and how Mary Magdalene reared his son for two years and resurrected his wife who had died in childbirth. Mary Magdalene's lengthy withdrawal from society is given short shrift in the *cywydd*, since her eremitic experiences are briefly summed up in one couplet which rather baldly states that she spent thirty years 'mewn rhyw ogof' (in some cave). This again suggests that the traditions associated with Sainte Baume were not considered to be particularly relevant to a Welsh audience. One could also argue that, to Gutun Ceiriog, her withdrawal from society was not as pertinent as her role as sinner and penitent. The main emphasis in the poem is on Mary's role as repentant sinner weeping salty tears at Christ's feet:

> Pan weles Mair yr Iesu
> Ofn y farn arni a fu
> Du law hallt a wylai hon
> Oi golwg uwch y galon
> Wylo ar ei draed alwyn
> A wnâi'r Fair wen er ei fwyn
> Golchi traed Crist yn ddistaw
> A'r dagrau'n llynnau 'mhob llaw.[74]

(When Mary saw Jesus
she was afraid of Judgement Day.
She cried black, salty rain
from her eyes above the heart.
Holy Mary cried a gallon [of tears]
on his feet for his sake.
She quietly washed his feet,
and the tears were [like] lakes in each hand.)

Since she herself was forgiven of her sins, she made an appropriate intercessor on behalf of all common sinners and was perhaps a more accessible role model than many of the virgin martyrs. Mary Magdalene, *castissima meretrix* (the most chaste prostitute), unlike many of the other Christian saints revered in the medieval period, was not perfect and was not without fault. Her medieval Life demonstrated that if Christ could forgive a reformed harlot, then there was hope for all repentant sinners regardless of the magnitude of their sins. Gutun Ceiriog notes that Mary Magdalene was afraid of Judgement Day. One might expect that a saint need have no fear of Judgement Day, yet Mary Magdalene's humility and humanity ensure that, faced with the Day of Judgement, she encounters the same fears and anxieties as any other Christian. In a similar vein, Martha is depicted as being terrified on her deathbed. In *Buched Martha* at midnight an ill wind extinguishes the lights that surround Martha's bed. Ill and afraid in the dark, surrounded by evil spirits holding written lists of her sins, she calls out to Christ who comes and comforts her:

> Ac yna yd ymdanges Iessu Grist idi ac y dywa6t 6rthi. 'Dabre,' heb ef 'vy llettywreic attaf. A thi a vydy gyt a mi yn y nef, kanys titheu amllettyeist inneu y gyt a thitheu gynt. Ar neb a alwo arnaf i yth en6 di mi ae g6aranda6af ef yrot ti.'[75]

> (And then Jesus Christ appeared to her and said to her: 'Come to me my hostess. And you will be with me in heaven, for previously you offered me accommodation with you. And I will listen to whoever calls upon me in your name because of you.')

Fear of dying, the terrifying prospect of Judgement Day and the uncertainty of its outcome must all have seemed relevant anxieties to a medieval audience who would, no doubt, have been able to identify easily with Martha in this scene. *Buched Martha* is also particularly relevant within a domestic setting, since Martha is rewarded for the generosity and hospitality that she showed towards Christ in her home at Bethany. Thus, *Buched Martha* stresses the importance of being a good host(ess) and emphasizes that Christ rewards generosity and hospitality in the Christian household.

Similarly, in *Buched Meir Vadlen* the Prince of Marseilles and his household are rewarded for the hospitality they extend to the saints: they eventually offer food, clothing and accommodation to Mary Magdalene and her companions and are rewarded accordingly. Indeed the episode relating the Prince of Marseilles's conversion and Mary Magdalene's relationship with his family is central to *Buched Meir Vadlen*. As early as the third century Origen identified Martha and her sister Mary Magdalene as representatives of the active and contemplative forms of the religious life. Yet in *Buched Meir Vadlen*, before Mary Magdalene retires to the wilderness to lead a contemplative existence, she leads a full and active life performing many miracles. The most important miracle story in the *buchedd* centres on the lay family, rewarded for their conversion and adherence to the Christian faith. The kind of miracles Mary Magdalene performs – wet-nursing, assisting during childbirth, healing and even looking after the prince of Marseilles's household and financial affairs during his absence – made her a particularly relevant saint within a lay household.

Furthermore, Mary Magdalene appears to have been considered an appropriate role model with which to compare married noblewomen in medieval Wales, and her role as myrrophore (ointment bearer) led to her specific association with healing. She is depicted carrying a jar of precious ointment on a fourteenth-century wall painting on the north wall of the chancel at Llantwit Major and she also appears on the panels of the canopy of honour in the church at Gyffin.[76] A leper hospital near the bottom of Heywood Hill in Tenby was founded *c.*1236 by Gilbert Mareschal and this appears to have been dedicated to Mary Magdalene.[77] In medieval Welsh poetry she is frequently referred to as 'meddyges Iesu'

(Christ's physician). In a *cywydd* to Hywel of Moelyrch who had injured his knee Guto'r Glyn compares Hywel's wife with Mary Magdalene 'meddyges Iesu' and requests that Elen heal her husband successfully with her precious ointment.[78] On another occasion he compares Siân, the wife of Sir Siôn Bwrch, with Mary Magdalene and claims that Siân's generous hospitality does wonders for the poet's physical ailments.[79]

There appear to be no surviving medieval artistic representations of Martha in Wales. Images at Gresford of a female saint carrying a bunch of keys are more likely to be St Sitha than Martha. Sitha is depicted on the font at Gresford and also in the east window of St Katherine's chapel, alongside St Apollonia (patron saint of toothache).[80] Martha may have become associated with St Sitha in the late medieval period, since Sitha, a domestic servant renowned for her piety, also became associated with domesticity and house husbandry.[81] Martha is rarely invoked in Welsh poetry. However, she is mentioned in a poem by Lewys Glyn Cothi written in order to wish Elliw ferch Henri a safe passage on return from her pilgrimage to Santiago de Compostella. Martha's perilous journey in a boat without oars or a sail seems to have made her an appropriate candidate for the task of ensuring that no storm arises during Elliw's journey across the sea.[82]

Thus from considering the context and transfer of the Welsh Lives of Mary Magdalene and Martha, and the use made of these two female saints within the secular poetic tradition, a tentative picture can begin to be sketched of their popularity and audience within medieval Wales. Martha appears to have always remained a minor character. Contingent conditions of textual transfer to Wales resulted in an atrophied Life which, in its extant form, may have further reduced its interest to a Welsh audience. Mary Magdalene, on the other hand, was relatively popular in late medieval Wales. The Middle Welsh *Buched Meir Vadlen* and *Buched Martha*, as we have seen, are not direct translations of the versions in the *Legenda aurea*, but probably stem from related texts. Four slightly different medieval versions of *Buched Meir Vadlen* exist while *Buched Martha* is found in only two medieval manuscripts and one of these is a fragmentary Life. Both the White Book of Rhydderch and the Red Book of

Talgarth, which appear to be household manuscripts, give an important indication of the literary interests and spiritual requirements of the Welsh gentry in the fourteenth and fifteenth centuries. The majority of the religious texts in these anthologies relate to the liturgical year in some manner and could have provided the laity (as well as the clergy)[83] with appropriate readings throughout the year, for example, on saints' feast-days. Texts such as *Buched Meir Vadlen*, with its particular emphasis on penitence, would also have provided the lay family with suitable reading material for penitential preparation prior to confession. The Fourth Lateran Council of 1215 stipulated that everyone should attend confession and receive communion at least once a year.[84] The Dominicans, who emphasized the importance to layfolk of confession and penitential practice, made Mary Magdalene the patron of their Order in 1297 and, no doubt, the Welsh Dominicans helped to diffuse her cult. Much of the legendary material in the White Book of Rhydderch has moral overtones and focuses on the importance of the family and appropriate social behaviour both within the kin group and the wider community. The Four Branches of the Mabinogi, for example, may be read as moral tales that highlight the heartache, humiliation, and disaster resultant from inappropriate social conduct and failure to respect bonds of kinship.[85] In the same vein, *Ystorya Bown o Hamtwn* (Bevis of Hampton), which is also included in the White Book, has been described as a pious romance 'about the founding of a family, in which marriage plays an important role'.[86] The Welsh Lives of Mary Magdalene and Martha, as we have seen, also focus on the Christian household and the importance of offering hospitality to others, while promising salvation and increased child-bearing capabilities to those who welcome the saints into their household. One can easily imagine that these *bucheddau* were considered to be suitable reading material for the whole family: not only Rhydderch ab Ieuan Llwyd who appears to have commissioned the White Book, but also his wives Margred ferch Gruffudd Gryg and Mawd ferch Sir William Clement, as well as his ten children.[87] Even in the sixteenth century Lives of the saints, such as *Buched Meir Vadlen* and *Buched Martha*, were considered to be both entertaining and edifying. A colophon in Llanstephan 117 names the scribe and hints at his motivation for copying such a collection of texts:

> Ieuan ap William ap dd: ap ejnws a jysgrivenodd y llyvyr hwn i gyd ari gost i hvn i gael o bobl y ddifyrwch o hono a lles yw heneidiav o hwn.[88]
>
> (Ieuan ap William ap D[afydd?] wrote this book, all at his own expense, so that people would get entertainment from it and that it might benefit their souls.)

The aim of this study has been to shed new light on the Middle Welsh Lives of Mary Magdalene and Martha and to highlight the importance and relevance of these religious texts within a lay context. One does not necessarily have to accept that these hagiographic texts were indicative of a renewed interest in the virgin life, or that they were read and enjoyed exclusively by young virgins and clerics (as previous readings have suggested). They may well have been read, or heard, copied and adapted for use by more than one kind of audience, but their context in the earliest extant manuscripts suggests a bias towards the pious family. They appear to have had a particular relevance for the lay household and may be read as containing relevant messages for the good Christian family as well as for all common sinners. The texts themselves would have been highly valued within the household and considered almost as holy relics, perhaps only being brought out on special occasions. To read or hear a reading of these Lives was to experience contact with the saints, and these particular biblical sisters, both the reformed harlot and the faithful hostess, who had experienced close personal relationships with Christ, were believed to be particularly powerful intercessors. Another 'foreign' saint whose Life was available in Middle Welsh and who was renowned for her intercessory powers forms the focus of the next chapter. An examination of the Welsh Life of Katherine will allow us to further develop suggestions put forward in this chapter concerning the intended audience of the Welsh Lives.

5

Buched Seint y Katrin: The Middle Welsh Life of Katherine of Alexandria and her Cult in Medieval Wales[1]

The cult of St Katherine of Alexandria transcended national barriers and enjoyed international popularity throughout Western medieval Europe.[2] In Wales devotion to Katherine may not have been actively promoted by the medieval dioceses of Wales in quite the same manner as the cults of some of the native saints, who enjoyed political promotion and cult status within their own particular dioceses (particularly during the late eleventh century and the twelfth). Nevertheless, by the fourteenth century Katherine appears to have become as fashionable a figure in Wales as she was elsewhere in Europe and her popularity increased towards the late Middle Ages. Her feast day on 25 November is recorded in the majority of late medieval Welsh calendars. However, in the *Vitae sanctorum Wallensium*, one of the earliest calendars, dating from about 1200, her feast has been added in a later hand, possibly in the mid-thirteenth century or even the fourteenth.[3] This seems to suggest that she was not well known in Wales until this period, when she became adopted as a popular patron and included in lists of predominantly Welsh saints. According to the Welsh genealogies recorded by Bartrum, the Welsh version of her name, Catrin (or Katrin), became increasingly popular in Wales, particularly between *c.*1350 and 1415.[4] This may be related to her increasing devotional profile from the fourteenth century onwards.

This chapter aims to provide a detailed overview of the cult of St Katherine in medieval Wales and synthesize as many of the extant Welsh sources as possible. It sets out to do this via the extant visual arts and church dedications, to be discussed directly below, and an examination of the textual evidence in the form of the Welsh prose Life, *Buched Seint y Katrin*, which constitutes the latter part of this chapter.[5] This peculiar prose version of Katherine's passion, its idiosyncrasies, tone and consumption will be analysed in some detail and it will be demonstrated how the Life is distinctive (or even unique). Consideration will also be given to its similarity to other versions of Katherine's Life (most notably an unusual fifteenth-century English verse Life which appears to have attracted even less attention then the Welsh *buchedd*). The extant medieval miscellanies, which contain the Middle Welsh Life of St Katherine, will be discussed and the popularity and representation of Katherine within a specifically Welsh context will be examined. However, in studying both the visual and textual evidence relating to the cult of St Katherine within Wales the aim is not to distil a 'caricature' of a distinctly Welsh Katherine from the available sources. On the contrary, it will be found that the cult of Katherine in medieval Wales displays much continuity with Katherine's cult in England and the rest of Europe. Thus, medieval Wales should be understood, not as a culturally isolated land, in which cult practice evolved peculiarly native mutations, but as a fully integrated member of the wider cultural currents effective across the whole of Christendom. Setting aside issues of national character or style, it would also be misleading to study the cult of Katherine within Wales as if it had a singular, clearly defined form. In Wales, as elsewhere, the figure of Katherine was multivalent and varied in relation to the differing social, cultural and regional contexts within which her cult was practised. Evidence for certain contexts (such as devotion to Katherine in the Welsh nunneries, for example) appears to have been lost, and inevitably the extant evidence leaves us with a fragmented, but nevertheless rich, picture of devotion to Katherine in Wales.

The lack of testamentary evidence from medieval Wales means that it is not possible to build up as detailed a picture of devotion to her as, for example, that which Katherine J. Lewis has presented for medieval England.[6] In particular, while the substantial testamentary evidence available for England indicates that iconic images of Katherine in wood, stone and alabaster existed in lay households and that she was also depicted on such household items as bowls, bed linen, wall hangings and jewellery, in Wales this particular kind of evidence from within the household is largely absent. Several visual representations of St Katherine have survived from medieval Wales, but virtually all of these are either associated with churches or found on or near religious sites. There is, however, a fairly wide range of extant material relating to the cult of St Katherine in Wales, which can be used to reconstruct the wider devotional and cultic environment in which the Welsh Life was read. For instance, individuals are known to have founded churches and hospitals in her honour or set up chantries as well as commemorating her by incorporating her image into the iconography displayed on their tombs or in medieval stained glass.

Visual representations

The surviving visual representations of Katherine extant in Wales date from the late fourteenth, fifteenth, and sixteenth centuries. Compared with images of other universal saints, Katherine has fared quite well in the medieval survivals from Wales. This is, no doubt, indicative of her popularity, and the fact that there were originally many more representations of her than there were of most other saints.[7] She appears as a single figure in various stained-glass windows and decorative panels on tombs, as well as in one full-length medieval wall painting. Iconic images carved in stone or moulded from pipe clay also exist and images of St Katherine or simply her iconographic emblem – the wheel – are also recorded on smaller items such as medieval seals, rings, and pilgrim badges. There are no elaborate visual narratives of the Life of St Katherine in Wales to compare with cycles of her Life surviving in English church wall paintings such as that at Sporle in Norfolk, for instance.[8] It is therefore not possible to draw any conclusions about the ways in which the complete narrative of her Life may have been rendered visually in medieval Wales, or to link *Buched Seint y Katrin* specifically with the visual sources.

A number of important medieval wall paintings have been discovered at the church of St Teilo, Llandeilo Tal-y-bont. These were discovered when fragments of plaster and lime-wash began to fall from the walls of the rapidly deteriorating building that had been badly vandalized and was suffering from subsidence. In 1985 The Museum of Welsh Life at St Ffagans, near Cardiff, was granted permission to dismantle the church for removal to the outdoor museum, and conservators from the University of Wales, Cardiff, painstakingly lifted the wall paintings from the decaying walls. There appear to have been at least four phases of decoration, two of which belong to the Pre-Reformation period. One of the earliest paintings is a full-length figure of St Katherine that was discovered on the east wall of the south aisle on the north side of the window (Plate 21). She is depicted holding a sword in her right hand and a large Katherine wheel emerges from behind her mantle on her left side. One can clearly see the 'danedd o dur' (teeth of steel) described in the Welsh Life on the rim of the wheel.[9] Whilst numerous saints are depicted holding the implements with which they were martyred, few hold both the instrument of their martyrdom (in Katherine's case the sword) and a weapon with which thousands of pagans were killed before their death.[10] All of the extant images from Wales include only one wheel, rather than the complicated machine consisting of four wheels that was invented by Maxentius' henchman Cursates. Katherine has long flowing hair, and wears a crown surrounded by an *aureola*. She is clad in a long pink dress with fashionably flared sleeves, and over her dress she wears a mantle. The saint has a high forehead and there are no remnants of a veil or wimple. The figure is boldly outlined in black. A. J. Parkinson has proposed that whilst the costume suggests a late fourteenth-century date, the details of the eyes indicate a slightly later date.[11] The beauty and simplicity of the boldly outlined figure is not dissimilar to an earlier figure of St Katherine found at Cold Overton in Leicestershire.[12]

The Llandeilo Tal-y-bont Katherine has been compared to representations of the saint in other media, some of which post-date the wall painting, for example, the early sixteenth-century woodcut published in Richard Pynson's *The Lif of Saincte Kateryne*.[13] In the woodcut the figure is reversed, so that Katherine holds the sword in her left hand and the wheel appears on her right. At her feet is the defeated Maxentius. The base of the Llandeilo mural is well worn and there appear to be no traces of her persecutor lying at her feet.[14] The woodcut in Pynson's Life is almost identical to the one that precedes the Breton Life of Katherine, printed in 1576 for Bernard de Leau, and other similar examples are extant.[15] However, since single figures of St Katherine are ubiquitous, it is almost impossible to pinpoint exact parallels and patterns of transmission. However, in the case of this representation of St Katherine, some tentative suggestions have been made. William Gefferey, who died in 1503, left £6. 6*s*. 8*d*. to the church at Llandeilo Tal-y-bont. He also left a number of books, which included woodcut illustrations, to Pilton church and the church library at Swansea.[16] Although these do not contain identical illustrations, it has been suggested that the closest parallels for the passion cycle at Llandeilo Tal-y-bont are woodcut illustrations.[17]

Katherine is also depicted holding both a sword and a wheel in a late fifteenth-century stained-glass window in the north chapel of St Stephen's church at Old Radnor (Plate 22).[18] Once again Katherine is crowned Christ's virginal bride and has long flowing yellow hair. She wears neither a veil nor a wimple. An elaborately decorated yellow mantle covers her simple red dress and she clutches the spiked wheel in her left hand and the sword in her right hand. The figure is set against a background of *roses ensoleillées*, the badge of Edward IV (1461–83), and above the figure is a small *Agnus*

Dei. St Katherine is also depicted with a large spiked wheel emerging from her left side in late medieval stained glass at Llansanffraid Glan Conwy.[19] Alongside St Katherine is a portrait of John the Baptist. Although it is possible that the glass has been repositioned, Katherine does appear to have been associated with John the Baptist, perhaps because John was one of the most famed victims of beheading. In England, images of Katherine often appear on the alabaster heads of John the Baptist, which became popular with the laity in the late Middle Ages.[20] Katherine is depicted alongside a number of other saints, including native Welsh saints, in the tracery lights of the east window at the church of St Tyrnog, Llandyrnog, Denbighshire. She is accompanied by SS. Marchell of Llanfarchell (Tyrnog's sister), Gwenfrewy of Holywell and Frideswide of Oxford. In this instance we cannot rule out the possibility that the labels identifying the saints were added at a later date.[21] However, the iconography of St Katherine, at least, is unmistakeable. Extant panels of late medieval glass from the Church of St Cystennin, Llangystennin, include an image of Katherine holding a sword and a wheel alongside St George in full armour, St Peter with his keys, Christ rising from the tomb, and a mitred figure which has been interpreted as St Nicholas. The glass is no longer *in situ*. I tracked it down to a safe in the Church of St Michael and All Angels, Llandudno Junction.

The Life of St George has a great deal in common with the Life of Katherine: he too is summoned to sacrifice to Roman gods and when he refuses he is detained by a heathen ruler, tortured in a variety of ways including being strapped to a wheel with knife-like blades, and eventually he is decapitated.[22] If Mostyn Lewis and Madeleine Gray are correct in assuming that the mitred figure is St Nicholas,[23] then we have another saint from Llangystennin whose Life has parallels with St Katherine: Nicholas, like Katherine, exudes healing oil, although in Nicholas's case the oil is expelled from his head, rather than his breasts. Jacobus de Voragine drew comparisons between the two for their production of oil in his Life of St Katherine in the *Legenda aurea*. As we have seen in the previous chapter, St Katherine appears alongside other female saints' Lives in Welsh manuscripts, and similarly she is depicted with other virgin martyrs (Barbara, Margaret and Dorothy) in a glass panel that forms part of the vast east window at the Parish Church of All Saints, Gresford.[24] Thomas Stanley, Earl of Derby, commissioned the window in 1500. One might expect that his wife, Margaret Beaufort, would have influenced the scheme. However, in 1499 she had taken a vow of chastity and moved to Collyweston. St Katherine appears to have been one of Margaret Beaufort's favourite saints and she could quite well have been one of Thomas Stanley's favourites as well.[25] Among the effects of Margaret's private chapel was a cope worked with the figure of St Katherine, and she had an image of the saint in the closet next to her bedchamber.[26]

There was also a portrait of St Katherine in a medieval stained-glass window at Bangor Cathedral. Unfortunately the window is no longer extant, but it is recorded as depicting St Katherine alongside St Dwynwen, one of the daughters of Brychan Brycheiniog whom we encountered in Chapter 2. Browne Willis described the window depicting Katherine and Dwynwen in 1721 as bearing an inscription revealing the name of its donor, Rhisiart Cyffin, who became Dean of Bangor Cathedral *c.*1475.[27] Cyffin is described as 'the captain of Dwynwen and Deiniol' by the poet Guto'r Glyn who also refers to the extensive repair work undertaken during Cyffin's period as Dean. He seems to have been responsible for renovating the choir and eastern end of the cathedral and re-roofing this section with lead.[28] He appears to have had a special devotion to St Katherine, since not only did he choose to commission a portrait of her in stained glass, but he also founded a chantry in the cathedral in her honour. The chantry was endowed with tithes from the parishes of Llangoed, Llaniestyn and Llanfihangel Tynfelin and Rhisiart Cyffin was buried there, in the south transept, in 1502.[29]

An image of Katherine carved in stone is to be found on the tower of the Church of St Giles at Wrexham. The tower, which was completed around 1524, is considered to be one of the seven wonders of Wales, and twenty-seven of the thirty niches on the tower still contain large sculptures of saints. Katherine holding her wheel and her sword is positioned on the east face of the tower. A chronicle in Peniarth 20 records that on the feast of St Katherine in 1330 the steeple at Wrexham fell down.[30] Not surprisingly, when the building was restored an effigy of Katherine was included in the perpendicular tower and a chapel in the church was also dedicated to her.

Images of Katherine and the wheel have also been found on smaller objects such as rings and seals at various sites in Wales. A ring depicting St Katherine was found at the Cistercian abbey of Cymer, and was described in *Archaeologia Cambrensis* in 1866. Unfortunately the whereabouts of the ring are now unknown.[31] In 1935 a small clay-pipe figurine of St Katherine was found in a field at Newtown, Montgomeryshire. It is thought to date from the late fourteenth or early fifteenth century and is assumed to have come from the church at Newtown. The figure which measures a little over three inches shows Katherine wearing a long robe resting her right hand on a sword and holding a book in her other hand. The wheel rests at her feet. Unfortunately the head of the statue is missing, but it can be seen that Katherine has long, flowing hair.[32] The image, which is made from pipe clay formed in a mould and fired, would have been far cheaper to produce than a statue carved in stone and gives an idea of how people of lesser means could, nonetheless, afford to own a representation of their favoured saint.[33] An early fourteenth-century seal depicting Katherine holding a wheel in her left hand and a sword in her right hand was found in the parish of Mathern. The legend reads 'SC'A KATERINA ORA PRO ME'. Since there is nothing to indicate the ownership of this personal seal, it is not possible to ascertain why Katherine was chosen specifically as a patron. She appears to have been a relatively popular choice for inclusion on seal matrices elsewhere in Europe, since similar examples are found on personal, ecclesiastical and monastic seals in Italy, Germany, France, Sweden, England and Scotland.[34] Jeremy Davis suggests that seals depicting popular saints such as St Katherine would have formed part of a seal-engraver's general stock rather than have been engraved to order, and that the Mathern seal was probably mislaid by an individual visiting the bishop of Llandaff's palace at Mathern.[35] A late medieval pilgrim badge depicting a wheel with knife-like blades was found on Newgale beach, Pembrokeshire, by Colin Scale. Other artefacts associated with pilgrimages have been discovered at Newgale, and possibly indicate that this may have been a landing place connecting with the pilgrim routes of Pembrokeshire. Although rare within Wales, similar pilgrim badges are found in England, and a significant number of souvenirs depicting the Katherine wheel have been discovered in London.[36]

St Katherine also appears on a number of alabaster tomb panels including the Bulkeley tomb in the parish church of St Mary and St Nicholas at Beaumaris, where it was originally placed next to a figure of St George.[37] She also appears on the tomb of Richard Herbert of Coldbrook in the priory church at Abergavenny and the tomb of the Whites at St Mary's Church, Tenby. On the tomb of John White and his wives Margaret Phelp and Christina Einon at Tenby Katherine is depicted clutching her sword in one hand, whilst she jabs Maxentius in the guts with the tip of her sword and tramples on him (Plate 23). Images of Katherine defeating Maxentius and using her sword as a weapon are quite common outside of Wales. Karen A. Winstead's work on images of Katherine in English manuscripts highlights a number of examples of visual representations of Katherine in which she not only stabs Maxentius in the side, the cheek or the groin, but also wields her sword above her head ready for combat. The sword may also be considered a symbol of her sovereignty.[38] John White appears to have chosen the image of St Katherine and the other saintly figures depicted on his tomb, as well as the image of himself during his lifetime, since the area on the tomb where the date of his death was to be inserted has been left blank. His first wife, Margaret, and his father, Thomas White, both died in 1482, and it is therefore probable that John commissioned the tombs and chose the iconography at that time, with the intention of being buried there himself.[39] Huw Meirion Edwards's work on Welsh elegiac poetry has demonstrated that literary memorials to the dead were occasionally commissioned, composed and authorized whilst their subjects were still alive.[40] One might expect that reasonably wealthy individuals who held prominent posts in society would also be keen to have a say in their final visual memorials – their tombs. Tombs acted as both a status symbol and also a spiritual investment. Saintly figures such as St Katherine were an obvious choice for a tomb, since, as we shall see, in her final prayer Katherine requests that all who have faith in her and commemorate her passion, be granted eternal salvation. All those who look upon an image of St Katherine with her sword and wheel are reminded of her passion, and the events of her Life are crystallised in a single image.[41] In addition to being reminded of Katherine's martyrdom, the viewer is also reminded to pray for the soul of the dead person within the memorial. On John White's tomb two female figures kneel at Katherine's side in an attitude of prayer. Thus when prayers were not actually being offered in church for the salvation of his soul, visually on his tomb prayers were continually (in the process of) being offered and Katherine was permanently worshipped. Other figures on adjacent panels are also depicted in prayer. These may well represent his wife and children, or other members of his family, or they may possibly represent the congregation.

Church dedications

At present there are seventeen churches dedicated to St Katherine in Wales, but only three of these are medieval foundations: St Katherine's Church at Cricieth in Gwynedd, the parish church at Granston, Pembrokeshire and Llan-faes on Anglesey.[42] Although the present-day church at Llan-faes is a Victorian building, it replaces a medieval structure, which appears to have been dedicated to St Katherine, possibly from the thirteenth century. It is referred to in *Valor Ecclesiasticus* as 'Ecclia Sce Katine Dec' and the advowson of the church at Llan-faes belonged to Penmon priory.[43] In a document relating to the visitation of the Bishop of Bangor in 1623 Llan-faes is referred to as 'Llan Saint y Katherin'.[44] Interestingly there is another Llan-faes near Brecon which also appears to have had a Katherine dedication. John Leland (1506–52) refers to the church and hospital of 'S. Catarine' in the parish of Llan-faes:

> The paroch of Llanuays. Llan Chirch . . . It standeth betwixt the river of Uske and Tyrtarelle Brooke, that [is] about the lower ende of the toun of Brekenok. In the est [east] suburbe ys an hospitale with a chapel.[45]

Very little is known of this hospital and it is not listed in Knowles and Hadcock's *Medieval Religious Houses England and Wales*, although they provide a list of hospitals in Wales.[46] It is possible that St Katherine's hospital was a relatively new foundation in Leland's day. In 1527/8 John Richard, of Brecon, left 12*d.* to the hospital of St Katherine and a further 26*s.* 8*d.* for the building of the hospital.[47]

Uncovering extinct chapels once dedicated to St Katherine is somewhat more difficult. There was a chapel of St Katherine on the small island still called St Catherine's off Tenby. This was mentioned in a survey of the town in 1586.[48] There appears to have been another chapel in Pembrokeshire dedicated to Katherine at Milford Haven. The chapel was derelict by 1644 and was being used as a powder magazine.[49] Christopher Saxton's county maps of 1579 record only three 'Sct Katerens': at Granston, St Katherine's Island, and Cricieth.[50] It has been suggested that an earlier church at Cricieth was originally dedicated to one or more Welsh saints and that the present church was rededicated to St Katherine in the thirteenth century.[51] This seems to be supported by the presence of a holy well in the area, known as 'Ffynnon y Saint' (the Well of the Saints), which only became associated with Katherine in the modern period; on Easter mornings keys as well as pins were thrown into the well 'to solace St Katherine'.[52] She does not seem to have been frequently associated with holy wells, although, as we shall see, the *buchedd* emphasizes her healing properties and this is reiterated in the writings of contemporary poets. I have been unable to locate any wells in Wales actually dedicated to Katherine, and the well at Cricieth seems to be the only one associated with her.

As mentioned above, it is likely that the church at Cricieth was originally dedicated to another saint, rather than to St Katherine.[53] Gresham and Ward suggest that the dedications to Katherine at Cricieth and Llan-faes may well be attributed to Llywelyn ap Iorwerth (1173–1240) who was responsible for building the castle at Cricieth and establishing a major port at Llan-faes.[54] If this were the case, his choice of an internationally popular saint, who was very much in vogue in the thirteenth century, would have been 'in keeping with Llywelyn's modernistic approach'.[55] Given the role of the Norman nobility in disseminating the cult of St Katherine, Llywelyn may also have been aware that devotion to her was part of an expression of power and status, which he also wished to impress upon others.[56]

Thus we can see that, despite the comparative dearth of testamentary sources, there is enough evidence remaining to give an idea of how popular the cult and image of St Katherine was in medieval Wales. This popularity is further underlined by the frequency with which her Welsh Life is to be found in manuscripts. For the remainder of this chapter we will consider the content and context of this Life, exploring the ways in which the Welsh text presents her in ways that diverge from the more standard narrative current in later medieval Europe.

The Middle Welsh Life of Katherine

As we have already noted, the Life of St Katherine was first translated into Middle Welsh some time before the mid-fourteenth century. In all, the Middle Welsh Life of Katherine is now preserved in seventeen handwritten manuscripts that date from the mid-fourteenth to the nineteenth century (see Table 1).[57] All of the Welsh manuscripts preserve a similar version of the Life, although their orthography differs and rewording, summarizing and even certain omissions can be found.[58] J. E. Caerwyn Williams identified three recensions.[59] Any significant differences will be referred to below, but, on the whole, the Life as it appears in all the Welsh manuscripts narrates the same events, in the same order. Significantly for our purposes, they share the same peculiarities which are not to be found in the majority of the Latin and vernacular versions of Katherine's legend, including the Irish and Breton versions of her passion, thus presenting an unusual version of the Life of St Katherine, certain details of which can be considered unique.[60] In order to demonstrate this, we shall now examine the ways in which the Welsh Life differs from other more popular and (in scholarly terms) more well-known versions of Katherine's Life, including the Vulgate, the *Legenda aurea,* and the Middle English versions found in the *South English Legendary* and Mirk's *Festial.*[61] Like these versions of the Life *Buched Seint y Katrin* focuses primarily on Katherine's (Catrin's) *passio* and does not describe her mystical marriage to Christ.[62]

The narrator is not named and it is not claimed that he (or she) was an eyewitness to the events recounted. The reference to Catrin's parentage is so brief that it is confusing: 'Merch y vrenhin constantinobyl. Alexand^r y gel6ir yn llatin.' (Daughter of the king of Constantinople, called Alexand(er/ria) in Latin).[63] Rees and Bell take 'Alexand^r' to refer to her father, Alexander, rather than his kingdom Alexandria.[64] An alternative reading could be that the author/translator assumes that 'Alexand^r' is the Latin name for Constantinople. In the vast majority of Katherine legends, Katherine is the daughter of Costus, one of the kings of Alexandria. She is usually orphaned. However, since *Buched Seint y Katrin* does not mention this, one could assume that her father is still alive. The Auchinleck *Seynt Katerine* and the Northern Homily Cycle suggest that Katherine's father is still alive at the time of her martyrdom, and this is specifically stated in the unusual Middle English account found in Oxford, Bodley MS 779.[65] The Welsh *buchedd* refers only briefly to Catrin's father in order to establish her royal status. He is not mentioned again in the narrative and no reference is made to her mother. In an early fifteenth-century Welsh poem by Siôn ap Hywel, Catrin's mother is referred to as 'Leoneisa', but this name does not occur in the *buchedd.*[66] Llanstephan 28 at first appears to contain a brief reference to her foster mother, 'y mamaeth', which has been crossed out. However, on closer inspection, it becomes apparent that this is part of a line from the Middle Welsh Life of Margaret of Antioch, which claims that Margaret was reared by her foster mother following the death of her real mother. This is obviously a scribal error. Having begun a new page, Gutun Owain, the scribe of

Llanstephan 28, started to copy a section from *Buched Margred*.[67] No extended genealogy is given in *Buched Seint y Katrin*, and it is not claimed that the saint is related to Constantine the Great, as in other versions of the Life.[68]

No details relating to Catrin's education are provided, which is very unusual. For example, the *Northern Homily Life* and an anonymous fifteenth-century verse Life are the only Middle English versions which make no reference at all to her having been educated.[69] Hence there is no opportunity to suggest that Catrin rejects her secular education for religious instruction, although, again, this is a point that is made explicit in other versions of the Life.[70] As Catrin, unlike Katherine of the *Legenda aurea*, for example, is therefore not presented as having received a university-style education, this could be taken as an indication that Catrin is deliberately being presented as a less academic figure in order to render her a more accessible model for lay readers. She is, nevertheless, described as being inherently wise and, as we shall see, capable of outwitting the most prestigious philosophers in the land. In the Welsh Life her wisdom stems from her unwavering faith rather than a classical and religious education.

The legend begins, as do most of the Welsh Lives of female saints (and of virgin martyr saints more generally), shortly after the saint has reached puberty, or marriageable age. According to Peniarth 5 and the earlier Welsh manuscripts, Catrin is eighteen years old when she decides to dedicate her virginity to God. This agrees with the Vulgate version and the vast majority of the Lives of Katherine. However, in Llanstephan 28, Peniarth 27, Cardiff 2.629 and Llanstephan 117 Catrin is twelve years old.[71] As already noted, Catrin's conversion and mystical marriage to Christ are absent from the Welsh text. This is, perhaps, not surprising since, for example, these elements did not become a particularly popular part of her Life in Middle English until the fifteenth century.[72] What is surprising, however, is that at no point does the *buchedd* refer to Christ as Catrin's spiritual spouse. Her love of God is frequently stated,[73] but Christ is not specifically described as her lover or eternal husband, in which respect the Welsh Life deviates from most other versions.[74] Again, this may be intended to make Catrin appear less like a nun or other professed religious woman, and more like a lay person.[75]

When Maxen organizes a great feast and instructs all the inhabitants of his country to make offerings to his pagan gods (in the Welsh text referred to as Apolin/Apollo, Thervagawnt/ Termagant and Iolkyn), Catrin does not go willingly to Alexandria to remonstrate with Maxen, as in the standard versions, but is summoned when she fails to arrive at the sacrifice. Catrin is thrown into prison where she is entertained by angels and it is at this point in the narrative that two formulae occur: one that describes Maxen's anger and frustration prior to Catrin's imprisonment, and the other that refers to the indescribable scene of joy and merriment in the prison:

> Maxen a littyaud yn vaur pan dy6at hi o du6. Ac yna y gelwis ef atta6 rei o^{e} wassannaeth6yr. ac erchi . . .[76]

> (Maxen became very angry when she referred to God and summoned some of his assistants and requested . . .)

The first formula occurs three times in the text. On the first occasion, it precedes Catrin's imprisonment; on the second occasion, it is a prelude to a severe beating suffered by Catrin; and finally, a slight variation on the formula precedes a description of the torturing of the queen.[77] On each occasion Maxen consults his advisors and the formula introduces a violent scene. However, Catrin is not described as suffering during her imprisonment. As in the majority of the Katherine legends, Catrin is imprisoned twice and a bright light illuminates her dark cell; however, the Welsh Life places particular emphasis on the joy experienced in the prison:

> Yr egylyon a doethant attei. a ry6 le6enyd a 6naethant yr vor6yn hyt nat oes dyn yn y byt a alley y dy6edut. na challon y vedylya6. nac yscolheic y esgriuenu.[78]

> (The angels came to her and gave the maiden such joy as no man in the world could describe, nor heart contemplate, nor scholar convey in writing.)

Unlike other versions, no mention is made of Catrin's wounds in prison; the angels come to entertain her rather than anoint her injuries. It is the rapturous noise, rather than the bright light, coming from the jail that attracts Porffir's attention during Catrin's second period of incarceration. Despite the reintroduction of the formula, claiming that no man can describe such a joyous scene, Porffir immediately hurries off to see the queen and describes what he has witnessed: 'ac ynteu a aeth at y vrenhines. ac a vanaga6d idi y lle6enyd a gigleu ef yn yr eol'.[79] (and he went to the queen and told her about the joy he had heard in the jail).

An abbreviated account of Catrin's debate with the philosophers follows her first period of imprisonment. They are here described as 'athra6on goreu oe wlat o dilechtit. ac o ystronomy' (the best scholars in logic and astronomy in his country) and no specific number of scholars is given.[80] They do not complain that it is far too easy for them to argue with a girl, only that Catrin should begin the debate. The argument that takes place between Catrin and one of the philosophers centres on the miracle of the virgin birth and Christ's humanity and divinity as in other versions. In line with the omission of references to her academic education it is not claimed that Catrin is familiar with the work of Homer, Aristotle, Galen, and Plato: she is merely described as 'mor6yn doeth' (a wise maiden).[81] When she suggests that the principal philosopher becomes her disciple, he is converted to Christianity and the other scholars immediately follow suit.

Maxen offers to take Catrin as his wife. He is, of course, already married and already has a queen, but this is not one of the reasons given for Catrin's refusal. Indeed, at this point in the narrative, Maxen's wife has not even been mentioned. The audience is not introduced to the queen until she visits Catrin during her second period of incarceration. Catrin rejects Maxen's proposal and empty promises, pointing out rather sardonically that he has only just threatened to hang her, and reiterates her total devotion to the Lord. Catrin is then beaten mercilessly and a vivid description of her bruises is provided. They are compared to violets in a topos common in ascetic writings:[82]

> Heb ohir kymer6ch yr ynvyt honn a dody6ch hi 6rth brenn yn r6ym. a meyd6ch hi a g6yeil hyt ban debyccoch ch6i y mar6. ar

g6yr dr6c hynny ae maeda6d hi yny reda6d y g6aet allan oe chorff. ym pob lle mal y rettey d6fyr y gaeaf. Hyny yttoed y chna6t g6ynt [sic.] hi yn velyn vegys y violet.[83]

(Without delay, take this fool and tie her to a tree, and beat her with rods until she appears to be dead. And those evil men beat her until blood flowed from every part of her body, just as water flows in winter, and until her white skin became yellow, [with bruises] like violet[s].)

The Welsh *buchedd* does not mention that Maxen has temporarily left the palace when Porffir and the queen visit Catrin during her second period of incarceration; only that they visit her in secret, in the hope that the king will not find out about their visit. They are subsequently converted to Christianity and the queen immediately goes to see Maxen and informs him of their visit, telling him that he is mistreating Catrin and that she no longer believes in Termagant and Apollo. He orders his men to beat the queen, hang her by her hair, cut off her breasts and feed her body to the dogs. When Porffir scorns Maxen and criticizes him for not burying his queen's body, Maxen orders his men to kill the steward. At this point, *Buched Seint y Katrin* differs significantly from the majority of the other versions of Katherine's Life, since Porffir decides to retaliate, picks up a ladder, slays four thousand of Maxen's men and wounds another four thousand. Maxen is terrified of Porffir and believes that he too is about to be slain by the steward. However, Catrin intervenes and reminds Porffir of Christ's suffering. She suggests that it is inappropriate for him to fight back and recommends that he suffer martyrdom gracefully. Porffir casts down the ladder, which breaks into pieces, and submits to Maxen, who commands Porffir and the queen to be decapitated. In Cardiff 2.629 Maxen disposes of Porffir and the queen in the same manner as the philosophers: he burns them to death.[84] Angels deliver their souls to Christ.

In the vast majority of versions of the Life of St Katherine, Porphirius does not retaliate. The Welsh Life is unique in Porffir's choice of weapon, but there are a few other versions of the Life which relate the incident. In a thirteenth-century

German verse Life, Porphirius slays four thousand of Maxentius' men with a pole and is reprimanded for his behaviour by Katherine.[85] However, the German Life does not agree with the Welsh *buchedd* in other respects. A closer parallel for the Welsh Life is to be found in an unusual fifteenth-century English verse Life in which Porphirius grabs a shield and a sword and slays four thousand of Maxentius' men. Maxentius is terrified and fears for his own Life, but Porphirius throws down his shield when Katherine advises him not to fight. This English Life will be discussed in greater detail below. All of the Welsh manuscripts agree in their description of this incident and refer to Porffir's weapon as a ladder ('ysgaul/yscol/ysgol'). The description of the ladder breaking into pieces precedes the description of the broken wheels, where the same word 'dryllev' is used to describe the fragments. This perhaps conjures up an image of the wooden rungs on the ladder smashing as the ladder hits the ground, in similar fashion to the way in which the wooden spokes of the Katherine wheel break into fragments as the knife-like steel blades are hurled into the crowd. Another possible interpretation is that 'ysgaul' represents a mistranslation or a copyist's error. One could speculate that the word that should have appeared in the Welsh text, or indeed may have appeared in the original version, is 'ysguyd', the Middle Welsh word for shield. However, although a shield is a suitable object for self-defence, on its own it is not an appropriate weapon with which to slay four thousand men and injure another four thousand.

Another way in which the Welsh Life differs from the standard narrative is that it changes the order in which the events are related. In *Buched Seint y Katrin* the queen and Porffir are disposed of before Cursattes conceives of the idea of torturing Catrin on four wheels with metal teeth. Therefore the queen is tortured and decapitated before Maxen offers to spare Catrin's life 'o achaus dy decceti' (because of your beauty).[86] This could imply that in the Welsh Life Maxen's motivation for disposing of the queen is somewhat different from in the other Lives, since he does this at the first possible opportunity. Having rid himself of the queen, he is presumably free to marry Catrin. However, he does not propose to her again, and he only offers to spare her life on condition that she worships his pagan gods. The narrator emphasizes that this promise is false, and Catrin also accuses Maxen of lying. His primary motivation is to convert Catrin to his faith and break her devotion to Christianity, rather than to pollute her virginity.

In the Welsh text Catrin prays on the wheel that God may show mercy on her soul. She does not request that the wheels are broken and believes that she is about to be baptized in her own blood. The number of onlookers killed by fragments of the broken wheel is yet another example of the way in which the Welsh Life deviates from the standard Life of St Katherine. The number of pagans slaughtered by fragments of the wheel is usually forty thousand, but Catrin's wheel slays fifty thousand.[87] Ieuan ap William, the scribe of Cardiff 2.629, has sketched a small wheel in the margin near the account of Cursattes and his invention as though to act as a marker and draw the reader's attention to this particularly important section in the narrative.[88] The poet Lewys Môn (*fl.*1485–1527) refers to Catrin's tenacity in the face of imminent torture on the wheel in one of his poems, but he does not mention the number of pagans killed during the spectacle.[89]

Before she is beheaded, Catrin asks her executioner to delay his task so as to grant her enough time for her final prayer. She requests that God grant salvation for all good Christians, and heal all those who visit her tomb. She asks God to forgive her tormentors in words that provide a direct parallel with Christ's final words on the Cross (Luke xxiii:34): 'madeu vdunt eu ffolinep h6nn cany vdunt beth y maent yn y wneuthur'[90] (forgive them this foolishness for they know not what they do). Then she tells her executioner to behead her and milk, rather than blood, flows from the wound. As noted by de Voragine in the *Legenda aurea* version of her Life, this parallels St Paul's martyrdom in the Apocryphal Acts of St Paul where milk is described as flowing from Paul's severed head.[91] Angels arrive to guide her soul to heaven and her body is buried on Mount Sinai. Four streams of oil, flowing from her breasts, issue forth from her grave and heal innumerable sick people who visit the site.[92]

The detail provided in the Welsh Life here is very unusual. Oil usually flows from Katherine's tomb and from her bones, but not from her breasts. In the Middle English version of the legend which seems to be closely connected to the Welsh version oil is also said to issue from her breasts, as discussed below. But it is only in the Welsh version of the legend that this seems to become a standard element. This contention is further supported by the fact that the image of oil flowing from St Katherine's breasts was certainly current amongst medieval Welsh poets who demonstrate a familiarity with the Welsh version of Katherine's passion. For example, Lewys Glyn Cothi, in a poem praising Gwilym ap Gwallter and his wife Siwan Du, refers to the vigorous flow of oil from St Catrin's breasts, and associates this with the generous quantity of wine that he receives at Gwilym and Siwan's house.[93] Lewys Môn also refers to the oil exuding from Catrin's tomb in an elegy to the saint's namesake, Catrin ferch Morgan of Radyr, although he does not specifically mention that the oil flows from St Catrin's breasts.[94] In two other poems Lewys Glyn Cothi associates Catrin with wine and compares Elin ferch Llywelyn and Gwenhwyfar wraig Gruffudd Derwas to St Catrin because they provide him with copious quantities of different wines.[95] Praising married noblewomen for their hospitality and generosity in providing wine, and comparing them to female saints, are common *topoi* in medieval Welsh poetry. However, Catrin in particular appears to have been associated with wine, generosity and fecundity, and this seems to have been linked to the oil that flowed from her body.[96] Wine, water, oil and milk, on occasions, appear to be interchangeable in poetic imagery, and Welsh holy wells associated with saints are frequently described as flowing with milk or wine.[97] The famous Marian holy well at Pen-rhys, which is discussed in Chapter 1, is one such example. Rhisiart ap Rhys describes the spring water as 'llaeth i redeg/ o'th fronnau doeth, forwyn deg' (milk running from your wise breasts, pretty virgin), and elsewhere in the poem he refers to the water as white wine.[98] Christine James suggests that, although Rhisiart's description does not have to be taken literally, it may imply that the water once flowed from the statue's breasts.[99] Indeed, a similar fountain at Llanfihangel y

Bont-faen in the Vale of Glamorgan consists of a stone carving of a bare-breasted figure of St Anne, the Virgin Mary's mother; at one time, water used to flow from the holes in the statue's breasts.[100] The fifteenth-century poet Siôn ap Hywel also mentions Catrin's breasts in association with healing in a poem about the saint. He refers specifically to her 'iach fron' (healthy breast), and hopes that she will listen to his plea for salvation since she herself suffered physical pain and torment.[101] In this context, it is not surprising that the Welsh Life of Katherine claims that the oil flows from Catrin's breasts, or that this rather unusual bodily fluid was considered to have healing powers.

Within virgin martyr Lives, including the Life of St Katherine, breasts more usually feature as a site of torture than of healing. For instance, as was mentioned in Chapter 2, both SS. Agatha and Barbara have their breasts amputated because, like Catrin, they refuse to sacrifice to pagan gods and refuse to marry their tormentors.[102] Agatha's breasts regrow and heal miraculously during the period of time she spends in prison. However, in the standard Life of Katherine it is the queen, rather than the saint, who has her nipples and breasts brutally removed by the tyrant.[103] Although in the Welsh version it is not clear if Maxen carries out his plan to amputate the queen's breasts since, having ordered his men to do so, he is interrupted by Porffir's protestations and a massacre ensues. There is certainly no specific description of the event.

This method of torture is displaced from the saint to another character, and one could argue that it would make more sense if Catrin's breasts, rather than the queen's, were removed. It is almost as if the narrator of the Welsh *buchedd* assumes that Catrin's breasts had previously been injured in some way, and that the healing oil is indicative of their wholesome and healthy state following the saint's death. Could the poet Siôn ap Hywel have been aware of this when he referred to Catrin's 'healthy breast'? One could tentatively suggest that the additional detail at the end of the Welsh Life stems from a confusion between the descriptions of Catrin's torture and the queen's ordeal. Indeed, the narrative's treatment of the queen in the *buchedd* is confused and sometimes contradictory. For instance, Maxen asks Catrin to marry him when he already has a wife, rather than waiting until after her death as in other versions. Similarly, the queen returns to be decapitated with Porffir, despite the fact that the *buchedd* has just provided details relating to her intended torture and execution as well as a discussion on her burial. Presumably Maxen only threatens to throw her body to the dogs. In other less concise versions of the Life of Katherine, for example, the late Middle English prose Life, the queen has a much clearer and more significant role to play than in the Welsh *buchedd*.[104] Although no account of Katherine's Life exists in which her breasts are removed, we could speculate that there may once have been a version in which Katherine, rather than the queen, was tortured in this way, or at least this may have been one of the ways in which oral versions of her legend may have been (mis)remembered.

Although, the Welsh *buchedd* contains a number of deviations from the standard Life of St Katherine, and the narrative seems disordered in places, there is, as has already been noted, an extant Middle English verse Life which closely resembles it.[105] The English Life is extant in two fifteenth-century manuscripts, Cambridge, University Library, MS Ff.2.38 and Oxford, Bodleian Library, MS Rawlinson Poetry 34.[106] The version in Rawlinson Poetry 34 is approximately sixty lines shorter than the same text in the Cambridge manuscript, but otherwise the texts are virtually identical. As mentioned earlier, this unusual verse Life of St Katherine seems to have attracted little scholarly attention.[107] It shares a number of peculiarities with the Welsh *buchedd*. Both texts refer to a Latin original and very likely derive from a common source.[108] A similarly brief and confusing description of Katherine's parentage is provided: 'The kyngys doghtur [daughter] of Costentyne, / Of Alysaundur, as seythe the latyne',[109] and no specific details are provided relating to Katherine's education. As in the Welsh Life, Katherine is summoned by Maxentius and she refuses to sacrifice to his gods (here referred to as Tarmagaunt/Termagant, Apolyne/Apollo and Mahowne/Mahound). A similarly graphic description of Katherine's beating is provided, although her bruises are not compared to violets as in the Welsh text.

Angels twice entertain her in prison and on both occasions a similar formula is repeated to describe the indescribable scenes of joy:

> Aungels come to hur adowne
> And soche yoye made in prysone,
> Bothe be day and be nyghte,
> That all þe men y-borne ne myȝt
> That yoye telle nor that blys
> That was ther-yn, wyth-owt mys.[110]

> (Angels came down to her
> and such joy was had in the prison,
> both during the day and at night,
> that no man could accurately describe
> the joy nor the bliss
> that was experienced there.)

As in the Welsh text, Porphirius goes to inform the queen of what he has heard, rather than what he has seen, and Maxentius is presumably still in Alexandria when they visit Katherine. Maxentius also offers to make Katherine his wife before he disposes of the queen. Following the torturing of the queen, Porphirius complains that she has not been given a proper burial and, as we have already seen, when Maxentius commands that Porphirius be slain, the steward grabs a shield and a sword and slays four thousand of Maxentius' men. The English text, however, does not claim that he injures a further four thousand men. Porphyrius and the queen are not decapitated; instead they are drawn by Maxentius' horses. As in the Welsh *buchedd*, the queen is disposed of prior to the incident involving the four wheels, rather than afterwards, as is more usually the case. Katherine believes that she is to be baptized in her own blood, but angels break the wheels and the fragments kill forty thousand spectators (compared to fifty thousand in the Welsh *buchedd*). Katherine's final prayer resembles the Welsh version, and she asks forgiveness for her tormentors. Following her burial on Mount Sinai, four streams of oil flow from her tomb. The English text also claims that the oil flows from Katherine's breasts: 'Fowre stremys, sothe hyt ys, / Renne owt of the tombe, ywys, / Of oyle fro the maydenys breste.'[111] (Four streams of oil, from the maiden's breast, so it is, ran out of the tomb).

The resemblance between the English verse Life and the Welsh *buchedd* is far too striking to be attributed to mere coincidence. Although one is written in verse and the other is a prose text, they agree fairly closely in terms of content and order of events, and they appear to have been produced for similar audiences. They both contain a high percentage of dialogue, and have a tendency to summarize the lengthy theological debates. In both passions the action is fast moving and punctuated by the various violent episodes. Both the Welsh and the English texts include an additional outbreak of violence, since they recount the incident in which Porffir/Porphirius murders four thousand men before he is put to death. Bray compares Porphirius' reaction with Peter's attempted reprisal against the high priest, when Peter picks up a sword in retaliation, but is reprimanded by Christ (John xviii:10–11).[112] There are, however, a number of minor differences between the Welsh and the English texts and it is more likely that they stem from a common original than that one is a translation of the other. Middle Welsh hagiographic texts are usually assumed to be translations or adaptations of earlier Latin or vernacular equivalents, but in this case the Welsh *buchedd* antedates the English text. Nevertheless, the verse Life is unlikely to be a translation of the prose *buchedd*. Bray suggests that the two extant English manuscripts were not made from closely affiliated texts and that they probably constitute the remains of a larger manuscript tradition.[113] Rarely are the Welsh Lives as idiosyncratic as the Welsh version of the Life of St Katherine, for they normally follow the standard Lives of the internationally popular saints.[114] However, *Buched Seint y Katrin* appears to stem from a more unusual account of Katherine's Life that was current in both Wales and England in the fourteenth and fifteenth centuries. Although it apparently enjoyed much more currency and popularity in Wales than in England, given that the Welsh version survives in nine manuscripts which predate 1550, whereas the English version is only extant in two (as compared to over twenty manuscripts of the English prose Life, for example).

McSparran and Robinson suggest that Cambridge Ff.2.38 which contains this unusual Middle English version of the Life of Katherine 'was intended as a reading book for all members of a family'.[115] Significantly Cambridge Ff.2.38 contains a mixture of romances and popular pious legends that are similar to the blend of secular tales and religious texts found in the White Book of Rhydderch (Peniarth 4 and 5). These household manuscripts have a number of features in common, including the arrangement of their contents that, broadly speaking, proceeds from religious material to moral tales and secular romances. They also share a number of texts including the Lives of Katherine, Margaret and Mary Magdalene, the Assumption of the Virgin Mary, the Fifteen Signs before Doomsday and an account of Bevis of Hampton. Although they preserve different versions of these texts and the native Welsh legendary material is naturally unique to the Welsh source, these anthologies do give an indication of the literary interests and spiritual requirements of middling-status readers in the fourteenth and fifteenth centuries.[116] The White Book of Rhydderch has even more texts in common with the Auchinleck Manuscript (Edinburgh, National Library of Scotland, Advocates MS 19.2.1), another medieval miscellany that contains the Life of Katherine and appears to have been compiled for the education, entertainment and spiritual welfare of a lay family of some means.[117] Bray emphasizes the influence of secular romances on the Lives of Katherine found in Cambridge Ff.2.38 and the Auchinleck MS, suggesting a 'certain secularisation in tone: they are written as adventure stories with the saint as the protagonist'.[118] This is equally applicable to the Welsh *buchedd*, which is a compact, fast-moving and violent version of Katherine's passion. While it preserves all the episodes of violence and torture, it omits, as we have seen, the introductory material relating to Catrin's youth and her grounding in classical education. Catrin is wise and intelligent, but her debate with the philosophers is expressed in simplistic terms and constitutes more a proclamation of her faith than the in-depth theological debate that one finds, for instance, in the Vulgate Life.[119] Although the Welsh Life does not place heavy intellectual demands on its audience, the moral content of the Life is certainly not discarded. Catrin's debate with the philosophers is simplified, but it is not as brief as in the Auchinleck MS, and the narrator's address at the beginning of *Buched Seint y Katrin* demands that his audience *understands* the significance of Catrin's experiences:

> Argluydi guerendeuch a dyelluch yr hynn a dy6edir y6ch or wyry vendigeit a el6ir katrin.[120]

> (Lords, listen and understand what is said about the blessed virgin called Catrin.)

The opening lines in which the narrator addresses an actual audience construct a setting in which the Life is being read aloud. To some extent this should be read as a literary trope, rather than as direct evidence that the Life was intended to be read aloud. Its middling-status readers would probably have read the Life to themselves, but there may also have been occasions on which it was actually read out for the benefit and entertainment of the wider household. Similarly, the address to 'Lords' should not necessarily be taken as literally referring specifically to a projected audience of male aristocrats (although there probably were some amongst its readership), but perhaps to an audience of some wealth who liked to think of themselves as significant. Lords, moreover, does not necessarily exclude ladies: indeed it is likely that men and women of gentry or aristocratic background were the intended recipients. So this address, in combination with the evidence of the wider manuscript contents, as discussed in the previous chapter, confirms a contention made at the outset: that the Welsh Lives of Katherine, Mary Magdalene and Martha were not specifically intended for religious virgins (as previous readings have too readily suggested) but were designed to function as part of the moral and spiritual education of lay readers.

As we have seen in the previous chapter, Lives of other saints included in the White Book of Rhydderch appear to have a particular relevance for the Christian family. The Life of Martha stresses the importance of being a good host/ess and emphasizes that Christ rewards generosity and hospitality in the Christian household. The most important miracle story in the Welsh Life of Mary Magdalene centres on a lay family, rewarded for their conversion and adherence to the Christian faith. The kind of miracles Mary Magdalene performs – wet nursing, assisting during childbirth, healing and even looking after the prince of Marseilles's household and financial affairs during his absence – also make her a particularly relevant saint within a domestic setting.[121] Catrin herself, although she is a virgin martyr, is a religious heroine whose wisdom, faith and chastity provided an appropriate role model for lay-women and adolescents in noble families.[122] Medieval Welsh poets appear to have been familiar with the Welsh version of her passion and to have considered Catrin as an appropriate role model with which to compare the generosity and virtuousness of married laywomen. To possess, read or listen to a reading of the Life of Katherine was to commemorate the saint and thus fulfil the stipulations laid down by Katherine in her final prayer. Commemoration led to intercession and, in turn, intercession led to salvation.

The *buchedd* places particular emphasis upon the strength of Catrin's faith in the face of adversity and her ultimate transformation into powerful intercessor via her martyrdom. It is noticeably less concerned with issues such as her education, virginity and marriage to Christ.[123] Although Catrin's devotion to the virgin Life is briefly mentioned at the beginning of the text, it does not play a central role in the Life. Unlike many of the traditions associated with native Welsh saints (e.g. Gwenfrewy), in the case of Catrin it is her adherence to the Christian faith, rather than the virgin life, that she continually has to defend. Catrin is an exemplar to all Christians and Maxen, her persecutor, is portrayed as the enemy of all Christians. In her final prayer she asks for mercy not only for her own soul, but also 'y bob Cristaun a gredont ynot ti yn gatarnn'[124] (for all Christians who firmly believe in you). In a similar vein, the narrator/translator requests that 'we' may be treated mercifully and 'dyuot y diwed da'[125] (come to a good end). In the focus and tone of *Buched Seint y Katrin* it may therefore be possible to discern an awareness of the contemporary cultural context of the text's consumption and use, which could be interpreted as representing a bias towards the pious family as opposed to the cloistered life.

6

The Desire to Corrupt: Convent and Community in Medieval Wales[1]

The aim of this chapter is to investigate the history of the Welsh nunneries and to examine the possible roles women played in relation to religious life in medieval Wales. The objective is not to present any definitive conclusions, but to explore tentative interpretations in the light of the extant sources. Relatively little is known about communities of religious women in medieval Wales. Although, as we have seen, Wales boasts a wealth of native female saints (from the fifth to the seventh centuries), the importance of contemporary holy women in medieval Wales appears to have been negligible. Indeed, there were remarkably few formal communities of religious women. An attempt will be made here to shed some light on the convents of medieval Wales, by examining the documentary and literary evidence, and suggestions will be proposed to explain their scarcity. This will involve studying and attempting to interpret possible social and cultural attitudes, within the wider community, concerning nuns and female religious activity more generally. In addition to considering all the extant documentary evidence available for the nunneries, we will also focus on the Poets of the Gentry and the poets' perception of the female religious as corruptible virgin. Poetry forms a vital source as it represents a tradition that lies outside of the direct province of religious activity and, thus, may provide some insight into a more secular mentality. The Bardic Grammars suggest that nuns should be praised for their devotion to God and their holy way of life, yet medieval poetry reflects nothing but a desire to pollute the brides of Christ. More frequently it is the secular Christian wife who is praised for her piety and Christian virtue. Women may have been too important within the social, political and economic concerns and interests of the secular community to have been actively encouraged to retreat to more isolated and rarefied religious environments. This chapter examines the possibility that private devotion rather than claustration was the mode of religious expression preferred for Welsh women.

Female monasticism: the convents of medieval Wales

If we are to begin to build up a picture of the nature of female monasticism and the kind of religious opportunities available to Welsh women, it is necessary to review the data relating to the number and type of religious establishments within medieval Wales. It is informative to compare and contrast this evidence with that available for England, Ireland and Scotland. It has often been noted by medieval historians that there were fewer monastic establishments for women than there were for men.[2] It is not surprising, then, that there were fewer nunneries than monasteries in medieval Wales.[3] Yet the lack of provision made for women wishing to follow a religious vocation in Wales is quite astonishing. Whilst there were approximately one hundred and fifty nunneries in late medieval England,[4] about sixty-four in Ireland[5] and fifteen in Scotland,[6] there appear to have been only three enduring nunneries in post-Conquest Wales: two Cistercian abbeys and a Benedictine priory.

Let us consider the evidence for these Welsh nunneries in greater depth. The Cistercian abbey for women at Llanllŷr in Ceredigion was founded before 1197 by the Lord Rhys as a daughter-house to Strata Florida abbey. There was another Cistercian house for women at Llanllugan in Cydewain (now Powys), founded by Maredudd ap Rhobert probably some time between 1170 and 1190, although possibly later. It appears that there were strong links between the Cistercian nunneries of Wales and particular male abbeys. Llanllugan was placed under the jurisdiction of Strata Marcella. Before 1135 Richard de Clare settled Benedictine nuns at Usk and Richard Strongbow later granted an important charter to the priory which was confirmed in 1330 by Elizabeth de Burgh.[7]

The above nunneries seem to be safely vouched for by contemporary documentary and/or material evidence. However, further contenders are less reliable. Leland, writing *c.*1536–9, notes a ruined building at Llanrhystud and suggests that this may have been a nunnery.[8] However, it appears that he was referring to the ruins of Llanrhystud castle and buildings that had belonged to the Knights Hospitallers.[9] He also, incorrectly, suggests that Llansanffraid Cwmteuddwr was the location of another nunnery mentioned by Gerald of Wales. According to Gerald of Wales there was a Cistercian nunnery at Llansanffraid-yn-Elfael. In three different works he recounts the tale of how Enoc, abbot of Strata Marcella, assembled a community of virgins at Llansanffraid-yn-Elfael. Tempted by the beauty of one of the nuns, Enoc entered into a 'sordid' affair and eloped with the nun, only to regret bitterly his 'misdemeanour' and return repentant to his abbey.[10]

The three versions of the Enoc story, given by Gerald of Wales, vary in detail. Only in *Speculum Ecclesiae* is it stated that the nunnery was at Llansanffraid-yn-Elfael;[11] the other two versions do not mention the location of the nunnery. Whilst according to *Itinerarium Kambriae* Enoc is abbot of Strata Marcella, *Gemma Ecclesiastica* suggests that he is abbot of Whitland and *Speculum Ecclesiae* mentions only that he was an abbot from Powys. All these variations and vagaries do not enhance the confidence which we can place in Gerald's account as a historically rigorous record. As D. H. Williams points out, a Cistercian nunnery at Llansanffraid-yn-Elfael would probably have come under the auspices of Cwmhir abbey – not Strata Marcella.[12] There are also other contradictions in the tale which lead to a questioning of its historical utility. Whilst in the *Itinerarium* and *Speculum* Enoc elopes with a nun, in *Gemma Ecclesiastica* he also manages to impregnate a number of virgins at the convent, before throwing off the ecclesiastical habit:

> There is a story about an abbot Enoc who gathered together in Wales during our own time a group of virgins for the service of Christ. He at length succumbed to temptations and made many of the virgins in the convent pregnant. Finally, he ran around in a comical manner, throwing off the religious habit, and fled with one of the nuns. After he had spent many years in the service of the devil, he at last returned to his Order and the mother-house from which he had fled. The monastery [he returned to] was called Whitland. He was taken back, not without great compunction, and performed his penance with fitting devotion, according to the rigors of the Cistercian rule.[13]

The context of the Enoc tale within Gerald's texts should also be taken into account, as should the possible motives and meanings of Gerald's writings in relation to his social and cultural context. In *Itinerarium Kambriae* it is used to illustrate the wizard Meilyr's psychic powers, since he knew of the scandal before anyone else. In *Gemma Ecclesiastica* it is recounted amidst a number of other 'stories relevant to these matters of not fixing your gaze on and not living with women'.[14] In one such 'story' Gerald relates how Eliah, chaplain and steward of a community of women, was tempted with carnal desires and had to flee from the convent he had founded. Having witnessed three angels sever his testicles in a dream, he returned to the convent untroubled by lust. Gerald notes that his successor had the good sense not to live with the nuns, but to instruct them through the window of his cell. In this context, the narrative in which the Llansanffraid nunnery features can be seen as yet another example serving to illustrate the dangers felt to be involved in caring for a community of women. It is, perhaps, more indicative of male prejudice and of the fear felt by medieval clergy that religious women were a threat to their reputation, than it is of an eagerness to record the history of an otherwise unknown nunnery. Is it not plausible that sometimes fictional or semi-fictional characters and places were preferable within such tales of scandal and criticism? This is particularly likely if such criticism was too close to the mark for comfort and primarily designed to warn and instruct rather than to aggravate.

It is also possible that Gerald aimed to entertain rather than offend. Tales of sexually active nuns and pregnant abbesses were immensely popular in the Middle Ages, for example: the tale of the abbess who dons her lover's trousers on her head instead of her veil in Boccacio's *Decameron* and the history of the nun of Watton (although the latter does draw on historical events).[15] As we have seen in the chapter on the Welsh cult of the Virgin Mary, the tale of the pregnant abbess who was comforted by Mary was translated into Welsh and included in *Gwyrthyeu e Wynvydedic Veir* (The Miracles of the Blessed Virgin). The earliest extant Welsh text is found in Aberystwyth, NLW, MS Peniarth 14 (second half of the fourteenth century), although the miracles appear to have been translated into Welsh in the thirteenth century. The tale of the pregnant abbess was one of the most popular of the Virgin's miracles and is included in almost every collection.[16]

It is possible to interpret the 'history' of the Llansanffraid nunnery as belonging to a particular tale type. Whilst not wishing to state categorically that there was never a nunnery at Llansanffraid-yn-Elfael, it is worth questioning the validity of Gerald's tale and pointing out the contradictions within it. It has, perhaps, been too frequently recounted by modern historians who amalgamate the three versions into a neat tale of sexual scandal and avoid highlighting any of the contradictions in this unique source for another Welsh nunnery. It is recounted by J. E. Lloyd in his classic *History of Wales*[17] and thereafter it is a temptation to quote Lloyd's neat version, rather than refer to the various versions in Gerald of Wales's texts.[18] Saunders Lewis built up a complete picture of how a Dafydd ap Gwilym poem, which expresses the desire to corrupt one of the nuns of Llanllugan, was sung to the monks of Strata Marcella, where the tale of the errant abbot and the nun from Llansanffraid was still fresh in the memory.[19]

Somehow, this weaving together of sources and speculation produces a picture that is too simplistic and, possibly, quite inaccurate.

Economy and provision

The discussion so far has demonstrated that there were very few nunneries in post-Conquest Wales: probably only three long-standing establishments and possibly a fourth short-lived community. Let us now turn to a closely related feature of our evidence that also has a strong bearing upon our attempt to build up a picture of female monasticism in medieval Wales and the nature of provisions made and opportunities provided for female religious activity. Not only were Welsh nunneries few in number, but there appear to have been relatively few nuns in these communities despite the fact that Llanllugan and Llanllŷr are, rather surprisingly, given the status of abbeys.[20] It is possible that this can be attributed to the notion that all Cistercian houses were designated as abbeys.[21] However, this certainly does not seem to have been the case in England where only two Cistercian nunneries, Marham and Tarrant, were officially recognized as abbeys. The others, although sometimes described as abbeys in early charters, appear to have been priories.[22] This blurred categorization in relation to status can, perhaps, be attributed to the lack of official cognizance of the Cistercian nunneries. At any rate, regardless of their status, the Cistercian nunneries of Wales do not appear to have been large communities.

At the time of the suppression there were only three nuns at Llanllugan. Although the number of inmates at the suppression is usually substantially lower than the actual number reached at an earlier period, an assessment of 1377 reveals that there were only four nuns and an abbess at Llanllugan at that time.[23] Knowles and Hadcock suggest that there were sixteen nuns at Llanllŷr and about eight at the suppression, but, unfortunately, do not list documentary sources.[24] According to Dugdale's *Monasticon* the priory at Usk was founded for five nuns, but there certainly appear to have been more inmates than this at the time of Archbishop Peckham's

Visitation in 1284.[25] If we take Knowles and Hadcock's more optimistic estimate of thirteen, then we can precariously suggest that there were, at most, roughly thirty-five women living in religious communities in medieval Wales. Obviously, because of the paucity of primary sources, exact numbers are impossible to calculate. However, it is interesting to compare this rough estimate of the number of female religious in Wales with Eileen Power's estimate of the number of nuns in England at the Dissolution – between 1,500 and 2,000.[26] Before the end of this chapter we will examine why there were so few nunneries in Wales and suggest possible reasons for the lack of provision made for Welsh religious women.

Not only was female monasticism neglected in medieval Wales, the resultant paucity of sources has a legacy. Hence, nuns have also been neglected within much modern Welsh scholarship. Recent studies on the female religious highlight previous neglect of nunneries in more general studies of medieval monasticism – noting that the role of religious women has frequently been ignored or marginalized.[27] Gilchrist points out that the nunneries have often been dismissed as poor or failed monasteries and that, because of this, they have received little attention.[28] This is certainly true of the Welsh nunneries. Gerald of Wales described Llanllŷr as a small and poor house and Leland referred to Llanllugan as 'a veri little poore nunneri'.[29] In the nineteenth century Morris Charles Jones dismissed Llanllugan as 'an insignificant establishment'[30] and in the 1920s Eileen Power included Usk in her list of medieval English nunneries and only mentioned Llanllŷr and Llanllugan in her corrigenda.[31] In 1999 Lawrence Butler in an article on 'The Cistercians in Wales and Yorkshire' noted that Wales and Yorkshire had a similar number of Cistercian houses for men, but chose not to explore the reasons why there were fewer nunneries in Wales than Yorkshire:

> By contrast Wales had only two houses for Cistercian nuns while Yorkshire had twelve; their slight remains, especially in Wales, means that these nunneries will not be discussed here. Concentrating instead upon the houses for men, it is a question

> of exploring common trends or else highlighting disparate developments.[32]

Significant contributions to the study of the Welsh nunneries have been made by D. H. Williams and Helen Fulton who have published articles on the history of the nunneries and medieval Welsh poems to nuns respectively and my own work on the Welsh nunneries has also been published in Welsh.[33] R. Morgan has published an early Llanllugan charter and Madeleine Gray has considered the significance of the dedications to SS. Radegund and Mary Magdalene at Usk.[34] Whilst there is nothing to compare with Gilchrist's study of the archaeology of religious women in England, some excavation work has taken place at Usk.[35] Nevertheless, the Welsh nunneries, on the whole, have attracted little published research – possibly because there were so few and possibly because poverty has been considered a sign of insignificance.

The Welsh nunneries do appear to have been relatively poor. The net incomes of the convents of Llanllugan, Llanllŷr and Usk *c*.1535 were £22, £57 and £55 respectively.[36] Of the thirteen Cistercian abbeys in Wales whose net income *c*.1535 has been recorded, eight had incomes of £100–£200 and only two had incomes of less than £50.[37] This is constant with Gilchrist's findings concerning net incomes of Benedictine nunneries and monasteries in England *c*.1535: nunneries were generally poorer than monasteries for men.[38] Adequate endowment was, no doubt, difficult to sustain over long periods – in particular during times of political and economic upheaval. It is likely that nunneries were better endowed at certain periods than at others. War damage affected the Welsh nunneries, as it did other monastic establishments. In 1284 Llanllŷr was awarded forty marks' compensation for damage done to the nunnery during the Edwardian Conquest. Two Latin letters confirm that the abbess acknowledges receipt of the reparation.[39] Interestingly one of the letters is written on her behalf by John of Caeau, a monk of Strata Florida, and sealed with the seals of the abbots of Strata Marcella and Valle Crucis, because John of Caeau did not have the seal of the abbess with him at the time. Adam of Usk notes that 'none but virgins of noble birth' were received at the priory of

Usk and that, before the Glyndŵr Uprising, the priory had been sufficiently endowed.[40] However, in 1404 Adam of Usk petitioned the pope requesting that indulgences be granted in order to attract alms at St Radegund's chapel in the Benedictine priory of Usk. He states that:

> owing to the burnings, spoilings and other misfortunes which have been caused by the wars which raged in those parts, or otherwise, this same monastery hath come to such want that, unless ready help be forthwith found by your holiness, the sisterhood will be forced to beg for food and clothing, straying through the country, or to stay in the private houses of friends; whereby it is feared that scandals may belike arise.[41]

Interestingly, the success of his petition rests on the pope's desire for strict active enclosure and fear of scandal (again highlighting male preconceptions concerning the female religious).[42]

One of the complaints in Archbishop Peckham's visitation record in 1284 was that the nuns of Usk were wandering outside the confines of the nunnery and staying with layfolk. Other criticisms are mainly to do with economic affairs and he suggested the appointment of two Treasuresses.[43] In 1299 the abbess of Llanllŷr was acquitted by Queen Margaret of a fine for illegally felling an oak.[44] Criticism for felling trees appears in the visitation records of some of the English nunneries described by Eileen Power.[45] Once again it is likely that this illegal activity was brought about by financial hardship. John Nichols warns of the dangers of depending too heavily upon visitation records when building up a picture of life in the convent. As he points out, it is very easy to use the visitation records to create a negative impression of monastic standards, since the purpose of episcopal visitations was to criticize and suggest improvements – not to document achievements.[46]

So far we have considered evidence relating to the number of nunneries in medieval Wales, their population and economic status. We have also found it increasingly necessary to refer to social and cultural attitudes and relations of power when attempting to construct a picture of female monasticism. Let us now focus much more directly upon these social and cultural attitudes and the possible motives and purposes they represent, within both the religious and the secular communities of Wales, communities which were, of course, dominated by male concerns and power structures. It is easy to use the extant information available on the Welsh nunneries to build up a very negative picture of the few religious communities of women in medieval Wales; small communities of women who failed to manage their financial affairs, who chopped down trees illegally, wandered outside the convent, caroused with layfolk, eloped with abbots and, as we shall see, kept exotic pets, revealed one of the most erotic parts of their bodies – their foreheads – and agreed to make love in Welsh woodlands! Yet were the Welsh nunneries really this morally lax? What of the spiritual nature of their religious vocation – their contemplative lifestyle and their devotion to God? One of their saving graces is a bishop's licence which granted permission, as late as 1530, for an Augustinian nun of Limebrook (Katherine Dodd) to transfer to Llanllugan because she wished to lead 'a holier life'. The rule at Llanllugan was said to be 'stricter' and the religious life 'better and [more] frugal'.[47] This document, although late, provides a rare glimpse of a genuinely monastic lifestyle.

Sadly there are no descriptions of monastic life recorded by the nuns themselves. All extant evidence appears to have been recorded by men: the *vox feminae* is non-existent. This perhaps explains why so much of the extant evidence throws little light on the devotional nature of the nunneries. No devotional literature or mystical works by Welsh women have survived and it is quite possible that none were ever composed. It is not known whether the female religious received any kind of education – whether formal or informal, written or oral. It is not known whether nuns in Wales were Latin-literate or indeed literate at all. It is worth recalling that one of the letters sent to acknowledge the receipt of reparation for damage done to the nunnery at Llanllŷr, was written by a monk (John of Caeau) on behalf of the abbess.[48] It is not clear whether the other letter was written by the abbess herself or by someone else on her behalf. However, it appears to have been standard practice for a proctor to write letters of acquittal for war damages on behalf of abbots and abbesses.

A comparison of John of Caeau's letter with a similar letter, written on behalf of the abbot of Strata Florida, reveals the formulaic nature of this form of correspondence.[49] The only reference to religious literature being translated from Latin into Welsh for a Welsh woman is found at the beginning of the thirteenth-century Welsh translation of *Quicumque Vult* (Credo Athanasius Sant). Brother Gruffudd Bola notes that he is translating the text into Welsh for Efa ferch Maredudd so that she may read and understand it and that it might be spiritually beneficial to her.[50] Although she was not Latin-literate, Efa certainly seems to have been able to read. It is not known whether Efa was a nun, but interestingly, she was a descendant of the Lord Rhys who founded the nunnery at Llanllŷr.

Poems to nuns

Whilst there are no poems written by nuns in Wales and there are no *chansons de nonnes*, there are a number of *cywyddau* written to nuns and one fifteenth-century *cywydd gofyn* supposedly written on behalf of the abbess of Llanllŷr. *Cywyddau gofyn*, poems requesting gifts from patrons and Welsh nobility, occur frequently in the poetry of *Beirdd yr Uchelwyr* (The Poets of the Gentry).[51] One such poem by Huw Cae Llwyd requests a pet ape from Sir William Herbert, earl of Pembroke, as a gift for Annes, abbess of Llanllŷr. This particular *cywydd gofyn* is very unusual in that rather than praise the gift requested (as usually happens in a *cywydd gofyn*) the poet heaps scorn and derision on the animal:

> Cythraul llwyd, crinllwyd yw'r croen,
> Cleiriach gruddgrach, garweiddgroen.
> Gwrach foel yw goruwch y fainc,
> Gyrrai ofn i'r gwŷr ifainc.
> Gwar ymylgrach gŵr moelgryg,
> Ac ysbryd llun gwas brawd llyg.
> Mynach brwnt gyfeillach breg,
> lddew heb gael ei oddeg.
> Lledryn o bryf, lleidryn brwnt,

Lledrith goesfrith atgasfrwnt . . .
. . . Bryntach, anafach na neb,
Byr einioes ys bo i'r wyneb[52]

(Grey/brown[53] devil with crinkly brown skin,
old man with scabby cheeks and rough skin.
A bald witch above the bench,
used to frighten the young men.
Tonsured man with scabby sides on the nape of his neck,
with a spirit that resembles a lay brother's serving boy.
Foul monk, false friend,
Jew who hasn't been loved.
Infested animal skin, dirty, petty thief.
Odious, foul apparition with mottled legs . . .
Dirtier and more blemished than anyone.
May his face have a short life!)

Rather than wishing the animal a long life, as is customary in a *cywydd gofyn*, the closing line wishes him a short life. Although the poem is unusual within its genre, it is not unique. A similar poem by Robert Leiaf requests a pet ape for Huw Lewys and contains a similar derogatory description of the animal.[54] It appears, then, that the poem belongs to a particular topos and is, perhaps, satirical. It seems unlikely that Annes was present at the court of Sir William as Leslie Harries suggests: 'rhaid mai rywbryd rhwng 1461 a 1469 yr ymwelodd y lleian o ddyffryn Aeron â'r marchog enwog hwn yn ei lys ym Mrycheiniog'[55] (it must have been sometime between 1461 and 1469 that the nun from the Aeron valley visited this famous knight at his court in Breconshire). Not only would it have been inappropriate for an abbess to be visiting Sir William's court at Rhaglan – since she would have been breaking the rule of strict claustration – but it would also have been unseemly for her to request such a pet. Nevertheless, exotic pets, such as apes, do seem to have been popular in the Middle Ages and nuns were reprimanded for keeping them.[56] One needs to ask whether the abbess of a poorly endowed nunnery would have been in a position to sponsor poetry, and, if she was, whether she would have condoned a *cywydd* that cast her in such a negative light. However, since both William Herbert and the abbess are named, it is unlikely that the poem is purely a piece of fabrication on behalf of the poet. There must have been some connection between Sir William and Anne's or her family. Since the abbess of a nunnery would have been of gentle birth, one can easily imagine that William Herbert, who was, no doubt, acquainted with Abbess Annes's family, would have appreciated the humour of the *cywydd* – regardless of whether Annes genuinely expected to receive a pet ape.

A number of *cywyddau gofyn* written on behalf of men of the Church request gifts such as a goshawk, bows, a book on the Holy Grail and a poem praising God.[57] However, the majority of *cywyddau gofyn* written in connection with religious men request gifts from them. The most heavily requested gifts are horses and no less than eight *cywyddau* are extant which request horses from Dafydd ab Owain, abbot of the Cistercian abbey of Aberconwy.[58] No poems are extant which request gifts from abbesses or nuns. Considering how few nuns there were in Wales, this is not at all surprising. Furthermore, it is unlikely that they would have had the financial stability to offer gifts. Although the Bardic Grammars suggest that nuns should be praised in much the same way as religious men, vast differences exist between Welsh poetry to nuns and to men of the church. Whilst at least a hundred *awdlau* and *cywyddau* praise specific, named churchmen,[59] hardly any of the poems to nuns name their subjects – thus failing to identify them as historical characters.

According to the Bardic Grammars a nun should be praised for her holiness and pure way of life, her chastity and heavenly love of God and other spiritual virtues, just as a religious man is praised.[60] However, rather than praising nuns for their religious virtues, the *cywyddau* to nuns reflect only a desire to corrupt the brides of Christ. In the Dafydd ap Gwilym *cywydd*, mentioned above, the poet attempts to entice the abbess or one of the nuns into the leafy grove.[61] The poem is usually interpreted as seeking out the abbess, but Helen Fulton reinterprets the poem and suggests that the real target is the chantress – one practised in the art of love.[62] Given that there were so few nuns at Llanllugan in the fourteenth century, it is, of course, also possible that Dafydd was happy to entice any one of them. He refers to the sisters as 'Chwiorydd bedydd bob un i Forfudd' (god-sisters are they every one to Morfudd). Dafydd ap Gwilym mentions Morfudd, a married woman who appears frequently in his poetry.[63] Thus we are reminded that the poet is not merely eager to commit adultery against *Y Gŵr Eiddig* (The Jealous Husband), but that in this poem Dafydd's blasphemy increases in magnitude: he wishes to adulterate the brides of Christ.

Another *cywydd* which belongs to the Dafydd ap Gwilym apocrypha attempts to persuade a female religious to give up her monastic lifestyle:

Er Duw, paid â'r bara a'r dŵr
A bwrw ar gasau'r berwr.
Er Mair, paid â'r paderau main
A chrefydd mynaich eryfain.
Na fydd lân yn y gwanwyn,
Gwaeth yw lleianaeth na llwyn,
Gwarant Morwyn, â mantell
A gwerdd wisg, a urddai well.

Dyred i'r fedw gadeinog,
I grefydd y gwŷdd a'r gog –
. . . Duw a fyn, difai annerch,
A saint roi pardwn i serch.

(For God's sake give up the bread and water
and strive to hate cress.
For Mary's sake, dispense with stone beads
and the religion of carousing monks.
Do not be chaste in the spring-time,
a nun's life is worse than the grove:
the Virgin's guarantee, with mantle
and green gown, would confer greater honour.

Come to the spreading birch trees,
to the religion of the trees and the cuckoo –
God and the saints will want, perfect greeting
to give pardon to love.)[64]

The nun here is not so much an object of praise as the object of the poet's lust. In true courtly love tradition she is enticed into the woodland to make love. As Helen Fulton points out, the nuns' vows 'are not taken seriously by secular poets and they are wooed with offers of romantic love into abandoning their virginity, abandoning what amounts to a separatist position, and serving the patriarchy instead'.[65] Some late manuscript versions of the poem quoted above include the phrase 'gwra oedd well' (it were better to marry) thus promoting married life rather than a life of claustration.[66] In some manuscripts the poem ends by suggesting that the poet and the nun have had sexual relations whilst on pilgrimage to Rome and Santiago de Compostella.[67]

In another poem to a nun by Phylib Emlyn, the poet once again attempts to persuade the girl in question that she has chosen the wrong career.[68] Embittered by the fact that she has chosen claustration and turned her back on the life that she used to lead, he appears to attempt to win her back, or at least make her whole again. The nun is described as 'unllawog' (one-handed) and this rather unusual imagery extends throughout the poem, perhaps implying that the nun is somehow incomplete without her natural partner – not Christ, the eternal husband chosen by all female religious women – but the poet himself. The description of the 'lleian unllawog' (one-handed nun) appears to refer to Matthew 5:30: 'And if your right hand is your undoing, cut it off and fling it away; it is better for you to lose one part of your body than for the whole of it to go to hell.'[69] The nun appears to have cut her losses, repented of her former life and now 'ni wrhëir' – she no longer seeks a male partner, which saddens the poet as he imagines her in heaven physically maimed.

Other *cywyddau* suggest that the nuns are already sexually active. The Dafydd ap Gwilym *cywydd* mentions a nun with forehead revealed, friend of some sixty other darlings, and another poem from the Dafydd ap Gwilym apocrypha uses the rhetorical device of *occupatio* to deny that the poet has been having sexual relations with a nun. The more frequently that this is denied the stronger the suggestion that it is true.[70]

Another poem attributed to Hywel ap Dafydd ab Ieuan ap Rhys in some manuscripts plays on the juxtaposition of black and white in a nun's colouring – her black veil and her white skin suggesting both purity and potential sinfulness.[71] The poem consists mainly of a detailed description of the girl's face, framed by her black clothing. The poet laments that she has been blackened around her face and that he cannot see her forehead. Nowhere in the poem is it specifically stated that the girl is a nun, one can only infer this from the description of her clothing.

Clothing is all important when identifying the subjects of other more ambiguous *cywyddau* which may, or may not, describe women who belong to religious Orders. The main problem here is to establish to what extent uniformity of religious habit was current within the Cistercian and Benedictine Orders and within what period. Whilst the Benedictines are traditionally thought of as wearing black, the Cistercian habit is usually described as white – 'rhai lliwgalch' (chalk-white ones) according to Dafydd ap Gwilym.[72] However, Thompson points out that nuns described as 'moniales albae' (white nuns) do not necessarily belong to the Cistercian Order. One could add that women described as wearing black are not necessarily Benedictine nuns. Some attempts to establish uniformity of habit are apparent in the thirteenth century when the Cistercian General Chapter decreed that a cowl should be worn, or a cloak, but not both and that nuns' veils must be black.[73] A fifteenth-century stained-glass window at Llanllugan depicts a female religious wearing a white gown and wimple and a blue hooded cloak – presumably blue represents black (Plate 24).[74]

A complex poem attributed to Dafydd ab Edmwnd describes a woman, called Gwenonwy, dressed in pure black.[75] The poet, who is pining for the woman's love, laments the woman's choice of black clothing (as in the poem mentioned above) and suggests that it would be better if she wore green. This particular idea is reminiscent of one of the poems in the Dafydd ap Gwilym apocrypha: 'A gwerdd wisg, a urddai well' (green gown would confer greater honour). However, the fact that the woman is dressed in black does not necessarily mean that she is a nun. Another possible interpretation of this rather ambiguous poem is that it may describe a widow who is unobtainable because she is still mourning her husband.[76]

Gilbert Ruddock suggests that a *cywydd* by lolo Goch to a young girl, 'I Ferch', describes a nun.[77] Although she wears a pale headdress and carries a rosary it does not necessarily, follow that she is a nun. Headdresses, wimples and veils were all worn by secular noblewomen, who also possessed rosaries.[78] The remaining description of her attire – scarlet gown,[79] fur-trimmed garment, golden sleeves and rings – certainly seems to suggest that she is not a member of a religious Order. As Ruddock points out, nuns were often criticized for wearing their own clothing, but the unorthodoxy of this attire does little to suggest that the young girl described here is a nun. No phrase in the poem implies that this shy girl, with lowered eyes, is sexually experienced or rebellious, as one might expect if she were wearing clothing unsuited to her vocation.[80] The fact that she has never known a man implies only that she is a virgin:

> Brwynengorff heb rin ungwr . . .
> . . . Duw a'i gwnaeth, arfaeth eurfab,
> Myn delw Bedr, ar fedr ei Fab.
> Pentyriais gerdd, pwynt dirym,
> Puntur serch, pond trahaus ym
> Dybio cael, bu hael baham,
> Gytgwsg â'm dyn lygatgam?

> (Reed-like body which no man has ever known . . .
> God made her, golden son's purpose,
> by Peter's image, for His son.
> I have heaped up poetry, helpless state,
> pencil of love, is it not presumptuous of me
> to imagine getting, it was a noble reason,
> to sleep with my girl with the lowered eyes?)[81]

The suggestion that God made her especially for His son is more suggestive of a bride of Christ, but again this may simply refer to her pure, virginal state.

'Pererindod Merch', another Dafydd ap Gwilym poem, describes a pilgrimage from Anglesey to St Davids.[82] The girl in this poem is referred to as a nun and, whilst this is a strong possibility, it may also be interpreted as metaphor. In the same way that the girl has not literally killed the poet, she is, perhaps, not literally a nun. As with many of these ambiguous poems, it is virtually impossible to decide with any authority whether the girl referred to actually belongs to religious Orders; nor, perhaps, is it important to do so since the poet may not have a particular female in mind. Since most of the 'nuns' described in Welsh poetry belong to the *Canu Serch* tradition (courtly love poetry) rather than *Canu Mawl* (more formal praise poetry) they are not identifiable as particular individuals. Instead, they pertain to a virginal type: pure and potentially corruptible, yet often unobtainable.

The corruptibility of virginity is depicted not only in poems to nuns (or possible nuns) but in *cywyddau* to young devout virgins. In a fifteenth-century *cywydd* by Hywel Dafi the poet looks through a keyhole and sees a young girl reciting psalms, kneeling in front of a statue of the Virgin Mary. The blasphemous nature of the imagery is startling:

Rhwng dwy lenlliain feinon
och fis haf na chefais hon,
a'i bwrw rhwng dau bared
i'r llawr a'i dwyfraich ar lled;
offrwm, liw blodau effros,
ar dalau y gliniau'n glos,
a hon o'i bodd yn goddef,
a rhoddi naid rhyddi a nef;
disgyn rhwng ei dwy esgair,
addoli fyth i'r ddelw Fair.

(Between two fine bed-curtains
if only I could have her in a summer month,
and throw her between two walls
to the ground with her arms outstretched;
I'd offer, colour of euphrasy flowers,
on my knees up close,
and she'd let me willingly,
and I'd leap between her and heaven;
coming down between her legs
I'd worship forever Mary's image.)[83]

The type of religious location in which the girl is viewed is not clear. Does Hywel Dafi see the girl through the keyhole of a convent church, a parish church or a private chapel? The reference to 'her speech in a golden book' possibly suggests that she is holding a psalter or a Book of Hours often used by women for private devotion. However, despite the fact that much of the contents of Books of Hours was translated into Welsh in the Middle Ages, no Books of Hours in the vernacular are extant.[84]

Poems to married noblewomen

Bearing in mind that there were so few nunneries in medieval Wales, it seems likely that private devotion rather than claustration was the mode of religious expression generally preferred for Welsh women, Although Welsh poetry to nuns does not take their religious vocation seriously, a number of praise poems and elegies to married noblewomen, for example, Elsbeth Mathau, Mabli ferch Gwilym, Gwladus ferch Syr Dafydd Gam and Annes of Caerleon, praise their Christian virtues, their generosity, chastity and religious devotion.[85] Many are compared to female saints and from some are requested gifts that would have been considered appropriate gifts for women of the church to offer. For example, Lewys Glyn Cothi requests a curtain depicting the Virgin Mary, Christ, the twelve apostles and both male and female saints from Annes of Caerleon and in an *awdl* he thanks Efa ferch Llywelyn for a rosary.[86] Unlike the vast majority of the poems to nuns, these poems specifically identify their subjects: they are 'real' women and their lineages can frequently be traced in the Welsh genealogies.

Two *marwnadau*, or elegies, to Welsh noblewomen – Nest Stradling and Gwenllian ferch Rhys – seem to suggest that they retired to the convent after the death of their husbands.[87] Nest, the wife of Siôn Stradling from Westplas, is described as a nun from Gwent and it is emphasized that she was chaste when she passed away:

> Y wraig falch orau ag fu
> oedd ddiweirferch pan ddarfu.

Lleian o Went â llu Non,
lletyodd dillad duon.[88]

(The proud wife – the best that ever there was –
was a chaste girl when she passed away.
Nun from Gwent, with Non's host;
she gave shelter to black clothes.)

No mention is made of any particular religious house and the reference to her as a nun may be taken to mean that she remained chaste – that is, that she did not remarry – after the death of her husband. In her *marwnad* her body is described as going to join her husband's but, rather confusingly, in Siôn's *marwnad* Nest is also described as being in heaven.[89] There seems to be some confusion, then, over who died first. It seems likely that Nest died shortly after her husband and if she did spend any time in religious Orders, it is unlikely to have been for long. The elegy places great emphasis on her Christian beliefs, her charity work and her importance as a wife and mother. It is probable that most of her charitable acts took place whilst she was married and religious devotion and marriage are portrayed as compatible and harmonious.

Gwenllian ferch Rhys, like Nest, is described as joining her husband after death and both elegies link the women with St Non.[90] Although it is said that Gwenllian ascends to the rank of virgins, she is also mentioned as joining Non's choir in heaven. As we have seen in Chapter 3, Non, the mother of St David, is one of the few female saints who was not a virgin, since her sanctity was closely related to her maternity. By comparing these women with Non, the poets place emphasis on both their holiness and their maternity. E. D. Jones suggested that Rhys ap Dafydd was Gwenllian's father and that, although she was engaged to Dafydd, she died young before getting married.[91] However, as Dafydd Johnston has shown, Rhys ap Dafydd was her son, not her father, and this opinion is supported by the genealogies.[92] Poems to Gwenllian's son, Rhys, are extant by Lewys Glyn Cothi and there are also poems to her husband, Dafydd ap Tomas, by Guto'r Glyn.[93] Gwenllian is not referred to as a nun in the poems to her son, and it is debatable whether she ever spent any period of time in a nunnery during widowhood. The word 'lleianaeth' (female monasticism), which occurs in her elegy may be used metaphorically to refer to her piety and chastity after she lost her husband. She is portrayed as having been particularly devout from an early age, and this is perhaps why E. D. Jones incorrectly assumed that she had died a young virgin:

> Ymarfer o'i phaderau,
> hynny a wnaeth honno'n iau.
> Tua'r nef troi a wnâi,
> tua'r eglwys y treiglai.[94]
>
> (Practising with her rosary,
> this is what she did when she was younger.
> She would turn towards heaven.
> She would wander towards the church.)

In a *cywydd* to Rhys ap Dafydd Gwenllian is praised for healing the poet Lewys Glyn Cothi. No mention is made of any formal religious vocation in this poem and the main aim of the *cywydd* is to praise Rhys ap Dafydd and the household at Blaen Tren, Llanybydder.[95]

Pious noblewomen are frequently compared to female saints in Welsh poetry – often to Non and Elen (Helen), the mother of Constantine, who is accredited with finding the true cross.[96] Ann, countess of Rhaglan, is compared to SS. Martha, Mary and Anne and, as she takes responsibility for the court at Rhaglan following the death of her husband, she is described by Guto'r Glyn as 'Elen wych Raglan . . . Ac ail gwraig i gael y groes'[97] (Great Elen of Rhaglan . . . And the second woman to find the cross). Nest of Caeo, the wife of Dafydd, is likened to SS. Non, Ffraid (Brigid), Anne and Frideswide in her elegy and she is praised for her generosity and charity work, providing the poor and sick with food and money.[98]

One could argue that one might expect the poets to compare married noblewomen to female saints in their elegies and praise their generosity and charitable acts. Afterall, the Bardic Grammars recommend that poets praise noblewomen for their 'haelioni' (generosity).[99] Nevertheless, one is frequently given the impression that the descriptions are not merely reinforcing poetic stereotypes and that in many instances where the woman is named we are given some insight into her reputation and, on occasions, allowed to glimpse her genuine religious beliefs and witness instances of private devotion. Mabli ferch Gwilym, for example, is praised for giving to the poor and caring for the elderly, but the poet also refers to her Christian knowledge: 'a gair y Iesu a garasoch' (and you loved the word of Jesus), 'a galw y Iesu a glywasoch' (and you heard Jesus's call), 'â gwersau Iesu ymgroesasoch' (and you welcomed the lessons taught by Jesus).[100] It would simply be unnecessary for a poet to praise a woman's religious devotion in detail, if she were not a devout Christian.

Occasionally the Poets of the Gentry refer to pilgrimages made by medieval women, for example, when Elliw ferch Henri goes on pilgrimage to Santiago de Compostella[101] or Elsbeth Mathau of Radyr visits the Virgin's holy well at Pen-rhys and leaves a substantial offering. At her court in Radyr Elsbeth offered hospitality to other pilgrims visiting Pen-rhys and her unwavering devotion to this particular holy site led to her salvation according to the poet Rhisiart ap Rhys:

Pen-Rhys o'i llys a'i llaswyr,
pwys dau gant mewn pyst o gŵyr.
Diffrwyth oedd weled offrwm
dieithr ei haur da a thrwm.
Ei mawr fraint gyda Mair fry,
y mae'i henaid am hynny.[102]

(From her court and psalter Pen-Rhys [received]
two hundred pounds in wax candles.
It was futile to see her unusual offering
of good, heavy gold.
Her great reward is that her soul
is with Mary on high because of this.)

As we saw in Chapter 3, Lewys Glyn Cothi provides a valuable description of Edudful ferch Gadwgan's pilgrimage to St Non's well and chapel near St Davids and witnesses the acts of devotion she performed there before progressing to the cathedral where she kisses St David's relics.[103] The poem is an important witness to medieval women's religious devotion and the practice of pilgrimage in medieval Wales. Interestingly, the poet is keen to emphasize not only Edudful's religious faith, but also her maternity. She is associated with Non and the Virgin Mary, two maternal saints, and the fact that she calls upon the saints every Sunday is claimed by the poet to ensure that her sons will enjoy longevity. Assigning one's daughter to a nunnery was frequently seen as a spiritual investment: the daughter's prayers would benefit the souls of all the family who had made this commitment and sacrifice. In the poem to Edudful the mother's spirituality extends spiritual rewards to her sons and the whole family is blessed as a result of her religious devotion – devotion which, nevertheless, does not involve retiring to a nunnery. Edudful's faith is depicted as sincere, since she comes 'i wir weddïaw' (to truly pray or sincerely pray) and her genuine religious convictions are portrayed as being incorporated naturally into her everyday life.

In a stained-glass window at the Church of St Cadwaladr, Llangadwaladr, Anglesey (*c.*1490) Elen, the wife of Owain ap Meurig ap Llywelyn, is depicted kneeling behind her husband with her hands together in an attitude of prayer (Plate 25). The image crystallizes many of the attitudes and desires of the Welsh gentry during this period. Owain is depicted dressed in military regalia illustrating his respectability and social status as well as hinting at his bravery and confirming his masculinity and military prowess. Elen, on the other hand, is depicted wearing simple clothing and a white veil suggesting humility, chastity and piety as she kneels obediently near her husband. Owain's parents, Meurig and his wife Marged, are depicted in the same window and it would appear that the portrait was commissioned during Owain and Elen's lifetime, shortly after Meurig died *c.*1480–90. The idealized image, therefore, depicts the pair in exactly the manner they wished since they, no doubt, approved the portraits. There is not a great deal of difference between the way in which Elen is portrayed (Plate 25) and the way in which the female religious depicted in stained glass at the convent church at Llanllugan is depicted (Plate 24). However, Elen is a married woman who had fourteen children and her religious devotion is here depicted as being compatible with marriage. Elen outlived her husband and her grief on losing Owain is described in an elegy by Lewys Daron.[104] The poets Tudur Aled and Lewys Môn also commemorate the couple.[105] It is also worth noting that it was not unusual for the Boduan family to sponsor their parish church at Llangadwaladr rather than make a more permanent commitment to a religious house, a point which will be discussed in more detail below when we consider why there were so few religious houses for women in Wales.

Women who are described as healing the poets, or their husbands, are frequently compared to Mary Magdalene – 'meddyges Iesu' (Christ's physician). As we saw in Chapter 4, in two separate *cywyddau* Guto'r Glyn compares both Elen wraig Hywel o Foelyrch and Siân wraig Syr Siôn Bwrch to Mary Magdalene. Elen is praised for her special healing ointment which will heal her husband's injured knee and Siân is also compared to St Gwenfrewy.[106] The hospitality, wine and mead that Siân offers the poet is said to be medically more effective than the healing waters of Gwenfrewy's well.[107] Guto'r Glyn appears to have turned either to married noblewomen or to Welsh abbots for healthcare, but not to the female religious. When the poet breaks a rib he turns to Dafydd ab Ieuan, abbot of Valle Crucis, for support and it was to this abbey that Guto'r Glyn retired in old age.[108] Although he wrote a number of poems to men of the church, none of his works are addressed to specific religious women.

As we have seen, many of the native Welsh saints are associated with healing and their holy wells were popular places of pilgrimage for the sick. However, the role of healer is not recorded as being performed by medieval Welsh nuns and the poets turn either to the hospitality of male abbots or married noblewomen for their healthcare.

The Hospitallers: women and healing

Gilchrist observes that in medieval England hospitals offered a more flexible religious life to a wider spectrum of women: some were semi-monastic and more akin to the *via media* of the beguines.[109] Whilst women's contributions to the healing of the sick are apparent in medieval England, there is, as yet, no concrete evidence of similar institutions in Wales being run specifically by religious women, but is this due to a lack of extant sources?[110]

The 'Sister's House' which belonged to the commandery of the Hospital of St John of Jerusalem at Slebech, Pembrokeshire, has been interpreted in a variety of different ways and scholars have failed to reach a consensus regarding the function of this complex of ruined buildings. The ruins at Minwear are positioned on the south bank of the Eastern Cleddau directly opposite the Hospitallers' church at Slebech, but separated from the main site by the river. The main building has been variously interpreted as a barn, a hospice or a hostel for female pilgrims.[111] The name 'Systerne House' was recorded in 1546 and this gave rise to the suggestion that there must once have been a cistern on the site which fed a mill, although there are no longer any remains of a mill. The fact that the site is known locally as the 'Sisters' House' has also lead to the assumption that it must have been specifically associated with women, but if this were the case, were these female members of the Order, women who helped nurse the sick or female pilgrims seeking accommodation? Is the name 'Sisters' House' merely a corruption of 'Systerne House'?

The Royal Commission Inventory for Pembrokeshire dismissed the idea that there was ever a house for females of the Order of St John at Slebech, concluding instead that female pilgrims on their way to St Davids may have been housed separately in the 'Sisters' House' away from the main site.[112] Helen Nicholson, who has carefully surveyed the site and analysed all previous interpretations of the 'Sisters' House', demonstrates that the main building does share certain characteristics with other European hospices or infirmaries and argues that these were multifunctional, providing accommodation for pilgrims, caring for the sick and elderly and providing medical care. She, however, rejects the idea that the 'sisters' were women employed by the Order to nurse the sick and favours instead the hypothesis that women who were associated with the Hospitallers at Slebech, but who were not fully professed members of the Order, dwelt in the 'Sisters' House':

> There is no evidence in the report of 1338 that the Hospital of St John of Jerusalem at Slebech employed women to help to look after the sick or pilgrims. It is possible that the 'sisters' of the 'Sisters' House' were female associates, such as female corrodary-holders, women who had given gifts to the order and were now living in a house belonging to the order and under the order's protection, but not on the main site, to keep them segregated from the male members of the order. In this respect they were in a similar position to the pilgrims: under the order's protection and care, but segregated from the order. It would have been logical to place all these dependent but segregated persons together in the same complex of buildings. If the 'sisters' at Slebech lived in the same complex of buildings as the pilgrims, it was reasonable to name the pilgrims' complex 'the Sisters' House.[113]

The argument that women associated with the Hospitallers at Slebech were not fully professed members of the Order and that they were, therefore, likely to be overlooked in official records is convincing.[114] Comparisons with Ireland, where documents reveal that there were 'sisters' belonging to the Order, although officially there were no houses for Hospitaller sisters in Ireland, are particularly pertinent here.[115] One does not necessarily need to reject the notion that women nursed the sick in Wales on the ground that no written references to this are extant. If there were women living at Slebech/Minwear who had chosen to associate themselves with the religious Order, but had not officially taken vows, then they were unlikely to be leading a purely contemplative lifestyle and I see no reason why they would not have nursed the sick or assisted at the hospice where they resided. Nevertheless, the fact remains that the notion that women were associated with the Hospital of St John of Jerusalem at Slebech hinges only on the name of the associated site at Minwear, and it is a pity that more substantial evidence to corroborate this does not appear to be available at present.

Why were there so few nunneries in medieval Wales?

The poetic evidence suggests that the vast majority of Welsh women were encouraged to lead chaste but not celibate religious lives within marriage, whilst a few may have retired to the convent after the death of their husbands, having reached the end of their reproductive careers. On the whole, though, there does not seem to have been much encouragement for Welsh women to devote their virginity to Christ and retire to the convent at an early age – for virginity was both a precious and a saleable commodity.

One must exercise great caution when dealing with native Welsh law. It is not certain to what extent it reflects actual practice and it is also difficult to date with any accuracy, since late manuscripts contain archaic elements.[116] However, it is worth noting that according to the tractate *Cyfraith y Gwragedd* (The Law of Women) a fee, called *amobr*, was payable to a woman's lord on the loss of virginity.[117] This fee varied according to the woman's status:

> Amobyr merch maer kyghella6r, punt. Amobyr merch maer, chweugeint. Amobyr merch penkenedyl, chweuge*in*t a phunt. Amobyr merch uchel6r, chweugeint. Amobyr merch mab eillt, pedwar ugeint. Amobyr merch alltut, pedeir ar ugeint. Amobyr merch pob pe*n*ns6yda6c, herwyd rei punt, herwyd ereill chweugeint. Amobyr merch pob un o'r s6ydogyon ereill, herwyd rei chweuge*in*t, herwyd ereill tri ugeint. Amobr merch kaeth, deudec k*einya6c*.

> (The *amobr* of a *maer cynghellor's* daughter, a pound. The *amobr* of a *maer's* daughter, six score pence. The *amobr* of the daughter of the head of a kindred, a pound and six score pence. The *amobr* of an *uchelwr's* daughter, six score pence. The *amobr* of a villein's daughter, four score. The *amobr* of a foreigner's daughter, twenty-four. The *amobr* of the daughter of any chief official, according to some a pound, according to others six score. The *amobr* of the daughter of any of the other officials, according to some six score, according to others three score. The *amobr* of a slave's daughter, twelve pence.)[118]

It is probable that *amobr* was payable more than once – for illicit sexual relations as well as loss of virginity.[119] R. R. Davies suggests that this became a lucrative source of income for the territorial lord. If this really were the case, then it is little wonder that Welsh lords were reluctant to establish foundations in which women could remain perpetual virgins. In 1334 the surveyor of Denbigh calculated the return on *amobr* at £41 annually and in 1395 in Kidwelly it was calculated at £21. 6*s*. 8*d*.[120] These sums are substantial – especially considering that the net incomes of the nunneries at Llanllugan, Llanllŷr and Usk in 1535 were £22, £57 and £55 respectively.[121]

Women were instrumental in the founding of a number of medieval English nunneries.[122] Wealthy widows seem to have been particularly fond of patronizing religious houses: often retiring to the convent after the death of their husbands. Thompson notes that several nunneries founded jointly by husband and wife were, in fact, located on land that had formed part of the wife's dowry.[123] Although women in England had minimal rights to inheritance, according to feudal law daughters could inherit land and property in the absence of male heirs. In 1317 Elizabeth de Burgh inherited one-third of the Clare lands in the partition of her brother's inheritance.[124]

Elizabeth de Burgh, who confirmed an important charter to Usk priory in 1330, is also recorded as entertaining the Benedictine nuns of Usk and she also remembered them in her will, leaving the sisters £6 13*s*. 4*d*. and two cloths of gold.[125] According to Welsh law women could not inherit land nor could they receive a dower in land on their husbands' death.[126] The Welsh equivalent of dowry – *argyfrau* – appears to have consisted of moveable goods, rather than land and property. Despite the fact that some families managed to circumvent the laws of inheritance,[127] it seems likely that Welsh women, on the whole, were not in a position to offer land for the founding of nunneries.

Nevertheless, there are examples of Welsh women and Anglo-Norman women who married Welsh nobility who managed to procure land and there are even occasionally documented cases when women who were landowners benefited from collecting *amobr*.[128] Gwenyth Richards in her fascinating thesis on women in thirteenth-century Wales discusses instances when women of the upper classes – often female relations within the Welsh royal families – sought to protect their families' interests and safeguard their lands or have their own lands and rents returned when they had been seized by a third party.[129] Gwenllian, Gwladus, Elen, Margaret and Angharad, the five daughters of Llywelyn ap Iorwerth (1173–1240), all possessed land: whilst the first four daughters married Anglo-Norman barons, Angharad appears to have married a Welshman, Maelgwn Fychan, son of Maelgwn ap Rhys Gruffudd.[130] Although no documents are extant which indicate whether the women ever made donations to religious houses for women, Margaret Clifford left a will requesting that her heart be buried at Aconbury priory church near Hereford and she made a bequest to cover alms and funeral expenses.[131] Clearly these women were needed by Llywelyn ap Iorwerth to form political alliances via marriage and he sought to arrange the best possible marriages for all of his daughters (whether they were legitimate or illegitimate). There were no superfluous or unwanted daughters who could be assigned to nunneries. As we shall see below, the only women of the Royal House of Gwynedd who were committed to nunneries were sent there by the English monarchy, following the demise of Llywelyn ap Gruffudd (*c*.1225–82).

In 1273 Angharad (the granddaughter of Angharad ferch Llywelyn ap Iorwerth) was granted the commote of Anhuniog by her husband Owain ap Maredudd of Ceredigion. Although Owain was keen to see that dower provision was made to his wife, the deed also set out that if Angharad took another husband, died without an heir by Owain or took religious vows, then she would forfeit the commote.[132] The charter is interesting not only because it is another example of a husband making territorial provision for his wife which appears to contradict the Welsh Law of Women, but it also indicates that it was at least conceivable that Angharad might consider entering a religious community. Nevertheless, Angharad was not granted the freedom of choosing to become a nun and grant dower lands to a nunnery and following the death of her husband Owain she married Walter de Pedwardyn.[133]

Jennifer Ward proposes a variety of relationships that existed between English noblewomen and religious houses. She suggests that whilst women of the higher nobility often preferred to exercise patronage over religious houses, women of the lower nobility and of the gentry turned their attention to their parish churches.[134] Given that there were so few wealthy women of the higher nobility and so few nunneries in medieval Wales, one could speculate that the parish church rather than the convent was more likely to receive religious patronage. Women who wished to share in the spiritual benefits of religious endowment and arrange, for example, for prayers or requiem masses to be said for their souls or for their families' souls may well have made donations to their parish churches, given gifts, set up or been included in chantries. Sustained endowment of religious houses was, perhaps, out of reach of most Welsh women's capabilities.

Many reasons can be proffered as to why there were so few nunneries in medieval Wales. The Order most favoured by the Welsh princes and the Welsh nobility was the Cistercian Order and Cistercian hostility towards the creation of new foundations for women has frequently been noted by medieval historians.[135] In 1220 and 1225 the Cistercians attempted to ban the admission of existing nunneries to the Order and in 1228 the building of entirely new Cistercian nunneries was forbidden.[136] Communities of religious women were dependant upon the services of a priest for Mass and confession and there were strong links between the Cistercian nunneries of Wales and the male abbeys responsible for them. In 1222 Cistercian abbots petitioned the pope requesting that they should not be forced to send monks to live at women's houses, as this endangered both their souls and the reputation of their Order.[137] No doubt, the tale of the Llansanffraid nunnery did little to promote the establishment of further communities of women in Wales. In 1216 the Cistercians laid down restrictions on how near a nunnery could be to a male abbey and how near it could be to another nunnery.[138] The accumulation of land was also an important feature of the

Cistercian Order and the creation of more nunneries would have meant greater competition for land and appropriated churches. Gerald of Wales records that Strata Florida stole some of the property of Llanllŷr after the death of Lord Rhys.[139]

The Benedictine Order, popular in England, does not seem to have been favoured by the native Welsh princes and nobility. It is quite likely that the Benedictine nuns of Usk were of Norman rather than of Welsh descent. In Wales there was not the same diversity of Orders open to women as there was elsewhere. Ironically, one of the few Welsh women we know of who joined another Order was Gwenllian, daughter of Llywelyn ap Gruffudd, the last Prince of Wales.[140] According to *Brut y Tywysogyon* (The Chronicle of the Princes) after her father was killed she was sent, against her will, to a convent in England. In fact, this was the Gilbertine Order at Sempringham (the only Order to have originated in England):

> Ac yna y gwnaethpwyt priodas Lywelin ac Elienor yg Kaer Wynt, ac Edwart, vrenhin Lloegyr, yn costi y neithawr ehun yn healaeth. Ac o'r Elienor honno y bu y Lywelin verch a elwit Gwenlliant. A'r dywededic Elienor a uu varw y ar etiued; ac y hagkladwyt ymanachloc y Brodyr Troetnoeth yn Llann Vaes yMon. A'r dywededic Wenlliant, gwedy marw y that, a ducpwyt yg keith[i]wet y Loeger; a chynn amser oet y gwnaethpwyt ynn vanaches o'e hanuod.

> (And then the marriage of Llywelyn and Eleanor was solemnized at Winchester, with Edward, king of England, himself liberally defraying the costs of the wedding banquet. And by that Eleanor Llywelyn had a daughter called Gwenllïan. And the said Eleanor died in childbirth; and she was interred in the monastery of the Barefooted Friars at Llan-faes in Anglesey. And the said Gwenllïan, after the death of her father, was taken into captivity to England; and before coming of age she was made a nun against her will.)[141]

She remained there all of her life and died in 1336 at the age of fifty-five. Her cousin Gwladus ferch Dafydd ap Llywelyn was sent to the Gilbertine priory of Sixhills and died one year before Gwenllian. Dafydd ap Llywelyn's other five daughters, of whom very little is known, all appear to have been forced to enter the same religious Order, either at Sixhills or Alvingham priory also in North Lincolnshire.[142] Brian Golding in a section on involuntary residents of the Gilbertine Order notes that: 'saddest of all the inmates of Gilbertine priories were the daughters of enemies of the realm placed there for safe-keeping.'[143] Clearly Edward I wanted to ensure that none of the daughters of Llywelyn or Dafydd had offspring and the lineage of the Welsh rulers of Gwynedd came to an abrupt end. Unlike the Cistercian Order which had close links with Welsh nobility and sponsored Welsh literature, the Gilbertine Order was firmly rooted in England and North Lincolnshire was far enough away from Wales to sever any links, particularly when this was coupled with the strict enclosure that the priories offered. Gwenllian and Gwladus may not have chosen a religious vocation of their own volition, but it is certainly likely that reared from a tender age in a spiritual environment, religion became their genuine vocation.

As of yet no evidence exists to suggest that Welsh women followed less orthodox religious vocations such as those of the beguine, the sister in a hospital, the hermit or the anchorite. Considering that medieval Wales had a thriving tradition of Welsh women saints (Dwynwen, Gwenfrewy, Melangell, Non, Tegfedd and Eluned, for example),[144] most of whom were consecrated virgins, astonishingly little provision was made for those who wished to follow in their footsteps.[145] Whilst numerous men of the Church are named in Welsh praise poetry, the religious vocation of the nebulous nuns is not taken seriously. Nuns – the ultimate in forbidden fruit – made excellent subjects for Welsh courtly love poetry because not only did they remain anonymous, but they barely existed. They belonged more to the erotica of the imagination than to any social reality. It can be postulated that Welsh women were generally encouraged to worship within the confines of marriage, rather than in a community of religious females. Women of the upper echelons of society appear to have been too important in the political and economic life of Wales to be allowed to retire to a convent, since they were needed to form valuable marital alliances. Unless new evidence is uncovered to suggest alternative, less institutionalized forms of religious activity in Wales – such as anchoritic activity – then it appears that the monastic life was rarely a genuine vocation for Welsh women.

Notes

Introduction

1 Although publications in the field are too numerous to provide a comprehensive bibliography here, I shall refer to some of the main examples: Eileen Power, *Medieval English Nunneries* c.*1275 to 1535* (Cambridge: Cambridge University Press, 1922); Barbara Newman, *Sister of Wisdom: St Hildegard's Theology of the Feminine* (Aldershot: Scolar Press, 1987); Caroline Walker Bynum, *Holy Feast and Holy Fast: the Religious Significance of Food to Medieval Women* (Berkeley, CA and London: University of California Press, 1988); Sharon K. Elkins, *Holy Women of Twelfth-century England* (Chapel Hill, NC and London: University of California Press, 1988); Sally Thompson, *Women Religious: the Founding of English Nunneries after the Conquest* (Oxford: Clarendon, 1991); *Sainted Women of the Dark Ages*, ed. and trans. Jo Ann McNamara, J. E. Halborg and E. G. Whatley (Durham and London: Duke University Press, 1992); Roberta Gilchrist, *Gender and Material Culture: the Archaeology of Religious Women* (London: Routledge, 1994); Juliette Dor, Lesley Johnson and Jocelyn Wogan-Browne (eds), *New Trends in Feminine Spirituality: the Holy Women of Liège and their Impact* (Brussels: Brepols, 1999); Kathleen Coyne Kelly, *Performing Virginity and Testing Chastity in the Middle Ages* (London and New York: Routledge, 2000); Elizabeth Spearing (ed.), *Medieval Writings on Female Spirituality* (London: Penguin, 2002); Anke Bernau, Ruth Evans and Sarah Salih (eds), *Medieval Virginities* (Cardiff: University of Wales Press, 2003); Liz Herbert McAvoy and Mari Hughes-Edwards (eds), *Anchorites, Wombs and Tombs: Intersections of Gender and Enclosure in the Middle Ages* (Cardiff: University of Wales Press, 2005).

2 Diane Watt, *Secretaries of God: Women Prophets in Late Medieval*

and Early Modern England (Woodbridge: The Boydell Press, 1997); Karen A. Winstead, *Virgin Martyrs: Legends of Sainthood in Late Medieval England* (Cornell: Cornell University Press, 1997); Rosalynn Voaden, *God's Words, Women's Voices: the Discernment of Spirits in the Writing of Late-Medieval Women Visionaries* (Woodbridge: York Medieval Press, 1999); Katherine J. Lewis, *The Cult of St Katherine of Alexandria in Late Medieval England* (Woodbridge: The Boydell Press, 2000); Jocelyn Wogan-Browne, *Saints' Lives and Women's Literary Culture c.1150–1300: Virginity and its Authorizations* (Oxford: Oxford University Press, 2001); Virginia Nixon, *Mary's Mother: Saint Anne in Late Medieval Europe* (University Park, Pa: Pennsylvania State University Press, 2004).

3 Valuable publications on various aspects of women's history in medieval Wales including the legal status of women, literary representations, women writers and female literacy include: D. Jenkins and M. E. Owen (eds), *The Welsh Law of Women* (Cardiff: University of Wales Press, 1980); M. Haycock, 'Merched drwg a merched da: Ieuan Dyfi v. Gwerful Mechain', *Ysgrifau Beirniadol*, 16 (1990), 97–110; M. Haycock, 'Defnydd hyd Ddydd Brawd: rhai agweddau ar y ferch ym marddoniaeth yr Oesoedd Canol', in Geraint H. Jenkins (ed.), *Cymru a'r Cymry 2000 / Wales and the Welsh 2000* (Aberystwyth: CAWCS, 2001), pp. 41–70; K. Curtis *et al.*, 'Beirdd benywaidd yng Nghymru cyn 1800', *Y Traethodydd*, 141 (1986), 12–27; H. Fulton, 'Medieval Welsh poems to nuns', *Cambridge Medieval Celtic Studies*, 21 (1991), 87–112; S. Davies, 'Y ferch yng Nghymru yn yr Oesoedd Canol', *Cof Cenedl*, 9 (1994), 3–32; Dafydd Johnston, 'Gwenllïan ferch Rhirid Flaidd', *Dwned*, 3 (1997), 27–32; Ceridwen Lloyd-Morgan, 'More written about than writing? Welsh women and the written word', in Huw Pryce (ed.), *Literacy in Medieval Celtic Societies* (Cambridge: Cambridge University Press, 1998), pp. 149–65; *Gwaith Gwerful Mechain ac Eraill*, ed. Nerys Ann Howells (Aberystwyth: CAWCS, 2001); *Beirdd Ceridwen: Blodeugerdd Barddas o Ganu Menywod hyd tua 1800*, ed. Cathryn A. Charnell-White (Llandybïe: Cyhoeddiadau Barddas, 2005); Elisa Moras, ' "Mabddysg oedd iddi rhoddi yn rhwydd": nawdd barddol gan wragedd yn yr Oesoedd Canol', *Llên Cymru*, 28 (2005), 26–52.

4 P. H. Cullum and Katherine J. Lewis (eds), *Holiness and Masculinity in the Middle Ages* (Cardiff: University of Wales Press, 2004). Pioneering work on masculinity and Welsh literature has been undertaken by Chandler and Moras: Kirstie Siân Chandler, 'Masculinity and medieval Welsh literature' (unpublished doctoral thesis, University of Wales, Aberystwyth, 2004) and Elisa Moras, 'Gwrywdod, gwroldeb a gwrhydri yn y Canu Cynnar', *Llenyddiaeth Mewn Theori*, 2 (2007), 35–85.

5 Hilda Graef, *Mary, A History of Doctrine and Devotion*, 2 vols (London: Sheed and Ward, 1963); Marina Warner, *Alone of All Her Sex: the Myth and the Cult of the Virgin Mary* (London: Picador, 1976); Penny Schine Gold, *The Lady and the Virgin: Image, Attitude*

and Experience in Twelfth-Century France (Chicago: University of Chicago Press, 1985); Peter O'Dwyer, *Mary: A History of Devotion in Ireland* (Dublin: Four Courts, 1988); Mary Clayton, *The Apocryphal Gospels of Mary in Anglo-Saxon England* (Cambridge: Cambridge University Press, 1998); Sarah Jane Boss, *Empress and Handmaid: On Nature and Gender in the Cult of the Virgin Mary* (London: Cassell, 2000); Mary F. Foskett, *A Virgin Conceived: Mary and Classical Representations of Virginity* (Bloomington: Indiana University Press, 2002); Teresa Reed, *Shadows of Mary: Reading the Virgin Mary in Medieval Texts* (Cardiff: University of Wales Press, 2003); Bissera V. Pentcheva, *Icons and Power: the Mother of God in Byzantium* (University Park PA: Pennyslvania State University, 2006).

6 Andrew Breeze, 'The girdle of Prato and its rivals', B, 33 (1986), 95–100; 'The Virgin's tears of blood', *Celtica*, 20 (1988), 110–14; 'The Virgin's rosary and St Michael's scales', *Studia Celtica*, 24 (1989–90), 91–8; 'The Blessed Virgin's Joys and Sorrows', *Cambridge Medieval Celtic Studies*, 19 (1990), 41–54; 'The instantaneous harvest', *Ériu*, 41 (1990), 81–93; 'The Virgin Mary, daughter of her Son', *Études Celtiques*, 27 (1990), 267–87; 'Two bardic themes: the Trinity in the Blessed Virgin's womb', *Celtica*, 22 (1991), 1–15; 'Two bardic themes: the Virgin and child and *AVE*-EVA', *Medium Ævum*, 63 (1994), 17–33.

7 Christine James, 'Pen-rhys: mecca'r genedl', in Hywel Teifi Edwards (ed.), *Cwm Rhondda* (Llandysul: Gomer, 1995), pp. 27–71.

8 Madeleine Gray, 'Pen-rhys: the archaeology of a pilgrimage', *Morgannwg*, 40 (1996), 10–32 and *Images of Piety: the Iconography of Traditional Religion in Late Medieval Wales*, BAR British Series 316 (Oxford: Archaeopress, 2000).

9 Jane Cartwright, *Y Forwyn Fair, Santesau a Lleianod: Agweddau ar Wyryfdod a Diweirdeb yng Nghymru'r Oesoedd Canol* (Cardiff: University of Wales Press, 1999), pp. 14–75.

10 For editions of these Lives, see *Rhigyfarch's Life of St. David*, ed. J. W. James (Cardiff: University of Wales Press, 1967); *The Welsh Life of St David*, ed. D. Simon Evans (Cardiff: University of Wales Press, 1988); *Vitae Sanctorum Britanniae et Geneaologiae*, ed. and trans. A. W. Wade-Evans (Cardiff: University of Wales Press, 1944); *Liber Landavensis*, ed. W. J. Rees (Llandovery: Society for the Publication of Ancient Welsh Manuscripts, 1840). There is no extant Latin equivalent of *Hystoria o Uched Beuno*; for an edition of the Welsh Life of Beuno see *Vitae Sanctorum*, pp. 16–22. For editions of a number of Welsh poems to saints see D. J. Jones, 'Cerddi'r saint a'r bucheddau cyfatebol' (unpublished M. A. thesis, University of Wales, Aberystwyth, 1929). For an introduction to the development of Welsh hagiography see J. E. Caerwyn Williams, 'Bucheddau'r saint: eu cefndir a'u datblygiad fel llên', B, 11 (1944), 149–57; for a useful overview of the Welsh Lives see D. Simon Evans, 'Y Bucheddau', in Geraint Bowen (ed.), *Y Traddodiad Rhyddiaith yn yr Oesau Canol* (Llandysul: Gomer, 1974), pp. 245–73.

11 Sabine Baring-Gould and John Fisher, *The Lives of the British Saints*, 4 vols (London: Cymmrodorion, 1907–13); Elissa R. Henken, *Traditions of the Welsh Saints* (Cambridge: D. S. Brewer, 1987).

12 See, for example, T. Charles-Edwards, *Saint Winefride and her Well: the Historical Background* (London: Catholic Truth Society, 1962); F. Winward, 'The Lives of St. Wenefred (BHL 8847–8851)', *Analecta Bollandiana*, 117 (1999), 100–3; *Two Mediaeval Lives of Saint Winefride*, trans. Ronald Pepin and Hugh Feiss (Toronto: Peregrina Publishing, 2000); Lisa Eryl Jones, 'Golygiad o *Fuchedd Gwenfrewy*' (unpublished M.Phil. thesis, University of Wales, Cardiff, 2000); Huw Pryce, 'A new edition of the *Historia divae Monacellae*', *Montgomeryshire Collections*, 82 (1994), 23–40; W. J. Britnell and K. Watson, 'Saint Melangell's shrine, Pennant Melangell', *Montgomeryshire Collections*, 82 (1994), 147–66. See also, T. Thornley Jones, 'The daughters of Brychan Brycheiniog', *Brycheiniog*, 17 (1976–7), 17–58. Although this article provides some valuable information on the daughters of Brychan Brycheiniog, its main emphasis is on the early history of Breconshire and the 'blood relationships' between saintly and legendary characters.

13 There is some uncertainty as to whether or not St David was canonized by Pope Calixtus II (1119–24). *Councils and Ecclesiastical Documents Relating to Great Britain and Ireland*, ed. A. W. Haddan and W. Stubbs, 3 vols (Oxford: Clarendon Press, 1869–78), vol. 1, p. 316 and *Episcopal Acts and Cognate Documents Relating to Welsh Dioceses 1066–1272*, ed. James Conway Davies, 2 vols ([Cardiff]: Historical Society of the Church in Wales, 1946–8), 1(1), p. 136, n. 887. Giraldus Cambrensis put forward a proposal to canonize Caradog in 1200, but he was unsuccessful. St Caradog, who died in 1124, is an unusual case, since all of the other medieval Welsh saints belong to the early Middle Ages. He was buried in St Davids Cathedral. Some Welsh Catholic martyrs have been canonized in the modern period: for example, Richard White, who was put to death in 1584, was canonized by Pope Paul VI in 1970.

14 Anneke B. Mulder-Bakker (ed.), *Sanctity and Motherhood: Essays on Holy Mothers in the Middle Ages* (New York and London: Garland Publishing, 1995), p. 4.

15 A survey of previous publications on the Welsh nunneries is provided in Chapter 6.

Chapter 1

1 *Gwaith Siôn Ceri*, ed. A. Cynfael Lake (Aberystwyth: CAWCS, 1996), p. 149.

2 *Gramadegau'r Penceirddiaid*, ed. G. J. Williams and E. J. Jones (Cardiff: University of Wales Press, 1934), p. 15.

3 For Bishop Hugh Latimer's correspondence concerning Pen-rhys see

Letters and Papers, Foreign and Domestic, of the Reign of Henry VIII, arranged and catalogued by James Gairdner (London: HMSO, 1892–3), vol. 13, i, p. 134; and for Bishop William Barlow's letter to Cromwell regarding Our Lady of the Taper at Cardigan, see *Three Chapters of Letters relating to the Suppression of Monasteries*, ed. Thomas Wright (London: Camden Society, 1843), pp. 183–7. On the images, see below.

4 Glanmor Williams, *The Welsh Church from Conquest to Reformation* (Cardiff: University of Wales Press, 1976), p. 481. A. W. Wade-Evans, 'Parochiale Wallicanum', *Y Cymmrodor*, 22 (1910), 22–124, lists 149 churches and chapels dedicated to Mary. This excludes modern foundations. The Transnational Database and Atlas of Saints' Cults (TASC) has 364 entries on Marian dedications in Wales and the Marches: *http://www.le.ac.uk/elh/grj1/database/dedwales.html.* See also Graham Jones, *Saints of Wales: An Inventory of Religious Dedications* (Aberystwyth: Celtic Studies Publications, forthcoming).

5 Frances Jones, *The Holy Wells of Wales* (Cardiff: University of Wales Press, repr. 1992), p. 45, Map 4. While this volume remains a classic, it is by no means a fully comprehensive guide to the holy wells of Wales; in particular, there are many omissions in relation to north Wales. For a critique of the study see Tristan Gray Hulse, 'The documentation of Ffynnon Ddeier: some problems reconsidered', *Living Spring Journal*, 2 (2002), *http://www.bath.ac.uk/lispring/journal/front.html.* For a detailed study of Marian wells in Pembrokeshire see Julie Trier, 'A study of holy wells in Pembrokeshire including those of Our Lady and St David and their possible association with pilgrimage routes to St Davids', 2 vols (unpublished M.Phil. thesis, University of Wales, Lampeter, 2004).

6 *The Book of Llan Dâv*, ed. J. G. Evans and J. Rhŷs (Oxford: imprinted at Gloucester by John Bellows, 1893), p. 231; Wendy Davies, *An Early Welsh Microcosm: Studies in the Llandaff Charters* (London: Royal Historical Society, 1978), pp. 182–3; R. W. D. Fenn and J. B. Sinclair, 'St Michael, Our Lady, and St Cadoc: some ancient Monmouthshire dedications', *The Monmouthshire Antiquary*, 16 (2000), 99–106 (104).

7 See Nancy Edwards and Alan Lane (eds), *The Early Church in Wales and the West* (Oxford: Oxbow Monograph 16, 1992).

8 O'Dwyer, *Mary: A History of Devotion in Ireland.*

9 For details on the Welsh calendars and which Welsh manuscripts refer to the feasts of the Virgin see Cartwright, *Y Forwyn Fair*, pp. 180–6.

10 Cambridge, University Library, MS Ff.4.42, fol. 1^{r}. Ifor Williams, 'Naw englyn y Juvencus', B, 6 (1931–3), 205–24 (206). See also the editions and discussions in *Blodeugerdd Barddas o Ganu Crefyddol Cynnar*, ed. Marged Haycock ([Felindre, Abertawe (Swansea)]: Cyhoeddiadau Barddas, 1994), pp. 3–16, and Helen McKee, *The Cambridge Juvencus Manuscript Glossed in Latin, Old Welsh, and Old Irish Text and Commentary* (Aberystwyth: CMCS Publications, 2000), pp. 15–18, 81.

11 N. G. Costigan, *Defining the Divinity: Medieval Perceptions in Welsh Court Poetry* (Aberystwyth: CAWCS, 2002), p. 161.

12 *Gwaith Bleddyn Ddu*, ed. R. Iestyn Daniel (Aberystwyth: CAWCS, 1994), p. 21.

13 He emphasizes her descent from Jesse: *Gwaith Hywel Swrdwal a'i Deulu*, ed. Dylan Foster Evans (Aberystwyth: CAWCS, 2000), p. 79.

14 For a detailed discussion of the origins and development of the apocrypha from the second to the eleventh centuries, including the Syriac, Greek, Coptic and Latin evidence, see Clayton, *The Apocryphal Gospels*.

15 For editions see Mary Williams, 'Llyma Vabinogi Iessu Grist' and 'Buched Meir Wyry', *Revue Celtique*, 33 (1912), 184–207, 207–38; and for 'Buched Anna' see Jones, 'Cerddi'r saint', pp. 38–44. A new edition is currently being compiled by Carol Thomas, '*Buched Anna, Buched Meir Wyry* a *Llyma Vabinogi Iessu Grist*: agweddau ar destunau apocryffaidd' (unpublished doctoral thesis to be submitted to the University of Wales, Lampeter). In most medieval Welsh texts Mary's mother is referred to as 'Anna' rather than 'Anne'.

16 J. E. Caerwyn Williams, 'Welsh translations of *Pseudo-Matthaei Evangelium sive liber de ortu Beatae Mariae et infantia Salvatoris*', *Proceedings of the Irish Biblical Association*, 17 (1994), 102–25.

17 Williams, 'Llyma Vabinogi Iessu Grist', 210.

18 Ibid., 211. The angel tells Joachim 'a ry6 hat a rodet yt. y kyury6 ny bu eiroet' (and some seed was given to you. The like of which has never existed before).

19 Graef, *Mary*, vol. 1, p. 221.

20 Quoted in Giovanni Miegge, *The Virgin Mary. The Roman Catholic Marian Doctrine*, trans. Waldo Smith (London: Lutterworth Press, 1955), p. 114.

21 Jones, 'Cerddi a bucheddau'r saint', p. 39.

22 *Gwaith Hywel Swrdwal*, p. 85. I have chosen the reading in London, BL, MS Add. 31056, 44^{r} 'heb ffydd dda' (without good faith) which implies a slight criticism of Joachim and makes more sense in this context than 'nid eisiau fydd dda' (not needing good faith).

23 *Gwaith Ieuan Tew Brydydd Hen o Gydweli*, ed. Owen Thomas (Aberystwyth: CAWCS, forthcoming). I am grateful to my colleague, Owen Thomas, for providing me with a copy of his edition prior to publication. For another example see *Gwaith Barddonol Howel Swrdwal a'i Fab Ieuan*, ed. J. C. Morrice (Bangor: Welsh MSS Society, 1908), p. 5. This poem has now been rejected from the Hywel Swrdwal canon: *Gwaith Hywel Swrdwal*, pp. 12–13.

24 Williams, 'Llyma Vabinogi', 197.

25 P. R. Davis and S. Lloyd-Fern, *Lost Churches of Wales and the Marches* (Stroud: Sutton, 1990), p. 71.

26 Williams, 'Buched Meir', 214.

27 *Iolo Goch: Poems*, ed. and trans. Dafydd Johnston (Llandysul: Gomer, 1993), pp. 128–9; *The Poetical Works of Dafydd Nanmor*,

ed. Thomas Roberts and Ifor Williams (Cardiff: University of Wales Press, 1923), p. 92.

28 *Gwaith Dafydd ab Edmwnd*, ed. Thomas Roberts (Bangor: Welsh Manuscripts Society, 1914), p. 117.

29 *Iolo Goch: Poems*, pp. 126–7.

30 Miegge, *The Virgin Mary*, p. 41.

31 W. B. Smith, 'The theology of the virginity *in partu* and its consequences for the Church's teaching on chastity', *Marian Studies*, 31 (1980), 99–110 (109).

32 Warner, *Alone of All Her Sex*, p. 20.

33 Cf. Clayton, *The Apocryphal Gospels*, p. 23. *Libri de natiuitate Mariae: Libellus de natiuitate santae Mariae*, ed. R. Beyers, Corpus Christianorum Series Apocryphorum 10 (Turnhout: Brepols, 1997).

34 *Gwaith Hywel Swrdwal*, p. 86.

35 Warner, *Alone of All Her Sex*, p. 19. See also Miegge, *The Virgin Mary*, p. 29.

36 Aberystwyth, NLW, MS 4973B, fol. 377^{r}. Aberystwyth, NLW, MSS Peniarth 191 and Peniarth 192 also record this tradition. In Peniarth 192 a later hand has added to the front cover: 'Service Book, great part from the Primer of David Ddu of Hiraddug. Hengwrt M. S. 433'.

37 *Gwassanaeth Meir sef Cyfieithiad Cymraeg Canol o'r Officum Parvum Beatae Mariae Virginis*, ed. Brynley F. Roberts (Cardiff: University of Wales Press, 1961), pp. lxxv–lxxx.

38 See, for example, the Pembroke Hours, a fifteenth-century illustrated psalter made in the Low Countries, and the Louthe Hours, which includes an image of its patron, Sir John Dwnn, kneeling in prayer at the foot of an illumination depicting the Annunciation: Peter Lord, *The Visual Culture of Wales: Medieval Vision* (Cardiff: University of Wales Press, 2003), pp. 252–63 (p. 255 for the Annunciation scene).

39 G. F. Warner, *A Descriptive Catalogue of Illuminated Manuscripts in the Library of C. W. Dyson Perrins* (Oxford: Oxford University Press, 1920), pp. 59–61; Daniel Huws, *Medieval Welsh Manuscripts* (Cardiff: University of Wales Press and the National Library of Wales, 2000), p. 19. Huws notes that Isabella was married to William Godynogh, who appears in documents relating to Conwy (ibid., p. 19, n. 36).

40 E. J. M. Duggan, 'Notes concerning the "Lily Crucifixion" in the Llanbeblig Hours', *Journal of the National Library of Wales*, 27 (1991), 39–48.

41 Sarah Jane Boss, *Mary* (London and New York: Continuum, 2003), p. 2 discusses a lily crucifixion found in a sequence of paintings in the Lady Chapel at St Helen's church at Abingdon, Oxfordshire.

42 This ordeal is similar to a test described in the Old Testament when a jealous husband doubts his wife's fidelity (Numbers 5: 16–31).

43 Williams, 'Buched Meir', 220.

44 On this and other virginity tests in medieval Welsh texts see Jane Cartwright, 'Virginity and chastity tests in Middle Welsh prose', in

Bernau, Evans and Salih (eds), *Medieval Virginities*, pp. 56–79. This incident is similar to one described in *Transitus Mariae* when a Jewish priest's hand sticks to the Virgin's bier and he is in terrible pain until he announces that he believes in her virginity in partu and post partum. See below.

45 *Gwaith Iorwerth Fynglwyd*, ed. Howell L. Jones and E. I. Rowlands (Cardiff: University of Wales Press, 1975), p. 96.

46 Anne Elizabeth Jones, 'Gwilym Tew: astudiaeth destunol a chymharol o'i lawysgrif Peniarth 51, ynghyd ag ymdriniaeth â'i farddoniaeth' (unpublished doctoral thesis, University of Wales, Bangor, 1980), p. 448.

47 *Iolo Goch: Poems*, pp. 128–9.

48 *Cywyddau Iolo Goch ac Eraill*, ed. H. Lewis, T. Roberts and I. Williams (Cardiff: University of Wales Press, 1937), p. 96.

49 Warner, *Alone of All Her Sex*, p. 339.

50 Boss, *Empress and Handmaid*, pp. 64–6, 187–96; Cf. Boss, *Mary*, pp. 102–4, where it is argued that the generating action of God is manifested fully in Mary's virginal motherhood.

51 See, for example, *Woman Defamed and Woman Defended*, ed. Alcuin Blamires (Oxford: Clarendon, 1992); Howard R. Bloch, *Medieval Misogyny and the Invention of Western Romantic Love* (Chicago and London: University of Chicago Press, 1991).

52 Williams, 'Buched Meir', 223.

53 Graham C. G. Thomas, 'Mair a'r afallen', B, 24 (1970–2), 459–60.

54 *Gwaith Tudur Aled*, ed. T. Gwynn Jones, 2 vols (Cardiff: University of Wales Press, 1926), vol. 1, p. 128.

55 *Cywyddau Iolo Goch ac Eraill*, p. 94.

56 *Ludus Coventriae or the Plaie called Corpus Christi*, ed. Katherine Salter Block, EETS, 120 ES (1922).

57 *Selections from the Hengwrt MSS Preserved in the Peniarth Library*, ed. and trans. Robert Williams and G. Hartwell Jones, 2 vols (London: T. Richards and B. Quaritch, 1876–92), vol. 2, p. 244.

58 For example, Gwlydd Mair (Anagallis arvensis, Scarlet Pimpernel), Gwlydd Melyn Mair (Lysimachia nemorum, Yellow Pimpernel), Gwlydd Mair y Gors (Anagallis tenella, Bog Pimpernel), Mantell Fair (Alchemilla, Lady's Mantle), Briallu Mair (Primula veris, Cowslip), Briallu Mair Disawr (Primula elatior, Oxlip), Clustog Fair (Armeria maritima, Thrift), Chwys Mair (Ranunculus bulbosus, Bulbous Buttercup), Tafol Mair (Rumex conglomeratus, Clustered Whorled Dock), Ysnoden Fair (Cyperus longus, Galingale), Ysgallen Fair (Sambuscus ebulus, Dwarf Elder), Gwlyddyn Mair Beryw (Anagallis foemina, Blue Pimpernel), Helygen Mair (Myrica gale, Bog Myrtle), Mari Waedlyd (Amaranthus caudatus, Love-lies-bleeding) and Eirin Mair (Ribes uva-crispa, Gooseberry). See R. G. Ellis, *Flowering Plants of Wales* (Cardiff: National Museum of Wales, 1983) and Gwenllian Awbery, *Blodau'r Ardd a'r Maes ar Lafar Gwlad* (Llanrwst: Gwasg Carreg Gwalch, 1995). In the Lady Chapel at Llandaf

Cathedral a reredos by Frank Roper illustrates various flowers associated with Mary in Welsh.

59 The poem has been edited and translated into modern Welsh by Marged Haycock: *Blodeugerdd Barddas o Ganu Crefyddol*, pp. 121–35. The relevant section of the poem has also been translated into English by Andrew Breeze, 'The instantaneous harvest', 81–93, who discusses other versions of the miracle including thirteenth-century visual representations.

60 K. Jackson, 'A note on the miracle of the instantaneous harvest', B, 10 (1939–41), 203–7, and 'Some fresh light on the miracle of the instantaneous harvest', *Folklore*, 51 (1940), 203–10.

61 Breeze, 'The instantaneous harvest'. D. Simon Evans also suggested that the miracle originated in the Celtic Church: D. Simon Evans, *Medieval Religious Literature* (Cardiff: University of Wales Press, 1986), p. 17.

62 Lord, *Medieval Vision*, p. 158.

63 For a comparison of the different Welsh versions see J. E. Caerwyn Williams, '*Transitus Beatae Mariae* a thestunau cyffelyb', B, 18 (1959), 131–57.

64 A. Wenger, *L'Assomption de la très-sainte Vierge dans la tradition byzantine du VIe au Xe siècle* (Paris: Archives de l'Orient chrétien 5, 1955), p. 278. On the sermon and early beliefs relating to the Assumption see Graef, *Mary*, vol. 1, pp. 133–8.

65 J. E. Caerwyn Williams, 'Rhyddiaith grefyddol Cymraeg Canol', in Geraint Bowen (ed.), *Y Traddodiad Rhyddiaith yn yr Oesau Canol* (Llandysul: Gomer, 1974), pp. 312–408 (pp. 331–6).

66 Williams, '*Transitus*', 150.

67 Ibid., 150.

68 Cf the discussion on the burial site in Clayton, *The Apocryphal Gospels*, pp. 79–83.

69 Williams, '*Transitus*', 147.

70 Ibid., 151.

71 Mostyn Lewis, *Stained Glass in North Wales up to 1850* (Altrincham: John Sherratt & Son Ltd, 1970), Plate 22; Gray, *Images of Piety*, Plate 13b.

72 Gray, *Images of Piety*, p. 12, Plate 1b.

73 Aberystwyth, NLW, MS Llanstephan 117, pp. 139–40: the manuscript is now badly stained in parts; Williams, '*Transitus*', 137.

74 *Iolo Goch: Poems*, pp. 108–9.

75 Ibid., pp. 128–9.

76 *Gwaith Syr Phylib Emlyn, Syr Lewys Meudwy a Mastr Harri ap Hywel*, ed. M. Paul Bryant-Quinn (Aberystwyth: CAWCS, 2001), p. 133.

77 *Gwaith Bleddyn Ddu*, p. 30.

78 M. R. James, *The New Apocryphal Testament* (Oxford: Clarendon Press, 1953), p. 218.

79 See also the discussion on this manuscript and the Lives of Mary Magdalene and Martha in Chapter 4.

[80] Graef, *Mary*, vol. 1, p. 138.

[81] Warner, *Alone of All Her Sex*, pp. 278–9; Breeze, 'The girdle of Prato'.

[82] Lewis Haydn Angell, '*Gwyrthyeu e Wynvydedic Veir*: astudiaeth gymharol ohonynt fel y'u ceir hwynt yn llawysgrifau Peniarth 14, Peniarth 5 a Llanstephan 27' (unpublished M. A. thesis, University of Wales, Cardiff, 1938), pp. 49–50. Angell includes Latin versions of the miracles for comparison with the Welsh texts. Cf. also the comparison between the Welsh versions and Latin *Transitus* B in Williams, '*Transitus*', 140–2.

[83] Ingo Mittendorf, 'The Middle Welsh Mary of Egypt and the Latin source for of the *Miracles of the Virgin Mary*', in E. Poppe and B. Ross (eds), *The Legend of Mary of Egypt in Medieval Insular Hagiography* (Dublin: Four Courts Press, 1996), pp. 205–36 (pp. 210–18).

[84] This is not including the *Transitus*.

[85] Angell, '*Gwyrthyeu*', p. 66.

[86] Ibid., p. 66. The text has also been edited by Gwenan Jones, 'Gwyrthyeu y Wynvydedic Veir', B, 9 (1938–9), 144–8, 334–41, B, 10 (1939), 21–33 (21–2 on the pregnant abbess).

[87] Angell, '*Gwyrthyeu*', p. 58.

[88] On the Welsh Life of Mary of Egypt and her association with Mary Magdalene, see Chapter 4.

[89] Angell, '*Gwyrthyeu*', p. 83.

[90] On the Irish phenomena, see Chris Maunder, 'Apparitions of Mary in late twentieth-century Ireland: visions and reflections Part 1', *Maria*, 1 (1990), 69–85.

[91] On the Poets of the Gentry and the cultural, historical and religious background to this period in Wales, see Dafydd Johnston, *Llên yr Uchelwyr: Hanes Beirniadol Llenyddiaeth Gymraeg 1300–1525* (Cardiff: University of Wales Press, 2005).

[92] *Gwaith Llywelyn Fardd I ac Eraill o Feirdd y Ddeuddegfed Ganrif*, ed. Kathleen A. Bramley *et al.* (Cardiff: University of Wales Press, 1994), p. 455, p. 477, n. 293.

[93] *Gwaith Dafydd Benfras ac Eraill o Feirdd Hanner Cyntaf y Drydedd Ganrif ar Ddeg*, ed. N. G. Costigan *et al.* (Cardiff: University of Wales Press, 1995), p. 66.

[94] *Gwaith Casnodyn*, ed. R. Iestyn Daniel (Aberystwyth: CAWCS, 1999), p. 74; *Gwaith Bleddyn Ddu*, p. 17.

[95] R. T. Davies, 'A study of the themes and usages of medieval Welsh religious poetry 1100–1450', (unpublished B. Litt. dissertation, Oxford University, 1958–9), pp. 88–9.

[96] Graef, *Mary*, vol. 1, p. 85.

[97] *The Elucidarium and other tracts in Welsh from Llyvyr Agkyr Llandewivrevi A. D. 1346*, ed. John Morris Jones and John Rhŷs (Oxford: Clarendon, 1869), p. 17.

[98] *Concerning Virgins in St Ambrose: Select Works and Letters, A Select Library of Nicene and Post-Nicene Fathers of the Church*, ed.

P. Schaff and H. Wace, 10 vols (New York: The Christian Literature Company, 1896), vol. 6, pp. 29–30.

99 *Gwaith Gronw Gyriog, Iorwerth ab y Cyriog ac Eraill*, ed. Rhiannon Ifans *et al*., (Aberystwyth: CAWCS, 1997), p. 39.

100 Breeze, 'Two bardic themes: the Trinity', 27.

101 *Gwaith Gruffudd ap Maredudd II: Cerddi Crefyddol*, ed. Barry J. Lewis (Aberystwyth: CAWCS, 2005), p. 83.

102 *Gwaith Sefnyn, Rhisierdyn ac Eraill*, ed. Nerys Ann Jones and Erwain Haf Rheinallt (Aberystwyth: CAWCS, 1996), pp. 151–9, 186–9.

103 *Iolo Goch: Poems*, pp. 128–9.

104 *Gwaith Gruffudd Llwyd a'r Llygliwiaid Eraill*, ed. Rhiannon Ifans (Aberystwyth: CAWCS, 2000), p. 193

105 *Casgliad o Waith Ieuan Deulwyn*, ed. Ifor Williams (Bangor: Welsh Manuscripts Society, 1909), p. 99.

106 Sabine Baring-Gould and John Fisher, *The Lives of the British Saints*, 4 vols (London: Cymmrodorion, 1907–13) vol. 4, pp. 376–7.

107 Gray, *Images of Piety*, p. 10. See also Lord, *Medieval Vision*, p. 154.

108 Clayton, *The Cult of the Virgin Mary*, p. 6.

109 *Iolo Goch: Poems*, pp. 128–9.

110 *Cywyddau Iolo Goch ac Eraill*, p. 96.

111 *Gwaith Sefnyn*, p. 152.

112 Davies, 'A study of the themes and usages', p. 90.

113 *The Elucidarium*, p. 159.

114 *Gwaith Sefnyn*, p. 191, n. 61. On 'gwydr' meaning 'bright, shining' see *Geirfa Barddoniaeth Gynnar Gymraeg*, ed. J. Lloyd-Jones (Cardiff: University of Wales Press, 1931–63), col. 729.

115 In the Life of St David, for example, Non gives birth outside in a thunderstorm, but the immediate area around her shines with bright sunlight. On Non, see Chapter 3.

116 The Woman of the Apocalypse is also taken as a personification of the Church. By the Middle Ages the woman clothed in the sun was often interpreted as Mary and Mary was frequently depicted as the body of the Church itself.

117 Williams, 'Buched Meir', 214.

118 Jones, 'Cerddi'r saint', p. 41.

119 *Gwaith Gruffudd ap Maredudd II*, pp. 79–80.

120 *Cywyddau Iolo Goch ac Eraill*, p. 322.

121 *Gwaith Llywelyn Brydydd Hoddnant, Dafydd ap Gwilym, Hillyn ac Eraill*, ed. Ann Parry Owen (Aberystwyth: CAWCS, 1996), p. 141.

122 *Gwaith Bleddyn Ddu*, p. 21.

123 Ibid., p. 17.

124 *Gwaith Hywel Swrdwal*, p. 80.

125 R. Geraint Gruffydd, 'Dafydd Ddu o Hiraddug', *Llên Cymru*, 18 (1995), 205–20.

126 *Gramadegau'r Penceirddiaid*, p. 15.

127 *Ymborth yr Enaid*, ed. R. Iestyn Daniel (Cardiff: University of Wales Press, 1995), pp. 17–22.

128 Aberystwyth, NLW, MS Llanstephan 47B, pp. 153–6.

[129] Ibid., p. 156.
[130] G. Ruddock, 'Prydferthwch merch yng nghywyddau serch y bymthegfed ganrif', in John Rowlands (ed.), *Dafydd ap Gwilym a Chanu Serch yr Oesoedd Canol* (Cardiff: University of Wales Press, 1975), pp. 95–119. (pp. 98–102).
[131] James, 'Pen-rhys', p. 46.
[132] The explanation is given in a prose prologue to the poem: a short version of the prologue is found in London, BL, MS Add. 14866, fols 25^{r}–26^{r} (dated 1587) and a longer version is found in Aberystwyth, NLW, MS Peniarth 111, pp. 286–91 (dated *c.*1610). For a full transcription and translation see E. J. Dobson, 'The hymn to the Virgin', *Transactions of the Honourable Society of Cymmrodorion* (1954), 70–124 (99–100, 111–12).
[133] Tony Conran, 'The hymn to the Virgin', *Welsh Writing in English*, 1 (1995), 5–22 (15 for trans.); See also Dobson, 'The hymn to the Virgin', 101, and *Gwaith Hywel Swrdwal*, p. 124.
[134] Conran, 'The hymn to the Virgin', 14.
[135] Reed, *Shadows of Mary*, p. 77.
[136] On medieval medical ideas relating to conception and pregnancy, see Danielle Jacquart and Claude Thomasset, *Sexuality and Medicine in the Middle Ages*, trans. Matthew Adamson (Cambridge: Polity Press, 1988).
[137] *Gwaith Gruffudd ap Maredudd II*, p. 75.
[138] Brynley F. Roberts, 'Gweddi Boneffas Bab', B, 16 (1956), 271–3 (272).
[139] *Gwaith Cynddelw Brydydd Mawr*, ed. Nerys Ann Jones and Ann Parry Owen, 2 vols (Cardiff: University of Wales Press, 1995), vol. 2, p. 336.
[140] Costigan, *Defining the Divinity*, pp. 69–70.
[141] *Casgliad o Waith Ieuan Deulwyn*, pp. 99–100.
[142] *Cywyddau Iolo Goch ac Eraill*, p. 96.
[143] Johan Henrick Cornell, *The Iconography of the Nativity of Christ* (Uppsala: Uppsala Universitets årsskrift, 1924), p. 12.
[144] Lord, *Medieval Vision*, p. 156.
[145] *Gwaith Bleddyn Fardd a Beirdd Eraill Ail Hanner y Drydedd Ganrif ar Ddeg*, ed. Rhian M. Andrews *et al.* (Cardiff: University of Wales Press, 1996), p. 359.
[146] *Medieval Welsh Poems*, trans. Joseph P. Clancy (Dublin: Four Courts Press, 2003), p. 166.
[147] *Gwaith Bleddyn Fardd*, pp. 359–60.
[148] *Medieval Welsh Poems*, pp. 167–8.
[149] *Hen Gerddi Crefyddol*, ed. Henry Lewis (Cardiff: University of Wales Press, 1931), p. xiv.
[150] *Blodeugerdd Barddas o Ganu Crefyddol*, p. 269.
[151] *Gwaith Dafydd Benfras*, pp. 139–40.
[152] *Gwaith Meilyr Brydydd a'i Ddisgynyddion ynghyd â dwy awdl fawl ddienw o Ddeheubarth*, ed. J. E. Caerwyn Williams with the help of

Peredur Lynch and R. Geraint Gruffydd (Cardiff: University of Wales Press, 1994), p. 523.

153 Costigan, *Defining the Divinity*, p. 47.

154 *Gwaith Dafydd Epynt*, ed. Owen Thomas (Aberystwyth: CAWCS, 2002), p. 27.

155 *Gwaith Syr Phylib Emlyn*, p. 132.

156 Breeze, 'The Virgin's rosary'.

157 *Casgliad o Waith Ieuan Deulwyn*, pp. 97–8.

158 On the topos, see Breeze, 'The Virgin's tears of blood'.

159 *Cywyddau Iolo Goch ac Eraill*, p. 94.

160 *Gwaith Gruffudd Llwyd*, pp. 124–31. On Morgan ap Dafydd's case, see ibid., pp. 240–2.

161 *Gwaith Lewys Glyn Cothi*, ed. Dafydd Johnston (Cardiff: University of Wales Press, 1995), p. 189; *Gwaith Lewys Morgannwg*, ed. A. Cynfael Lake, 2 vols (Aberystwyth: CAWCS, 2004), vol. 2, p. 507; *Gwaith Deio ab Ieuan Du a Gwilym ab Ieuan Hen*, ed. A. Eleri Davies (Cardiff: University of Wales Press, 1992), pp. 12–13.

162 Thomas Roberts, 'Cywyddau pererindod', *Y Traethodydd*, 13 (1944), 28–39 (29).

163 Thomas Charles-Edwards, 'Pen-rhys: y cefndir hanesyddol 1179–1538', *Efrydiau Catholig*, 5 (1951), 24–39; G. J. Williams, 'Atodiad: cywyddau ac awdlau Pen-rhys', *Efrydiau Catholig*, 5 (1951), 40–5; Silas M. Harris, 'Y Wyry Wen o Ben-rhys. Our Lady of Pen-rhys', *Welsh Saints and Shrines*, 1 (1951), 1–3; James, 'Pen-rhys', pp. 27–71; Johnston, *Llên yr Uchelwyr*, p. 217.

164 Jones, 'Gwilym Tew', p. 447.

165 *Gwaith Lewys Morgannwg*, vol. 2, p. 503.

166 Ibid., vol. 2, p. 507.

167 James, 'Pen-rhys', pp. 45–6.; *Gwaith Rhys Brydydd a Rhisiart ap Rhys*, collected by John Morgan Williams and ed. Eurys I. Rolant (Cardiff: University of Wales Press, 1976), pp. 13–14.

168 Jones, 'Gwilym Tew', p. 448.

169 James, 'Pen-rhys', pp. 33–4; Terry John and Nona Rees, *Pilgrimage: A Welsh Perspective* (Llandysul: Gomer, 2002), pp. 112–16. See also Gray, 'Pen-rhys'.

170 See, for example, the crowned and enthroned Virgin on the seal of an anonymous abbot of Strata Florida in Cartwright, *Y Forwyn Fair*, Plate 3.

171 John and Rees, *Pilgrimage*, p. 87.

172 D. H. Williams, 'Llantarnam Abbey', *The Monmouthshire Antiquary*, 2 (1967), 131–48 (144).

173 *Gwaith Lewys Morgannwg*, vol. 2, p. 503.

174 Nest Scourfield, 'Gwaith Ieuan Gethin ab Ieuan ap Lleision, Llywelyn ap Hywel ab Ieuan ap Gronw, Ieuan Du'r Bilwg, Ieuan Rudd a Llywelyn Goch y Dant' (unpublished M.Phil. thesis, University of Wales, Swansea, 1992), p. 53.

175 Ibid., p. 45.

176 *Letters and Papers,* vol. 13, i, p. 437.

[177] *Three Chapters of Letters*, pp. 183–4.
[178] Ibid., p. 186.
[179] Giraldus Cambrensis, *The Journey Through Wales and The Description of Wales*, trans. Lewis Thorpe (London: Penguin, 1978), p. 172.
[180] *Three Chapters of Letters*, p. 186.
[181] Ibid., p. 187.
[182] H. Maynard Smith, *Pre-Reformation England* (London: Macmillan & Co. Ltd, 1938), p. 178.
[183] On Gwenfrewy, see Chapter 2 in the present volume.
[184] Peter Mullen, *Shrines of Our Lady. A Guide to Fifty of the World's Most Famous Marian Shrines* (London: Piatkus, 1998), pp. 178–80.
[185] Ibid., pp. 176–7. The Sisters of Nazareth moved on and I am very grateful to Sister Patricia, one of the Sisters of Loreto, who cares for the shrine for providing me with information.
[186] Cambrian Archaeological Society, 'Carmarthen Meeting – Report, Friday, August 20th 1875', *Archaeologia Cambrensis*, 6 (1875), series 4, 412–13; D. Ambrose Jones, 'Miscellanea', *Archaeologica Cambrensis*, 2 (1922), series 7, 415.
[187] *Gwaith Dafydd ap Gwilym*, pp. 259–60. I am grateful to Dylan Foster Evans for drawing my attention to this reference when he was preparing a new edition and translation of the poem: see now http://www.dafyddapgwilym.net (number 89). As noted by Foster Evans, since Dafydd may be referring to Mael Maelienydd ap Cadfael, whom the poet Lewys Glyn Cothi associates with Elfael, it is possible that the image may have been in the hundred of Elfael.
[188] *Dafydd ap Gwilym: His Poems*, trans. Gwyn Thomas (Cardiff: University of Wales Press, 2001), p. 191.
[189] *Gwaith Dafydd ap Gwilym*, p. 519, n. 3.
[190] For an image of the Christ figure, see Lord, *Medieval Vision*, p. 172.
[191] University of Wales, Bangor, MS Gwyneddon 4, pp. 69–70; NLW, MS, Peniarth 221, pp. 207–9; NLW Peniarth 64, p. 36; NLW, MS 6209E, pp. 249–50. I am grateful to Barry Lewis for drawing this poem to my attention. Gwilym Tew refers to Maelienydd in his awdl to Mary of Pen-rhys: Jones, 'Gwilym Tew', p. 447.
[192] M. Paul Bryant-Quinn, ' "Enaid y gwir goleuni": y Grog yn Aberhonddu', *Dwned*, 2 (1996), 51–93; Ann Parry Owen, 'Englynion Dafydd Llwyd ap Gwilym Gam i'r Grog o Gaer', *Ysgrifau Beirniadol*, 21 (1996), 15–36; Christine James, '"Y grog ddoluriog loywrym": golwg ar y canu i grog Llangynwyd', *Llên Cymru*, 29 (2006), 64–109.
[193] Smith, *Pre-Reformation England*, pp. 178–9.
[194] *Gwaith Tudur Aled*, vol. 2, p. 349.
[195] John and Rees, *Pilgrimage*, p. 87.
[196] *Gwaith Hywel Swrdwal*, p. 86; *The Poetical Works of Dafydd Nanmor*, p. 82.
[197] John and Rees, *Pilgrimage*, p. 89.
[198] 'Trŵn' usually means 'throne' and probably indicates that the Virgin was enthroned at Llanystumdwy, as was the image at Pen-rhys.

However, another meaning of 'trŵn' is 'firmament'. See, for example, Rhys Goch Eryri's second response to Llywelyn ab y Moel in *Gwaith Rhys Goch Eryri*, ed. Dylan Foster Evans (Aberystwyth: CAWCS, forthcoming), poem 8, ll.43–8: I am grateful to Ann Parry Owen for this reference. Thus, 'Mary of the Firmament' is another possible translation.

199 Aberystwyth, NLW, MS Llanstephan 134, p. 63.

200 The place name is split in two by the interjection. 'Llan', meaning 'church', as well as forming the first element in the place name 'Llanystumdwy'.

201 Aberystwyth, NLW, MS Llanstephan 134, p. 63.

202 Elsbeth Wendy Owen Davies, 'Testun beirniadol o waith Hywel Rheinallt ynghyd â rhagymadrodd, nodiadau a geirfa' (unpublished M. A. thesis, University of Wales, Aberystwyth, 1967), p. 2.

203 Davies, 'Testun beirniadol o waith Hywel Rheinallt', p. 2.

204 Scourfield, 'Gwaith Ieuan Gethin', p. 54.

205 James, 'Pen-rhys', pp. 38–9.

206 Davies, 'Testun beirniadol o waith Hywel Rheinallt', p. 2.

207 On Dwynwen see Chapter 2 in the present volume.

208 Ibid., p. 3.

209 Frank Ward, *The Lakes of Wales* (London: Herbert Jenkins Ltd, 1931), p. 144.

210 *Gwaith Meilyr Brydydd*, p 102.

211 Jones, *Holy Wells of Wales*, p. 47; John and Rees, *Pilgrimage*, pp. 120–2.

212 *Gwaith Hywel Swrdwal*, p. 79. Aberystwyth, NLW, MS 13079B, fol. 51^{r}, states 'Mair o Gymry deg' (Mary from fair Wales).

213 Davies, 'Testun beirniadol o waith Hywel Rheinallt', p. 2.

214 *Gramadegau'r Penceirddiaid*, p. 15.

215 Jones, 'Gwilym Tew', p. 434.

216 *Iolo Goch: Poems*, pp. 116–17.

217 Scourfield, 'Gwaith Ieuan Gethin', p. 50.

Chapter 2

1 This is an expanded and revised version of an article which first appeared in *Medium Ævum*, 71 (2002), 1–28.

2 See, for example, E. G. Bowen, *The Settlements of the Celtic Saints in Wales* (Cardiff: University of Wales Press, 1954) and *Saints, Seaways and Settlements in the Celtic Lands* (Cardiff: University of Wales Press, 1977).

3 Kathleen Hughes, 'The Celtic Church: is this a valid concept?', *Cambridge Medieval Celtic Studies*, 1 (1981), 1–20; Wendy Davies, 'The myth of the Celtic Church', in Edwards and Lane (eds), *The Early Church in Wales and the West*, pp. 12–21.

[4] Ian Bradley, *The Celtic Way* (London: Darton, Longman and Todd, 1993); the quotation appears on the book's cover.

[5] Ian Bradley, *Celtic Christianity: Making Myths and Chasing Dreams* (Edinburgh: Edinburgh University Press, 1999), p. vii.

[6] See the Introduction to the present volume for a survey of work undertaken in the field.

[7] J. W. Willis Bund, 'Some characteristics of Welsh and Irish saints', *Archaeologia Cambrensis*, 11 (1894), series 5, 276–91 (279–80).

[8] G. H. Doble, *S. Nectan, S. Keyne and the Children of Brychan in Cornwall*, Cornish Saints Series 25 (Exeter: Sydney Lee, 1930), p. 47.

[9] G. H. Doble, *Lives of the Welsh Saints*, ed. D. Simon Evans (Cardiff: Cardiff University of Wales Press, 1971), p. 66.

[10] David H. Farmer, *The Oxford Dictionary of Saints*, 3rd edn (Oxford: Oxford University Press, 1992), pp. 55 and 500. In 1992 the front cover was redesigned to include a nun as well as a monk.

[11] See also Farmer's comments on Ninnoc (one of the daughters of Brychan Brycheiniog): 'Her memory is kept alive by various images of her and by her feast on 4 June. There is also a worthless legendary Life.' Ibid., p. 358.

[12] J. Wyn Evans, 'The early Church in Denbighshire', *Transactions of the Denbighshire Historical Society*, 35 (1986), 61–81 (65).

[13] *Trioedd Ynys Prydein. The Welsh Triads*, ed. and trans. Rachel Bromwich (Cardiff: University of Wales Press, 1978), p. 201.

[14] *Early Welsh Genealogical Tracts*, ed. P. C. Bartrum (Cardiff: University of Wales Press, 1966), pp. 14–16. See also pp. 17–19, 81–4.

[15] Bowen, *Settlements of the Celtic Saints*, p. 26.

[16] For a list of the varying numbers of Brychan's children see Jones, 'The daughters of Brychan Brycheiniog', 18–19. For translations of *De situ Brecheniauc* and *Cognacio Brychan*, see A. W. Wade-Evans, 'The Brychan Documents', *Y Cymmrodor*, 19 (1906), 18–50, and on the dating and historical background to the texts see Charles Thomas, *And Shall These Mute Stones Speak?* (Cardiff: University of Wales Press, 1994), pp. 131–62.

[17] Joanna Mattingly, 'Pre-Reformation saints' cults in Cornwall, with particular reference to the St Neot windows', in Jane Cartwright (ed.) *Celtic Hagiography and Saints' Cults* (Cardiff: University of Wales Press, 2003), pp. 249–70 (p. 260 and Figure 14.11).

[18] *Vitae Sanctorum*, pp. xix and 318.

[19] Giraldus Cambrensis, *The Journey through Wales and The Description of Wales*, trans. Lewis Thorpe (Harmondsworth: Penguin, 1978), pp. 91–2.

[20] For example, Aberystwyth, NLW, MSS Peniarth 27i, Peniarth 60, Peniarth 186 and Peniarth 187. For a composite calendar listing the feasts of female saints and details of the Welsh sources, see Cartwright, *Y Forwyn Fair*, pp. 180–6.

[21] On the nunnery at Usk, see Chapter 6.

[22] William Worcestre, *Itineraries*, ed. J. H. Harvey (Oxford: Clarendon, 1969), p. 155.

23 *Gwaith Tudur Aled*, vol. 2, p. 524.

24 Baring-Gould and Fisher, *Lives of the British Saints*, vol. 3, p. 191, n. 2.

25 See *Acta Sanctorum*, ed. C. de Smedt *et al.*, November, vol. 1 (Paris: Apud Victorem Palme, 1887), pp. 691–731 for editions of both Lives. The anonymous *vita*, found in London, British Library, MS Cotton Claudius A.v, has been edited and translated by Wade-Evans, *Vitae Sanctorum*, pp. 288–309, and for English translations of Prior Robert's *vita* as well as the anonymous Life, see *Two Mediaeval Lives*. The Welsh Life is preserved in Aberystwyth, National Library of Wales, MSS Peniarth 27, Peniarth 225, Llanstephan 34 and Llanstephan 104. See Table 1 for its context in the Welsh manuscripts. For an edition and more detailed discussion of the Welsh manuscripts see Jones, 'Golygiad o *Fuchedd Gwenfrewy*'.

26 Cf St David's attendance at the synod of Llanddewibrefi.

27 *Supplementary Lives in Some Manuscripts of the Gilte Legende*, ed. Richard Hamer and Vida Russell, EETS os 315 (Oxford: Oxford University Press, 2000), pp. 39–43. I am grateful to Vida Russell for her helpful comments on the Middle English versions of the Life (personal communication).

28 G. Hartwell Jones, *Celtic Britain and the Pilgrim Movement*, *Y Cymmrodor*, 23 (London: Cymmrodorion, 1912), pp. 401–2; Jones, 'Cerddi'r saint', pp. 127–33; *Gwaith Ieuan Brydydd Hir*, ed. M. Paul Bryant-Quinn (Aberystwyth: CAWCS, 2000), pp. 141–5; *Gwaith Tudur Aled*, vol. 2, pp. 523–6; *Cywyddau Iolo Goch ac Eraill*, pp. 104–6; *Gwaith Siôn ap Hywel ap Llywelyn Fychan*, ed. A. Cynfael Lake (Aberystwyth: CAWCS, 1999), pp. 73–5. There are also allusions to Gwenfrewy and her healing well in other poems: see, for example, *Gwaith Guto'r Glyn*, ed. John Llywelyn Williams and Ifor Williams (Cardiff: University of Wales Press, 1961), pp. 120, 123.

29 Oxford, Bodleian Library, MS Rawlinson B464, fol. 29^{r}; Nancy Edwards and Tristan Gray Hulse, 'A fragment of a reliquary casket from Gwytherin, North Wales', *The Antiquaries Journal*, 72 (1992), 91–101. The dating of the reliquary relies not on radiocarbon dating, but on a comparison of the metal roundels depicted in Lhuyd's drawing with similar roundels on Anglo-Saxon reliquaries. See also L. Butler and J. Graham-Campbell, 'A lost reliquary casket from North Wales', *The Antiquaries Journal*, 70 (1990), 40–8.

30 *Gwaith Tudur Aled*, vol. 2, p. 526.

31 *Gwaith Siôn ap Hywel*, p. 70.

32 David H. Williams, *Catalogue of Seals in the National Museum of Wales*, 2 vols (Cardiff: National Museum of Wales, 1998), vol. 2, p. 59, E486.

33 Lewis, *Stained Glass in North Wales*, pp. 9–12, 52, Plates 35 and 53; Gray, *Images of Piety*, pp. 27, 34–6.

34 See, for example, Glanmor Williams, 'The tradition of St David in Wales', in O. W. Jones and D. Walker (eds), *Links with the Past:*

Swansea and Brecon Historical Essays (Llandybïe: Christopher Davies, 1974), pp. 1–20; Evans, 'Y Bucheddau', pp. 245–73; Wendy Davies, 'Property rights and property claims in Welsh "Vitae" of the eleventh century', *Hagiographie, Cultures et Sociétés, IVe–XIIe siècles* (Paris: Études augustiniennes, 1981), pp. 515–33; Elissa R. Henken, *Traditions of the Welsh Saints* (Cambridge: D. S. Brewer, 1987), pp. 5–6.

35 *Two Mediaeval Lives*, p. 111.

36 See also the discussion on Cricieth church in Chapter 5: it appears to have been dedicated to one or more native saints prior to the thirteenth century when it became associated with St Katherine.

37 Cartwright, *Y Forwyn Fair*, Plate IV.

38 Britnell and Watson, 'Saint Melangell's shrine' 147–66. For an account of the restoration of the church at Pennant Melangell, see the interview with Rev. Evelyn Davies in Peter Lord, *The Visual Culture of Wales: Medieval Vision*, CD-ROM (Cardiff: University of Wales Press, 2004).

39 *The Letter Book of Lewis Sabran, S. J. (Rector of St. Omers College) October 1713 to October 1715*, ed. Geoffrey Holt, Catholic Record Society (Records Series), vol. 62 (St Albans: Catholic Record Society Publications, 1971), pp. 8, 36–7, 53, 58, 66, 78, 80, 95–7, 99, 101, 104, 108–10, 112, 118, 272, 277.

40 Ibid., pp. 58, 78.

41 Ibid., p. 95.

42 Tristan Gray Hulse presented an excellent paper on the relics: ' "Visting a dry skull": aspects of the cult of relics in post-Reformation Wales', unpublished paper delivered at the conference on Celtic Hagiography and Saints' Cults, University of Wales, Lampeter, 8–10 September 2000.

43 *Gwaith Lewys Glyn Cothi*, pp. 25, 333; *Gwaith Guto'r Glyn*, pp. 120, 171, 284.

44 Cardiff, Central Library, MS 3.11, p. 1 (incomplete); London, BL, Harley MS 2059, fol. 111^{r-v} (incomplete); Aberystwyth, NLW, MS 1506C, part iii, pp. 38–41; Aberystwyth, NLW, MS 1641B i, pp. 63–8; R. Williams, 'Historiae Monacellae', *Archaeologia Cambrensis*, 3 (1848), 139–42.

45 C. A. Ralegh Radford and W. J. Hemp, 'Pennant Melangell: the church and the shrine', *Archaeologia Cambrensis*, 108 (1959), series 5, 81–113 (82); Pryce, 'A new edition of the *Historia divae Monacellae*', 30.

46 M. H. Ridgway, 'Furnishings and fittings at Pennant Melangell church', *Montgomeryshire Collections*, 82 (1994), 127–38 (130–5).

47 Pryce, 'A new edition of the *Historia divae Monacellae*', 40.

48 Ibid., p. 40.

49 *Vitae Sanctorum*, pp. 292–3.

50 *The Welsh Life of St David*, ed. D. Simon Evans (Cardiff: University of Wales Press, 1988), p. 6.

51 *Iolo Manuscripts. A Selection of Ancient Welsh Manuscripts*, ed.

Taliesin Williams (Llandovery: William Rees, 1848), pp. 107–8, 120. On Iolo Morganwg see Geraint H. Jenkins (ed.), *A Rattleskull Genius: The Many Faces of Iolo Morganwg* (Cardiff: University of Wales Press, 2005); Cathryn Charnell-White, *Bardic Circles: National, Regional and Personal Identity in the Bardic Vision of Iolo Morganwg* (Cardiff: University of Wales Press, 2007); Mary-Ann Constantine, *The Truth Against the World: Iolo Morganwg and Romantic Forgery* (Cardiff: University of Wales Press, 2007).

52 *Iolo Manuscripts*, p. 121.

53 Ibid., p. 131.

54 *Vitae Sanctorum*, p. 283.

55 Jones, 'Cerddi'r saint', pp. 185–7.

56 The word 'eurgrair' literally means 'golden relic', but it can also be used to describe something precious. An alternative interpretation of the first line of this poem could read as follows: 'Talking of the most treasured St Margaret'. Cf. 'Y Tad iawngrair' (the most treasured father) in Iolo Goch's 'Cywydd y Llafurwr': *Iolo Goch: Poems*, pp. 116–17. Theodosius is traditionally Margaret's father, although the reference to 'Vorach' is peculiar. Perhaps the poet intended to refer to Antioch.

57 Melville Richards, 'Buchedd Fargred', B, 9 (1939), 324–34 (332).

58 Ibid., 329.

59 For the Lives of Agatha and Barbara, see William Caxton, *The Golden Legend or Lives of the Saints as Englished by William Caxton*, ed. F. S. Ellis, 7 vols (London: J. M. Dent, 1900), vol. 3, pp. 32–9, vol. 4, pp. 198–205; Jacobus de Voragine, *The Golden Legend*, trans. William Granger Ryan, 2 vols (Princeton: Princeton University Press, 1993), vol. 1, pp. 154–7.

60 *The Poetical Works of Dafydd Nanmor*, pp. 500–1.

61 *Gwaith Lewys Morgannwg*, vol. 1, p. 55.

62 Lewis, *Stained Glass in North Wales*, Plates 16 and 17. She also appears in the east window, although I believe that this particular section of glass is modern and may have been added to the medieval window when it was transformed into a Te Deum window in 1867.

63 I. B. Jones, 'Hafod 16 (A mediaeval Welsh medical treatise)', *Études Celtiques*, 7 (1955–6), 46–75, 270–339 (74).

64 *Rhyddiaith Gymraeg: Y Gyfrol Gyntaf Detholion o Lawysgrifau 1488–1609*, ed. T. H. Parry-Williams (Cardiff: University of Wales Press, 1954), pp. 18–22.

65 Jane Cartwright, 'Santesau Ceredigion', *Ceredigion*, 14 (2001), 1–36 (21, Plate 5).

66 See Haycock, 'Merched drwg a merched da', 80–3.

67 *Gwaith Tudur Aled*, vol. 2, p. 523.

68 For example, *Gwaith Iolo Goch*, p. 3; *Gwaith Dafydd Gorlech*, ed. Erwain H. Rheinallt (Aberystwyth: CAWCS 1997), p. 46; *Gwaith Lewys Môn*, ed. Eurys I. Rowlands (Cardiff: University of Wales Press, 1975), p. 85.

69 Geoffrey of Monmouth, *The History of the Kings of Britain*, trans.

Lewis Thorpe (Harmondsworth: Penguin, 1987), pp. 140–3; *Brut Dingestow*, ed. Henry Lewis (Cardiff: University of Wales Press, 1942), p. 78.

70 Elissa R. Henken, *The Welsh Saints: A Study in Patterned Lives* (Cambridge: D. S. Brewer, 1991), pp. 1–14 and 'The saint as folk hero: biographical patterning in Welsh hagiography', in P. K. Ford (ed.), *Celtic Folklore and Christianity* (Santa Barbara: McNally and Loftin, 1983), pp. 58–74.

71 Images of Katherine and George also appear on the fifteenth-century alabaster tomb of the Bulkeleys at Beaumaris, Anglesey. Although the figures now appear on opposite sides of the tomb, they were originally situated next to each other, and the tomb, no doubt, has been repositioned in the church, dismantled and re-erected. See Chapter 5. On the cult of St George see Samantha J. E. Riches, *St George: Hero, Martyr and Myth* (Stroud: Sutton, 2000).

72 Elissa R. Henken, 'Folklore of the Welsh Saints', 2 vols (unpublished M. A. thesis, University of Wales, Aberystwyth, 1982), vol. 1, pp. 13–14. See also Henken's comments on the biographical pattern of the Welsh women saints, *The Welsh Saints*, pp. 6–9.

73 For a typical profile of the female virgin martyr saint in twelfth- and thirteenth-century vernacular literature, see Jocelyn Wogan-Browne, 'Saints' lives and the female reader', *Forum for Modern Language Studies*, 37 (1991), 314–32 (315).

74 R. H. Bloch, 'Chaucer's maiden's head: *The Physician's Tale* and the poetics of virginity', *Representations*, 28 (1989), 113–34 (120).

75 *Vitae Sanctorum*, p. 291.

76 Bloch, 'Chaucer's maiden's head', 117.

77 *Gwaith Iorwerth Fynglwyd*, p. 94. On the Irish Lives of St Brigid of Kildare, see *Bethu Brigte*, ed. Donncha Ó hAodha (Dublin: Dublin Institute for Advanced Studies, 1978). For further evidence of the Welsh interest in St Birgitta of Sweden (1303–73) see the Middle Welsh version of the fifteen prayers attributed to her: Brynley F. Roberts, 'Pymtheg Gweddi San Ffraid a'r Pardwn', B, 14 (1956), 254–68.

78 Jane Tibbets Schulenburg, 'The heroics of virginity. Brides of Christ and sacrificial mutilation', in Mary Beth Rose (ed.), *Women in the Middle Ages and the Renaissance, Literary and Historical Perpectives* (Syracuse: Syracuse University Press, 1986), pp. 29–72.

79 David Knowles, *The Monastic Order in England* (Cambridge: Cambridge University Press, 1940), p. 101.

80 Schulenburg, 'The heroics of virginity'.

81 Aberystwyth, NLW, MS Llanstephan 117, p. 72. On the calendars, see Cartwright, *Y Forwyn Fair*, p. 183.

82 Davies, 'Testun beirniadol o waith Hywel Rheinallt', p. 3.

83 *Iolo Manuscripts*, p. 84.

84 Daniel Huws, 'The earliest Bangor missal', *National Library of Wales Journal*, 27 (1991), 113–28.

85 *Vitae Sanctorum*, p. 137.

86 *Gwaith Syr Dafydd Trefor*, ed. Rhiannon Ifans (Aberystwyth: CAWCS, 2005), p. 67.

87 *Gwaith Dafydd ap Gwilym*, p. 257.

88 *Dafydd ap Gwilym: His Poems*, pp. 189–90.

89 *Gwaith Dafydd Llwyd o Fathafarn*, ed. W. Leslie Richards (Cardiff: University of Wales Press, 1964), p. 14.

90 H. Owen, 'Llanddwyn Island', *Transactions of the Anglesey Antiquarian Society and Field Club*, (1920), 1–32 (15–16).

91 *Gwaith Dafydd Llwyd*, p. 118.

92 *Vitae Sanctorum*, p. 27.

93 For *Vita sancti Cadoci* see ibid., pp. 24–141 and for *Vita sancti Gundleii* see ibid., pp. 172–93.

94 *Early Welsh Genealogical Tracts*, pp. 14–20.

95 The link between virginity and feminine sanctity has been stressed by numerous authors. On the Lives of Frankish women from the sixth and seventh centuries see *Sainted Women of the Dark Ages*; also on female sanctity in Carolingian Europe see J. M. H. Smith, 'The problem of feminine sanctity in Carolingian Europe, *c*.780–920', *Past and Present*, 146 (1995), 3–37; on virgin sanctity in twelfth- and thirteenth-century England see Wogan-Browne, *Saints' Lives and Women's Literary Culture* and on feminine sanctity in late medieval England see Winstead, *Virgin Martyrs*. On sanctity, masculinity and virginity see Bernau, Evans and Salih (eds), *Medieval Virginities*, pp. 102–39; Cullum and Lewis (eds), *Holiness and Masculinity*, pp. 10–13.

96 Willis Bund, 'Some characteristics of Welsh and Irish saints', 279–80.

97 Rhyddlad's feast is mentioned in two calendars: Aberystwyth, NLW, MS Peniarth 172, p. 46 and London, BL, MS Additional 14882, fol. 43^r. The feast of Callwen and Gwenfyl on 1 November is mentioned only in Aberystwyth, NLW, MS Cwrtmawr 44, p. 5. The feast of Gwenfaen on 4 November is mentioned only in Aberystwyth, NLW, MS Peniarth 186, p. 11, and a later hand has altered the name to Gwenfrewy.

98 St Gwenog is invoked several times in two manuscript copies of the laws of Hywel Dda written by the same scribe: Aberystwyth, NLW, MS Llanstephan 116 and London, BL, MS Additional 22356. The first manuscript also refers to St Gwnnen whose unique dedication is found at Llanwnnen, a neighbouring church in the same parish. On this basis, Christine James has suggested that the scribe was a native of the Teifi valley: 'Ysgrifydd anhysbys: proffil personol', *Ysgrifau Beirniadol*, 23 (1997), 44–72. References to Gwnnen (or Gwynnen) in the poetry of Lewys Glyn Cothi suggest that this saint was male; see *Gwaith Lewys Glyn Cothi*, p. 222. For a more detailed discussion of the cults of Gwenog and Gwnnen see Cartwright, 'Santesau Ceredigion', 1–36.

99 *Breuddwyd Maxen*, ed. Ifor Williams (Bangor: Jarvis & Foster, 1908); T. Gwynn Jones, '*Ystorya Addaf a Val a Cauas Elen y Grog*:

tarddiad, cynnwys ac arddull y testunau Cymraeg a'u lledaeniad' (unpublished M. A. thesis, University of Wales, Aberystwyth, 1936).

100 R. Sharpe, 'Some medieval miracula from Llandegley (Lambeth Palace Library, MS 94 fols. 153v–155r)', B, 37 (1990), 166–76.

101 There was a Benedictine priory at Usk and two Cistercian houses for women at Llanllugan and Llanllŷr. In Chapter 6, I attempt to explain why there were so few nunneries in medieval Wales.

102 This is generally true of the male saints as well. On the unusual case of St Caradog (*ob.* 1124) see Baring-Gould and Fisher, *Lives of the British Saints*, vol. 2, pp. 75–8. Nevertheless, ample provision was made in Wales for men who wished to enter the monastic profession. David Knowles and R. Neville Hadcock, *Medieval Religious Houses: England and Wales* (London: Longman, 1953), list sixty-three monastic establishments for men in Wales, including abbeys, priories, alien priories, friaries and cells.

Chapter 3

1 A slightly different version of this chapter appeared in J. Wyn Evans and Jonathan M. Wooding (eds), *St David of Wales: Cult, Church and Nation* (Woodbridge: Boydell and Brewer, 2007), pp. 182–206.

2 For example, London, BL, MS Cotton Vespasian Axiv, fol. 2^{r} (Latin) and Aberystwyth, NLW, MS Peniarth 60, p. 54 (Welsh).

3 William Worcestre records that the feast of St Non was celebrated at Launceston in Cornwall on 3 July and it appears to have been celebrated at Altarnun on 15 June. Worcestre, *Itineraries*, p. 83.

4 Jones, 'Golygiad o Fuchedd Gwenfrewy', p. 154. I have added emphasis here.

5 Corinne Saunders, *Rape and Ravishment in the Literature of Medieval England* (Cambridge: D. S. Brewer, 2001), p. 125.

6 Kelly, *Performing Virginity*, pp. 42–3.

7 London, BL, MS Royal 13 Ci, fol. 180^{v}. I am indebted to my colleague Janet Burton for her transcription and translation of this text. Thanks also to David Noy for checking the translation. See also Michael J. Curley, 'Five *lecciones* for the feast of St Nonita: a text and its context', *Cambrian Medieval Celtic Studies*, 43 (2002), 59–75.

8 E. Ernault, 'La vie de sainte Nonne', *Revue Celtique*, 8 (1887), 230–301, 405–91; Yves Le Berre, Bernard Tanguy and Yzes-Pascal Castel, *Buez Santez Nonn. Mystère breton. Vie de sainte Nonne* (Minihi-Levenez: CRBC, 1999).

9 I intend to publish a separate study on Non's cult in Ireland and Cornwall at a future date.

10 E. G. Bowen, 'Celtic saints in Cardiganshire', *Ceredigion*, 1 (1950–1), 3–17 (15). See also Map I.5.

11 *Rhigyfarch's Life of St. David*, p. 6; *The Welsh Life*, p. 3.

12 Giraldus Cambrensis, *Giraldi Cambrensis Opera*, ed. J. S. Brewer,

J. F. Dimock and G. F. Warner (London: Longman, 8 vols (1861–91), vol. 3, p. 384; *Life of St. David*, trans. A. W. Wade-Evans (London: SPCK, 1923), p. 9; see also the discussion on Hen Fynyw (pp. 83–6) and *Vita Sancti Patterni: the Life of Saint Padarn and the Original 'Miniu'*, ed. and trans. Charles Thomas and David Howlett (Lampeter: Trivium Publications, 2003), p. 101.

13 For an illustration of the window see Cartwright, 'Santesau Ceredigion', Plate 3.

14 Anon., 'Folk-lore of the Cardiganshire coast', *Welsh Gazette*, 18 January 1912. See also *Welsh Gazette*, 4 January and 11 January 1912.

15 P. Ó Riain, 'The Church in Ceredigion in the early Middles Ages: b. The saints of Cardiganshire', in *Cardiganshire County History I*, ed. J. L. Davies and D. P. Kirby (Cardiff: University of Wales Press, 1994), pp. 378–96 (p. 394).

16 On the 'patterned life' see Henken, *The Welsh Saints: A Study in Patterned Lives*.

17 Cambrensis, *The Journey Through Wales*, p. 161.

18 Baring-Gould and Fisher, *The Lives of the British Saints*, vol. 4, p. 22–3; Elizabeth de Guise, *The Story of St Non the Mother of St David* (Tenby: Everdrake Press, no date), p. 5. Farmer, *Oxford Dictionary of Saints*, p. 358.

19 G. H. Doble, *Saint Nonna*, Cornish Saints Series 16, (Liskeard: Philp & Sons, 1928). In the Life recorded by Albert Le Grand the patron of Penmarch is named Vouga; see *Les vies des saints de la Bretagne Armorique par Fr Albert Le Grand*, ed. D.-L. M. de Kerdanet (Brest: Anner, 1837).

20 Charles Thomas (personal communication). See also Elizabeth Okasha, *Corpus of Early Christian Inscribed Stones of South-west Britain* (London and New York: Leicester University Press, 1993), pp. 299–301.

21 Doble, *Saint Nonna*, pp. 4–5.

22 D. S. Hague, 'St Non's Chapel, Llanon', unpublished document, SN 56 NW, RCAHMW.

23 Anon., 'Ancient church to be rescued from neglect', *Western Mail*, 12 July 1988.

24 R. Suggett, 'Neuadd', unpublished document in RCAHMW archive. For a photograph of the building see Cartwright, 'Santesau Ceredigion', Plate 1.

25 *Welsh Gazette*, 18 January 1912.

26 George Eyre Evans, *Cardiganshire: A Personal Survey of Some of its Antiquities, Chapels, Churches, Fonts, Plate and Registers* (Aberystwyth: Welsh Gazette, 1903), pp. 176–7.

27 Anon., 'Aberystwyth meeting report', *Archaeologia Cambrensis*, 14 (1897), series 5, 164–6; Anon., 'St David and Cardiganshire', *Welsh Gazette*, 29 February 1912, which includes an imaginative sketch by Dora Jones; Argus, 'Correspondence', *Transactions of the Cardiganshire Antiquarian Society*, 1, no. 3 (1913), p. 36; E. Lewes, 'Image of

St Non, at Llanon, Cardiganshire', *Archaeologia Cambrensis*, 19 (1919), series 6, 32–3.

28 For an image of the stone see Cartwright, 'Santesau Ceredigion', Plate 2. Cf. Jørgen Anderson, *The Witch on the Wall. Medieval Erotic Sculpture in the British Isles* (London: Allen and Unwin, 1977); M. Freeman, 'A Sheela-na-Gig from Llanon, Llansanffraid, Ceredigion', *Archaeologia Cambrensis*, 149 (2000), 14–19. I am grateful to Michael Freeman for sharing with me his detailed knowledge of the Llanon site prior to the publication of this article.

29 See, for example, Mary-Ann Constantine, 'Saints behaving badly: sanctity and transgression in Breton popular culture', in Cartwright (ed.), *Celtic Hagiography and Saints' Cults*, pp. 198–215 (pp. 201–2). On the destruction and disfigurement of Sheela-na-gigs see Anderson, *The Witch on the Wall*, pp. 27–31.

30 Iwan Wmffre, *The Place-Names of Cardiganshire*, 3 vols, BAR British Series 379 (II) (Oxford: Archaeopress, 2004), vol. 2, p. 729; Ó Riain, 'The saints of Cardiganshire', p. 390.

31 François Falc'hun, *Dirinon* (La Guerche-de-Bretagne: Ouest France, 1986), p. 3; Le Berre *et al.*, *Buez*, p. 11.

32 *Gwaith Ieuan ap Llywelyn Fychan, Ieuan Llwyd Brydydd a Lewys Aled*, ed. M. Paul Bryant-Quinn (Aberystwyth: CAWCS, 2003), pp. 109, 151, nn. 68 and 70. Possibly Curig is also mentioned here because he was renowned for curing blindness.

33 *Gwaith Lewys Glyn Cothi*, p. 72

34 J. C. Davies, *Folk-Lore of West and Mid-Wales* (Aberystwyth: Welsh Gazette, 1911), p. 303.

35 I collected various oral traditions associated with the female saints of Wales by means of a questionnaire sent out to vicars in Wales in 1992. I am grateful to J. H. Gravell, the former vicar of Llan-non, for this information.

36 T. O'Loughlin, 'Rhygyfarch's *Vita Dauidis*: an *apparatus biblicus*', *Studia Celtica*, 32 (1998), 179–88.

37 *Life of St. David*, p. 6.

38 Personal communication.

39 S. Baring-Gould, 'Exploration of St. Non's Chapel, near St. Davids', *Archaeologia Cambrensis*, 15 (1898), series 5, 345–8 (347).

40 A. W. Wade-Evans, 'Rhygyfarch's Life of Saint David', *Y Cymmrodor*, 24 (1913), 1–73 (37–8).

41 Nancy Edwards, 'Monuments in a landscape; the early medieval sculpture of St David's', in Helena Hamerow and Arthur MacGregor (eds), *Image and Power in the Archaeology of Early Medieval Britain: Essays in Honour of Rosemary Cramp* (Oxford: Oxbow, 2001), pp. 53–77 (pp. 56–8).

42 *Cywyddau Iolo Goch ac Eraill*, pp. 242–3. The first line could also be translated as: 'At the church of the everlasting cross'. By the 1870s the stone had been set into the east face of the building.

43 Le Berre *et al.*, *Buez*, pp. 154–5.

[44] Browne Willis, *A Survey of the Cathedral Church of St David's* (London: R. Gosling, 1717), p. 53.
[45] J. Wyn Evans (personal communication).
[46] Richard Fenton, *A Historical Tour Through Pembrokeshire* (London: Longman, Hurst, Rees, Orme & Co., 1811), p. 113.
[47] Baring-Gould, 'Exploration of St. Non's Chapel', p. 346.
[48] *Gwaith Lewys Glyn Cothi*, p. 371.
[49] B. G. Charles, *George Owen of Henllys: A Welsh Elizabethan* (Aberystwyth: NLW, 1973), pp. 184–5. Willis, *Survey*, pp. 52–3.
[50] Fenton, *Historical Tour*, pp. 112–13.
[51] Doble, *Saint Nonna*, p. 8.
[52] See John Morgan-Guy, 'Shrine and counter-shrine in 1920s and 1930s Dewisland?', in Evans and Wooding (eds), *St David of Wales*, pp. 286–95.
[53] Personal communication.
[54] 'Yues' has been interpreted by the editors of the *Buez* as 'yuerdon' (Ireland); see Le Berre *et al.*, *Buez*, p. 115.
[55] On the Breton ceiling paintings discussed below he is referred to as 'Mobvs'.
[56] Le Berre *et al*, *Buez*, pp. 156–9.
[57] Non has also become associated with another stone at Dirinon, which, it is claimed, bears the imprints of her knees. See the images and interviews on Non's cult in Brittany that I contributed to Lord, *The Visual Culture of Wales*, CD-ROM; Le Berre *et al.*, *Buez*, p. 4, and J. Abgrall, 'Les pierres à empreintes – les pierres à bassins', *Bulletin de la société archéologique du Finistère*, 17 (1890), 62–72 (66–7).
[58] Le Berre *et al.*, *Buez*, p. 161
[59] Ibid., p. 132.
[60] Ibid., p. 115.
[61] Ibid., pp. 172–3.
[62] R. Perrott, 'The tomb of Ste. Nonne, at Dirinon, in Britanny [sic.]', *Archaeologia Cambrensis*, 3 (1857), series 3, 249–58 (250).
[63] Le Berre *et al.*, *Buez*, pp. 12 and 37.
[64] Ibid., pp. 11 and 14.
[65] When I asked the vicar of Dirinon if he thought the reliquary contained the bones of St Non or St David, he replied that it contained both. The reliquary is labelled as both 'le reliquaire de sainte Nonne' and 'le reliquaire de saint Divy' in Le Berre *et al*, *Buez*, pp. 39 and 96. See Jean-Yves Cozan *et al*, *La Bretagne au temps des Ducs* (Daoulas: Centre Culturel Abbaye de Daoulas, 1991), pp. 147–8 for images of other reliquaries of a very similar style made at Morlaix.
[66] There is, however, an intriguing reference to a book relating the translation of SS. Andrew, David and Non in the *Liber Communis*: W. B. Jones and E. A. Freeman, *The History and Antiquities of St. David's* (London: J. H. & J. Parker, 1856; 1998 edn), p. 380.
[67] Worcestre, *Itineraries*, p. 62.

68 Exeter Cathedral Library MS 3672A. Curley, 'Five *Lecciones*', 66, n. 29. There is a medieval image believed to represent St Non in stained glass at her church at Altarnun. Joanna Mattingly, however, has suggested that this is more likely to be an image of St John the Evangelist (personal communication).

69 Le Berre *et al.*, *Buez*, pp. 21–31.

70 The paintings were restored in 1961 and again 1998. See the images in ibid., pp. 49–70, and those I contributed to Lord, *The Visual Culture of Wales*, CD-ROM.

71 The two *epitomae* (BHL 2108 and parts of BHL 2109) were published in *Acta Sanctorum*, ed. J. Bollandus *et al.*, March, vol. 1 (Antwerp: Jacobus Meurs, 1668).

72 It is referred to as the nunnery in Le Berre *et al.*, *Buez*, p. 54.

73 Cf Davidstow and Altarnun in Cornwall.

74 B. L. Olson and O. J. Padel, 'A tenth-century list of Cornish parochial saints', *Cambridge Medieval Celtic Studies*, 12 (1986), 33–71 (67).

75 See the discussion on the Welsh and Breton traditions associated with SS. Cadfan and Tysilio in N. A. Jones and M. E. Owen, 'Twelfth-century Welsh hagiography: the *Gogynfeirdd* poems to saints', in Cartwright (ed.), *Celtic Hagiography and Saints' Cults*, pp. 45–76 (pp. 47–8, 66–8).

76 Le Berre *et al.*, *Buez*, pp. 123–36.

77 *Life of St. David*, pp. 3–4.

78 Le Berre *et al.*, *Buez*, p. 136.

79 Augustine, *City of God*, ed. and trans. David Knowles and Henry Bettenson (Harmondsworth: Penguin, 1972), p. 26.

80 Le Berre *et al.*, *Buez*, p. 134.

81 London, BL, MS Royal 13 C.i, fol. 180^{v}.

82 *Gwaith Dafydd Llwyd*, p. 47.

83 Jocelyn Wogan-Browne, 'The virgin's tale', in Ruth Evans and Leslie Johnson (eds), *Feminist Readings in Middle English Literature: The Wife of Bath and All her Sect* (London: Routledge, 1994), pp. 165–94.

84 *The Irish Penitentials*, ed. L. Bieler, *Scriptores Latini Hiberniae* (Dublin: Dublin Institute for Advanced Studies, 1963) vol. 5, p. 81.

85 *Two Lives of Gildas by a Monk of Ruys and Caradoc of Llancarfan*, trans. Hugh Williams (Felinfach: Llanerch, 1990), pp. 88–91.

86 *Gwaith Dafydd Llwyd*, p. 46; Henken, *Traditions of the Welsh Saints*, p. 36.

87 *Gwaith Iorwerth Fynglwyd*, p. 96. See Chapter 1 in the present volume.

88 *Life of St. David*, p. 33; *The Welsh Life*, p. 1.

89 *Vitae Sanctorum*, p. 16.

90 *Rhyddiaith Gymraeg*, p. 37.

91 *Lives of S. Ninian and S. Kentigern Compiled in the Twelfth Century*, ed. Alexander Penrose Forbes (Edinburgh: Edmonston and Douglas, 1874), pp. 123–33.

92 Ibid., pp. 33–119; Anon., *Two Celtic Saints: The Lives of Ninian and Kentigern* (Felinfach: Llanerch, 1989), pp. 29–119.
93 Alan Macquarrie, *The Saints of Scotland: Essays in Scottish Church History AD 450–1093* (Edinburgh: John Donald, 1997), p. 119.
94 Anon., *Two Celtic Saints*, pp. 30–1.
95 Le Berre *et al.*, *Buez*, p. 155.
96 On the Middle Welsh version, see Chapter 1 in the present volume and Williams, 'Buched Meir'.
97 P. Ó Riain, 'Irish saints' Genealogies', *Nomina*, 7 (1983), 23–9 (23).
98 *Trioedd*, p. 201; *Early Welsh Genealogical Tracts*, pp. 16, 20.
99 This would require a thorough, international survey which is beyond the scope of this chapter.
100 Mulder-Bakker (ed.), *Sanctity and Motherhood*, p. 4.
101 On the Middle Welsh Life, see Chapter 2 in the present volume.
102 de Voragine, *The Golden Legend*, vol. 1, pp. 27–9.
103 See the discussion on the *topos* of the menaced virgin in Kelly, *Performing Virginity*, pp. 42–62.
104 In Brittany the cult of St Anne is particularly strong: indeed it is even claimed that Anne was a Breton.
105 *Gwaith Lewys Glyn Cothi*, p. 108.
106 See the discussion on Welsh poetry to pious married noblewomen in Chapter 6 of the present volume.

Chapter 4

1 An earlier version of this chapter appeared in Jane Cartwright (ed.), *Celtic Hagiography and Saints' Cults* (Cardiff: University of Wales Press, 2003), pp. 77–101.
2 J. E. Caerwyn Williams, 'Buchedd Catrin Sant', B, 25 (1973), 247–68 (249); Williams, *The Welsh Church*, p. 103; Evans, *Medieval Religious Literature*, p. 76.
3 *Medieval English Prose for Women, Selections from the Katherine Group and Ancrene Wisse*, ed. Bella Millett and Jocelyn Wogan-Browne (Oxford: Clarendon Press, 1990). Bella Millett, 'The audience of the saints' lives of the Katherine Group', *Reading Medieval Studies*, 16 (1990), 127–56, argues that although *Ancrene Wisse* was produced originally for three sisters, it was modified for a larger number of recluses and also used by a wider audience. See also Cate Gunn, 'Beyond the tomb: *Ancrene Wisse* and lay piety', in Liz Herbert McAvoy and Mari Hughes-Edwards (eds), *Anchorites, Wombs and Tombs: Intersections of Gender and Enclosure in the Middle Ages* (Cardiff: University of Wales Press, 2005), pp. 161–71.
4 *Virgin Lives and Holy Deaths*, ed. and trans. G. Burgess and J. Wogan-Browne (London: J. M. Dent, 1996); Jocelyn Wogan-Browne, '"Clerc u lai, muïne u dame"; women and Anglo-Norman hagiography in the twelfth and thirteenth centuries', in C. M. Meale (ed.),

Women and Literature in Britain, 1150–1500 (Cambridge: Cambridge University Press, 1993), pp. 61–85; Lesley J. Smith and Jane H. M. Taylor (eds), *Women, the Book and the Godly: Selected Proceedings of the St Hilda's Conference*, 1993, (Cambridge: D. S. Brewer, 1995).

5 Katherine J. Lewis, 'Model girls? Virgin-martyrs and the training of young medieval women in late medieval England', in Katherine J. Lewis *et al.* (eds), *Young Medieval Women* (Stroud: Sutton, 1999), pp. 25–46.

6 I have used Daniel Huws's dating of the Welsh manuscripts as far as possible, and where this is not available, I have referred either to the dates given in the later manuscripts or to J. Gwenogvryn Evans, *Report on Manuscripts in the Welsh Language*, 2 vols, (London, 1899–1903). See Huws, *Medieval Welsh Manuscripts*, pp. 57–64. The Lives in Table 1 are listed in the order that they occur in the manuscripts.

7 On the Welsh Life of Gwenfrewy, see Jones, 'Golygiad o Fuchedd Gwenfrewy'. On the different manuscript versions see especially pp. 28–31, 249–31.

8 Angell, '*Gwyrthyeu*'; Mittendorf, 'Mary of Egypt'.

9 On the White Book of Rhydderch, see Huws, *Medieval Welsh Manuscripts*, pp. 227–45.

10 Williams, 'Rhyddiaith', pp. 331–6.

11 On the Middle Welsh texts relating to Mary, see Chapter 1 in the present volume.

12 Brynley F. Roberts, 'Un o lawysgrifau Hopcyn ap Thomas o Ynys Dawe', B, 22 (1967), 223–8 (224).

13 G. Charles-Edwards, 'The scribes of the Red Book of Hergest', *National Library of Wales Journal*, 21 (1987–8), 246–50; Christine James, 'Llwyr wybodau, llên a llyfrau: Hopcyn ap Thomas a'r traddodiad llenyddol Cymraeg', in Hywel Teifi Edwards (ed.), *Cwm Tawe* (Llandysul: Gomer, 1993), pp. 4–44.

14 *Lives of the Cambro British Saints*, ed. and trans. William J. Rees (Llandovery: W. Rees, 1853), pp. 219–31; Melville Richards, 'Buchedd Fargred', B, 9 (1939), 324–34; B, 10 (1939) 53–9, and B, 13 (1949), 65–71.

15 *Lives of the Cambro*, pp. 211–18; *Vita Sancti Tathei and Buched Seint y Katrin*, ed. H. Idris Bell (Bangor: Welsh MSS Society, 1909), pp. 31–9; Williams, 'Buchedd Catrin'; Catherine E. Byfield, 'A new edition of *Buched Seint y Katrin*' (unpublished M.Phil. thesis, to be submitted to Cardiff University).

16 Angell, '*Gwyrthyeu*'; Jones, 'Gwyrthyeu'; M. Richards, 'Buchedd Mair o'r Aifft', *Études Celtiques*, 2 (1937), 45–9; Mittendorf, 'Mary of Egypt'.

17 D. J. Jones, 'Buchedd Mair Fadlen a'r *Legenda aurea*', B, 4 (1929), 325–39.

18 Aberystwyth, NLW, Idris Foster's papers, Box 20.

19 I am currently working on editions and translations of the two Lives

and am grateful to the Arts and Humanities Research Council for a period of study leave.

20 Jones, 'Buchedd Mair Fadlen', p. 330, n. 1.

21 Evans, *Report*, vol. 1, part ii, p. 310.

22 Mittendorf, 'Mary of Egypt', p. 208.

23 L. Duchesne, 'La légende de Sainte Marie-Madeleine', in L. Duchesne, *Fastes Episcopaux de l'Ancienne Gaule*, 3 vols (Paris: Albert Fontemoing, 1907–15), vol. 1, pp. 321–60 (p. 358); William Caxton, *A Critical Edition of the Legend of Mary Magdalene From Caxton's Golden Legend of 1487*, ed. D. A. Mycoff (Salzburg: University of Salzburg, 1985), p. 14.

24 J. Misrahi, 'A *vita sanctae Mariae Magdalenae (B. H. L. 5456)* in an eleventh-century manuscript', *Speculum*, 18 (1943), 335–9 (336–7).

25 *An Old English Martyrology*, ed. G. Herzfeld (London: K. Paul, Trench, Trübner & Co., 1900).

26 P. Ó Riain, *Anglo-Saxon Ireland: The Evidence of the Martyrology of Tallaght*, H. M Chadwick Memorial Lectures 3, (Cambridge: Department of Anglo-Saxon, Norse and Celtic, University of Cambridge, 1993), p. 19.

27 Aberystwyth, NLW MS Peniarth 187, fol. 4[v], refers to 'Dychweliad Mair Fadlen'. This calendar is, however, fairly late (*c.*1596).

28 Examples of this pattern can be seen in the Lives of Katherine, Margaret and Gwenfrewy. On the fragmentary evidence for other Welsh virgin martyrs (e.g. Maches, Tudful and Dunod), see Chapter 2.

29 David Mycoff, *The Life of Saint Mary Magdalene and of Her Sister Martha* (Kalamazoo: Cistercian Publications, 1989), pp. 1–2. For a detailed discussion on the theories of unity and plurality see Susan Haskins, *Mary Magdalen Myth and Metaphor* (New York: Riverhead Books, 1993), pp. 1–29.

30 Haskins, *Mary*, p. 13.

31 Ibid., pp. 171–3; V. Saxer, *Le culte de Marie Madeleine en Occident des origines à la fin du moyen âge* (Auxerre-Paris: Publications de la Société des Fouilles Archéologiques et des Monuments Historiques de l'Yonne-Librairie Clavreuil, 1959), pp. 217–24.

32 A. Hufstader, 'Lefèvre d'Étaples and the Magdalen', *Studies in the Renaissance*, 16 (1969), 31–60.

33 For a more detailed discussion on the development of the legend, see Caxton, *A Critical Edition*, pp. 7–24.

34 Saxer, *Le culte*.

35 Jacobus de Voragine, *Legenda Aurea*, ed. T. Graesse (Dresden: impensis librariae Arnoldianae 1850), pp. 407–17, 444–7; de Voragine, *The Golden Legend*, vol. 1, pp. 374–83; vol. 2, pp. 23–6 (for English translations).

36 *The Early South English Legendary or Lives of Saints I MS. Laud, 108, in the Bodleian Library*, ed. Carl Horstmann, EETS, os, 86 (London: N. Trübner & Co., 1887), pp. 462–80; *South English*

Legendary, ed. Charlotte D'Evelyn and Anna J. Mill, EETS, ES, 235–5, 244 (London: Oxford University Press, 1956–9), vol. 1, pp. 340–8.

37 Nicholas Bozon, *Three Saints' Lives by Nicholas Bozon*, ed. M. A. Klenke (New York: St Bonaventure 1947), pp. 3–25, 45–59.

38 On the French and Spanish manuscripts see *The Lives of St Mary Magdalene and St Martha*, ed. J. R. Smith (Exeter: University of Exeter, 1989), pp. xviii–xxvii.

39 J. Zupita, 'Das leben der heiligen Maria Magdalena', *Archiv für das Studium der neuren Sprächen und Litteraturen*, 47 (1893), 207–24.

40 Caxton, *A Critical Edition*, pp. 117–44.

41 *Altenglische Legenden*, ed. Carl Horstmann (Heilbronn: Neue Folge, 1881), pp. 81–92.

42 *Sammlung Altenglischer Legenden*, ed. Carl Horstmann (Heilbronn: Neue Folge, 1878), pp. 163–70.

43 John Mirk, *Festial*, ed. Theodor Erbe, EETS, ES, 96 (London: Trübner, 1905), pp. 203–8.

44 Osbern Bokenham, *Legendys of Hooly Wummen*, ed. Mary S. Serjeantson (London: Oxford University Press, 1938), pp. 136–72.

45 Richard Spalding, *Speculum Sacerdotale*, ed. Edward H. Weatherly, EETS, OS, 200 (London: Oxford University Press, 1936), pp. 170–4.

46 P. Meyer, 'Légendes pieuses en provençal', *Histoire littéraire de la France*, 32 (1898), 78–100; *The Middle Low German Version of the Legend of Mary Magdalen*, ed. C. E. Eggert (Bloomington: The Journal of Germanic Philology Press, 1902), pp. 152, 212–13. The Middle Low German version, which omits the pre-ascension material and Magdalene's sojourn in the desert, appears to be an adaptation of a thirteenth-century verse Life by a Norman clerk called Guillaume.

47 Trinity College Dublin, MS H. ii. 15a, p. 95. *Legends of the Saints in the Scottish Dialect of the Fourteenth-Century*, ed. W. M. Metcalfe, 3 vols (Edinburgh and London: Scottish Text Society, 1891–6), vol. 1, p. vii. On associations between Mary Magdalene and the Breton ballad *Mari Kelenn* see Mary-Ann Constantine, *Breton Ballads* (Aberystwyth: CMCS Publications, 1996).

48 Caxton, *A Critical Edition*, pp. 25–7.

49 The orthography in Llanstephan 34 has been revised considerably.

50 Llanstephan 34, pp. 376–7. A cross appears in the manuscript before Mary's name.

51 Peniarth 27ii, p. 52.

52 Mirk, *Festial*, p. 203.

53 Llanstephan 27, fol. 132^{v}. I have added punctuation.

54 de Voragine, *The Golden Legend*, vol. 1, p. 378.

55 'Meis pur rien ne volt demorer / Dieu le voleit sanz nule fayle; / Ceo mustra bien par mervayle.' (But she was not at all inclined to remain behind. God wished it so without doubt; He showed it plainly by a miracle.) Bozon, *Three Saints' Lives*, p. 13.

56 Llanstephan 27, fol. 134^{r}.

57 de Voragine, *The Golden Legend*, vol. 1, p. 380. In the Anglo-Norman Life the priest's dwelling is twelve furlongs from Mary Magdalene's abode. Bozon, *Three Saints' Lives*, p. 18.

58 Cardiff 2.629, fols 69^{v}–70^{r}. Prior to the event she has not seen the face of any man for thirty years.

59 In *Pedeir Keinc y Mabinogi* Pwyll encounters Hafgan, king of the otherworld, in a clearing in woodland: *Pedeir Keinc y Mabinogi*, ed. Ifor Williams (Cardiff: University of Wales Press, 1930), p. 1, and in the Latin Life of Melangell, Brochfael Ysgithrog comes across St Melangell whilst he is out hunting in the woods. She has led a solitary existence for fifteen years during which time she has not seen the face of any man (Pryce, 'A new edition', pp. 39–40). On the relationship between the forest and the otherworld in medieval Welsh literature see also P. L. Williams, '"Ar ganghennau'r gynghanedd": agweddau ar y goedwig yn llenyddiaeth yr Oesoedd Canol', *Dwned*, 6 (2000), 55–76.

60 The cave at Sainte Baume, reputed to be the site of Mary Magdalene's hermitage, appears to have been associated with the Virgin Mary until *c.*1170. See Haskins, *Mary*, p. 117.

61 de Voragine, *The Golden Legend*, vol. 2, p. 24

62 Richards, 'Buchedd Fargred', 331.

63 Llanstephan 34, p. 379. The relevant fragment of text is missing in the incomplete version in Peniarth 5 and the phrase is absent in Llanstephan 27.

64 Llanstephan 27, fol. 137^{r}. Cf. Cardiff MS 2.633, p. 352: 'A phoyd drwy nerth y vendigedig Vair, ag eiriol y vendigedig santes honno a rrad yr Ysbryd Glan y delom ninneu i vuchedd dragywydd heb dranc, heb orffen, amen.' (And through the strength of blessed Mary, the intercession of that blessed saint [i.e. Martha] and the grace of the Holy Spirit may we attain everlasting life forever, without end, amen.)

65 Cartwright, *Y Forwyn Fair*, p. 183.

66 S. Thomas, 'Land occupation, ownership and utilisation in the parish of Llansantffraid', *Ceredigion*, 3 (1956–9), 124–55 (127).

67 *Canu Rhydd Cynnar*, ed. T. H. Parry-Williams (Cardiff: University of Wales Press, 1932), pp. 289–91; Jones, 'Celtic Britain', pp. 318–19.

68 NLW, Slebech Park Papers and Documents, 247A. Trier, 'A study of holy wells'.

69 Wiliam Middleton refers to a well dedicated to Mary Magdalene in a sixteenth-century poem which criticises idolatry and worship of holy wells, although he does not mention the well's location. Ifor Williams, 'Protestaniaeth Wiliam Middleton', B, 8 (1936), 242–7 (243).

70 Jones, *Saints*. I am grateful to Graham Jones for sharing his work on dedications with me prior to the publication of this volume.

71 Edward Lhuyd, *Parochialia*, ed. R. H. Morris (London: T. & T. Clark, 1909–11), pp. 116–17.

72 For a similar motif involving pigs see Karen Jankulak, 'Alba Longa in the Celtic regions? Swine, saints and Celtic hagiography', in Cartwright (ed.), *Celtic Hagiography and Saints' Cults*, pp. 271–84.

[73] Baring-Gould and Fisher, *Lives of the British Saints*, vol. 4, p. 426.

[74] Jones, 'Buchedd Mair Fadlen', 328.

[75] Llanstephan 27, fol. 136ᵛ.

[76] Gray, *Images of Piety*, Plate 58b (for the image at Llantwit Major). Madeleine Gray suggests that the fragmentary figure of another female saint, also on the north wall of the chancel at Llantwit Major, is a painting of the Virgin Mary whose 'presence here may indicate the location of a temporary Easter sepulchre'. She also proposes that the head of a female saint in the north window of the chancel at Treuddyn may possibly depict Mary Magdalene, since it is similar in style to the depiction of Mary Magdalene at Grappenhall (Cheshire): ibid., p. 23. However, stylistic similarities do not necessarily indicate that this is the same saint, for similar cartoons are known to have been used to depict different saints.

[77] J. Cule, 'Some early hospitals in Wales and the border', *National Library of Wales Journal*, 20 (1977–8), 97–130 (110).

[78] *Gwaith Guto'r Glyn*, p. 119. The Virgin Mary rather than Mary Magdalene is referred to as 'meddyges' (a physician) in other poems from this period. For example, when Hywel Sele falls from his horse and injures his leg an anonymous poet appeals to the Virgin to heal Hywel's leg with ointment: *Gwaith Llywelyn Goch ap Meurig Hen*, ed. Dafydd Johnston (Aberystwyth: CAWCS, 1998), p. 77. See also *Gwaith Ieuan Brydydd Hir*, p. 72.

[79] *Gwaith Guto'r Glyn*, p. 123. Mary Magdalene is referred to as 'meddyges Duw i hunan' ('the physician of God himself') in the anonymous free-metre poem mentioned above: *Canu Rhydd*, p. 289.

[80] Gray, *Images of Piety*, Plate 25.

[81] St Petronilla is also depicted holding keys. Both Petronilla and Sitha appear on a screen at North Elham and in this instance both saints are named. E. G. Tasker, *Encyclopaedia of Medieval Church Art* (London: B. T. Batsford, 1993), pp. 157, 160–1.

[82] *Gwaith Lewys Glyn Cothi*, p. 189.

[83] Huws, *Medieval Welsh Manuscripts*, p. 245, suggests that the quires which contain the Lives of the female saints in Peniarth 5 were composed as part of a separate programme and that they were 'written presumably for use by a cleric'.

[84] Haskins, *Mary*, p. 133. On the Dominicans at St Maximin see ibid., p. 129.

[85] Rhiannon M. M. Davies, 'The moral structure of *Pedeir Keinc y Mabinogi*' (unpublished doctoral thesis, University of Wales, Cardiff, 1993).

[86] Cambridge University Library MS Ff.2.38, intro. Frances McSparran and P. R. Robinson (London: Scolar Press, 1979), p. xi. As we shall see in the next chapter, Cambridge Ff.2.38, a Middle English household manuscript, has a great deal in common with the White Book of Rhydderch including an unusual fifteenth-century verse Life of St Katherine, which is similar to the earlier Middle Welsh prose Life. Its copy of the Life of Mary Magdalene is from Mirk's *Festial*.

[87] According to his genealogy in Lewis Dwnn, *Heraldic Visitations of Wales*, 2 vols (Llandovery: W. Rees, 1846), vol. 1, pp. 45, 85, Rhydderch married twice and had ten children, but the same text (vol. 1, p. 131), suggests that he had a third wife called Annes, and that she was the mother of the poet Ieuan ap Rhydderch. See also *Cywyddau Iolo Goch ac Eraill*, pp. xxiv–xxv. Ceridwen Lloyd-Morgan notes that the White Book may have been produced for Rhydderch's wife. See Lloyd-Morgan, 'More written about than writing?', pp. 149–65, for a valuable discussion on issues relating to women's literacy in medieval Wales.

[88] Evans, *Report*, vol. 2, p. 568. The manuscript is now badly stained; in large sections (including the pages which contain the Lives of Mary Magdalene and Martha), only fragments of red ink are legible.

Chapter 5

[1] An earlier version of this chapter appeared in Jacqueline Jenkins and Katherine J. Lewis (eds), *St Katherine of Alexandria: Texts and Contexts in Western Medieval Europe* (Turnhout: Brepols, 2003), pp. 53–86.

[2] For a detailed discussion of the cult in its European context see Jenkins and Lewis (eds), *St Katherine*.

[3] London, BL, MS Cotton Vespasian Axiv; Silas M. Harris, 'The kalendar of the *Vitae Sanctorum Wallensium*', *Journal of the Historical Society of the Church in Wales*, 111 (1953), 3–53; Marie Anne Mayeski, '"The right occasion for the words": situating Ælred's homily on Saint Katherine', *Cistercian Studies Quarterly*, 33 (1998), 45–60 (46).

[4] *Welsh Genealogies* AD *300–1400*, ed. Peter C. Bartrum, 11 vols (Cardiff: University of Wales Press, 1974–80), in particular vol. 5. Although the genealogies are not comprehensive, they do give some indication of the popularity of personal names in Wales throughout the Middle Ages. See also Meredith Cane, 'Personal names of women in medieval Wales, Cornwall and Brittany 400–1400 A.D.' (unpublished M.Phil. thesis, University of Wales, Aberystwyth, 1999).

[5] I gave a paper on visual representations of St Katherine at the Centre for Advanced Welsh and Celtic Studies' Forum on the Visual Culture of Wales in September 2001 and I am grateful to members of the audience for their comments and suggestions. Some of the photographs I have taken of female saints and discussions of their related iconography appear in Lord, *The Visual Culture of Wales*, CD-ROM. An edition and English translation of *Buched Seint y Katrin*, based on London, BL, MS Cotton Titus D.xxii (dating from the first half of the fifteenth century), was published in 1853 by W. J. Rees, but this was 'so full of blunders', to use Idris Bell's expression, that Bell published another edition, based on the same manuscript, in 1909. *Lives of the*

Cambro, pp. 211–18, 531–9; *Vita Sancti Tathei*, pp. 31–9 (p. v). Bell was unaware that the text was extant in other Welsh manuscripts, but in 1973 J. E. Caerwyn Williams published a list of the manuscripts that contained *Buched Seint y Katrin* and provided an edition of the text based on Peniarth 5: Williams, 'Buchedd Catrin'. A new edition of the Life which includes transcriptions of all the extant manuscripts, full critical apparatus, and an English translation of the text is currently being compiled by Catherine E. Byfield and it is anticipated that the completed project will be available on CD-ROM. Byfield, 'A new edition of *Buched Seint y Katrin*'.

6 Lewis, *The Cult of St Katherine*, especially pp. 40–4, 114–25, 191–4. On extant Welsh wills see Helen Chandler, 'The will in medieval Wales up to 1540' (unpublished M.Phil. thesis, University of Wales, Aberystwyth, 1992).

7 This seems a more likely explanation than that images of St Katherine have simply survived more frequently than those of many other universal saints.

8 On the Sporle cycle see Katherine J. Lewis, 'Pilgrimage and the cult of St Katherine in late medieval England', in Jenkins and Lewis (eds), *St Katherine*, pp. 37–52 (p. 42).

9 Williams, 'Buchedd Catrin', 267.

10 For further discussion of the significance of St Katherine's iconographic emblems see Karen A. Winstead, 'St Katherine's Hair', in Jenkins and Lewis (eds), *St Katherine*, pp. 171–99.

11 A. J. Parkinson, 'Llandeilo Talybont old church and wall-paintings in Wales' (Royal Commission on the Ancient and Historical Buildings of Wales, unpublished report, 1986). See also Gerallt D. Nash, 'Llandeilo Tal-y-bont' (unpublished leaflet on the church, 1996). I am extremely grateful to Dave Watkinson and Siobhan Stevenson for providing me with slides, taken by John Morgan, of the medieval mural of St Katherine from Llandeilo Tal-y-bont. I would also like to thank Joy Bowen and staff of the Historical Buildings Unit for allowing me access to the photographic archive and the information on Llandeilo Tal-y-bont kept at the Museum of Welsh Life, St Ffagans.

12 E. W. Tristram, *English Mediaeval Wall Painting the Thirteenth Century* (Oxford: Oxford University Press, 1950).

13 R. Pynson, *The Lif of Saincte Kateryne* (London: R. Pynson, 1505); Parkinson, 'Llandeilo Talybont', pp. 46–7.

14 For examples of Welsh images which do show St Katherine trampling Maxentius, see below.

15 *Buhez Cathell* (Cuburien, 1576), front page.

16 Chandler, 'The will in medieval Wales', pp. 49–51.

17 At the time of writing, the church of St Teilo is being re-erected at the Museum of Welsh Life and it has been proposed that reproductions of the wall paintings are reinstated in the church. These may include additional reconstructions based on late medieval woodcuts.

18 Although in Wales, Old Radnor is one of the border parishes that

now belongs to the diocese of Hereford, but probably belonged to the diocese of St Davids in the Middle Ages. On the church of St Stephen at Old Radnor, see J. B. Sinclair and R. W. D. Fenn, *Old Radnor Parish Church. A Short History* (Llandrindod Wells: Sayce Brothers, 1988).

19 The church was rebuilt in the 1840s, and two medieval panels of glass are all that remain of the original windows.

20 W. H. St John Hope, 'On the sculptured tablets called Saint John's Heads', *Archaeologia*, 52 (1890), series 2, 669–708 (706); Lewis, *The Cult of St Katherine*, p. 193.

21 Restoration work was carried out by Kempe in the late-nineteenth century. However, Kempe's restoration appears to have focused on rearranging the extant fragments in the Seven Sacraments window beneath the tracery lights. Lewis, *Stained Glass in North Wales*, pp. 55–9. For illustrations see Gray, *Images of Piety*, Plates 35 and 36.

22 Riches, *St George*.

23 Lewis, *Stained Glass in North Wales*, p. 66; Gray, *Images of Piety*, p. 28.

24 Lewis, *Stained Glass in North Wales*, Plate 20a; Gray, *Images of Piety*, Plate 20 (a). Fishbourne confirms that the east window, which now contains a total of 108 saints, martyrs, virgins, apostles and seraphim in the lower lights, originally only nominally expressed the adoration of all the saints and that it was completely transformed into a Te Deum window by Clayton and Bell in 1867. E. A. Fishbourne, 'Notes on the east window of the Church of All Saints, Gresford', *Archaeologia Cambrensis*, 7 (1907), series 6, 352–7. St Katherine occurs in one of the sections that appears to be largely medieval.

25 Michael K. Jones and Malcolm G. Underwood, *The King's Mother Lady Margaret Beaufort, Countess of Richmond and Derby* (Cambridge: Cambridge University Press, 1992), p. 150, suggest that whilst Margaret Beaufort's sponsorship of Welsh churches has been overplayed, Thomas Stanley's involvement has not always been fully recognized. On Margaret Beaufort's association with Gwenfrewy and the well chapel at Holywell, see Chapter 2 in the present volume.

26 Lewis, *The Cult of St Katherine*, p. 78.

27 I am extremely grateful to Enid Roberts for information about Bangor Cathedral, the stained glass and the chantry (personal communication). Browne Willis, *A Survey of the Cathedral Church of Bangor and the Edifices belonging to it* (London: R. Gosling, 1721), pp. 17–18, 96–8.

28 *Gwaith Guto'r Glyn*, pp. 245 and 247.

29 Browne Willis, *Survey*, pp. 18, 34–5.

30 Alfred N. Palmer, *The History of the Parish Church of Wrexham* (Wrexham and Oswestry: Woodall, Minshall and Thomas, 1886), p. 19.

[31] Anon., 'Machynlleth Meeting Report', *Archaeologia Cambrensis*, 12 (1866), series 3, 544–9.

[32] See H. Harold Hughes, 'Miscellanea', *Archaeologia Cambrensis*, 91 (1936), series 1, 134–6, which includes illustrations of the figurine.

[33] Its provenance is uncertain, but Mark Redknap believes that it belongs to a continental group of clay pipe images manufactured in the Rhineland and that it was probably imported to Wales. I am grateful to Mark Redknap for providing me with information on the figurine (personal communication).

[34] Katherine appears on two seals in the collection at the National Museum of Wales, but both of these seals are from England. Williams, *Catalogue of Seals*, vol. 2, pp. 13, 23. An image of Katherine with the wheel, but no sword, is found on the seal of the Benedictine priory of Polsoe, Devon; see Roger H. Ellis, *Catalogue of Seals in the Public Records Office. Monastic Seals I* (London: HMSO, 1986), p. 73. She is depicted on an oval seal, similar to the Mathern seal, holding both the sword and the wheel, on the prior's seal of the Dominican priory of St Katherine at Ayr: W. de Gray Birch, *Catalogue of Seals in the Department of MSS at the British Museum*, 6 vols (London: Printed by order of the trustees, 1887–1900), vol. 4, p. 132, see also pp. 84, 109, 150; vol. 5, pp. 377, 366, 367, 446, 889; vol. 4, pp. 176, 419, 427. On the relationship between the sealer and the saint in Sweden see Tracey R. Sands, 'The saint as symbol: the cult of St Katherine of Alexandria among medieval Sweden's high aristocracy', in Jenkins and Lewis (eds), *St Katherine*, pp. 94–6.

[35] I am grateful to Jeremy P. Davis for this information and for kindly sending me slides of the Mathern seal depicting St Katherine (personal communication). Other seal matrices have been discovered in the vicinity of Mathern; see Jeremy P. Davis, 'Gwent Seals: IX', *The Monmouthshire Antiquary*, 15 (1999), 19–21.

[36] I am grateful to Roy Lewis of the Pembrokeshire Prospector's Society and Mark Redknap of the Department of Archaeology and Numismatics at the National Museum and Gallery, Cardiff, for this information. Roy Lewis kindly sent me a photograph of the pilgrim badge (personal communication). On metal detector finds in Pembrokeshire, see Richard Blacklaw-Jones, *Pembrokeshire Past Lost and Found* (Pembrokeshire Prospectors, 1997). The Newgale badge is not illustrated in this booklet since it was found by a private individual. On badges found in London that depict the Katherine wheel, see Brian Spencer, *Pilgrim Souvenirs and Secular Badges* (Salisbury: Salisbury and South Wiltshire Museum, 1998).

[37] At Beaumaris the tomb appears to have been dismantled, removed form its original location within the church and reconstructed. It contains images of various saints. The figures of Katherine and George are now on opposite sides of the tomb, although they originally appear to have been next to each other. Charles R. Hand, 'Llanfaes friary and its mystery monuments', *Archaeologia Cambrensis*, 79 (1924), series 7, 125–88.

38 See Karen A. Winstead, 'St Katherine's Hair', in Jenkins and Lewis (eds), *St Katherine*, pp. 171–99 (pp. 196–7).

39 Edward Laws, *Church Book of St Mary the Virgin* (Tenby: John Leach, 1907), pp. 74–6.

40 Huw M. Edwards, 'Murnio marwnadau: golwg ar y ffug-farwnad yng nghyfnod y cywydd', *Dwned*, 5 (1999), 47–70.

41 Lewis, *The Cult of St Katherine*, pp. 11–12.

42 The vast majority of the other churches are nineteenth-century foundations and their dedications are sometimes associated with the name of their donors' wives or mothers, as at Baglan parish church, dedicated in March 1882.

43 W. Dugdale, *Monasticon Anglicanum*, ed. J. Caley *et al.*, 6 vols (London: Longman, 1655–73; 1817–30 edn); H. L. J. [sic.] 'Mona Mediaeva No. XII Penmon Priory', *Archaeologia Cambrensis*, 6 (1849), series 1, 44–60 (57).

44 Anon., 'Llanllyfni Papers', *Archaeologia Cambrensis*, 11 (1863), series 3, 280–6 (238).

45 John Leland, *The Itinerary of John Leland in or about the Years 1535–43*, ed. Lucy Toulmin Smith (London: George Bell & Sons, 1906), p. 105.

46 Knowles and Hadcock, *Medieval Religious Houses*, p. 105.

47 NLW Penpont Supplementary 274; Chandler, 'The will in medieval Wales', p. 175.

48 Arthur Leach, 27 February 1941, Museum archive N41/39, Tenby Museum and Art Gallery.

49 Although in the absence of early documentation relating to the dedication, it is possible that the inhabitants of Milford Haven simply referred to the chapel as 'Old St Katherine's' as a means of comparison with the modern church dedicated to Katherine in the new town. J. F. Rees, 'Miscellanea', *Archaeologia Cambrensis*, 2 (1922), series 7, 394–5.

50 *Christopher Saxton's Sixteenth-Century Maps. The Counties of England and Wales*, intro. William Ravenhill (Shrewsbury: Chatsworth Library, 1992), Maps 92/93, 98/99.

51 M. A. Ward, 'St. Catherine's Church, Cricieth', *Caernarvonshire Historical Society Transactions*, 58 (1997), 7–34 (8–10). In 1306, the township at Cricieth was recorded as 'Merthir' (Merthyr); this term usually implies that the local church or cemetery once possessed the physical remains of a saint or martyr, and inevitably these were not the relics of St Katherine.

52 Jones, *Holy Wells of Wales*, p. 153.

53 Ward, 'St. Catherine's Church', 8–9.

54 C. A. Gresham, 'Tre Ferthyr and the development of Cricieth', B, 27 (1966), 5–36 (6–7); Ward, 'St Catherine's Church', 10.

55 Ward, 'St Catherine's Church', 10.

56 On the Normans' involvement in the proliferation of the cult of St Katherine see Christine Walsh, 'The role of the Normans in the

development of the cult of St Katherine', in Jenkins and Lewis (eds), *St Katherine*, pp. 19–35.

57 Aberystwyth, NLW, MSS Peniarth 5, fols 21v–23r (*c*.1350); Llanstephan 27, fol. 131 (*c*.1400); Peniarth 15, pp. 138–44 (turn of fourteenth/fifteenth century); NLW 5267 B, fols 30r–34v (mid-fifteenth century); Llanstephan 28, pp. 167–76, 179–82 (second half of fifteenth century); Peniarth 27, part III, pp. 43–57 (second half of fifteenth century); Llanstephan 117, pp. 172–77 (*c*.1548); Llanstephan 34, pp. 24–35 (second half of sixteenth century); Peniarth 217, pp. 509–26 (*c*.1611); Llanstephan 187, pp. 87–101 (*c*.1634); NLW 552 B, fols 100r–103v (seventeenth century); NLW 6209 E, pp. 68–9 (seventeenth century); Llanstephan 104, pp. 197–216 (early-eighteenth century); Cwrtmawr 1155, pp. 58–64 (1810–90); London, BL, MS Cotton Titus D. xxii, fols 175v–185r (first half of the fifteenth century); Cardiff, Central Library, MS 2.629 (Hafod 19), pp. 120–32 (*c*.1536); Cardiff, Central Library, MS 2.633 (Hafod 23), pp. 358–76 (1604). The Welsh Life of St Katherine is incomplete in five manuscripts, two of which are seventeenth-century transcriptions of earlier manuscripts; Llanstephan 27, Llanstephan 28, Peniarth 217, NLW 552 B and NLW 6209 E.

58 In particular, Ieuan ap William demonstrates a tendency to abbreviate in Cardiff 2.629, and the text in NLW 552B is also a summarized version.

59 Williams, 'Buchedd Catrin', 259. The two oldest extant manuscripts, Peniarth 5 and Llanstephan 27, appear to stem from the same common original, although a substantial part of the text in Llanstephan 27 is missing. It begins with the scene in which angels are sent to break up the wheels on which Catrin is about to be tortured. NLW 6209E is an exact copy of this incomplete version, since it begins with the same fragment of a word found at the beginning of the surviving text in Llanstephan 27. Llanstephan 34 appears to be a copy (direct or indirect) of Peniarth 5, and Peniarth 217 is a copy that John Jones (*c*.1585–1657/8) of Gellilyfdy made of Llanstephan 34, although the final pages are missing. At the beginning of the eighteenth century, Llanstephan 34 was in the possession of Moses Williams and he also made a copy of the manuscript, now known as Llanstephan 104. Cwrtmawr 1155, in the handwriting of Robert Williams (1810–80) of Rhydycroesau, appears to be a copy of Peniarth 5, since it notes the start of each new page in its source and this corresponds to the layout of the text in Peniarth 5.

60 The Breton Life has been edited by E. Ernault, 'La vie de sainte Catherine', *Revue Celtique*, 8 (1887), 76–95. The Irish Life is extant in London, BL, MS Egerton 1781, fols 48r–49v, Dublin, Royal Irish Academy, MS Reeves 42, pp. 103–105, Trinity College Dublin, MS H. ii. 17, pp. 29–36, 45–6, 81–2.

61 *'Seinte Katerine' Re-Edited from MS Bodley 34 and the other Manuscripts*, ed. S. R. T. O. d'Ardenne and E. J. Dobson, EETS, os 887 (Oxford: Oxford University Press, 1981); de Voragine, *The*

Golden Legend, vol. 2, pp. 334–41; *The South English Legendary*, vol. 2, pp. 533–43; Mirk, *Festial*, pp. 275–7.

62 I shall use the Welsh names given to the characters when referring to their actions within the *buchedd*. Catrin and Katrin occur in Peniarth 5. Catrin is still a popular name in modern Wales.

63 Williams, 'Buchedd Catrin', 265. I shall use J. E. C. Williams's edition of the text, based on Peniarth 5, unless referring to significant deviations within the manuscripts.

64 Rees, *Lives of the Cambro*, p. 531, *Vita Sancti Tathei*, p. xi. Llanstephan 28, Peniarth 27, and Cardiff 2.629 have 'Alexandria', whereas Cardiff 2.633 and Llanstephan 187 (both in the hands of John Jones) make it clear that the text is referring to her father's name: 'merch oydd hi i vrennin Konstantinobyl, henw y brenin yn lladin oydd Alexander' (Cardiff 2.633, p. 358) (she was the daughter of the king of Constantinople. The king's name in Latin was Alexander).

65 Jennifer Relvyn Bray, 'The legend of St Katherine in later Middle English literature' (unpublished doctoral thesis, University of London, 1984), p. 206, suggests that the version found in Bodley 779 is a modified form of the *South English Legendary* Life, into which an additional 110 lines describing her mystical marriage have been inserted. The reference to Katherine's father occurs in the additional material.

66 *Gwaith Siôn ap Hywel*, p. 73.

67 Llanstephan 28 contains both the Lives of Katherine and Margaret, and they have been incorrectly bound so that leaves from *Buched Seint y Katrin* are interspersed at various points in *Buched Margred*.

68 See Lewis, *The Cult of St Katherine*, pp. 45–6.

69 Lewis, *The Cult of St Katherine*, pp. 132–4, 150–2. The fifteenth-century English verse Life will be discussed in greater detail below.

70 See, for example, Anke Bernau, 'A Christian *Corpus*: virginity, violence, and knowledge in the Life of St Katherine of Alexandria' in Jenkins and Lewis (eds), *St Katherine*, pp. 109–30 (p. 120).

71 Katherine is fourteen years old in the late Middle English prose legend and Caxton's *Lyf of Saint Katherine*; fifteen in the Auchinleck *Seynt Katerine* and seventeen in the Middle Breton passion.

72 Although the mystical marriage episode first appears in some Lives of St Katherine in the thirteenth century.

73 For example, 'Yr argl6yd a garaf i' (I love the Lord) and 'E boen ar dolur yd wyf i yn y odef yr careat du6' (I suffer this pain and torment for love of God): Williams, 'Buchedd Catrin', 266.

74 For the more usual identification of St Katherine as bride of Christ and even purveyor of husbands see Katherine J. Lewis, 'Pilgrimage and the cult of St Katherine in late medieval England', in Jenkins and Lewis (eds), *St Katherine*, pp. 37–52.

75 Cf. the Welsh and Latin Lives of Gwenfrewy and the Breton Life of

Non, which have lengthy sections describing how the saints were admitted to the religious profession and formerly chose to take the veil.

76 Williams, 'Buchedd Catrin', 265.

77 'Yna y llittyaud maxen yn vaur. ac y gel6is atta6 rei oe wassanaeth6yr. a dy6edut 6rthynt . . .' (Then Maxen became very angry and called some of his servants to him and said to them . . .) (prior to the beating); 'ac yna y dechreua6d maxen ynvedu. ac gal6 atta6 y wassanaeth6yr. ac erchi vdunt . . .' (and then Maxen started to get angry and called his servants to him and asked them . . .) (prior to the queen's torture): Williams, 'Buchedd Catrin', 266 and 267.

78 Ibid., 265. The formula occurs again during the second period of incarceration (266–7).

79 Ibid., 267

80 Ibid., 265.

81 Ibid., 266.

82 See, for example, Wogan-Browne, *Saints' Lives and Women's Literary Culture*, p. 178, n. 66.

83 A more literal translation, based on Cotton Titus D, xxii, is provided by Rees, *Lives of the Cambro*, p. 535: 'and her whole flesh was rendered yellow like violet'. Llanstephan 28 includes a more accurate description of bruises: 'hyd pann ydoedd ichnawd gwynn hi yn velyn las megys violed' (p. 174) (until her white skin became blue-yellow like violet[s]).

84 Cardiff, Central Library, MS 2.629, p. 123.

85 'Katharinen Marter', ed. Johann Lambel, *Germania*, 8 (1863), 129–86 (174). On the similarity between this Life and the Welsh version, see *Vita Sancti Tathei*, p. xiii.

86 Williams 'Buchedd Catrin', 268. Other versions of the Katherine legend, which relate the tale of the queen's martyrdom before the incident involving the wheels, include a German Life by Hermann von Fritslar and two fifteenth-century English works associated with the Midlands: a collection of sermons known as *Speculum Sacerdotale*, and an alliterative hymn by Richard Spalding. Hermann von Fritslar, 'Das Heiligenleben von Hermann von Fritslar', in Franz Pfeiffer (ed.), *Deutsche Mystiker des Vierzehnten Jahrhunderts*, Scientia Verlag, 1 (Leipzig: G. J. Göschen, 1845), pp. 255–6. *Speculum Sacerdotale* is extant in only one manuscript, London, BL, MS Additional 3671. It has been edited by Edward H. Weatherly, EETS, os 200 (London: Oxford University Press, 1936). On Richard Spalding's hymn, see *Three Alliterative Saints' Hymns: Late Middle English Stanzaic Poems*, ed. Ruth Kennedy, EETS, os 321 (Oxford: Oxford University Press, 2003), pp. 1–9.

87 'deg mil a deugeint'. *Vita Sancti Tathei*, p. xviii, n. 1. This was incorrectly interpreted by Rees as 'ten thousand and forty'. Rees, *Lives of the Cambro*, p. 537.

88 Cardiff 2.629, fol. 66^{r}.

89 *Gwaith Lewys Môn*, p. 142.

90 Williams, 'Buchedd Catrin', 268. A similar parallel is found towards the end of the Middle Welsh Life of Margaret of Antioch. Margred asks her executioner to wait a while whilst she prays. She then requests that he cut off her head with his sword, but the executioner, having been converted to Christianity during the saint's final prayer, refuses to decapitate her. Margred commands that he does as she says and asks God to forgive the executioner. Richards, 'Buchedd Fargred', 333–4.

91 On other martyrs who emit milk instead of blood from their wounds, see C. Grant Loomis, *White Magic: An Introduction to the Folklore of Christian Legend* (Cambridge, MA: The Mediaeval Academy of America, 1948), p. 79 and p. 189, n. 29.

92 The endings in Llanstephan 177 and NLW 552B are somewhat different from the other Welsh texts, since they are more concise versions. Llanstephan 117 does not name Sinai, and claims only that Catrin is buried on a mountain. Four streams of spring water issue forth from the mountain and oil flows from her grave. NLW 552B states only that Catrin was buried in a grave.

93 *Gwaith Lewys Glyn Cothi*, pp. 68–9.

94 *Gwaith Lewys Môn*, p. 142.

95 *Gwaith Lewys Glyn Cothi*, pp. 491 and 507. *Gwaith Lewys Môn*, p. 142.

96 Fecundity also plays a significant role in St Katherine's Norman miracles; see Walsh, 'The role of the Normans', p. 27.

97 On fountains of milk and wine, see the motif index in Henken, *The Welsh Saints*, p. 164. See also, Jones, *Holy Wells of Wales*, pp. 36–9 and R. Iestyn Daniel, 'Y ffynhonnau yng nghanu'r Cywyddwyr', *Dwned*, 7 (2001), 65–81.

98 *Gwaith Rhys Brydydd a Rhisiart ap Rhys*, p. 13.

99 James, 'Pen-rhys', p. 46.

100 For an illustration of St Anne's well at Llanfihangel y Bont-faen, see Cartwright, *Y Forwyn Fair*, Plate XI. Two stone carvings of St Anne survive: one is near the church (presumably still in its original location) and the other is in the garden opposite the church. It is likely that the stone carvings formerly stood back-to-back: John Morgan-Guy (personal communication).

101 *Gwaith Siôn ap Hywel*, pp. 74–5.

102 Caxton, *The Golden Legend*, vol. 3, pp. 32–9; vol. 6, pp. 198–205.

103 For a discussion of the ways in which the Empress 'stands in' for Katherine in this respect, see Samantha J. E. Riches, 'St George as a male virgin martyr', in Samantha J. E. Riches and Sarah Salih (eds), *Gender and Holiness: Men, Women and Saints in Late Medieval Europe* (London: Routledge, 2002), pp. 65–85, (p. 84, n. 43). In the Anglo-Norman Life of St George, Dacien has his wife's breasts ripped off when she renounces paganism. See Wogan-Browne, *Saints' Lives and Women's Literary Culture*, p. 113.

104 *St Katherine of Alexandria The Late Middle English Prose Legend in*

Southwell Minster MS 7, ed. Saara Nevanlinna and Irma Taavitsainen (Cambridge: D. S. Brewer, 1993).

105 *Vita Sancti Tathei*, pp. xiv–xix.

106 Bell was only aware of the Cambridge manuscript. He also thought that the Welsh *buchedd* was extant in only one manuscript. The English verse Life, based on Cambridge Ff.2.38, has been edited twice and a facsimile of this manuscript has also been published. *Altenglische Legenden*, pp. 260–4; *Cambridge University Library MS Ff.2.38*.

107 See the valuable discussion in Bray's thesis, 'The legend of St Katherine', pp. 107–13. Bray refers to the Welsh Life, but since her knowledge of the *buchedd* is largely dependant upon Bell's introduction, she is unaware that the Welsh text is extant in seventeen manuscripts, including Peniarth 5, which can be dated to the mid-fourteenth century. See also Lewis 'Model girls?', pp. 31–8 and Lewis, *The Cult of St Katherine*, pp. 207–15, who discusses the manner in which St Katherine is portrayed in household manuscripts such as Cambridge Ff.2.38.

108 Although, of course, they are not necessarily direct translations of a Latin text.

109 Compare with the quotation from the Welsh *buchedd* cited above. All quotations are from *Altenglische Legenden* (here p. 260).

110 Ibid., p. 260.

111 Ibid., p. 264.

112 Bray, 'The legend of St Katherine', p. 113.

113 Ibid., p. 110.

114 For example, the Middle Welsh Life of Mary of Egypt and the Welsh version of the Miracles of the Blessed Virgin Mary (of which the Life forms a part) appear to be a translation of the Latin Life found in Oxford, Balliol College MS 240, see Mittendorf, 'Mary of Egypt' and the discussion on the Welsh versions of texts associated with Mary in Chapter 1 of the present volume. The Middle Welsh Life of Martha is somewhat unusual though, since it omits one of the most important and interesting episodes in the legend, the slaying of the dragon of Tarascon. See Chapter 4 of the present volume.

115 Cambridge University Library MS Ff.2.38, p.xvii.

116 For the social status of the owners and readers of household books, drawn largely from the gentry or mercantile elites, see Lewis, *The Cult of St Katherine*, pp. 175–84.

117 *The Auchinleck Manuscript. National Library of Scotland Advocates' MS. 19.2.1*, intro. Derek Pearsall and I. C. Cunningham (London: Scolar Press, 1977). The Auchinleck Manuscript and the White Book share the following texts: the Lives of Katherine, Margaret, Mary Magdalene and Adam and Eve; St Patrick's Purgatory; the Assumption of the Virgin Mary; one of the Virgin's miracles and Bevis of Hampton.

118 Bray, 'The legend of St Katherine', p. 233.

119 For a translation of the Vulgate version of the debate, see *Anchoritic*

Spirituality Ancrene Wisse and Associated Works, trans. and intro. Anne Savage and Nicholas Watson (New York: Paulist Press, 1991), pp. 268–73.

120 Williams, 'Buchedd Catrin', 265.

121 See Chapter 4.

122 Lewis, 'Model girls?'.

123 For a detailed discussion of the motif of St Katherine's virginity see Bernau, 'A Christian *Corpus*'.

124 Williams, 'Buchedd Catrin', 268.

125 Ibid., 268.

Chapter 6

1 This chapter is a revised and updated version of an article which first appeared in Diane Watt (ed.), *Medieval Women in their Communities* (Cardiff: University of Wales Press, 1997), pp. 20–48.

2 For example, Gilchrist, *Gender and Material Culture*, p. 61, notes that in later medieval England monasteries for men and friaries outnumbered nunneries by six to one.

3 Knowles and Hadcock, *Medieval Religious Houses*, list sixty-three monastic establishments for men in Wales (including abbeys, priories, alien priories, friaries and cells). Williams, *The Welsh Church*, p. 347, notes that there were forty-seven religious houses left in Wales by the beginning of the Tudor period (including the three nunneries). He points out that there were far fewer monasteries in Wales than in England and that Wales was probably supporting as many monastic houses as it could manage due to economic and geographical constraints.

4 Gilchrist, *Gender and Material Culture*, pp. 36–9. There were also eighteen double houses, six nuns' cells attached to male houses and four 'quasi-double' houses. In all, Knowles and Hadcock, *Medieval Religious Houses*, pp. 251–89, list 184 entries under 'Houses of Nuns' and thirteen double houses. Some houses were ephemeral and others may be counted several times since they were attributed to more than one Order. Often no one official Order was adhered to, as some nunneries swapped allegiance between Benedictine and Cistercian. Of the many female houses in England that claimed to be Cistercian, only two were officially recognized by the Order: Thompson, *Women Religious*, p. 99, but see also Constance Hoffman Berman, 'Were there twelfth-century Cistercian nuns?', in Constance Hoffman Berman (ed.), *Medieval Religion: New Approaches* (New York and London: Routledge, 2005), pp. 217–48.

5 G. Carville, 'Cistercian nuns in medieval Ireland: Plary Abbey, Ballymore, County Westmeath', in J. A. Nichols and L. T. Shank (eds), *Medieval Religious Women III, Hidden Springs: Cistercian Monastic Women* (Kalamazoo: Cistercian Publications, 1995),

pp. 63–84 (p. 65). Gilchrist, *Gender and Material Culture*, p. 40, states that there were sixty-two. More are listed in A. Gwynn and R. N. Hadcock, *Medieval Religious Houses: Ireland* (Dublin: Irish Academic Press, 1988), pp. 307–26. Again, some were short-lived. The vast majority of female houses in Ireland were Arrouasian and followed the Augustinian Rule.

6 D. E. Easson, 'The nunneries of medieval Scotland', *Scottish Ecclesiological Society Transactions*, 13.2 (1940–1), 22–38 (22). More are listed in D. E. Easson, *Medieval Religious Houses: Scotland* (London: Longmans, 1957), pp. 12–30, and Gilchrist, *Gender and Material Culture*, p. 39, states that there were thirteen.

7 D. H. Williams, 'Cistercian nunneries in medieval Wales', *Citeaux*, 26 (1975), 155–74 (157 and 163); D. H. Williams, *The Welsh Cistercians*, 2 vols (Caldey Island: Cistercian Publications, 1984), vol. 1, p. 11; D. H. Williams, 'Usk nunnery', *Monmouthshire Antiquary*, 4 (1980), 44–5 (44); F. G. Cowley, *The Monastic Order in South Wales 1066–1349* (Cardiff: University of Wales Press, 1977), pp. 37–8; Fulton, 'Medieval Welsh poems to nuns', 94. Morgan suggests *c.*1216–17 as a date for Maredudd ap Rhobert's charter. Maredudd's charter may have acted as confirmation of Llanllugan's lands rather than as a foundation charter: R. Morgan, 'An early charter of Llanllugan nunnery', *Montgomeryshire Collections*, 73 (1985), 116–19 (117–19).

8 Leland, *The Itinerary*, pp. 123–4.

9 George Owen, *The Description of Penbrokshire*, ed. H. Owen, 4 vols (London: Cymmrodorion Record Series, 1892–1936), vol. 4, p. 459.

10 Cambrensis, *Opera*, vol. 2, p. 248; vol. 4, pp. 168–9; vol. 6, p. 59.

11 Cambrensis, *Opera*, vol. 4, pp. 168–9. I am grateful to Professor John Percival for his translation of *Speculum Ecclesiae*.

12 Williams, 'Cistercian nunneries', 156.

13 Giraldus Cambrensis, *Gerald of Wales: The Jewel of the Church, a translation of Gemma Ecclesiastica*, trans. J. J. Hagen (Leiden: Lugduni Bavatorum, 1979), pp. 188–9. For the Latin text see Cambrensis, *Opera*, vol. 2, p. 248.

14 Cambrensis, *Gerald of Wales: The Jewel of the Church*, pp. 185–9.

15 For details on the former see Power, *Medieval English Nunneries*, pp. 522–3, and on the latter see G. Constable, 'Ailred of Rievaulx and the nun of Watton: an episode in the early history of the Gilbertine order', in D. Baker (ed.), *Medieval Women* (Oxford: Basil Blackwell, 1978), pp. 205–26.

16 Angell, '*Gwyrthyeu*', pp. 15, 66. On this legend and the Welsh *Gwyrthyeu* see Chapter 1 in the present volume.

17 J. E. Lloyd, *A History of Wales*, 2 vols (London: Longmans, 1911), vol. 2, p. 599.

18 See, for example, Fulton, 'Medieval Welsh poems to nuns', 95.

19 Saunders Lewis, 'Dafydd ap Gwilym', *Llên Cymru*, 2 (1953), 199–208 (205–6).

20 Williams, 'Cistercian nunneries'; Williams, *Welsh Cistercians*, vol. 1,

10–11. They are listed as priories in Knowles and Hadcock, *Medieval Religious Houses*, p. 272.

21 M. Fontette, *Les Religieuses à l'âge classique du droit canon. Recherches sur les structures juridiques des branches féminines des ordres* (Paris: Bibliothêque de la Société d'Histoire Ecclesiastique de la France, 1967), p. 34.

22 Thompson, *Women Religious*, pp. 97–100.

23 D. R. Thomas, *The History of the Diocese of St Asaph*, 3 vols (Oswestry: Caxton Press, 1908–13), vol. 1, p. 485; Williams, 'Cistercian nunneries', 158.

24 Knowles and Hadcock, *Medieval Religious Houses*, p. 274.

25 Dugdale, *Monasticon Anglicanum*, vol. 4, p. 591. See also Knowles and Hadcock, *Medieval Religious Houses*, p. 267. On Peckham's visitation, see *Registrum Epistolarum Fratris Johannis Peckham Archiepiscopi Cantuariensis (1279–92)*, ed. C. T. Martin, 3 vols (London, 1882–5), vol. 3, pp. 805–6; Williams, 'Usk Nunnery', 44; Power, *Medieval English Nunneries*, pp. 223–4.

26 Power, *Medieval English Nunneries*, p. 3. For an estimate of the number of Welsh clergy, 1377–81, see J. C. Russell, *British Medieval Population* (Albuquerque: University of New Mexico Press, 1948), p. 326, and for details of the number of monks in Wales at the end of the Middle Ages see Williams, *The Welsh Church*, pp. 561–3.

27 Thompson, *Women Religious*, p. 1; P. D. Johnson, *Equal in Monastic Profession: Religious Women in Medieval France* (Chicago: University of Chicago Press, 1991), p. 3; J. Burton, *Monastic and Religious Orders in Britain 1000–1300* (Cambridge: Cambridge University Press, 1994), p. 85.

28 Gilchrist, *Gender and Material Culture*, pp. 22–5.

29 Cambrensis, *Opera*, vol. 4, pp. 152–3; Leland, *Itinerary*, p. 55.

30 M. C. Jones, 'Some account of Llanllugan nunnery', *Montgomeryshire Collections*, 2 (1869), 301–10 (301).

31 Power, *Medieval Nunneries*, p. 692.

32 Lawrence Butler, 'The Cistercians in Wales and Yorkshire', *Archaeologia Cambrensis*, 148 (1999), 1–21.

33 Williams, 'Cistercian nunneries'; Williams, 'Usk Nunnery'; Fulton, 'Medieval Welsh poems to nuns'; Cartwright, *Y Forwyn Fair*, pp. 134–76.

34 Morgan, 'An early charter'; Madeleine Gray, 'Women of holiness and power: the cults of St Radegund and St Mary Magdalene at Usk', *The Monmouthshire Antiquary*, 18 (2002), 13–22.

35 See N. Maylan, 'Excavations at St Mary's Priory, Usk', *The Monmouthshire Antiquary*, 9 (1993), 29–41; G. Mein, 'Usk Priory: an unrecorded excavation', *The Monmouthshire Antiquary*, 9 (1993), 43–5.

36 Knowles and Hadcock, *Medieval Religious Houses*, pp. 255, 272.

37 Knowles and Hadcock, *Medieval Religious Houses*, pp. 112–15, Abbey Dore on the medieval ecclesiastical boundary between England and Wales could also be considered. Its income *c*.1535 was £101.

38 Gilchrist, *Gender and Material Culture,* pp. 41–4, 61.

39 *Littere Wallie*, ed. J. Goronwy Evans (Cardiff: Cardiff University of Wales Press, 1940), pp. 89, 132–3. I am grateful to Professor John Percival for translating these letters.

40 Adam of Usk, *Chronicon Adæ de Usk*, ed. and trans. Sir Edward Maunde Thompson (London: H. Frowde, 1904), p. 268.

41 Ibid., p. 268.

42 On strict claustration see Jane Tibbets Schulenburg, 'Strict active enclosure and its effects on the female monastic experience (500–1100)', in J. A. Nichols and L. T. Shank (eds), *Medieval Religious Women I: Distant Echoes* (Kalamazoo: Cistercian Publications, 1984), pp. 51–86.

43 *Registrum Epistolarum*, vol. 3, pp. 805–6; Power, *Medieval English Nunneries*, 223–4, 348; Williams, 'Usk Nunnery', 44.

44 Williams, 'Cistercian nunneries', 164.

45 Power, *Medieval English Nunneries*, p. 205.

46 J. A. Nichols, 'Medieval Cistercian nunneries and English bishops', in Nichols and Shank (eds), *Medieval Religious Women I*, pp. 237–49 (p. 245).

47 A. T. Bannister, '*Registrum Caroli Bothe*', *Canterbury and York Series*, 28 (1921), 241–2; Williams, 'Cistercian nunneries', 159.

48 *Littere Wallie*, pp. 89, 32–3.

49 S. W. Williams, *The Cistercian Abbey of Strata Florida: Its History and an Account of the Recent Excavations Made on its Site* (London: Whiting & Co., 1889), pp. xlviii–l; *Littere Wallie*, pp. 90–1. Compare also *Littere Wallie*, pp. 76, 84, 96–7, 174.

50 S. J. Williams, 'Rhai cyfeithiadau', in Bowen (ed.), *Y Traddodiad Rhyddiaith*, pp. 304–5.

51 On the *cywydd gofyn*, see Bleddyn Owen Huws, 'Astudiaeth o'r canu gofyn a diolch rhwng *c.*1350 a *c.*1630' (unpublished doctoral thesis, University of Wales, Bangor, 1994) and *Detholiad o Gywyddau Gofyn a Diolch*, ed. Bleddyn Owen Huws (Felindre, Swansea: Cyhoeddiadau Barddas, 1998).

52 Catrin T. B. Davies, 'Cerddi'r tai crefydd', 2 vols (unpublished M. A. thesis, University of Wales, Bangor, 1972), vol. 1, p. 95. See also *Gwaith Huw Cae Llwyd ac Eraill*, ed. L. Harries (Cardiff: University of Wales Press, 1953), pp. 69–71.

53 'Llwyd' can mean grey or brown. It can also mean sacred and the poet, aware of this ambiguity, is perhaps hinting at its rather ironic religious connotations.

54 *Detholiad o Gywyddau Gofyn*, pp. 59–60.

55 *Gwaith Huw Cae Llwyd*, p. 17.

56 For example, Archbishop Peckham forbade the abbess of Romsey to keep monkeys or dogs in her chamber. Power, *Medieval English Nunneries*, p. 306.

57 Davies, 'Cerddi'r tai crefydd', vol. 1, pp. 132–3, 142–4, 223–47.

58 Ibid., vol. 1, pp. 64–77, 81–2; Huws, 'Astudiaeth', p. 82; *Detholiad o Gywyddau Gofyn*, pp. 66–8.

[59] See Davies, 'Cerddi'r tai crefydd'.
[60] *Gramadegau'r Penceirddiaid*, pp. 16, 35, 56.
[61] *Gwaith Dafydd ap Gwilym*, pp. 298–9; Fulton, 'Medieval Welsh poems to nuns', 105–7.
[62] Fulton, 'Medieval Welsh poems to nuns', 88–9.
[63] See, for example, *Gwaith Dafydd ap Gwilym*, pp. 216–17, 227–9, 266–7.
[64] Fulton, 'Medieval Welsh poems to nuns', 107–8.
[65] Ibid., 103.
[66] Ibid., 101, n. 30.
[67] *The Oxford Book of Welsh Verse*, ed. Thomas Parry (Oxford: Oxford University Press, 1989), pp. 106–7; *Cywyddau Dafydd ap Gwilym a'i Gyfoeswyr*, ed. I. Williams and R. Thomas (Bangor: Evan Thomas, 1914), pp. 10–11.
[68] *Gwaith Syr Phylib Emlyn*, pp. 25–8.
[69] Ibid., p. 62.
[70] Fulton, 'Medieval Welsh poems to nuns', 93–4.
[71] Ibid., 103.
[72] This may refer to the colour of their skin rather than their habit.
[73] Thompson, *Women Religious*, p. 100.
[74] Lewis, *Stained Glass in North Wales*, p. 68. It is possible that the figure represents the donor of the window. I am grateful to David O'Connor for his comments on photographs of the window.
[75] London, BL, MS Additional 14999, fol. 104 $^{r-v}$.
[76] I am grateful to Graham Thomas of the National Library of Wales for help while transcribing the poem. I am also grateful to Dafydd Johnston for sharing with me his ideas on this poem and for many helpful comments on other aspects of the poetry discussed in this article.
[77] G. Ruddock, 'Cywydd i grefyddes?', *Llên Cymru*, 12 (1972), 117–20; *Gwaith lolo Goch*, pp. 101–3.
[78] See N. Truman, *Historical Costuming* (London: Sir Isaac Pitman and Sons, 1936; 1966 edn), pp. 41–2; M. Sichel, *Costume Reference 1: Roman Britain and the Middle Ages* (London: B. T. Batsford, 1977), p. 1. Numerous references are made to rosaries in Welsh poetry. Lewys Glyn Cothi thanks Efa ferch Llywelyn for providing him with a rosary and Syr Dafydd Trefor composed a *cywydd gofyn* requesting a rosary from Marged ferch Wiliam ab Wiliam: *Gwaith Lewys Glyn Cothi*, pp. 406–7; *Gwaith Syr Dafydd Trefor*, pp. 61–3.
[79] 'Ysgarladwisg' may refer to the type of material rather than its colour, *Gwaith lolo Goch*, p. 325, n. 42, but see also *Canu Maswedd yr Oesoedd Canol/Medieval Welsh Erotic Poetry*, ed. and trans. Dafydd Johnston (Cardiff: Tafol, 1991), p. 589.
[80] Compare the reference to 'dyn eglur dâl' – the nun with forehead revealed – in the Dafydd ap Gwilym *cywydd*, Fulton, 'Medieval Welsh poems to nuns', 106.
[81] *lolo Goch Poems*, pp. 100–3.
[82] *Gwaith Dafydd ap Gwilym*, pp. 269–70.

83 *Canu Maswedd*, pp. 58–61.
84 See the discussion on the Llanbeblig Hours in Chapter 1.
85 For these poems, see *Gwaith Rhys Brydydd a Rhisiart ap Rhys*, pp. 50–2; *Gwaith Lewys Glyn Cothi*, pp. 137–9, 247–8, 268–9.
86 *Gwaith Lewys Glyn Cothi*, pp. 268–9, 406–7.
87 *Gwaith Rhys Brydydd a Rhisiart ap Rhys*, pp. 34–6; *Gwaith Lewys Glyn Cothi*, pp. 107–8.
88 *Gwaith Rhys Brydydd a Rhisiart ap Rhys*, p. 34.
89 The poem to her husband is described as a praise poem, rather than an elegy, in the manuscript, *Gwaith Rhys Brydydd a Rhisiart ap Rhys*, pp. 33–4, 77, nn. 53–5.
90 *Gwaith Lewys Glyn Cothi*, p. 108.
91 *Lewys Glyn Cothi (Detholiad)*, ed. E. D. Jones (Cardiff: University of Wales Press, 1984), p. 171.
92 *Gwaith Lewys Glyn Cothi*, p. 545; *Welsh Genealogies*, vol. 2, Elystan Glodrydd 51.
93 *Gwaith Lewys Glyn Cothi*, pp. 100–6; *Gwaith Guto'r Glyn*, pp. 32–7.
94 *Gwaith Lewys Glyn Cothi*, p. 108.
95 Ibid., p. 100.
96 On the Welsh version of St Helen and the Holy Cross, see Jones, '*Ystorya Addaf a Val a Cauas Elen y Grog*'.
97 *Gwaith Guto'r Glyn*, pp. 139–41.
98 *Gwaith Lewys Glyn Cothi*, p. 97. On Welsh women donating clothing see Haycock, 'Defnydd hyd Ddydd Brawd', pp. 58–66.
99 *Gramadegau'r Penceirddiaid*, p. 56.
100 *Gwaith Lewys Glyn Cothi*, pp. 137–8.
101 Ibid., p. 189. On Elliw ferch Henri's sea journey, see Chapter 4.
102 *Gwaith Rhys Brydydd a Rhisiart ap Rhys*, p. 51.
103 *Gwaith Lewys Glyn Cothi*, pp. 371–2.
104 *Gwaith Lewys Daron*, ed. Cynfael Lake (Cardiff: University of Wales Press, 1994), p. 44.
105 *Gwaith Tudur Aled*, vol. 2, pp. 365–7; *Gwaith Lewys Môn*, pp. 28–35. See also Dafydd Wyn Wiliam, *Plasty Prysaeddfed Bodedern, Braslun o'i Hanes* (Llangefni: O. Jones, 1984).
106 *Gwaith Guto'r Glyn*, pp. 118–19, 123–5.
107 Ibid., pp. 123–5.
108 Davies, 'Cerddi'r tai crefydd', vol. 1, pp. 130–1; *Gwaith Guto'r Glyn*, p. xvi.
109 Gilchrist, *Gender and Material Culture*, pp. 172–6. On the beguine religious life see also Dor, Johnson and Wogan-Browne (eds), *New Trends in Feminine Spirituality*.
110 For a list of hospitals in medieval England and Wales see Knowles and Hadcock, *Medieval Religious Houses*, pp. 313–410.
111 Edward Laws *et al.*, *An Archaeological Survey of Pembrokeshire 1896–1907* (Tenby: John Leach, 1908), p. 121; RCAHMW, *An Inventory of the Ancient Monuments in Wales and Monmouthshire VII – County of Pembroke* (London: HMSO, 1925) pp. 232–4; Helen

Nicholson, 'The Sisters' House at Minwear, Pembrokeshire: analysis of the documentary and archaeological evidence', *Archaeologia Cambrensis*, 151 (2002), 109–38 (112–13).

112 RCAHMW, *An Inventory*, p. 234

113 Nicholson, 'The Sisters' House', 132.

114 Ibid., 132.

115 National Library of Malta, Valetta Archives of Malta 321, fol. 147^{r-v}; Nicholson, 'The Sisters' House', 132.

116 M. E. Owen, 'Y Cyfreithiau – (1) Natur y testunau', in Geraint Bowen (ed.), *Y Traddodiad Rhyddiaith yn yr Oesau Canol* (Llandysul: Gomer, 1974), pp. 196–219. A list of the manuscripts (twelfth–fifteenth century) is provided by Owen (pp. 201–2).

117 For a definition of *amobr*, see Jenkins and Owen (eds), *The Welsh Law of Women*, p. 190; see also pp. 73–5.

118 Ibid., pp. 172–3.

119 At least, this certainly seems to have been the case in the March, where *amobr* was paid for each sexual encounter until the woman's family declared her a common prostitute; see R. R. Davies, *Lordship and Society in the March of Wales 1282–1400* (Oxford: Clarendon Press, 1978), p. 137. See also Jenkins and Owen (eds), *The Welsh Law of Women*, pp. 88–90.

120 Davies, *Lordship and Society*, p. 137.

121 Knowles and Hadcock, *Medieval Religious Houses*, pp. 255, 272.

122 See details given in Thompson, *Women Religious*, pp. 167–76; Gilchrist, *Gender and Material Culture*, p. 50; Burton, *Monastic and Religious Orders in Britain*, pp. 91–3. For a discussion of English noblewomen and religious patronage see Jennifer C. Ward, 'English noblewomen and the local community in the later Middle Ages', in *Medieval Women in their Communities*, ed. Diane Watt (Cardiff: University of Wales Press, 1997), pp. 186–203 (pp. 192–3).

123 Thompson, *Women Religious*, p. 177.

124 Ward, *English Noblewomen*, p. 6. Edward I arranged that the Clare estates be held jointly by husband and wife when his daughter, Joan of Acre, married Gilbert, earl of Gloucester, in 1290, Ward, *English Noblewomen*, pp. 26–7.

125 PRO E101/93/4, m. 5. Ward, 'English noblewomen', discusses Elizabeth de Burgh's relationship with other religious houses, such as the Minoresses' convent, and it appears that this became the home of a number of other noblewomen. In her will Elizabeth's main bequests went to the London house of Minoresses and de Clare Hall: Jennifer C. Ward, 'Elizabeth de Burgh and Usk castle', *The Monmouthshire Antiquary*, 18 (2002), 13–22 (22).

126 R. R. Davies, 'The status of women and the practice of marriage in late-medieval Wales', in Jenkins and Owen (eds), *The Welsh Law of Women*, pp. 93–114 (pp. 100–2).

127 Ibid., pp. 100–2; A. D. Carr, *Medieval Anglesey* (Llangefni: Anglesey Antiquarian Society, 1982), pp. 156–60.

128 *Calendar of Ancient Petitions relating to Wales*, ed. William Rees

(Cardiff: University of Wales Press, 1975), p. 441; *The Welsh Assize Roll 1277–1284*, ed. James Conway Davies (Cardiff: University of Wales Press, 1940), pp. 287–8.

129 Gwenyth Richards, 'From footnotes to narrative: Welsh women in the thirteenth century' (unpublished doctoral thesis, University of Sydney, 2005).

130 Ibid., pp. 46–76. Rhys ap Gruffudd was the Lord Rhys, founder of Llanllŷr nunnery. There is some ambiguity concerning the daughters of Llywelyn ap Iorwerth and whether they were the daughters of Joan or Tangwystl. The Patent Rolls suggest that he had another daughter called Susanna: *Patent Rolls of the Reign of Henry III Preserved in the Public Record Office A. D. 1225–1232* (London: HMSO, 1903), p. 230.

131 M. Sheehan, *The Will in Medieval England* (Toronto: Pontifical Institute of Mediaeval Studies, 1963), Appendix B; Richards, 'From footnotes to narrative', pp. 70–2.

132 J. Beverley Smith, 'Dower in thirteenth-century Wales: a grant of the commote of Anhuniog, 1273', B, 30 (1983), 348–55.

133 At least this was certainly to be discouraged, as one might expect, during her husband's lifetime, since the lands were to revert to him according to the charter. The commote of Anhuniog was amongst lands forfeited to the Crown. Ibid., p. 353.

134 Ward, 'English noblewomen', p. 196.

135 Thompson, *Women Religious*, p. 213; Sally Ward, 'Why English nunneries had no history: a study of the problems of the English nunneries founded after the Conquest', in Nichols and Shank (eds), *Medieval Religious Women I*, pp. 131–49; Fulton, 'Medieval Welsh poems to nuns', 96–7.

136 Williams, 'Cistercian nunneries', 155.

137 Thompson, 'Why English nunneries had no history', p. 134. On the differences between the twelfth and thirteenth centuries and the practices of the Cistercians in relation to nunneries, see Hoffman Berman, 'Were there twelfth-century Cistercian nuns?'.

138 Williams, 'Cistercian nunneries', 155.

139 Cambrensis, *Opera*, vol. 4, pp. 152–3. On Cistercian lands owned by the different religious houses, see D. H. Williams, *Atlas of Cistercian Lands in Wales* (Cardiff: University of Wales Press, 1990).

140 Efa, daughter of William Marshall, earl of Pembroke, may have retired to the priory of the Augustinian nuns at Cornworthy in Devon after her husband, William de Braose, was hanged in 1230 by Llywelyn ap Iorwerth: Thompson, *Women Religious*, p. 172.

141 *Brut y Tywysogyon or The Chronicle of the Princes*, ed. and trans. Thomas Jones (Cardiff: University of Wales Press, 1955), pp. 262–5.

142 Oxford, Bodleian Library, MS Laud Misc. 642, fol. 149. J. Beverley Smith, *Llywelyn ap Gruffudd Prince of Wales* (Cardiff; University of Wales Press, 1998), pp. 579–80; Brian Golding, *Gilbert of Sempringham and the Gilbertine Order c.1130–c.1300* (Oxford: Clarendon

Press, 1995), p. 153. For a more detailed profile of these women, see Richards, 'From footnotes to narrative', pp. 210–24.

143 Golding, *Gilbert of Sempringham*, p. 153.

144 According to William Worcestre (1415–*c*.1485), the body of St Elvetha (Eluned) lay in the priory church at Usk: Worcestre, *Itineraries*, p. 155. On Eluned and the native female saints of Wales see Chapter 2.

145 Wales had to wait until the eighteenth century for its next prominent religious woman – Ann Griffiths (1776–1805).

Bibliography

Manuscripts

Aberystwyth, NLW, MS 552B
Aberystwyth, NLW, MS 1506C
Aberystwyth, NLW, MS 1641B
Aberystwyth, NLW MS 4973B
Aberystwyth, NLW, MS 5267B
Aberystwyth, NLW, MS 6209E
Aberystwyth, NLW, MS 13079B
Aberystwyth, NLW, MS Cwrtmawr 44
Aberystwyth, NLW, MS Cwrtmawr 1155
Aberystwyth, NLW, MS Llanstephan 3
Aberystwyth, NLW, MS Llanstephan 27 (the Red Book of Talgarth)
Aberystwyth, NLW, MS Llanstephan 28
Aberystwyth, NLW, MS Llanstephan 34
Aberystwyth, NLW, MS Llanstephan 47B
Aberystwyth, NLW, MS Llanstephan 104
Aberystwyth, NLW, MS Llanstephan 116
Aberystwyth, NLW, MS Llanstephan 117
Aberystwyth, NLW, MS Llanstephan 134
Aberystwyth, NLW, MS Llanstephan 187
Aberystwyth, NLW, MS Peniarth 4
Aberystwyth, NLW, MS Peniarth 5
Aberystwyth, NLW, MS Peniarth 14
Aberystwyth, NLW, MS Peniarth 15
Aberystwyth, NLW, MS Peniarth 20
Aberystwyth, NLW, MS Peniarth 23
Aberystwyth, NLW, MS Peniarth 27

Aberystwyth, NLW, MS Peniarth 57
Aberystwyth, NLW, MS Peniarth 60
Aberystwyth, NLW, MS Peniarth 111
Aberystwyth, NLW, MS Peniarth 172
Aberystwyth, NLW, MS Peniarth 186
Aberystwyth, NLW, MS Peniarth 187
Aberystwyth, NLW, MS Peniarth 191
Aberystwyth, NLW, MS Peniarth 192
Aberystwyth, NLW, MS Peniarth 217
Aberystwyth, NLW, MS Peniarth 225
Aberystwyth, NLW, MS Penpont Supplementary 274
Cambridge, University Library, MS Ff.2.38
Cambridge, University Library, MS Ff.4.42
Cardiff, Central Library, MS 2.629
Cardiff, Central Library, MS 2.633
Cardiff, Central Library, MS 3.11
Cardiff, Central Library, MS 3.242
Edinburgh, National Library of Scotland, MS Advocates 19.2.1
Lambeth, Lambeth Palace Library, MS 94
London, BL, MS Additional 14866
London, BL, MS Additional 14882
London, BL, MS Additional 14999
London, BL, MS Additional 22356
London, BL, MS Additional 31056
London, BL, MS Cotton Claudius A.v
London, BL, MS Cotton Cleopatra C. X
London, BL, MS Cotton Titus D. xxii
London, BL, MS Cotton Vespasian Axiv
London, BL, Harley MS 2059
London, BL, MS Royal 13 Ci
Oxford, Balliol College, MS 240
Oxford, Bodleian Library, MS Laud Misc. 642
Oxford, Bodleian Library, MS Rawlinson B464
Oxford, Bodleian Library, MS Rawlinson Poetry 34.
Oxford, Jesus College, MS 111 (the Red Book of Hergest)
Paris, Bibliothèque Nationale de France, MS fonds celtique 5

Reference

Birch, W. de Gray, *Catalogue of Seals in the Department of MSS at the British Museum*, 6 vols (London: printed by order of the trustees, 1887–1900).

Ellis, Roger H., *Catalogue of Seals in the Public Records Office. Monastic Seals I* (London: HMSO, 1986).

Evans, J. Gwenogvryn, *Report on Manuscripts in the Welsh Language*, 2 vols (London, 1899–1903).

Farmer, D. H., *The Oxford Dictionary of Saints*, 3rd edn (Oxford: Oxford University Press, 1992).

Gazetteer of Welsh Place-names, A, ed. E. Davies (Cardiff: University of Wales Press, 1957).

Geirfa Barddoniaeth Gynnar Gymraeg, ed. J. Lloyd-Jones (Cardiff: University of Wales Press, 1931–63).

Tasker, E. G., *Encyclopaedia of Medieval Church Art* (London: B. T. Batsford, 1993).

Warner, G. F., *A Descriptive Catalogue of Illuminated Manuscripts in the Library of C. W. Dyson Perrins* (Oxford: Oxford University Press, 1920).

Welsh Genealogies AD *300–1400*, ed. Peter C. Bartrum, 11 vols (Cardiff: University of Wales Press, 1974–80).

Williams, David H., *Catalogue of Seals in the National Museum of Wales*, 2 vols (Cardiff: National Museum of Wales, 1998).

Printed primary sources

Acta Sanctorum, ed. J. Bollandus *et al.*, March, vol. 1 (Antwerp: Jacobus Meurs, 1668).

Acta Sanctorum, ed. C. de Smedt *et al.*, November, vol. 1 (Paris: Apud Victorem Palme, 1887).

Adam of Usk, *Chronicon Adæ de Usk*, ed. and trans. Sir Edward Maunde Thompson (London: H. Frowde, 1904).

Altenglische Legenden, ed. Carl Horstmann (Heilbronn: Neue Folge, 1881).

An Old English Martyrology, ed. G. Herzfeld (London: K. Paul, Trench, Trübner & Co., 1900).

Anchoritic Spirituality Ancrene Wisse and Associated Works, trans. and intro. Anne Savage and Nicholas Watson (New York: Paulist Press, 1991).

Ancrene Riwle, The, trans. M. B. Salu (London: Burns and Oates, 1955).

Ancrene Riwle, English Text of the, The, ed. A. Zetterson, EETS, os, 274 (Oxford: Oxford University Press, 1976).

Angell, Lewis Haydn, '*Gwyrthyeu e Wynvydedic Veir:* astudiaeth gymharol ohonynt fel y'u ceir hwynt yn llawysgrifau Peniarth 14, Peniarth 5 a Llanstephan 27' (unpublished M. A. thesis, University of Wales, Cardiff, 1938).

Anon., *Two Celtic Saints: The Lives of Ninian and Kentigern* (Felinfach: Llanerch, 1989).

Auchinleck Manuscript, The. National Library of Scotland Advocates' MS. 19.2.1, intro. Derek Pearsall and I. C. Cunningham (London: Scolar Press, 1977).

Augustine, *City of God*, ed. and trans. David Knowles and Henry Bettenson (Harmondsworth: Penguin, 1972).

Beirdd Ceridwen: Blodeugerdd Barddas o Ganu Menywod hyd tua 1800, ed. Cathryn A. Charnell-White (Llandybïe: Cyhoeddiadau Barddas, 2005).

Bethu Brigte, ed. Donncha Ó hAodha (Dublin: Dublin Institute for Advanced Studies, 1978).

Blodeugerdd Barddas o Ganu Crefyddol Cynnar, ed. Marged Haycock ([Felindre, Abertawe (Swansea)]: Cyhoeddiadau Barddas, 1994).

Bokenham, Osbern, *Legendys of Hooly Wummen*, ed. Mary S. Serjeantson (London: Oxford University Press, 1938).

Book of Llan Dâv, The, ed. J. G. Evans and J. Rhŷs (Oxford: imprinted at Gloucester by John Bellows, 1893).

Bozon, Nicholas, *Three Saints' Lives by Nicholas Bozon*, ed. M. A. Klenke (New York: St Bonaventure, 1947).

Breuddwyd Maxen, ed. Ifor Williams (Bangor: Jarvis & Foster, 1908).

Brut Dingestow, ed. Henry Lewis (Cardiff: University of Wales Press, 1942).

Brut y Tywysogyon or The Chronicle of the Princes, ed. and trans. Thomas Jones (Cardiff: University of Wales Press, 1955).

Buhez Cathell (Cuburien, 1576).

Byfield, Catherine E., 'A new edition of *Buched Seint y Katrin*' (unpublished M.Phil. thesis, to be submitted to Cardiff University).

Calendar of Ancient Petitions relating to Wales, ed. William Rees (Cardiff: University of Wales Press, 1975).

Cambrensis, Giraldus (= Gerald of Wales), *Giraldi Cambrensis Opera*, ed. J. S. Brewer, J. F. Dimock and G. F. Warner, 8 vols (London: Longman, 1861–91).

—— *The Journey through Wales and The Description of Wales*, trans. Lewis Thorpe (Harmondsworth: Penguin, 1978).

—— *Gerald of Wales: The Jewel of the Church, a translation of Gemma Ecclesiastica*, trans. J. J. Hagen (Leiden: Lugduni Batavorum, 1979).

Cambridge University Library MS Ff.2.38, intro. Frances McSparran and P. R. Robinson (London: Scolar Press, 1979).

Canu Maswedd yr Oesoedd Canol/Medieval Welsh Erotic Poetry, ed. and trans. Dafydd Johnston (Cardiff: Tafol, 1991).

Canu Rhydd Cynnar, ed. T. H. Parry-Williams (Cardiff: University of Wales Press, 1932).

Casgliad o Waith Ieuan Deulwyn, ed. Ifor Williams (Bangor: Welsh Manuscripts Society, 1909).

Caxton, William, *The Golden Legend or Lives of the Saints as Englished by William Caxton*, ed. F. S. Ellis, 7 vols (London: J. M. Dent, 1900).

—— *A Critical Edition of the Legend of Mary Magdalene From Caxton's Golden Legend of 1487*, ed. D. A. Mycoff (Salzburg: University of Salzburg, 1985).

Concerning Virgins in St Ambrose: Select Works and Letters, A Select Library of Nicene and Post-Nicene Fathers of the Church, ed. P. Schaff and H. Wace, 10 vols (New York: The Christian Literature Company, 1896).

Councils and Ecclesiastical Documents Relating to Great Britain and Ireland, ed. A. W. Haddan and W. Stubbs, 3 vols (Oxford: Clarendon Press, 1869–78).

Cywyddau Dafydd ap Gwilym a'i Gyfoeswyr, ed. I. Williams and R. Thomas (Bangor: Evan Thomas, 1914).

Cywydddau Iolo Goch ac Eraill, ed. H. Lewis, T. Roberts and I. Williams (Cardiff: University of Wales Press, 1937).

Dafydd ap Gwilym: His Poems, trans. Gwyn Thomas (Cardiff: University of Wales Press, 2001).

Davies, Catrin T. B., 'Cerddi'r tai crefydd', 2 vols (unpublished M. A. thesis, University of Wales, Bangor, 1972).

Davies, Elsbeth Wendy Owen, 'Testun beirniadol o waith Hywel Rheinallt ynghyd â rhagymadrodd, nodiadau a geirfa' (unpublished M. A. thesis, University of Wales, Aberystwyth, 1967).

Davis, Jeremy P., 'Gwent Seals: IX', *The Monmouthshire Antiquary*, 15 (1999), 19–21.

Detholiad o Gywyddau Gofyn a Diolch, ed. Bleddyn Owen Huws (Felindre, Swansea: Cyhoeddiadau Barddas, 1998).

de Voragine, Jacobus, *Legenda Aurea*, ed. T. Graesse (Dresden: impensis librariae Arnoldianae, 1850).

—— *The Golden Legend: Readings on the Saints*, trans. William Granger Ryan, 2 vols (Princeton: Princeton University Press, 1993).

Dugdale, W., *Monasticon Anglicanum*, ed. J. Caley, H. Ellis and B. Bandinel, 6 vols (London: Longman, 1655–73; 1817–30 edn).

Early South English Legendary or Lives of Saints I, The, MS. Laud, 108, in the Bodleian Library, ed. Carl Horstmann, EETS, os, 86 (London: N. Trübner & Co., 1887).

Early Welsh Genealogical Tracts, ed. Peter C. Bartrum (Cardiff: University of Wales Press, 1966).

Elucidarium and other tracts in Welsh from Llyvyr Agkyr Llandewivrevi A. D. 1346, The, ed. John Morris Jones and John Rhŷs (Oxford: Clarendon, 1869).

Episcopal Acts and Cognate Documents Relating to Welsh Dioceses 1066–1272, ed. James Conway Davies, 2 vols (Cardiff: Historical Society of the Church in Wales, 1946–8).

Ernault, E., 'La vie de sainte Catherine', *Revue Celtique*, 8 (1887), 76–95.

—— 'La vie de sainte Nonne', *Revue Celtique*, 8 (1887), 230–301, 405–91.

Geoffrey of Monmouth, *The History of the Kings of Britain*, trans. Lewis Thorpe (Harmondsworth: Penguin, 1987).

Gramadegau'r Penceirddiaid, ed. G. J. Williams and E. J. Jones (Cardiff: University of Wales Press, 1934).

Gwaith Barddonol Howel Swrdwal a'i Fab Ieuan, ed. J. C. Morrice (Bangor: Welsh MSS Society, 1908).

Gwaith Bleddyn Ddu, ed. R. Iestyn Daniel (Aberystwyth: CAWCS, 1994).

Gwaith Bleddyn Fardd a Beirdd Eraill Ail Hanner y Drydedd Ganrif ar Ddeg, ed. Rhian M. Andrews *et al.* (Cardiff: University of Wales Press, 1996).

Gwaith Casnodyn, ed. R. Iestyn Daniel (Aberystwyth: CAWCS, 1999).

Gwaith Cynddelw Brydydd Mawr, ed. Nerys Ann Jones and Ann Parry Owen, 2 vols (Cardiff: University of Wales Press, 1995).

Gwaith Dafydd ab Edmwnd, ed. Thomas Roberts (Bangor: Welsh Manuscripts Society, 1914).

Gwaith Dafydd ap Gwilym, ed. Thomas Parry (Cardiff: University of Wales Press, 1979).

Gwaith Dafydd Benfras ac Eraill o Feirdd Hanner Cyntaf y Drydedd Ganrif ar Ddeg, ed. N. G. Costigan *et al.* (Cardiff: University of Wales Press, 1995).

Gwaith Dafydd Epynt, ed. Owen Thomas (Aberystwyth: CAWCS, 2002).

Gwaith Dafydd Gorlech, ed. Erwain H. Rheinallt (Aberystwyth: CAWCS 1997).

Gwaith Dafydd Llwyd o Fathafarn, ed. W. Leslie Richards (Cardiff: University of Wales Press, 1964).

Gwaith Deio ab Ieuan Du a Gwilym ab Ieuan Hen, ed. A. Eleri Davies (Cardiff: University of Wales Press, 1992).

Gwaith Gronw Gyriog, Iorwerth ab y Cyriog ac Eraill, ed. Rhiannon Ifans *et al.* (Aberystwyth: CAWCS, 1997).

Gwaith Gruffudd ap Maredudd II: Cerddi Crefyddol, ed. Barry J. Lewis (Aberystwyth: CAWCS, 2005).

Gwaith Gruffudd Llwyd a'r Llygliwiaid Eraill, ed. Rhiannon Ifans (Aberystwyth: CAWCS, 2000).

Gwaith Guto'r Glyn, ed. John Llywelyn Williams and Ifor Williams (Cardiff: University of Wales Press, 1961).

Gwaith Gwerful Mechain ac Eraill, ed. Nerys Ann Howells (Aberystwyth: CAWCS, 2001).

Gwaith Huw Cae Llwyd ac Eraill, ed. L. Harries (Cardiff: University of Wales Press, 1953).

Gwaith Hywel Swrdwal a'i Deulu, ed. Dylan Foster Evans (Aberystwyth: CAWCS, 2000).

Gwaith Ieuan ap Llywelyn Fychan, Ieuan Llwyd Brydydd a Lewys Aled, ed. M. Paul Bryant-Quinn (Aberystwyth: CAWCS, 2003).

Gwaith Ieuan Brydydd Hir, ed. M. Paul Bryant-Quinn (Aberystwyth: CAWCS, 2000).

Gwaith Ieuan Tew Brydydd Hen o Gydweli, ed. Owen Thomas (Aberystwyth: CAWCS, forthcoming).

Gwaith lolo Goch, ed. D. R. Johnston (Cardiff: University of Wales Press, 1988).

Gwaith Iorwerth Fynglwyd, ed. Howell L. Jones and E. I. Rowlands (Cardiff: University of Wales Press, 1975).

Gwaith Lewys Daron, ed. Cynfael Lake (Cardiff: University of Wales Press, 1994).

Gwaith Lewys Glyn Cothi, ed. Dafydd Johnston (Cardiff: University of Wales Press, 1995).

Gwaith Lewys Môn, ed. Eurys I. Rowlands (Cardiff: University of Wales Press, 1975).

Gwaith Lewys Morgannwg, ed. A. Cynfael Lake, 2 vols (Aberystwyth: CAWCS, 2004).

Gwaith Llywelyn Brydydd Hoddnant, Dafydd ap Gwilym, Hillyn ac Eraill, ed. Ann Parry Owen (Aberystwyth: CAWCS, 1996).

Gwaith Llywelyn Fardd I ac Eraill o Feirdd y Ddeuddegfed Ganrif, ed. Kathleen A. Bramley *et al.* (Cardiff: University of Wales Press, 1994).

Gwaith Llywelyn Goch ap Meurig Hen, ed. Dafydd Johnston (Aberystwyth: CAWCS, 1998).

Gwaith Meilyr Brydydd a'i Ddisgynyddion ynghyd â dwy awdl fawl ddienw o Ddeheubarth, ed. J. E. Caerwyn Williams with the help of Peredur Lynch and R. Geraint Gruffydd (Cardiff: University of Wales Press, 1994).

Gwaith Rhys Brydydd a Rhisiart ap Rhys, collected by John Morgan Williams and ed. Eurys I. Rolant (Cardiff: University of Wales Press, 1976).

Gwaith Rhys Goch Eryri, ed. Dylan Foster Evans (Aberystwyth: CAWCS, forthcoming).

Gwaith Sefnyn, Rhisierdyn ac Eraill, ed. Nerys Ann Jones and Erwain Haf Rheinallt (Aberystwyth: CAWCS, 1996).

Gwaith Siôn ap Hywel ap Llywelyn Fychan, ed. A. Cynfael Lake (Aberystwyth: CAWCS, 1999).

Gwaith Siôn Ceri, ed. A. Cynfael Lake (Aberystwyth: CAWCS, 1996).

Gwaith Syr Dafydd Trefor, ed. Rhiannon Ifans (Aberystwyth: CAWCS, 2005).

Gwaith Syr Phylib Emlyn, Syr Lewys Meudwy a Mastr Harri ap Hywel, ed. M. Paul Bryant-Quinn (Aberystwyth: CAWCS, 2001).

Gwaith Tudur Aled, ed. T. Gwynn Jones, 2 vols (Cardiff: University of Wales Press, 1926).

Gwassanaeth Meir sef Cyfieithiad Cymraeg Canol o'r Officum Parvum Beatae Mariae Virginis, ed. Brynley F. Roberts (Cardiff: University of Wales Press, 1961).

Hen Gerddi Crefyddol, ed. Henry Lewis (Cardiff: University of Wales Press, 1931).

lolo Goch: Poems, ed. and trans. Dafydd Johnston (Llandysul: Gomer, 1993).

Iolo Manuscripts. A Selection of Ancient Welsh Manuscripts, ed. Taliesin Williams (Llandovery: William Rees, 1848).

Irish Penitentials, The, ed. L. Bieler, *Scriptores Latini Hiberniae* (Dublin: Dublin Institute for Advanced Studies, 1963), vol. 5.

Jones, Anne Elizabeth, 'Gwilym Tew: astudiaeth destunol a chymharol o'i lawysgrif Peniarth 51, ynghyd ag ymdriniaeth â'i farddoniaeth' (unpublished doctoral thesis, University of Wales, Bangor, 1980).

Jones, D. J. (= Gwenallt), 'Buchedd Mair Fadlen a'r *Legenda aurea*', B, 4 (1929), 325–39.

—— 'Cerddi'r saint a'r bucheddau cyfatebol' (unpublished M. A. thesis, University of Wales, Aberystwyth, 1929).

Jones, Gwenan, 'Gwyrthyeu y Wynvydedic Veir', B, 9 (1938–9), 144–8, 334–41, B, 10 (1939), 21–33.

Jones, I. B., 'Hafod 16 (a mediaeval Welsh medical treatise)', *Études Celtiques*, 7 (1955–6), 46–75, 270–339.

Jones, Lisa Eryl, 'Golygiad o *Fuchedd Gwenfrewy*' (unpublished M.Phil. thesis, University of Wales, Cardiff, 2000).

'Katharinen Marter', ed. Johann Lambel, *Germania*, 8 (1863), 129–86.

Legends of the Saints in the Scottish Dialect of the Fourteenth-Century, ed. W. M. Metcalfe, 3 vols (Edinburgh and London: Scottish Text Society, 1891–6).

Leland, John, *The Itinerary of John Leland in or about the Years 1535–43*, ed. Lucy Toulmin Smith (London: George Bell & Sons, 1906).

Les vies des saints de la Bretagne Armorique par Fr Albert Le Grand, ed. D.-L. M. de Kerdanet (Brest: Anner, 1837).

Letter Book of Lewis Sabran, The, S. J. (Rector of St. Omers College) October 1713 to October 1715, ed. Geoffrey Holt, Catholic Record Society (Records Series), vol. 62 (St Albans: Catholic Record Society Publications, 1971).

Letters and Papers, Foreign and Domestic, of the Reign of Henry VIII, arranged and catalogued by James Gairdner (London: HMSO, 1892–3), vol. 13.

Lewys Glyn Cothi (Detholiad), ed. E. D. Jones (Cardiff: University of Wales Press, 1984).

Lhuyd, Edward, *Parochialia*, ed. R. H. Morris (London: T. & T. Clark, 1909–11).

Liber Landavensis, ed. W. J. Rees (Llandovery: Society for the Publication of Ancient Welsh Manuscripts, 1840).

Libri de natiuitate Mariae: Libellus de natiuitate santae Mariae, ed. R. Beyers, Corpus Christianorum Series Apocryphorum 10 (Turnhout: Brepols, 1997).

Life of St. David, trans. A. W. Wade-Evans (London: SPCK, 1923).

Littere Wallie, ed. J. Goronwy Evans (Cardiff: Cardiff University of Wales Press, 1940).

Lives of St Mary Magdalene and St Martha, The, ed. J. R. Smith (Exeter: University of Exeter, 1989).

Lives of S. Ninian and S. Kentigern Compiled in the Twelfth Century, ed. Alexander Penrose Forbes (Edinburgh: Edmonston and Douglas, 1874).

Lives of the Cambro British Saints, ed. and trans. William J. Rees (Llandovery: W. Rees, 1853).

Ludus Coventriae or the Plaie called Corpus Christi, ed. Katherine Salter Block, EETS, ES, 120 (Oxford: Oxford University Press, 1922).

Medieval English Prose for Women: Selections from the Katherine Group and Ancrene Wisse, ed. Bella Millett and Jocelyn Wogan-Browne (Oxford: Clarendon Press, 1990).

Medieval Welsh Poems, trans. Joseph P. Clancy (Dublin: Four Courts Press, 2003).

Middle Low German Version of the Legend of Mary Magdalen, The, ed. C. E. Eggert (Bloomington: The Journal of Germanic Philology Press, 1902).

Mirk, John, *Festial*, ed. Theodor Erbe, EETS, ES, 96 (London: Trübner, 1905).

Okasha, Elizabeth, *Corpus of Early Christian Inscribed Stones of South-west Britain* (London and New York: Leicester University Press, 1993).

Owen, George, *The Description of Penbrokshire*, ed. H. Owen, 4 vols (London: Cymmrodorion Record Series, 1892–1936).

Oxford Book of Welsh Verse, The, ed. Thomas Parry (Oxford: Oxford University Press, 1989).

Patent Rolls of the Reign of Henry III Preserved in the Public Record Office A. D. 1225–1232 (London: HMSO, 1903).

Pedeir Keinc y Mabinogi, ed. Ifor Williams (Cardiff: University of Wales Press, 1930).

Poetical Works of Dafydd Nanmor, The, ed. Thomas Roberts and Ifor Williams (Cardiff: University of Wales Press, 1923).

Pryce, Huw, 'A new edition of the *Historia divae Monacellae*', *Montgomeryshire Collections*, 82 (1994), 23–40.

Pynson, R., *The Lif of Saincte Kateryne* (London: R. Pynson, 1505).

Registrum Epistolarum Fratris Johannis Peckham Archiepiscopi Cantuariensis (1279–92), ed. C. T. Martin, 3 vols (London, 1882–5).

Rhigyfarch's Life of St. David, ed. J. W. James (Cardiff: University of Wales Press, 1967).

Rhyddiaith Gymraeg: Y Gyfrol Gyntaf Detholion o Lawysgrifau 1488–1609, ed. T. H. Parry-Williams (Cardiff: University of Wales Press, 1954).

Richards, Melville, 'Buchedd Mair o'r Aifft', *Études Celtiques*, 2 (1937), 45–9.

—— 'Buchedd Fargred', B, 9 (1939), 324–34; B, 10 (1939) 53–9; and B, 13 (1949), 65–71.

St Katherine of Alexandria The Late Middle English Prose Legend in Southwell Minster MS 7, ed. Saara Nevanlinna and Irma Taavitsainen (Cambridge: D. S. Brewer, 1993).

Sainted Women of the Dark Ages, ed. and trans. Jo Ann McNamara, J. E. Halborg and E. G. Whatley (Durham and London: Duke University Press, 1992).

Sammlung Altenglischer Legenden, ed. Carl Horstmann (Heilbronn: Neue Folge, 1878).

Saxton, Christopher, *Christopher Saxton's Sixteenth-Century Maps. The Counties of England and Wales*, intro. William Ravenhill (Shrewsbury: Chatsworth Library, 1992).

Scourfield, Nest, 'Gwaith Ieuan Gethin ab Ieuan ap Lleision, Llywelyn ap Hywel ab Ieuan ap Gronw, Ieuan Du'r Bilwg, Ieuan Rudd a Llywelyn Goch y Dant' (unpublished M.Phil. thesis, University of Wales, Swansea, 1992).

'Seinte Katerine' Re-Edited from MS Bodley 34 and the other Manuscripts, ed. S. R. T. O. d'Ardenne and E. J. Dobson, EETS, os, 887 (Oxford: Oxford University Press, 1981).

Selections from the Hengwrt MSS Preserved in the Peniarth Library, ed. and trans. Robert Williams and G. Hartwell Jones, 2 vols (London: T. Richards and B. Quaritch, 1876–92).

South English Legendary, The, ed. Charlotte D'Evelyn and Anna J. Mill, EETS, ES, 235–6, 244, 3 vols (London: Oxford University Press, 1956–9).

Spalding, Richard, *Speculum Sacerdotale*, ed. Edward H. Weatherly, EETS, os, 200 (London: Oxford University Press, 1936).

Supplementary Lives in Some Manuscripts of the Gilte Legende, ed. Richard Hamer and Vida Russell, EETS, os, 315 (Oxford: Oxford University Press, 2000).

Thomas, Carol, '*Buched Anna*, *Buched Meir Wyry* a *Llyma Vabinogi Iessu Grist*: agweddau ar destunau apocryffaidd' (unpublished doctoral thesis to be submitted to the University of Wales, Lampeter).

Three Alliterative Saints' Hymns: Late Middle English Stanzaic Poems, ed. Ruth Kennedy, EETS, os 321 (Oxford: Oxford University Press, 2003).

Three Chapters of Letters relating to the Suppression of Monasteries, ed. Thomas Wright (London: Camden Society, 1843).

Trioedd Ynys Prydein. The Welsh Triads, ed. and trans. Rachel Bromwich (Cardiff: University of Wales Press, 1978).

Two Lives of Gildas by a Monk of Ruys and Caradoc of Llancarfan, trans. Hugh Williams (Felinfach: Llanerch, 1990).

Two Mediaeval Lives of Saint Winefride, trans. Ronald Pepin and Hugh Feiss (Toronto: Peregrina Publishing, 2000).

Virgin Lives and Holy Deaths, ed. and trans. G. Burgess and J. Wogan-Browne (London: J. M. Dent, 1996).

Vita Sancti Patterni: the Life of Saint Padarn and the Original 'Miniu', ed. and trans. Charles Thomas and David Howlett (Lampeter: Trivium Publications, 2003).

Vita Sancti Tathei and Buched Seint y Katrin, ed. H. Idris Bell (Bangor: Welsh MSS Society, 1909).

Vitae Sanctorum Britanniae et Geneaologiae, ed. and trans. A. W. Wade-Evans (Cardiff: University of Wales Press, 1944).

von Fritslar, Hermann, 'Das Heiligenleben von Hermann von Fritslar', in Franz Pfeiffer (ed.), *Deutsche Mystiker des Vierzehnten Jahrhunderts*, Scientia Verlag, 1 (Leipzig: G. J. Göschen, 1845), pp. 255–6.

Welsh Assize Roll 1277–1284, The, ed. James Conway Davies (Cardiff: University of Wales Press, 1940).

Welsh Life of St David, The, ed. D. Simon Evans (Cardiff: University of Wales Press, 1988).

Williams, G. J., 'Atodiad: cywyddau ac awdlau Pen-rhys', *Efrydiau Catholig*, 5 (1951), 40–5.

Williams, J. E. Caerwyn, '*Transitus Beatae Mariae* a thestunau cyffelyb', B, 18 (1959), 131–57.

—— 'Buchedd Catrin Sant', B, 25 (1973), 247–68.

Williams, Mary, 'Buched Meir Wyry', *Revue Celtique*, 33 (1912), 207–38.

—— 'Llyma Vabinogi Iessu Grist', *Revue Celtique*, 33 (1912), 184–207.

Williams, R., 'Historiae Monacellae', *Archaeologia Cambrensis*, 3 (1848), 139–42.

Woman Defamed and Woman Defended, ed. Alcuin Blamires (Oxford: Clarendon, 1992).

Worcestre, William, *Itineraries*, ed. J. H. Harvey (Oxford: Clarendon, 1969).

Ymborth yr Enaid, ed. R. Iestyn Daniel (Cardiff: University of Wales Press, 1995).

Zupita, J. 'Das leben der heiligen Maria Magdalena', *Archiv für das Studium der neuren Sprächen und Litteraturen*, 47 (1893), 207–24.

Secondary sources

Abgrall, J., 'Les pierres à empreintes – les pierres à bassins', *Bulletin de la société archéologique du Finistère*, 17 (1890), 62–72.

Anderson, Jørgen, *The Witch on the Wall. Medieval Erotic Sculpture in the British Isles* (London: Allen and Unwin, 1977).

Anon., 'Llanllyfni papers', *Archaeologia Cambrensis*, 11 (1863), series 3, 280–6.

Anon., 'Machynlleth meeting report', *Archaeologia Cambrensis*, 12 (1866), series 3, 544–9.

Anon., 'Aberystwyth meeting report', *Archaeologia Cambrensis*, 14 (1897), series 5, 164–6.

Anon., 'Folk-lore of the Cardiganshire coast', *Welsh Gazette*, 4 January, 11 January and 18 January 1912.

Anon., 'St David and Cardiganshire', *Welsh Gazette*, 29 February 1912.

Anon., 'Ancient church to be rescued from neglect', *Western Mail*, 12 July 1988.

Argus, 'Correspondence', *Transactions of the Cardiganshire Antiquarian Society*, 1, no. 3, (1913), p. 36.

Awbery, Gwenllian, *Blodau'r Ardd a'r Maes ar Lafar Gwlad* (Llanrwst: Gwasg Carreg Gwalch, 1995).

Bannister, A. T., '*Registrum Caroli Bothe*', *Canterbury and York Series*, 28 (1921), 241–2.

Baring-Gould, S., 'Exploration of St. Non's Chapel, near St. Davids', *Archaeologia Cambrensis*, 15 (1898), series 5, 345–8.

—— and Fisher, John, *The Lives of the British Saints*, 4 vols (London: Cymmrodorion, 1907–13).

Berman, Constance Hoffman, 'Were there twelfth-century Cistercian nuns?', in Constance Hoffman Berman (ed.), *Medieval Religion: New Approaches* (New York and London: Routledge, 2005), 217–48.

Bernau, Anke, 'A Christian *Corpus*: virginity, violence, and knowledge in the Life of St Katherine of Alexandria', in Jenkins and Lewis (eds), *St Katherine of Alexandria*, pp. 109–30.

——, Ruth Evans and Sarah Salih (eds), *Medieval Virginities* (Cardiff: University of Wales Press, 2003).

Blacklaw-Jones, Richard, *Pembrokeshire Past Lost and Found* (Pembrokeshire Prospectors, 1997).

Bloch, Howard R., *Medieval Misogyny and the Invention of Western Romantic Love* (Chicago and London: University of Chicago Press, 1991).

Bloch, R. H., 'Chaucer's maiden's head: *The Physician's Tale* and the poetics of virginity', *Representations*, 28 (1989), 113–34.

Boss, Sarah Jane, *Empress and Handmaid: On Nature and Gender in the Cult of the Virgin Mary* (London: Cassell, 2000).

—— *Mary* (London and New York: Continuum, 2003).

Bowen, E. G., 'Celtic saints in Cardiganshire', *Ceredigion*, 1 (1950–1), 3–17.

—— *The Settlements of the Celtic Saints in Wales* (Cardiff: University of Wales Press, 1954).

—— *Saints, Seaways and Settlements in the Celtic Lands* (Cardiff: University of Wales Press, 1977).

Bowen, Geraint (ed.), *Y Traddodiad Rhyddiaith yn yr Oesau Canol* (Llandysul: Gomer, 1974).

Bradley, Ian, *The Celtic Way* (London: Darton, Longman and Todd, 1993).

—— *Celtic Christianity: Making Myths and Chasing Dreams* (Edinburgh: Edinburgh University Press, 1999).

Bradney, A. J., *A History of Monmouthshire*, 3 vols (London: Mitchell, Hughes and Clarke, 1904–33).

Bray, Jennifer Relvyn, 'The legend of St Katherine in later Middle English literature' (unpublished doctoral thesis, University of London, 1984).

Breeze, Andrew, 'The girdle of Prato and its rivals', B, 33 (1986), 95–100.

—— 'The Virgin's tears of blood', *Celtica*, 20 (1988), 110–14.

—— 'The Virgin's rosary and St Michael's scales', *Studia Celtica*, 24 (1989–90), 91–8.

—— 'The Blessed Virgin's Joys and Sorrows', *Cambridge Medieval Celtic Studies*, 19 (1990), 41–54.

—— 'The instantaneous harvest', *Ériu*, 41 (1990), 81–93.

—— 'The Virgin Mary, daughter of her Son', *Études Celtiques*, 27 (1990), 267–87.

—— 'Two bardic themes: the Trinity in the Blessed Virgin's womb', *Celtica*, 22 (1991), 1–15.

—— 'Two bardic themes: the Virgin and child and *AVE*-EVA', *Medium Ævum*, 63 (1994), 17–33.

Britnell, W. J. and K. Watson, 'Saint Melangell's shrine, Pennant Melangell', *Montgomeryshire Collections*, 82 (1994), 147–66.

Bryant-Quinn, M. Paul, '"Enaid y gwir goleuni": y Grog yn Aberhonddu', *Dwned*, 2 (1996), 51–93.

Bund, J. W. Willis, 'Some characteristics of Welsh and Irish saints', *Archaeologia Cambrensis*, 11 (1894), series 5, 276–91.

Burton, J., *Monastic and Religious Orders in Britain 1000–1300* (Cambridge: Cambridge University Press, 1994).

Butler, Lawrence, 'The Cistercians in Wales and Yorkshire', *Archaeologia Cambrensis*, 148 (1999), 1–21.

Butler, L. and J. Graham-Campbell, 'A lost reliquary casket from North Wales', *The Antiquaries Journal*, 70 (1990), 40–8.

Bynum, Caroline Walker, *Holy Feast and Holy Fast: the Religious Significance of Food to Medieval Women* (Berkeley, CA and London: University of California Press, 1988).

Cambrian Archaeological Society, 'Carmarthen Meeting – Report, Friday, August 20th 1875', *Archaeologia Cambrensis*, 6 (1875), series 4, 412–13.

Cane, Meredith, 'Personal names of women in medieval Wales, Cornwall and Brittany 400–1400 A.D.' (unpublished M.Phil. thesis, University of Wales, Aberystwyth, 1999).

Carr, A. D., *Medieval Anglesey* (Llangefni: Anglesey Antiquarian Society, 1982).

Cartwright, Jane, 'Non – mam dda ddinam', *Barn*, 374 (1994), 57–9.

—— 'The desire to corrupt: convent and community in medieval Wales', in Diane Watt (ed.), *Medieval Women in their Communities* (Cardiff: University of Wales Press, 1997), pp. 20–48.

—— *Y Forwyn Fair, Santesau a Lleianod: Agweddau ar Wyryfdod a Diweirdeb yng Nghymru'r Oesoedd Canol* (Cardiff: University of Wales Press, 1999).

—— 'Santesau Ceredigion', *Ceredigion*, 14 (2001), 1–36.

—— 'Dead virgins: feminine sanctity in medieval Wales', *Medium Ævum*, 71 (2002), 1–28.

—— '*Buchedd Catrin*: a preliminary study of the Middle Welsh Life of St Katherine of Alexandria and her cult in medieval Wales', in Jenkins and Lewis (eds), *St Katherine*, pp. 53–86.

—— (ed.), *Celtic Hagiography and Saints' Cults* (Cardiff: University of Wales Press, 2003).

—— 'The harlot and the hostess: a preliminary study of the Middle Welsh Lives of Mary Magdalene and her sister Martha', in Cartwright (ed.), *Celtic Hagiography and Saints' Cults*, pp. 77–101.

—— 'Virginity and chastity tests in Middle Welsh prose', in Bernau, Evans and Salih (eds), *Medieval Virginities*, pp. 56–79.

—— 'The cult of St Non: rape, sanctity and motherhood in Welsh and Breton hagiography', in Evans and Wooding (eds), *St David of Wales*, pp. 182–206.

Carville, G., 'Cistercian nuns in medieval Ireland: Plary Abbey, Ballymore, County Westmeath', in J. A. Nichols and L. T. Shank (eds), *Medieval Religious Women III, Hidden Springs: Cistercian Monastic Women* (Kalamazoo: Cistercian Publications, 1995), pp. 63–84.

Chandler, Helen, 'The will in medieval Wales up to 1540' (unpublished M.Phil. thesis, University of Wales, Aberystwyth, 1992).

Chandler, Kirstie Siân, 'Masculinity and medieval Welsh literature' (unpublished doctoral thesis, University of Wales, Aberystwyth, 2004).

Charles, B. G., *George Owen of Henllys: A Welsh Elizabethan* (Aberystwyth: National Library of Wales, 1973).

Charles-Edwards, G., 'The scribes of the Red Book of Hergest', *National Library of Wales Journal*, 21 (1987–8), 246–50.

Charles-Edwards, Thomas, 'Pen-rhys: y cefndir hanesyddol 1179–1538', *Efrydiau Catholig*, 5 (1951), 24–39.

—— *Saint Winefride and her Well: the Historical Background* (London: Catholic Truth Society, 1962).

Charnell-White, Cathryn, *Bardic Circles: National, Regional and Personal Identity in the Bardic Vision of Iolo Morganwg* (Cardiff: University of Wales Press, 2007).

Clayton, Mary, *The Apocryphal Gospels of Mary in Anglo-Saxon England* (Cambridge: Cambridge University Press, 1998).

Conran, Tony, 'The hymn to the Virgin', *Welsh Writing in English*, 1 (1995), 5–22.

Constable, G., 'Ailred of Rievaulx and the nun of Watton: an episode in the early history of the Gilbertine order', in D. Baker (ed.), *Medieval Women* (Oxford: Basil Blackwell, 1978), pp. 205–26.

Constantine, Mary-Ann, *Breton Ballads* (Aberystwyth: CMCS Publications, 1996).

—— 'Saints behaving badly: sanctity and transgression in Breton popular culture', in Cartwright (ed.), *Celtic Hagiography and Saints' Cults*, pp. 198–215.

—— *The Truth Against the World: Iolo Morganwg and Romantic Forgery* (Cardiff: University of Wales Press, 2007).

Cornell, Johan Henrick, *The Iconography of the Nativity of Christ* (Uppsala: Uppsala Universitets årsskrift, 1924).

Costigan, N. G., *Defining the Divinity: Medieval Perceptions in Welsh Court Poetry* (Aberystwyth: CAWCS, 2002).

Cowley, F. G., *The Monastic Order in South Wales 1066–1349* (Cardiff: University of Wales Press, 1977).

Cozan, Jean-Yves *et al.*, La Bretagne au temps des Ducs (Daoulas: Centre Culturel Abbaye de Daoulas, 1991).

Cule, J., 'Some early hospitals in Wales and the border', *National Library of Wales Journal*, 20 (1977–8), 97–130.

Cullum, P. H. and Katherine J. Lewis (eds), *Holiness and Masculinity in the Middle Ages* (Cardiff: University of Wales Press, 2004).

Curley, Michael J., 'Five *lecciones* for the feast of St Nonita: a text and its context', *Cambrian Medieval Celtic Studies*, 43 (2002), 59–75.

Curtis, K. *et al.*, 'Beirdd benywaidd yng Nghymru cyn 1800', *Y Traethodydd*, 141 (1986), 12–27.

Daniel, R. Iestyn, 'Y ffynhonnau yng nghanu'r Cywyddwyr', *Dwned*, 7 (2001), 65–81.

Davies, J. C., *Folk-Lore of West and Mid-Wales* (Aberystwyth: Welsh Gazette, 1911).

Davies, Rhiannon M. M., 'The moral structure of *Pedeir Keinc y Mabinogi*' (unpublished doctoral thesis, University of Wales, Cardiff, 1993).

Davies, R. R., *Lordship and Society in the March of Wales 1282–1400* (Oxford: Clarendon Press, 1978).

—— 'The status of women and the practice of marriage in late-medieval Wales', in Jenkins and Owen (eds), *The Welsh Law of Women*, pp. 93–114.

Davies, R. T., 'A study of the themes and usages of medieval Welsh religious poetry 1100–1450' (unpublished B. Litt. dissertation, Oxford University, 1958–9).

Davies, S., 'Y ferch yng Nghymru yn yr Oesoedd Canol', *Cof Cenedl*, 9 (1994), 3–32.

Davies, Wendy, *An Early Welsh Microcosm: Studies in the Llandaff Charters* (London: Royal Historical Society, 1978).

—— 'Property rights and property claims in Welsh "Vitae" of the eleventh century', *Hagiographie, Cultures et Sociétés, IVe-XIIe siècles* (Paris: Études augustiniennes, 1981), pp. 515–33.

—— 'The myth of the Celtic Church', in Edwards and Lane (eds), *The Early Church in Wales and the West*, pp. 12–21.

Davis, P. R. and S. Lloyd-Fern, *Lost Churches of Wales and the Marches* (Stroud: Sutton, 1990).

de Guise, Elizabeth, *The Story of St Non the Mother of St David* (Tenby: Everdrake Press, no date).

Doble, G. H., *Saint Nonna*, Cornish Saints Series 16 (Liskeard: Philp & Sons, 1928).

—— *S. Nectan, S. Keyne and the Children of Brychan in Cornwall*, Cornish Saints Series 25 (Exeter: Sydney Lee, 1930).

—— *Lives of the Welsh Saints*, ed. D. Simon Evans (Cardiff: Cardiff University of Wales Press, 1971)

Dobson, E. J., 'The hymn to the Virgin', *Transactions of the Honourable Society of Cymmrodorion* (1954), 70–124.

Dor, Juliette, Lesley Johnson and Jocelyn Wogan-Browne (eds), *New Trends in Feminine Spirituality: the Holy Women of Liège and their Impact* (Brussels: Brepols, 1999).

Duchesne, L., 'La légende de Sainte Marie-Madeleine', in L. Duchesne, *Fastes Episcopaux de l'Ancienne Gaule*, 3 vols (Paris: Albert Fontemoing, 1907–15), vol. 1, pp. 321–60.

Duggan, E. J. M., 'Notes concerning the "Lily Crucifixion" in the Llanbeblig Hours', *Journal of the National Library of Wales*, 27 (1991), 39–48.

Dwnn, Lewis, *Heraldic Visitations of Wales*, 2 vols (Llandovery: W. Rees, 1846).

Easson, D. E., 'The nunneries of medieval Scotland', *Scottish Ecclesiological Society Transactions*, 13.2 (1940–1), 22–38.

—— *Medieval Religious Houses: Scotland* (London: Longmans, 1957).

Edwards, Huw M., 'Murnio marwnadau: golwg ar y ffug-farwnad yng nghyfnod y cywydd', *Dwned*, 5 (1999), 47–70.

Edwards, Nancy, 'Monuments in a landscape; the early medieval sculpture of St David's', in Helena Hamerow and Arthur MacGregor (eds), *Image and Power in the Archaeology of Early Medieval Britain: Essays in Honour of Rosemary Cramp* (Oxford: Oxbow, 2001), pp. 53–77.

—— and Tristan Gray Hulse, 'A fragment of a reliquary casket from Gwytherin, North Wales', *The Antiquaries Journal*, 72 (1992), 91–101.

—— and Alan Lane (eds), *The Early Church in Wales and the West* (Oxford: Oxbow Monograph 16, 1992).

Elkins, Sharon K., *Holy Women of Twelfth-Century England* (Chapel Hill, NC and London: University of California Press, 1988).

Ellis, R. G., *Flowering Plants of Wales* (Cardiff: National Museum of Wales, 1983).

Evans, D. Simon, 'Y Bucheddau', in Bowen (ed.), *Y Traddodiad Rhyddiaith*, pp. 245–73.

—— *Medieval Religious Literature* (Cardiff: University of Wales Press, 1986).

Evans, George Eyre, *Cardiganshire: A Personal Survey of Some of its Antiquities, Chapels, Churches, Fonts, Plate and Registers* (Aberystwyth: Welsh Gazette, 1903).

Evans, J. Wyn, 'The early Church in Denbighshire', *Transactions of the Denbighshire Historical Society*, 35 (1986), 61–81.

—— and Jonathan M. Wooding (eds), *St David of Wales: Cult, Church and Nation* (Woodbridge: Boydell and Brewer, 2007).

Falc'hun, François, *Dirinon* (La Guerche-de-Bretagne: Ouest France, 1986).

Fenn, R. W. D. and J. B. Sinclair, 'St Michael, Our Lady, and St Cadoc: some ancient Monmouthshire dedications', *The Monmouthshire Antiquary*, 16 (2000), 99–106.

Fenton, Richard, *A Historical Tour Through Pembrokeshire* (London: Longman, Hurst, Rees, Orme & Co., 1811).

Fishbourne, E. A., 'Notes on the east window of the church of All Saints, Gresford', *Archaeologia Cambrensis*, 7 (1907), series 6, 352–7.

Fontette, M., *Les Religieuses à l'âge classique du droit canon. Recherches sur les structures juridiques des branches féminines des ordres* (Paris: Bibliothêque de la Société d'Histoire Ecclesiastique de la France, 1967).

Foskett, Mary F., *A Virgin Conceived: Mary and Classical Representations of Virginity* (Bloomington: Indiana University Press, 2002).

Freeman, M., 'A Sheela-na-Gig from Llanon, Llansanffraid, Ceredigion', *Archaeologia Cambrensis*, 149 (2000), 14–19.

Fulton, H., 'Medieval Welsh poems to nuns', *Cambridge Medieval Celtic Studies*, 21 (1991), 87–112.

Garth, Helen M., *Saint Mary Magdalene in Mediaeval Literature* (Baltimore: Johns Hopkins University Press, 1950).

Gilchrist, Roberta, *Gender and Material Culture: the Archaeology of Religious Women* (London: Routledge, 1994).

Gold, Penny Schine, *The Lady and the Virgin: Image, Attitude and Experience in Twelfth-Century France* (Chicago: University of Chicago Press, 1985).

Golding, Brian, *Gilbert of Sempringham and the Gilbertine Order c.1130–c.1300* (Oxford: Clarendon Press, 1995).

Graef, Hilda, *Mary, A History of Doctrine and Devotion*, 2 vols (London: Sheed and Ward, 1963).

Gray, Madeleine, 'Pen-rhys: the archaeology of a pilgrimage', *Morgannwg*, 40 (1996), 10–32.

—— *Images of Piety: the Iconography of Traditional Religion in Late Medieval Wales*, BAR British Series 316 (Oxford: Archaeopress, 2000).

—— 'Women of holiness and power: the cults of St Radegund and St Mary Magdalene at Usk', *The Monmouthshire Antiquary*, 18 (2002), 13–22.

Gresham, C. A., 'Tre Ferthyr and the development of Cricieth', B, 27 (1966), 5–36.

Griffiths, R. A., 'Gentlemen and rebels in later medieval Cardiganshire', *Ceredigion*, 5 (1964–7), 143–67.

Gruffydd, R. Geraint, 'Dafydd Ddu o Hiraddug', *Llên Cymru*, 18 (1995), 205–20.

Gunn, Cate, 'Beyond the tomb: *Ancrene Wisse* and lay piety', in Herbert McAvoy and Hughes-Edwards (eds), *Anchorites, Wombs and Tombs*, pp. 161–71.

Gwynn, A. and R. N. Hadcock, *Medieval Religious Houses: Ireland* (Dublin: Irish Academic Press, 1988).

Hague, D. S., 'St Non's Chapel, Llanon', unpublished document, SN 56 NW, RCAHMW.

Hand, Charles R., 'Llanfaes friary and its mystery monuments', *Archaeologia Cambrensis*, 79 (1924), series 7, 125–88.

Harris, Silas M., 'Y Wyry Wen o Ben-rhys. Our Lady of Pen-rhys', *Welsh Saints and Shrines*, 1 (1951), 1–3.

—— 'The kalendar of the *Vitae Sanctorum Wallensium*', *Journal of the Historical Society of the Church in Wales*, 111 (1953), 3–53.

Haskins, Susan, *Mary Magdalen Myth and Metaphor* (New York: Riverhead Books, 1993).

Haslam, Richard, *The Buildings of Wales: Powys (Montgomeryshire, Radnorshire, Breconshire)* (Harmondsworth: Penguin, 1979).

Haycock, M., 'Merched drwg a merched da: Ieuan Dyfi v. Gwerful Mechain', *Ysgrifau Beirniadol*, 16 (1990), 97–110.

—— 'Defnydd hyd Ddydd Brawd: rhai agweddau ar y ferch ym marddoniaeth yr Oesoedd Canol', in Geraint H. Jenkins (ed.), *Cymru a'r Cymry 2000 / Wales and the Welsh 2000* (Aberystwyth: CAWCS, 2001), pp. 41–70.

Henken, Elissa R., 'Folklore of the Welsh saints', 2 vols (unpublished M. A. thesis, University of Wales, Aberystwyth, 1982).

—— 'The saint as folk hero: biographical patterning in Welsh hagiography', in P. K. Ford (ed.), *Celtic Folklore and Christianity* (Santa Barbara: McNally and Loftin, 1983), pp. 58–74.

—— *Traditions of the Welsh Saints* (Cambridge: D. S. Brewer, 1987).

—— *The Welsh Saints: A Study in Patterned Lives* (Cambridge: D. S. Brewer, 1991).

H. L. J. [sic.], 'Mona mediaeva no. XII Penmon Priory', *Archaeologia Cambrensis*, 6 (1849), series 1, 44–60.

Hope, W. H. St John, 'On the sculptured tablets called Saint John's Heads', *Archaeologia*, 52 (1890), series 2, 669–708.

Hufstader, A., 'Lefèvre d'Étaples and the Magdalen', *Studies in the Renaissance*, 16 (1969), 31–60.

Hughes, H. Harold, 'Miscellanea', *Archaeologia Cambrensis*, 91 (1936), series 1, 134–6.

Hughes, Kathleen, 'The Celtic Church: is this a valid concept?', *Cambridge Medieval Celtic Studies*, 1 (1981), 1–20.

Hulse, Tristan Gray, '"Visting a dry skull": aspects of the cult of relics in post-Reformation Wales', unpublished paper delivered at the conference on Celtic Hagiography and Saints' Cults, University of Wales, Lampeter, 8–10 September 2000.

—— 'The documentation of Ffynnon Ddeier: some problems reconsidered', *Living Spring Journal*, 2 (2002), www.bath.ac.uk/lispring/journal/front.html.

Huws, Bleddyn Owen, 'Astudiaeth o'r canu gofyn a diolch rhwng *c.*1350 a *c.*1630' (unpublished doctoral thesis, University of Wales, Bangor, 1994).

Huws, Daniel, 'The earliest Bangor missal', *National Library of Wales Journal*, 27 (1991), 113–28.

—— *Medieval Welsh Manuscripts* (Cardiff: University of Wales Press and the National Library of Wales, 2000).

Jackson, K., 'A note on the miracle of the instantaneous harvest', B, 10 (1939–41), 203–7.

—— 'Some fresh light on the miracle of the instantaneous harvest', *Folklore*, 51 (1940), 203–10.

Jacquart, Danielle and Claude Thomasset, *Sexuality and Medicine in the Middle Ages*, trans. Matthew Adamson (Cambridge: Polity Press, 1988).

James, Christine, 'Llwyr wybodau, llên a llyfrau: Hopcyn ap Thomas a'r traddodiad llenyddol Cymraeg', in Hywel Teifi Edwards (ed.), *Cwm Tawe* (Llandysul: Gomer, 1993), pp. 4–44.

—— 'Pen-rhys: mecca'r genedl', in Hywel Teifi Edwards (ed.), *Cwm Rhondda* (Llandysul: Gomer, 1995), pp. 27–71.

—— 'Ysgrifydd anhysbys: proffil personol', *Ysgrifau Beirniadol*, 23 (1997), 44–72.

—— '"Y grog ddoluriog loywrym": golwg ar y canu i grog Llangynwyd', *Llên Cymru*, 29 (2006), 64–109.

James, M. R., *The New Apocryphal Testament* (Oxford: Clarendon Press, 1953).

Jankulak, Karen, 'Alba Longa in the Celtic regions? Swine, saints and Celtic hagiography', in Cartwright (ed.), *Celtic Hagiography and Saints' Cults*, pp. 271–84.

Jenkins, D. and M. E. Owen (eds), *The Welsh Law of Women* (Cardiff: University of Wales Press, 1980).

Jenkins, Geraint H. (ed.), *A Rattleskull Genius: The Many Faces of Iolo Morganwg* (Cardiff: University of Wales Press, 2005).

Jenkins, Jacqueline, 'St Katherine's and laywomen's piety: the Middle English prose life in London, British Library, Harley MS 4012', in Jenkins and Lewis (eds), *St Katherine*, pp. 153–70.

—— and Katherine J. Lewis (eds), *St Katherine of Alexandria: Texts and Contexts in Western Medieval Europe* (Turnhout: Brepols, 2003).

John, Terry and Nona Rees, *Pilgrimage: A Welsh Perspective* (Llandysul: Gomer, 2002).

Johnson, P. D., *Equal in Monastic Profession: Religious Women in Medieval France* (Chicago: University of Chicago Press, 1991).

Johnston, Dafydd, 'Awdl Llywelyn Goch i Rydderch a Llywelyn Fychan', B, 35 (1988), 20–8.

—— 'Gwenllïan ferch Rhirid Flaidd', *Dwned*, 3 (1997), 27–32.

—— *Llên yr Uchelwyr: Hanes Beirniadol Llenyddiaeth Gymraeg 1300–1525* (Cardiff: University of Wales Press, 2005).

Jones, D. Ambrose, 'Miscellanea', *Archaeologica Cambrensis*, 2 (1922), series 7, 415.

Jones, Francis, *The Holy Wells of Wales* (Cardiff: University of Wales Press, repr. 1992).

Jones, G. Hartwell, *Celtic Britain and the Pilgrim Movement*, *Y Cymmrodor*, 23 (London: Cymmrodorion, 1912).

Jones, Graham, *Saints of Wales: An Inventory of Religious Dedications* (Aberystwyth: Celtic Studies Publications, forthcoming).

Jones, M. C., 'Some account of Llanllugan nunnery', *Montgomeryshire Collections*, 2 (1869), 301–10.

Jones, Michael K. and Malcolm G. Underwood, *The King's Mother Lady Margaret Beaufort, Countess of Richmond and Derby* (Cambridge: Cambridge University Press, 1992).

Jones, N. A. and M. E. Owen, 'Twelfth-century Welsh hagiography: the *Gogynfeirdd* poems to saints', in Cartwright (ed.), *Celtic Hagiography and Saints' Cults*, pp. 45–76.

Jones, T. Gwynn, '*Ystorya Addaf a Val a Cauas Elen y Grog*: tarddiad, cynnwys ac arddull y testunau Cymraeg a'u lledaeniad' (unpublished M. A. thesis, University of Wales, Aberystwyth, 1936).

Jones, T. Thornley, 'The daughters of Brychan Brycheiniog', *Brycheiniog*, 17 (1976–7), 17–58.

Jones, W. B. and E. A. Freeman, *The History and Antiquities of St. David's* (London: J. H. & J. Parker, 1856; 1998 edn).

Kelly, Kathleen Coyne, *Performing Virginity and Testing Chastity in the Middle Ages* (London and New York: Routledge, 2000).

Knowles, David, *The Monastic Order in England* (Cambridge: Cambridge University Press, 1940).
—— and R. Neville Hadcock, *Medieval Religious Houses England and Wales* (London: Longman, 1971).
Laws, Edward, *Church Book of St Mary the Virgin* (Tenby: John Leach, 1907).
—— *et al.*, *An Archaeological Survey of Pembrokeshire 1896–1907* (Tenby: John Leach, 1908).
Le Berre, Yves, *et al.*, *Buez Santez Nonn. Mystère breton. Vie de sainte Nonne* (Minihi-Levenez: CRBC, 1999).
Lewes, E., 'Image of St Non, at Llanon, Cardiganshire', *Archaeologia Cambrensis*, 19 (1919), series 6, 32–3.
Lewis, Katherine J., 'Model girls? Virgin-martyrs and the training of young medieval women in late medieval England', in Katherine J. Lewis *et al.* (eds), *Young Medieval Women* (Stroud: Sutton, 1999), pp. 25–46.
—— *The Cult of St Katherine of Alexandria in Late Medieval England* (Woodbridge: The Boydell Press, 2000).
—— 'Pilgrimage and the cult of St Katherine in late medieval England', in Jenkins and Lewis (eds), *St Katherine*, pp. 37–52.
Lewis, Mostyn, *Stained Glass in North Wales up to 1850* (Altrincham: John Sherratt and Son Ltd, 1970).
Lewis, Saunders, 'Dafydd ap Gwilym', *Llên Cymru*, 2 (1953), 199–208.
Lloyd, J. E., *A History of Wales*, 2 vols (London: Longmans, 1911).
Lloyd-Morgan, Ceridwen, 'More written about than writing? Welsh women and the written word', in Huw Pryce (ed.), *Literacy in Medieval Celtic Societies* (Cambridge: Cambridge University Press, 1998), pp. 149–65.
Loomis, C. Grant, *White Magic: An Introduction to the Folklore of Christian Legend* (Cambridge, MA: The Mediaeval Academy of America, 1948).
Lord, Peter, *The Visual Culture of Wales: Medieval Vision* (Cardiff: University of Wales Press, 2003).
—— *The Visual Culture of Wales: Medieval Vision* CD-ROM (Cardiff: University of Wales Press, 2004).
Macquarrie, Alan, *The Saints of Scotland: Essays in Scottish Church History AD 450–1093* (Edinburgh: John Donald, 1997).
McAvoy, Liz Herbert and Mari Hughes-Edwards (eds), *Anchorites, Wombs and Tombs: Intersections of Gender and Enclosure in the Middle Ages* (Cardiff: University of Wales Press, 2005).

McKee, Helen, *The Cambridge Juvencus Manuscript Glossed in Latin, Old Welsh, and Old Irish Text and Commentary* (Aberystwyth: CMCS Publications, 2000).

Mattingly, Joanna, 'Pre-Reformation saints' cults in Cornwall, with particular reference to the St Neot windows', in Cartwright (ed.) *Celtic Hagiography and Saints' Cults*, pp. 249–70.

Maunder, Chris, 'Apparitions of Mary in late twentieth-century Ireland: visions and reflections Part 1', *Maria*, 1 (1990), 69–85.

Mayeski, Marie Anne, '"The right occasion for the words": situating Ælred's homily on Saint Katherine', *Cistercian Studies Quarterly*, 33 (1998), 45–60.

Maylan, N., 'Excavations at St Mary's Priory, Usk', *The Monmouthshire Antiquary*, 9 (1993), 29–41.

Mein, G., 'Usk Priory: an unrecorded excavation', *The Monmouthshire Antiquary*, 9 (1993), 43–5.

Meyer, P., 'Légendes pieuses en provençal', *Histoire littéraire de la France*, 32 (1898), 78–100.

Miegge, Giovanni, *The Virgin Mary. The Roman Catholic Marian Doctrine*, trans. Waldo Smith (London: Lutterworth Press, 1955).

Millett, Bella, 'The audience of the saints' lives of the Katherine Group', *Reading Medieval Studies*, 16 (1990), 127–56.

Misrahi, J., 'A *vita sanctae Mariae Magdalenae (B. H. L. 5456)* in an eleventh-century manuscript', *Speculum*, 18 (1943), 335–9.

Mittendorf, Ingo, 'The Middle Welsh Mary of Egypt and the Latin source of the *Miracles of the Virgin Mary*', in Erich Poppe and Bianca Ross (eds), *The Legend of Mary of Egypt in Medieval Insular Hagiography* (Blackrock: Four Courts, 1996), pp. 205–36.

Moras, Elisa, '"Mabddysg oedd iddi rhoddi yn rhwydd": nawdd barddol gan wragedd yn yr Oesoedd Canol', *Llên Cymru*, 28 (2005), 26–52.

—— 'Gwrywdod, gwroldeb a gwrhydri yn y Canu Cynnar', *Llenyddiaeth Mewn Theori*, 2 (2007), 35–85.

Morgan, R., 'An early charter of Llanllugan nunnery', *Montgomeryshire Collections*, 73 (1985), 116–19.

Morgan-Guy, John, 'Shrine and counter-shrine in 1920s and 1930s Dewisland?', in Evans and Wooding (eds), *St David of Wales*, pp. 286–95.

Mulder-Bakker, Anneke B. (ed.), *Sanctity and Motherhood: Essays on Holy Mothers in the Middle Ages* (New York and London: Garland Publishing, 1995).

Mullen, Peter, *Shrines of Our Lady. A Guide to Fifty of the World's Most Famous Marian Shrines* (London: Piatkus, 1998).

Mycoff, David, *The Life of Saint Mary Magdalene and of Her Sister Martha* (Kalamazoo: Cistercian Publications, 1989).

Nash, Gerallt D., 'Llandeilo Tal-y-bont' (Museum of Welsh Folk Life, St Ffagans: unpublished leaflet, 1996).

Newman, Barbara, *Sister of Wisdom: St Hildegard's Theology of the Feminine* (Aldershot: Scolar Press, 1987).

Nichols, J. A., 'Medieval Cistercian nunneries and English bishops', in Nichols and Shank (eds), *Medieval Religious Women I*, pp. 237–49.

—— and L. T. Shank (eds), *Medieval Religious Women I: Distant Echoes* (Kalamazoo: Cistercian Publications, 1984).

Nicholson, Helen, 'The Sisters' House at Minwear, Pembrokeshire: analysis of the documentary and archaeological evidence', *Archaeologia Cambrensis*, 151 (2002), 109–38.

Nixon, Virginia, *Mary's Mother: Saint Anne in Late Medieval Europe* (University Park, PA: Pennsylvania State University Press, 2004).

O'Dwyer, Peter, *Mary: A History of Devotion in Ireland* (Dublin: Four Courts, 1988).

O'Loughlin, T., 'Rhygyfarch's *Vita Dauidis*: an *apparatus biblicus*', *Studia Celtica*, 32 (1998), 179–88.

Olson, B. L. and O. J. Padel, 'A tenth-century list of Cornish parochial saints', *Cambridge Medieval Celtic Studies*, 12 (1986), 33–71.

Ó Riain, P., 'Irish saints' Genealogies', *Nomina*, 7 (1983), 23–9.

—— *Anglo-Saxon Ireland: The Evidence of the Martyrology of Tallaght*, H. M Chadwick Memorial Lectures 3 (Cambridge: Department of Anglo-Saxon, Norse and Celtic, University of Cambridge, 1993).

—— 'The Church in Ceredigion in the early Middles Ages: b. The saints of Cardiganshire', in *Cardiganshire County History I*, ed. J. L. Davies and D. P. Kirby (Cardiff: University of Wales Press, 1994), 378–96.

Owen, Ann Parry, 'Englynion Dafydd Llwyd ap Gwilym Gam i'r Grog o Gaer', *Ysgrifau Beirniadol*, 21 (1996), 15–36.

Owen, E., 'The Cistercian nunnery of Llanllugan', *Montgomeryshire Collections*, 37 (1915), 1–13.

Owen, H., 'Llanddwyn Island', *Transactions of the Anglesey Antiquarian Society and Field Club* (1920), 1–32.

Owen, M. E., 'Y Cyfreithiau – (1) Natur y testunau', in Bowen (ed.), *Y Traddodiad Rhyddiaith*, pp. 196–219.

—— 'Y Cyfreithiau – (2) Ansawdd y rhyddiaith', in Bowen (ed.), *Y Traddodiad Rhyddiaith*, pp. 220–44.
Palmer, Alfred N., *The History of the Parish Church of Wrexham* (Wrexham and Oswestry: Woodall, Minshall and Thomas, 1886).
Parkinson, A. J., 'Llandeilo Talybont old church and wall-paintings in Wales' (Royal Commission on the Ancient and Historical Buildings of Wales, unpublished report, 1986).
Pentcheva, Bissera V., *Icons and Power: the Mother of God in Byzantium* (University Park PA: Pennyslvania State University, 2006).
Perrott, R., 'The tomb of Ste. Nonne, at Dirinon, in Britanny [sic.]', *Archaeologia Cambrensis*, 3 (1857), series 3, 249–58.
Power, Eileen, *Medieval English Nunneries c.1275 to 1535* (Cambridge: Cambridge University Press, 1922).
Radford, C. A. Ralegh and W. J. Hemp, 'Pennant Melangell: the church and the shrine', *Archaeologia Cambrensis*, 108 (1959), series 5, 81–113.
RCAHMW, *An Inventory of the Ancient Monuments in Wales and Monmouthshire VII – County of Pembroke* (London: HMSO, 1925).
Reed, Teresa, *Shadows of Mary: Reading the Virgin Mary in Medieval Texts* (Cardiff: University of Wales Press, 2003).
Rees, J. F., 'Miscellanea', *Archaeologia Cambrensis*, 2 (1922), series 7, 394–95.
Richards, Gwenyth, 'From footnotes to narrative: Welsh women in the thirteenth century' (unpublished doctoral thesis, University of Sydney, 2005).
Richards, R., *Church and Priory of S. Mary, Usk* (London: Bemrose and Sons, 1904).
Riches, Samantha J. E., *St George: Hero, Martyr and Myth* (Stroud: Sutton, 2000).
—— 'St George as a male virgin martyr', in Samantha J. E. Riches and Sarah Salih (eds), *Gender and Holiness: Men, Women and Saints in Late Medieval Europe* (London: Routledge, 2002), pp. 65–85.
Ridgway, M. H., 'Furnishings and fittings at Pennant Melangell church', *Montgomeryshire Collections*, 82 (1994), 127–38.
Roberts, Brynley F., 'Gweddi Boneffas Bab', B, 16 (1956), 271–3.
—— 'Pymtheg Gweddi San Ffraid a'r Pardwn', B, 16 (1956), 254–68.
—— 'Un o lawysgrifau Hopcyn ap Thomas o Ynys Dawe', B, 22 (1967), 223–8.

Roberts, D. H. E., 'Noddwyr y beirdd yn Sir Aberteifi', *Llên Cymru*, 10 (1968–9), 76–107.

Roberts, Thomas, 'Cywyddau pererindod', *Y Traethodydd*, 13 (1944), 28–39.

Ruddock, G., 'Cywydd i grefyddes?', *Llên Cymru*, 12 (1972), 117–20.

—— 'Prydferthwch merch yng nghywyddau serch y bymthegfed ganrif', in John Rowlands (ed.), *Dafydd ap Gwilym a Chanu Serch yr Oesoedd Canol* (Cardiff: University of Wales Press, 1975), pp. 95–119.

Russell, J. C., *British Medieval Population* (Albuquerque: University of New Mexico Press, 1948).

Sands, Tracey R., 'The saint as symbol: the cult of St Katherine of Alexandria among medieval Sweden's high aristocracy', in Jenkins and Lewis (eds), *St Katherine*, pp. 94–6.

Saunders, Corinne, *Rape and Ravishment in the Literature of Medieval England* (Cambridge: D. S. Brewer, 2001).

Saxer, V., *Le culte de Marie Madeleine en Occident des origines à la fin du moyen âge* (Auxerre-Paris: Publications de la Société des Fouilles Archéologiques et des Monuments Historiques de l'Yonne-Librairie Clavreuil, 1959).

Schulenburg, Jane Tibbets, 'Strict active enclosure and its effects on the female monastic experience (500–1100)', in Nichols and Shank (eds), *Medieval Religious Women I*, pp. 51–86.

—— 'The heroics of virginity. Brides of Christ and sacrificial mutilation', in Mary Beth Rose (ed.), *Women in the Middle Ages and the Renaissance, Literary and Historical Perspectives* (Syracuse: Syracuse University Press, 1986), pp. 29–72.

Sharpe, R., 'Some medieval miracula from Llandegley (Lambeth Palace Library, MS 94 fols. 153v–155r)', B, 37 (1990), 166–76.

Sheehan, M., *The Will in Medieval England* (Toronto: Pontifical Institute of Mediaeval Studies, 1963), Appendix B.

Sichel, M., *Costume Reference 1: Roman Britain and the Middle Ages* (London: B. T. Batsford, 1977).

Sinclair, J. B. and Fenn, R. W. D., *Old Radnor Parish Church. A Short History* (Llandrindod Wells: Sayce Brothers, 1988).

Smith, H. Maynard, *Pre-Reformation England* (London: Macmillan & Co. Ltd, 1938).

Smith, J. Beverley, 'Dower in thirteenth-century Wales: a grant of the commote of Anhuniog, 1273', B, 30 (1983), 348–55.

—— *Llywelyn ap Gruffudd Prince of Wales* (Cardiff: University of Wales Press, 1998).

Smith, J. M. H., 'The problem of feminine sanctity in Carolingian Europe *c.*780–920', *Past and Present*, 146 (1995), 3–37.

Smith, Lesley J. and Jane H. M. Taylor (eds), *Women, the Book and the Godly: Selected Proceedings of the St Hilda's Conference*, 1993 (Cambridge: D. S. Brewer, 1995).

Smith, W. B., 'The theology of the virginity *in partu* and its consequences for the Church's teaching on chastity', *Marian Studies*, 31 (1980), 99–110.

Spearing, Elizabeth (ed.), *Medieval Writings on Female Spirituality* (London: Penguin, 2002).

Spencer, Brian, *Pilgrim Souvenirs and Secular Badges* (Salisbury: Salisbury and South Wiltshire Museum, 1998).

Suggett, R., 'Neuadd', unpublished document in RCAHMW archive.

Thomas, Charles, *And Shall These Mute Stones Speak?* (Cardiff: University of Wales Press, 1994).

Thomas, D. R., *The History of the Diocese of St Asaph*, 3 vols (Oswestry: Caxton Press, 1908–13).

Thomas, Graham C. G., 'Mair a'r afallen', B, 24 (1970–2), 459–60.

Thomas, S., 'Land occupation, ownership and utilisation in the parish of Llansantffraid', *Ceredigion*, 3 (1956–9), 124–55.

Thompson, Sally, 'The problem of the Cistercian nuns in the twelfth and early thirteenth centuries', in D. Baker (ed.), *Medieval Women* (Oxford: Basil Blackwell, 1978), pp. 227–52.

—— 'Why English nunneries had no history: a study of the problems of the English nunneries founded after the Conquest', in Nichols and Shank (eds), *Medieval Religious Women: I*, pp. 131–49.

—— *Women Religious: the Founding of English Nunneries after the Conquest* (Oxford: Clarendon, 1991).

Trier, Julie, 'A study of holy wells in Pembrokeshire including those of Our Lady and St David and their possible association with pilgrimage routes to St Davids', 2 vols (unpublished M.Phil. thesis, University of Wales, Lampeter, 2004).

Tristram, E. W., *English Mediaeval Wall Painting the Thirteenth Century* (Oxford: Oxford University Press, 1950).

Truman, N., *Historical Costuming* (London: Sir Isaac Pitman and Sons, 1936; 1966 edn).

Voaden, Rosalynn, *God's Words, Women's Voices: The Discernment of Spirits in the Writing of Late-Medieval Women Visionaries* (Woodbridge: York Medieval Press, 1999).

Wade-Evans, A. W., 'The Brychan Documents', *Y Cymmrodor*, 19 (1906), 18–50.

—— 'Parochiale Wallicanum', *Y Cymmrodor*, 22 (1910), 22–124.

—— 'Rhygyfarch's Life of Saint David', *Y Cymmrodor*, 24 (1913), 1–73.

Walsh, Christine, 'The role of the Normans in the development of the cult of St Katherine', in Jenkins and Lewis (eds), *St Katherine*, pp. 19–35.

Ward, Frank, *The Lakes of Wales* (London: Herbert Jenkins Ltd, 1931).

Ward, Jennifer C., *English Noblewomen in the Later Middle Ages* (London: Longman, 1992).

—— 'Elizabeth de Burgh, Lady of Clare (d. 1360)', in C. M. Barren and A. F. Sutton (eds), *Medieval London Widows 1300–1500* (London: Hambledon Press, 1994), pp. 29–45.

—— 'English noblewomen and the local community in the later Middle Ages', in *Medieval Women in their Communities*, ed. Diane Watt (Cardiff: University of Wales Press, 1997), pp. 186–203

—— 'Elizabeth de Burgh and Usk castle', *The Monmouthshire Antiquary*, 18 (2002), 13–22 (22).

Ward, M. A., 'St. Catherine's Church, Cricieth', *Caernarvonshire Historical Society Transactions*, 58 (1997), 7–34.

Warner, Marina, *Alone of All Her Sex: the Myth and the Cult of the Virgin Mary* (London: Picador, 1976).

Watt, Diane, *Secretaries of God: Women Prophets in Late Medieval and Early Modern England* (Woodbridge: The Boydell Press, 1997).

Wenger, A., *L'Assomption de la très-sainte Vierge dans la tradition byzantine du VIe au Xe siècle* (Paris: Archives de l'Orient chrétien 5, 1955).

Wiliam, Dafydd Wyn, *Plasty Prysaeddfed Bodedern, Braslun o'i Hanes* (Llangefni: O. Jones, 1984).

Williams, D. H., 'Llantarnam Abbey', *The Monmouthshire Antiquary*, 2 (1967), 131–48.

—— 'Cistercian nunneries in medieval Wales', *Citeaux*, 26 (1975), 155–74.

—— 'Usk nunnery', *Monmouthshire Antiquary*, 4 (1980), 44–5.

—— *The Welsh Cistercians*, 2 vols (Caldey Island: Cistercian Publications, 1984).

—— *Atlas of Cistercian Lands in Wales* (Cardiff: University of Wales Press, 1990).

Williams, Glanmor, 'The tradition of St David in Wales', in O. W. Jones and D. Walker (eds), *Links with the Past: Swansea and*

Brecon Historical Essays (Llandybïe: Christopher Davies, 1974), pp. 1–20.

—— *The Welsh Church From Conquest to Reformation* (Cardiff: University of Wales Press, 1976).

Williams, Ifor, 'Naw englyn y Juvencus', B, 6 (1931–3), 205–24.

—— 'Protestaniaeth Wiliam Middleton', B, 8 (1936), 242–7.

Williams, J. E. Caerwyn, 'Bucheddau'r saint: eu cefndir a'u datblygiad fel llên', B, 11 (1944), 149–57.

—— 'Rhyddiaith grefyddol Cymraeg Canol', in Bowen (ed.), *Y Traddodiad Rhyddiaith*, pp. 312–408.

—— 'Welsh translations of *Pseudo-Matthaei Evangelium sive liber de ortu Beatae Mariae et infantia Salvatoris*', *Proceedings of the Irish Biblical Association*, 17 (1994), 102–25.

Williams, P. L., '"Ar ganghennau'r gynghanedd": agweddau ar y goedwig yn llenyddiaeth yr Oesoedd Canol', *Dwned*, 6 (2000), 55–76.

Williams, S. J., 'Rhai cyfeithiadau', in Bowen (ed.), *Y Traddodiad Rhyddiaith*, pp. 303–11.

Williams, S. W., 'Architectural notes upon Usk Church, Monmouthshire', *Archaeologia Cambrensis*, 3, (1886), series 5, 90–3.

—— *The Cistercian Abbey of Strata Florida: Its History and an Account of the Recent Excavations Made on its Site* (London: Whiting & Co., 1889).

Willis, Browne, *A Survey of the Cathedral Church of St David's* (London: R. Gosling, 1717).

—— *A Survey of the Cathedral Church of Bangor and the Edifices belonging to it* (London: R. Gosling, 1721).

Winstead, Karen A., *Virgin Martyrs: Legends of Sainthood in Late Medieval England* (Cornell: Cornell University Press, 1997).

—— 'St Katherine's Hair', in Jenkins and Lewis (eds), *St Katherine*, pp. 171–99.

Winward, F., 'The Lives of St. Wenefred (BHL 8847–8851)', *Analecta Bollandiana*, 117 (1999), 100–3.

Wmffre, Iwan, *The Place-Names of Cardiganshire*, 3 vols, BAR British Series 379 (II) (Oxford: Archaeopress, 2004).

Wogan-Browne, Jocelyn, 'Saints' lives and the female reader', *Forum for Modern Language Studies*, 37 (1991), 314–32.

—— '"Clerc u lai, muïne u dame"; women and Anglo-Norman hagiography in the twelfth and thirteenth centuries', in C. M. Meale (ed.), *Women and Literature in Britain, 1150–1500* (Cambridge: Cambridge University Press, 1993), pp. 61–85.

—— 'The virgin's tale', in Ruth Evans and Leslie Johnson (eds), *Feminist Readings in Middle English Literature: The Wife of Bath and All her Sect* (London: Routledge, 1994), pp. 165–94.
—— *Saints' Lives and Women's Literary Culture* c.*1150–1300: Virginity and its Authorizations* (Oxford: Oxford University Press, 2001).

Websites

http://www.dafyddapgwilym.net

Index